GOD AS REASON

GOD AS REASON

Essays in Philosophical Theology

VITTORIO HÖSLE

University of Notre Dame Press
Notre Dame, Indiana

Library of Congress Cataloging-in-Publication Data

Hösle, Vittorio, 1960–
God as reason : essays in philosophical theology / Vittorio Hösle.
     pages   cm
Includes bibliographical references and index.
ISBN-13: 978-0-268-03098-8 (pbk. : alk. paper)
ISBN-10: 0-268-03098-7 (pbk. : alk. paper)
1. Philosophical theology. 2. Philosophy and religion.   I. Title.
BT40.H67   2013
261.5'1—dc23
2012050650

CONTENTS

PREFACE

Philosophy and Christianity are both based on a special relationship to the Logos, that is, Reason, and yet they have often been inimical to each other. The deepest cause is that both have absolute claims to defend, and a plurality of absolute claims inevitably causes difficulties, if they contradict each other. Perhaps it is a wise solution to prevent any such contradiction by identifying what is ontologically absolute with what is epistemologically absolute, Reason, which forms the uncircumventable horizon within which alone any theory, and thus also any theory about God, can claim validity.

The essays collected in this book stem from a philosopher who understands his own systematic work in theoretical as well as practical philosophy as an offshoot of a tradition committed to a strong concept of reason, drawing inspiration especially from Plato, Giambattista Vico, and Georg Wilhelm Friedrich Hegel, on whom he has written some of his major works. This concept of reason entails not only a commitment to semantic as well as performative consistency as necessary conditions of truth, but also the defense of principles of uniformity as synthetic a priori conditions of experience and the trust that preferring simpler systems of concepts to more cumbersome ones, where both render equal justice to experience, is not a subjective idiosyncrasy, but captures the essence of reality. For practical reason, it entails a commitment to a universalist, even if not necessarily a formalist, ethics. To these principles of reason all traditions have to be critically subjected; for as much as reason genetically presupposes traditions, on the level of validity it enjoys autonomy.

At the same time, the author regards himself as a Christian, and the essays here presented, with two exceptions all written from 1997 to 2009 and all forming a consistent whole, are the attempt to find an interpretation of Christianity that is compatible with this commitment to reason. In a time of mindless religious fundamentalism, on the one hand, and aggressive atheism, on the other, perhaps such an attempt deserves some attention; it is at least a more plausible intermediate position than religious indifferentism, which is probably even worse than an atheism that at least shows interest in the question of God. For while the critics of religious fundamentalism are right to point to the forces of ignorance and hatred that drive the latter and that in fact are based more on self-deception than deception of others, the irreligious person seems to have difficulties understanding that religion will stay with us, outliving all grand theories of secularization, and that it will remain one of the most powerful motives in the human soul. It is much wiser to engage it productively with pure reason than to ignore it or even provoke it by silly insults of that dimension in which also the most humiliated person on the planet can cherish her own dignity.

The first part of this book deals with issues of philosophical theology. (The important question of what Christianity's specific contribution to morals and ethics is is ignored in this volume.) In the first, foundational chapter I discuss some of the challenges that an approach to Christianity committed to reason has to face—the issue of freedom and necessity in God, the problems of grace and miracles, the authority of the church, the figure of Christ. Without denying the obvious tensions, I defend the possibility of interpreting Christianity in such a way that the commitment to God as Reason remains possible. The second chapter addresses how the Darwinian revolution in our understanding of teleology has altered the prospects of theism. It argues that the strongest objections against the argument from design all antedate Charles Darwin and that nothing in Darwinism excludes a teleological interpretation of the world, which is indeed entailed by theism, even if it does not entail the latter. While I reject the argument from design as an independent argument, I insist that on the basis of a priori arguments, such as the ontological and the moral proofs, a teleological vision of the world may well be defended even after Darwin.

The third chapter addresses the main objection to theism—the theodicy problem—and debates three paradigmatic solutions, each of which entails a significantly different concept of God: those of Gottfried Wilhelm Leibniz, G. W. F. Hegel, and Hans Jonas. Despite the phenomenological evidence for Jonas's position, I suggest that only some form of synthesis of the Leibnizian and Hegelian solutions can work. Indeed, many of the metaphysical tenets defended in these essays are close to Leibniz's metaphysics, which remains unmatched in its simplicity, while Hegel's dialectic renders greater justice to the intricacies of the world and the undeniable presence of negativity. The problem of divine omnipotence inevitably leads to that of human freedom, which is discussed in the fourth chapter. It articulates a compatibilist concept of freedom, which, I think, has some advantages for the theological field, too. The commitment to the principle of sufficient reason is connected with some skepticism regarding an intuitionist epistemology, which starts from basic beliefs as ultimate facts. No doubt, such an epistemology can be used to justify religion; but its main problem is that it can be used to prop up almost any religion and even any irreligious view, as long as someone finds it evident and it cannot be shown to be inconsistent. Starting from basic beliefs may be inevitable, but at least as long as these beliefs are not shared by a universal community, it is hard to see how an approach that ultimately rests on them will be more than a dogmatism that can easily be challenged by another dogmatism relying on different basic beliefs. Nothing guarantees that views starting from different basic beliefs will ever converge.

Freedom is a property of the human mind, and thus every theory of freedom, compatibilist or not, has to address the issue of the place of mentality in nature. The fifth chapter outlines my ideas on the mind-body problem, which is obviously central for any philosophy of religion; for already early religion was based on an appreciation of the specific role of mind in nature. To deal with this issue, I deliberately chose the dialogue form also because it allowed me to represent the two positions I find most plausible while leaving where exactly my preference lies open. (The careful reader will probably discover which stance the author is inclined to favor.) My choice of the dialogue form is furthermore based on the conviction that the immanent confutation of the adversaries and the common discovery of uncircumventable premises is a sounder basis for philosophy in general, and philosophy of religion in particular, than the more Cartesian start from one's private evidences.

The sixth essay, finally, tries to draw lines between the three different provinces of religion, theology based on authoritative texts, and philosophy. For my enterprise it is crucial to distinguish between philosophical theology based on pure reason and the philosophy of religion and theology as cultural phenomena. These are in truth two very different disciplines that in the Anglo-American world are sometimes confused under the homonymous name of philosophy of religion. For religion is more than a system of thought; it is often based on authoritative texts, the proper exposition of which is the task of theology. Philosophy cannot presuppose the authority of these texts. But it must, first, explain why religion and theology start from such texts and how they have changed their interpretative methods over time. Second, even the philosopher is well advised to recognize that his own enterprise is an outgrowth of a tradition, even if of a tradition dedicated to reason alone. The second part of this volume thus deals with predecessors of a rationalist approach to faith, which in the earlier Christian tradition was more frequent than a theological doctrine based on Thomas Aquinas's strict demarcation of reason and faith has been willing to recognize. Besides interpretations of these canonical texts, the most fascinating of which are, hardly by chance if what I said before holds, written in dialogue form, I offer some general reflections on how to interpret authoritative religious texts and understand their interpretations.

The seventh chapter begins by sketching the various stances that philosophers have taken with regard to the Bible and traces the complex causes that have led to the rise of modern biblical criticism. Even if we may rightly lament the loss of certain interpretive possibilities that premodern hermeneutics had, no honest intellectual should reject modern criticism; it is bad theology that opposes religion to modern science, and it is even worse theology that wants to protect religion from modern historiography. We may, however, learn some lessons from Hans-Georg Gadamer's complex challenge to the modern hermeneutical tradition. In the eighth chapter I focus on the New Testament concept of *pneuma* and propose a pneumatological interpretation of Christianity, which can see in German idealism its legitimate heir. I do not deny that German idealism has given up, perhaps too quickly, three decisive concerns of the Christian tradition, but I argue for both the sincerity and the plausibility of the idealist conviction that their philosophy of mind (*Geist*) was the only way of continuing the inspiration by the *pneuma* so characteristic of the New Testament under the conditions of post-Kantian philosophy. We should not forget that Johann Gottlieb Fichte, Friedrich Wilhelm Joseph Schelling, and Georg Wilhelm Friedrich Hegel were trained as Christian theologians; in their eyes, they remained faithful to this tradition even when transforming it according to the demands of the spirit they felt operating in their age.

Chapter 9, co-authored with Bernd Goebel, and chapter 10 scrutinize the contemporary relevance of some of the most important texts in the history of rationalist Christian thought. Anselm's *Cur Deus homo* is shown to integrate pre-Kierkegaardian insights into its rationalist framework; thus it demonstrates that passionate existential commitment is compatible with trust in reason. Peter Abelard's, Ramon Llull's, Nicholas of Cusa's, and Jean Bodin's unmatched interreligious dialogues are not only in themselves classical texts; they tell a story about the decline of the possibility of interreligious conversation. Nicholas of Cusa's complex contribution to the genesis of a modern philosophy of mathematics as well as to the foundation of a natural science that has its ultimate justification in a rational theology is the subject of the eleventh chapter. I hesitated to include this essay written in 1988; but I finally decided to do so because Nicholas of Cusa remains the most brilliant exemplification of my thesis that modernity is Christianity's legitimate child. Both mathematical constructivism, so alien to the ancient world and at the root of Immanuel Kant's Copernican revolution, as well as the shift in categories that led to the scientific discoveries of the sixteenth and seventeenth centuries are anticipated by Nicholas, whose form of Christianity, even if profoundly inspired by the neo-Platonic tradition, is so much closer to our irredeemably modern sensibilities and insights than Aquinas's *Summa*. While I do agree with Hans Blumenberg's view on the centrality of Nicholas in the genesis of modernity, I do not share his view that Giordano Bruno represents progress compared to Nicholas of Cusa. The legitimacy of modernity consists not in breaking off all links with the

Christian Middle Ages, but in a careful transformation of its legacy. On the one hand, nothing in modern science and in modernity in general entails atheism; on this score, Blumenberg is wrong. Therefore, on the other hand, Christians are well advised not to try to retrieve a prescientific form of Christianity.

Even more they should shrink back from a glorification of archaic forms of religion; after all, the overcoming of bloody sacrifices through Jesus' self-sacrifice is one of the central points of Christianity. The twelfth essay contains a sharp rebuttal of Søren Kierkegaard's famous account of Abraham's attempted sacrifice of Isaac, while at the same time recognizing that the triumphalist philosophy of history of the Hegelians indeed misses something crucial. While working toward a rational comprehension of Christianity, Christians have to understand why a secular age became such a tempting possibility. For what the theodicy problem is for rational theology, the rise of atheism is for a philosophical understanding of religion as a historical phenomenon. Charles Taylor's *A Secular Age* is one of the most complex attempts to deal with this rise, and thus this book concludes with a detailed analysis of his secularization theory and the sketch of an alternative one, which dares see even atheism in a providential light.

The author of these essays was educated in Germany; five were originally written in German, one in Norwegian, and these six texts were translated by four different people, Benjamin Fairbrother, James Hebbeler, Jason Miller, and Jeremy Neill, into English. I have translated most quotes from classical texts into English myself and given the original in the footnotes, where sometimes original texts have remained untranslated, if they were not crucial for the argument in the main text. Even if I cut the original texts here and there to adjust them to this volume and added some new footnotes, the reader will feel the German origins of these texts, which often refer to secondary literature from Germany. I trust nevertheless that the points they are making will be perceived as worth considering also by readers belonging to different intellectual traditions. It is also worth mentioning that the author, today a Catholic, was in his formative years educated by Lutheran teachers. Probably Catholic readers will find too little submission to the authority of the church, while Protestants will dislike the strong commitment to reason and the downplaying of scriptural authority.

✦ I remember with gratitude Rev. Alois Högerle, who showed me in my childhood lived Catholic faith. A first interest in the theology of the Middle Ages was instilled in me by my teacher at the University of Freiburg Rev. Charles Lohr, SJ. In my time at the Forschungsinstitut für Philosophie in Hannover 1997–99 and, since 1999, at the University of Notre Dame, several people have contributed to directing my reflections more and more to the topic of the philosophy of religion: I feel the need to thank explicitly Rev. David Burrell, Friedrich Hermanni, Jan Hagens, Jennifer Herdt (whose comments on these essays were invaluable), Jonathan Israel, Gerald McKenny, Cyril O'Regan, Alvin Plantinga, Barbara and Mark Roche, H. E. Bishop Marcelo Sánchez Sorondo, Rev. Richard Schenk, OP, Leopold Stubenberg, Rev. Robert Sullivan, Joseph Wawrykow, and last, but not least, my wife Jieon Kim and our children Johannes, Paul, and hopefully soon Clara Hösle, born philosophical theologians, for many conversations—even if I know that, for very different reasons, each of them will reject many of my statements. And I thank all the editors of earlier volumes, who graciously permitted me to have my texts reprinted, as well as Bernd Goebel, who generously allowed me to include our essay on Anselm in this volume. I dedicate this volume to the memory of my friend Leif Hovelsen (1923–2011), whose paradoxical life as an itinerant Lutheran "monk," as he was called by his friends, remains awe-inspring whenever he appears to my memory, as he so often does.

PHILOSOPHICAL THEOLOGY

CHAPTER 1

—·—·—·—

The Idea of a Rationalistic Philosophy of Religion and Its Challenges

One of the most important intellectual changes that has occurred within the Catholic Church in the last decades is the shift away from fideism toward rationalism—or, to be more precise, and to use comparative rather than classificatory concepts, a move from a more fideistic to a more rationalistic stance.[1] For there is no sharp demarcation but rather a continuum between the two positions, and certainly not even John Paul II's encyclical *Fides et ratio* embraced rationalism tout court, even if it recognized its partial right in a quite surprising form. Also, Benedict XVI's Regensburg speech of September 2006 came astonishingly close to professing reason as the justifying criterion of religion (although this central point was neglected due to the fuss made over Benedict's perhaps unfortunate quote from Manuel II Paleologus). I use the words "surprising" and "astonishingly" because most strands of neo-scholasticism from the nineteenth century onward had been quite inimical to rationalism. They build on Thomas Aquinas's distinction between *praeambula ad articulos fidei* and *articuli fidei*[2] and insist that the latter could not, and should not, be justified by reason. Certainly, Aquinas thought that the existence of God was rationally demonstrable (and thus not an *articulus fidei*), and still in the nineteenth century, Gregory XVI condemned the doctrine, originally defended by Louis Eugène Bautain, that God's existence had to be accepted only on the basis of faith.[3] But it is fair enough to say that many theologians of the twentieth century were fideists even with regard to this most basic principle, although this attitude dramatically jeopardized the chances that theology might be taken seriously as a science: after all, why should one respect an alleged revelation from a being whose existence is dubious at best? Without philosophical propaedeutics, dogmatic theology lacks any rational foundation, and the crisis of fundamental theology, with its core discipline of a philosophical theology, cannot leave the rest of theology unchallenged. Radical fideism was particularly held by the theologians influenced by Søren Kierkegaard and the movement of so-called dialectical theology, but also by Catholic theologians, especially those under the spell of Martin Heidegger and his postmodernist successors.[4]

What brought about the aforementioned change? On the one hand, there is the old argument that the appeal to subjective faith does not warrant truth. This situation is not significantly altered by the appeal to a religious tradition shared by millions, for there are several such religious traditions whose truth claims are not logically compatible with each other. Besides, within the same tradition there are radically varying interpretations. On the basis of a universalist ethics there is even something insulting and immoral in the conviction that my religious tradition is superior to others for the simple reason that it happens to be *my* tradition; for other traditions may just as well use the same words against me. On the other hand, the more seriously the Christian tradition was studied, the more obvious it became that the Thomist position was not the only one. (And the older neo-scholasticism, which focused only on Aquinas, often enough did not even render justice to him.) In Christian (as in Islamic) theology, there had always been a rationalistic alongside the more or less fideistic strand,[5] and some of the greatest Christian theologians clearly had defended the position that the concrete contents of religious truth should be based on reason alone. They were not satisfied with the intermediate position, according to which there were rational (partly historical) arguments for believing in a revelation whose contents could not be accepted on the basis of reason alone. A rationalist position was particularly tempting in times in which there was a clear awareness that a legitimate interpretation of "revelation"—of scripture and tradition—was itself a work of reason. If the last meaning of scripture was allegorical, tropological, and anagogical, then this meaning had to be based on rational arguments, which alone could have the power to transcend literal meaning. Even acknowledging the rules of piety, the church, or scripture, as in the main work by Origen, the founding father of Christian theology,[6] did not mean much if the interpretation of these rules by intellectuals was regarded as superior to that by nonintellectual, ordained priests. There can be little doubt that the young (not the later) Augustine,[7] Johannes Scottus Eriugena, Anselm,[8] Peter Abelard (to a limited degree), the Victorines, Ramon Llull, and Nicholas of Cusa are rationalists in the sense that they acknowledge the authority of reason as the last tribunal of justification regarding the truths of religion. In this respect, they are not too distant from the decisive principle of Enlightenment, and this shows that Christian intellectuals from Late Antiquity and the Middle Ages were intellectually far more vivacious and diverse than the often submissive and unoriginal Catholic theologians after the Counter-Reformation. It is hardly accidental that Abelard, Llull, and Nicholas of Cusa are all authors of important interreligious dialogues (the genre being somehow prepared by Anselm's *Cur Deus homo*) since whoever tries to engage with persons from a different religious background can hardly appeal to his own faith, but must rely on rational arguments. Globalization, with its mixing of people from diverse religious traditions, is probably an important social cause for the resurrection of rationalism in the late twentieth century. In closed communities, the challenge of the other religions may be ignored; in a world in which various traditions interpenetrate each other, however, this is no longer feasible.

An important cause of the fideistic approach to religion was a deflated concept of rationality that identified reason with *scientific* reason, that is, with systematized experience, plus logic and mathematics. Since knowledge of God cannot be achieved by means of science, it was thought to be beyond the reach of reason. But even if some scientists try to monopolize the term "reason" for their own activities, it is not difficult to see that it is far from rational to submit to this claim. Reason is more comprehensive than science, as Immanuel Kant, the most important modern theorist of the complex architecture of reason, has masterfully shown. Ethics, for example, is a rational discipline, even if valuative claims cannot be reduced to descriptive ones such as those dealt with by science—this is David Hume's lasting insight.[9] At the same time, a dualistic theory is unsatisfying if there is no connection between descriptive and normative sentences, for after all, the Ought has to be implemented within the Is. But if the Ought does not follow from the Is, and at the same time the two spheres have to be connected, the Ought must determine at least some features of the Is. No doubt, the need to interpret the natural world as a place in which the demands of the Ought can be realized is one of the strongest arguments for a moral principle behind nature.[10] The argument does not show that all features of Being derive from the Ought, but at least partially determining powers have to be ascribed to the latter.

Also within the realm of theoretical reason alone there are arguments for a spiritual principle of all being. Mental states cannot be identified with physical ones, and while the former seem to supervene on the latter, it is at the same time inevitable that the ensuing mental states that grasp an argument are connected logically as much as by the fact that they are supervenient on ensuing electrochemical processes in a brain. There must be a correspondence between these two properties, and if we do not accept a causal force of the mental on the physical, such parallelism cannot be the result of evolutionary forces driven by natural selection.[11] This is, as is known, Gottfried Wilhelm Leibniz's reformulation of the teleological proof, and it seems to be immune to Hume's and Kant's attacks against that proof, not to speak of Charles Darwin's destruction of traditional physico-theology. For the argument, as I have just used it, in fact presupposes its destruction through the category of natural selection.[12]

The status of the ontological proof is still debated, but it is far from clear that it cannot be formulated in a cogent way. Alvin Plantinga's reconstruction is the most plausible candidate for a cogent version. It presupposes, as Leibniz already knew,[13] the central premise that "indeed unsurpassable greatness is possibly exemplified."[14] Of course, Plantinga is aware that this premise has to be granted; and indeed this seems to belong to the nature of all arguments: they start from premises in order to arrive at a conclusion, which one may always reject by denying at least one of the premises. One's proof may even be the other's *reductio ad absurdum:* if someone regards the conclusion as utterly implausible, he will regard the conjugation of those premises that lead to it as confuted.

There are, however, some assumptions that are conditions of possibility of certain mental activities regarded by most people as legitimate. Science, for example, presupposes the constancy of natural laws. This principle is not entailed by logic alone: for there is no contradiction in the assumption of sudden changes of natural laws; nor does it follow from experience. We do not know from experience what will happen in the future, and the distant past, which we did not witness, is reconstructed on the basis of this principle and thus not itself an argument for it. Science therefore presupposes some metaphysical principles that are themselves not grounded in experience or logic. Perhaps, however, they can be made plausible by appealing to some attributes of God, such as his being one and timeless,[15] and/or through the use of teleological arguments—only a nature with constant laws would allow finite rational beings to acquire knowledge and thus act morally responsibly. If the project of science presupposes arguments of this sort, then scientific rationality is not the most basic form of rationality, but is grounded in some antecedent form of reason. This would explain the well-known historical fact that the scientific revolution was due to deeply pious persons such as René Descartes, Galileo Galilei, Johannes Kepler, and Isaac Newton, who regarded their scientific project as a consequence of their religious convictions.

It would be important for the revival of a rationalist philosophy of religion to show that the project of science becomes far more plausible and rational when certain of its presuppositions are made explicit, namely, those that are connected to classical assumptions of rational theology. Still, a stubborn skeptic could deny the validity of science and thus of its presumed basis, rational theology. But that which not even the skeptic can deny is the existence of truth and its in-principle intelligibility because this is the transcendental presupposition of all claims. The strongest proof of God—because it would not start from a premise open to

doubt—would certainly be one that showed that the ideas of truth and
its intelligibility make sense only if the world is an expression of an absolute mind.[16] I myself have argued that our capacity of having a priori
knowledge, which at the same time cannot be consistently understood as
being a merely subjective knowledge, shows that the world is necessarily
structured in a way that corresponds to the conceptual demands of a
mind. Since this is a property of the world that our finite minds cannot
bestow on it, it must come from a Mind antecedent to the world, that is,
from a divine Mind.[17] It is not the purpose of this essay to elaborate the
basic arguments and ideas of rational theology. What should already be
clear, however, is that any attempt to make sense of religious traditions
would be well advised to study carefully the aforementioned arguments.
Certainly some disagreements on the divine attributes and God's relations to the world are inevitable since the divine radically transcends
human nature, particularly its temporality, which permeates all our cognitive efforts. Two famous issues concern whether God is omnipotent, and
whether divine omnipotence entails human freedom in the compatibilist
form or allows for a libertarian form. But it would be intellectual suicide
to radicalize this insight to some form of negative theology that denies
any intelligibility to God. For such an unintelligible God might well be
evil or perhaps identical with matter. The basic properties of God that
alone warrant awe for him are his rationality and morality—indeed, he is
the standard of all our claims to morality and reason.

The philosophers who have contributed most to the development of
rational theology (as distinguished from a theology that takes tradition
and revelation into account) are certainly Plato, Leibniz, and Georg Wilhelm Friedrich Hegel. We owe to Plato the insights that our knowledge is
not reducible to empirical knowledge (even if he may well err in denying
any empirical knowledge) and that we have a knowledge of the Idea of
the Good, which transcends the factual world and cannot be identified
with our mental acts either.[18] The *Timaeus* (29e ff.) offers a picture of the
world as a place in which the Idea of the Good realizes itself—the basic
structures of the world are as they are because they realize value; ontology is rooted in axiology. Plato, however, does not yet have a theory of
mentality; the only dualism he knows is that between the ideas and the
physical world. Leibniz, on the contrary, has an elaborate theory of sub-

jectivity, which is integrated into an axiological worldview. As a good Lutheran, however, he does not have an ontology of universals; and this is a serious threat to axiology, which seems to presuppose that values actually exist. The other great step in Leibniz's unfolding of the idea of rational theology is his use of a metaphysics of possible worlds, which is indispensable if we want to ascribe choice to God.

There are three reasons Hegel's philosophy is of enormous importance to every person interested in rational theology, and particularly in a philosophical justification of basic Christian tenets.[19] The first is that Hegel's complex metaphysics acknowledges three strata of being—ideal, natural, and mental being. This is itself not accepted as mere fact, but connected to a theory of concept formation that is both epistemological and ontological and tries to be a rational transformation of the Christian belief in a Trinitarian God who creates the world according to a triadic pattern. Second, Hegel is the first great philosopher who offers an elaborate metaphysics of history, still alien to both Plato and Leibniz. He is able to make philosophical sense of the historical development of Christianity, which can easily disturb traditional Christians, when they become aware of it. Third, Hegel insists that God is Reason. By doing so, he continues a tradition that begins already with the Gospel of John, but there is little doubt that he alters it profoundly. God is no longer a being external to finite humans; he is grasped through reflection on one's own true self, one's own reason. Fundamentally, *Hegel identifies the transcendental with the transcendent*: what is a condition of possibility of our own thought—the system of basic categories—is something absolute because it cannot be negated. God cannot be different from it. Of course, Hegel recognizes that his reconstruction of our basic categories is not identical with the true set of basic categories, but he rests convinced that the ideal set of categories would be the core of any rational concept of God.[20]

It is this claim that provoked the revolt against Hegel. A further reason was that Hegel's theism is non-eschatological and does not have place for an immortality of the soul. It speaks, incidentally, for Hegel's dialectic reconstruction of the history of philosophy that his utmost rationalism in religious matters was followed by one of the most radical forms of fideism, namely, Kierkegaard's philosophy of religion. In the following, I discuss some of the objections that are voiced against theological rationalism; I answer them from a rationalist point of view. Probably the most important criticisms are the following. First, rationalism subjects God to reason, divinizes human reason, and does not render justice to our experience of finitude and sinfulness (I). Second, rationalism does not allow us to reconstruct the concept of grace (II). Third, the authority of the church or scripture is inevitably corroded by the project of rationalism (III). While these three objections can also be used by non-Christian theists against their own rationalist philosophies, the fourth and final one is specific to Christianity. It simply states that rationalism cannot render justice to the figure of Christ (IV).[21]

I.

Why is it, despite these objections, so difficult to get rid of rationalism? Before I try to tackle the various objections, let me state that the price of giving up rationalism can be very high. This is best shown by Kierkegaard's *Frygt og Bæven* (*Fear and Trembling*).[22] If God is not bound by reason and morality, but, as the voluntarist tradition teaches, it is his will that determines what is rational and good, then it may well be moral to kill one's own innocent son, if God so orders. It is not difficult to see that such an attitude is detrimental to all normal moral convictions: jihadist terrorists can find in it their justification. Certainly, reasonable voluntarists will deny that jihadists are authorized by God, but the point is that they do not have anything more to offer than their subjective conviction against the others' subjective conviction. For a rationalist, refuting the jihadists' claim is easy. It is impossible that God may have authorized the jihadists since their acts are against the moral law and the moral law belongs to God's essence. There are good reasons for seeing in the later doctrine of the *potentia absoluta* and in the breakdown of the essentialist tradition, to which Aquinas still belongs, one of the most dangerous events in the history of philosophical theology—and this not only with regard to religion, but also to public life. For the whole idea of natural law presupposes some form of essentialism, and whoever thinks that it is God's arbitrary will that makes something good will easily grant human sovereigns the same capacity. Thomas Hobbes, after all, is deeply rooted in the religious voluntarist tradition.[23] If someone accepts orders from a divine tyrant, he may easily subject himself to human tyrants as well. The refusal of rational scrutiny is not a respectable act of faith, but a betrayal of a faculty that most intensely connects humans with God—this is the rationalists' viewpoint. Whether the latter is circular or not depends on whether there can be an ultimate foundation of the basic principles of reason, a question that I cannot pursue here, even if I support an affirmative answer.[24]

Of course, the voluntarist is moved by the reflection that binding God by logic or morality means limiting him by something external to him, thus depriving him of absolute omnipotence. The only answer to this objection can be that logical truths, the moral law, and perhaps all the *eide* and laws of being are not antecedent to God, but *are* themselves God. This seems, however, to transform God into a set of absolute Truths. One does not see how he can still be something like a person. As we have seen before, in the Platonic tradition true being is conceived after the pattern of ideas. The demiurge in the *Timaeus* is probably nothing other than the mythical symbolization of the active aspect in the Idea of the Good. I have already conceded that Plato is unable to capture the specific form of being of finite subjectivity, and so it should not come as a surprise that he has difficulty ascribing full-fledged subjectivity to God, even if in the *Sophist* he struggles with the issue. But whoever recognizes that mentality is an irreducible form of being, and that it is axiologically superior to non-mental being, cannot avoid interpreting God as Mind. Still, it is clear that not only the range, but also the nature, of the divine Mind is quite different from that of the human mind. God is not only non-spatial (and thus not a body); he is, as the overwhelming part of the tradition has recognized, non-temporal as well. And that is the reason it can be an expression of profound religiosity if one hesitates to ascribe personality to God. This became particularly true in the twentieth century since the phenomenological analysis of personhood by Edmund Husserl, Max Scheler, and Martin Heidegger insisted so emphatically on the temporal features of human persons that it seemed difficult to attribute personality to an atemporal being. Nevertheless, God's being must be closer to mental than to physical being. He must be some form of atemporal Reason in which the various ideas are connected. For if one accepts the idea that the starting point of ultimate foundation is the reflection on what one necessarily presupposes while raising certain claims, then God is not simply Truth, but the Subject that claims and grasps this Truth at the same time. The Christian doctrine of immanent Trinity has tried to render justice to the intuition that in God *noesis* and *noema* are two aspects of the same being.

It may be surprising that God's being combines traits of logical and mental being. Is the distinction between *noesis* and *noema* not something basic that cannot be given up? Well, something that is basic for finite beings may not be so for the Absolute. No doubt, any rational theory of God is obliged to respect the principle of non-contradiction. But Georg Cantor's set theory is consistent, even if for infinite sets certain truths can be proven that would be absurd for finite sets. Our common-day ontology is based on physical objects; it probably does not render justice to mental substances, and it certainly fails to capture the peculiar form of being of the Absolute. Already Augustine avers that God is identical with his properties, even if this contradicts Aristotle's substance ontology.[25]

Although the core of God is Reason, God must be ascribed will, for he must be able to equally think all possible worlds—thus what leads to the creation of the real world cannot be an act of thinking, but an act of will. Of course, his will must be informed by reason: *if* God is a perfectly good and omnipotent Creator (which is not the only reasonable concept of God), he cannot choose among all possible worlds a world that does not have maximal value. But there may well be several worlds with maximal value; nothing guarantees that there is only one such world, as Leibniz and the young Kant[26] assumed. In this case God may even exert some form of the *liberum arbitrium indifferentiae*.[27] God furthermore may know emotions—stable mental states of great intensity such as love and happiness, which we experience as the most valuable ones in the complex world of our own mental states. But he cannot know affects since they change in time; it is a crude anthropomorphism to ascribe wrath and jealousy to God, as Lactantius has done.

By interpreting God as Reason, he is no longer conceivable as something external to us, the way a physical object or even another person is. He is not outside us, but is to be found inside our core. We start to grasp

him by reflecting on what makes us able to raise claims of truth and justice. Although a transcendental interpretation of God seems to violate
normal religious feelings, it shows a surprising similarity to one of the
most important strands in religious life—mysticism. Both the transcendental philosopher of religion and the mystic see an ultimate convergence between theonomy and autonomy: by obeying God, we gain our
true self; and we get to God by trying to capture what forms the core of
our self. It is well known that Hegel saw in Meister Eckhart one of his
predecessors.[28]

The idea that God is to be found within the self, however, does not
at all entail that the self is identical with God. Whenever we analyze the
self, we experience it as a strange mixture of opposite qualities: radical
temporality *and* the capacity to grasp timeless truths, unwillingness or
inability to conform to the demands of the moral law *and* recognition of
its unconditional validity. The self is clearly not divine—but there is
something divine in it. And it is only because of this divine spark that we
are able to acknowledge our distance from the divine. Far from making
us forget our finitude, it is the awareness of the divine core of the self
that makes us painfully aware of the inappropriateness of our normal
mental life with regard to God. But it is also this spark that gives us the
hope that our mental life may be rendered more worthy of its core. If
mentality is not regarded as identical with its physical substratum, there is
also the reasonable possibility that this process of mental and moral
growth may be continued after the death of our body. A dualist interpretation of mind is, as Descartes knew,[29] probably a necessary, never a
sufficient, condition for belief in immortality. According to the aforementioned principles, a sufficient condition could only be found in axiological considerations. And one must recognize that there are axiological
arguments that speak against immortality.[30] The attitude that regards itself entitled to a reward for one's moral deeds is not noble; the heroic
self-sacrifice has another dignity if it is done without any hope for one's
own advantage, but only out of respect for the moral law. On the other
hand, eschatological hope is morally legitimate if it concerns someone
else, such as the victims of history. The injustices that we witness in this
world are quite monstrous, and even if there are good arguments to believe that without them some important virtues would not come into

existence—for example, endurance presupposes sufferance, and forgive-ness presupposes sin[31]—this consequentialist justification of the suffer-ings of the innocent for the sake of the whole can hardly be the last word. If God is a Kantian and not a utilitarian, he will hardly be satisfied with the instrumentalization of the less fortunate persons without any form of compensation for them.

II.

Grace is a central concept of religion, and it is often regarded as incom-patible with a rationalist theology. For according to such an approach, there are reasons for God's creating the world as it is; since he is rational, he has to follow these reasons and is not free to reject them. But when we cannot experience the good that we receive from him as a free gift, we are less motivated to accept with humility all that we are and have. The problem of this objection is not only that it implies an enormous pride in one's own humility, which is modestly opposed to the arrogance of reason in people like Plato and Leibniz. Readers of Charles Dickens's *David Copperfield* have probably kept not too affectionate a memory of Uriah Heep's ostentatious humility, which always smacks of performa-tive contradiction. The more serious flaw is that the objection is based on a complete misunderstanding of the rationalist position. When rational-ist theology speaks of God's necessary creation of the world, it clearly does not mean that the world is logically necessary. Baruch Spinoza may have thought so, but one did not even need Leibniz's superior logical in-telligence to understand that this cannot be the case: other worlds are logically possible. It would be even less appropriate to think of a nomo-logical necessity: in the creation of the world, the choice of the laws of nature is at stake; thus they cannot constrain the Creator. What is meant by necessity in God comes closest to what we experience as moral neces-sity: the good person cannot really commit a murder; it is her own nature that prevents her from doing so. Analogously, if God is perfectly good, it follows from the goodness of his nature that he has to create a world that could not be better. This necessity is an intrinsic necessity, and thus si-multaneously a manifestation of freedom. In his influential book on God as mystery of the world,[32] Eberhard Jüngel has averred that God is more than necessary. But either he means what I have just said, namely, that God's necessity is compatible with freedom, in which case his point is correct, but unoriginal; it has been made by the tradition of Christian rational theology—from Anselm[33] to Hegel—from which Jüngel wants to break. Or he means something different. The only meaningful reconstruction I can offer would be that God's creation of the world is a supererogatory act. For indeed supererogatory norms are not easy to capture in the usual triadic system of deontic logic: they are not obligatory, nor does saying that they are permissible render justice to their specific difference. Whence this peculiar status? It has to do with the limits of human nature: even if in a given situation it would be morally better to sacrifice one's life (for example, because it could save many innocent lives), an ethical doctrine usually cannot prescribe such an act since our drive for self-preservation is too strong. But the limits of human nature do not apply to God; thus there is no way to reconstruct Jüngel's statement through the appeal to supererogatory norms. It is true that religious persons are often characterized by an uncommon capacity of engaging in supererogatory acts; however, it would be an anthropomorphism to transfer this concept to God.

The concept of grace has not only the presumed function of granting God utmost liberty; it often gives the recipient of grace the feeling of being something special, even if at the same time the conviction of not having deserved the grace elicits profuse humility. This can be understood on the basis of common human experiences: when we receive the same as others or something that is due to us, we do not think that we are an object of special affection; but when we are privileged, we feel loved by the person who so treats us. And this is precisely the problem of focusing on the concept of grace: often enough, one who does so sees in pure accidents of life something that is aiming at him, and him alone, and wants to build up a special relationship to God, even at the expense of others, who are regarded as less worthy of grace. The correct concept of God's relation to humankind, however, can only be that he aims at realizing as much value as possible; whatever share falls to oneself must be gratefully accepted, but true gratitude must react to the whole world as a divine gift.

Nevertheless, one cannot deny that there is a legitimate place for the experience of grace. Even if all persons who exist are there because they belong to the best possible world (or the one of the worlds with maximal value that God has chosen), there is still the undeniable fact that not all persons have the same degree of proximity to God. If someone happens to be relatively close to God—let us assume she is Mother Teresa—she can still ask herself: if Mother Teresa necessarily belongs to the world to be created by God, why have *I* become Mother Teresa? Indexicality is a notoriously murky issue, and it may be that for a divine Mind the problem does not exist. But for a finite consciousness with first-person access to herself, it clearly does; and since there can be no objective answer, even a rationalist can concede that reflection on this question triggers an experience of grace. If such an experience transforms itself into the desire to give to others in exchange for the divine gift of one's core self (it is a gift, for one has not created oneself), then we can assume that this both corresponds to the divine will and contributes to a deepening of one's autonomy. For we become autonomous only by transforming, as far as we can, what we have received into something of our own making. Again, autonomy and theonomy converge.

Closely connected to the issue of grace is the problem of miracles. The concept is notoriously difficult to define. First, the statement of facts is not easy, and in the case of events long past, is almost never beyond reasonable doubt; second, if extraordinary facts can be proven to occur, the question inevitably arises whether they can be explained by natural laws (including laws correlating mind and body) perhaps yet unknown to us. There is the further problem that an absolute Mind should not need miracles in the sense of ad hoc interventions. After all, we admire a watchmaker the more, the less often we have to bring our watch to him for repair. Baden Powell has expressed the argument this way: "It is derogatory to the idea of Infinite power and wisdom, to suppose an order of things so imperfectly established that it must be occasionally interrupted and violated when the necessity of the case compelled."[34] The decisive point for a religious person is that nature manifests a moral order. Whether such manifestations happen in accordance with known laws or through their violation should not matter. Indeed, John Henry Newman deliberately disconnects the concept of miracle from the idea

that it has to occur against laws of nature. "There will be no need of analyzing the causes, whether supernatural or natural, to which they are to
be referred. They may, or they may not, in this or that case, follow or
surpass the laws of nature, and they may do so plainly or doubtfully, but
the common sense of mankind will call them miraculous; for by a miracle
is popularly meant whatever be its formal definition, an event which im-
presses upon the mind the immediate presence of the Moral Governor
of the world."[35]

In this sense a person whose life is saved through a surprising event
or who, on account of an important encounter, discovers what her real
vocation is, that is, how she can make the best of the talents she has, may
well see a miracle at work. If that motivates her to achieve her moral best,
there is no reason she should refrain from thinking so. A decisive criterion in the choice of the world to be created is certainly that nature serves
moral purposes, and therefore such events may well have been one of the
reasons God chose such a world. But they are causally connected to
many other events, and we can never exclude the possibility that God did
not choose them primarily for their own sake, but because they prepare,
or follow from, other events with a higher value. Wanting to exclude this
would indeed be a sign of vanity, of making oneself the center of the
universe.

It cannot come as a surprise that conversions are often perceived as
being connected with miraculous events. But what makes Augustine's
Confessions the extraordinary book that it is is the fact that the hearing of
the voice singing *"Tolle lege"* and the opening of the Bible (VIII 12, 29)
are only the last triggering events in a long story that prepares the conversion with psychological necessity. The Christian mother, the death of
the close friend (IV 4, 7), the disappointment by Manichee authorities (V
7, 12), the intellectual and personal model represented by Ambrose (VI
3, 3f.), the disgust with worldly ambition (VI 6, 9), the appropriation of
Platonism (VII 9, 14), and finally the conversion stories about Victori-
nus, Antony, and Ponticianus's colleagues (VIII 2ff., 3ff.) are all decisive
steps, to which almost anything could have been added in order to trig-
ger Augustine's own conversion. The "miracle" is far less relevant than
its prehistory. And in fact, the true miracle is not the mysterious voice
but the structure of the human mind that even in a time as shallow as

that of Late Antiquity cannot be deprived of its desire and its capacity to return to its divine principle. The history of Christianity with its extraordinary ability for regeneration is in this sense miraculous, and the more miraculous, the less unexplainable facts have occurred in it.[36]

III.

Why does a rationalist need a church, a tradition, a scripture? Again, let me begin with a reflection on the price one has to pay if one exempts church, tradition, or scripture from the tribunal of reason. In many aspects, it is even higher than if one embraces a voluntarist concept of God. For the voluntarist critic of the jihadist terrorist can deny that the latter is fulfilling God's will (even if he does not have a cogent argument against it). After all, a claim that God speaks directly to a person, without the mediation of reasons, is unverifiable (at least from the outside), and thus even a voluntarist can deny the authority of alleged revelations that another pretends to have received. He is not able to reject them based on content—since everything is possible for God. But neither is he bound to assume that they stem from the ultimate source of validity. The situation changes, however, when the ultimate source is a church—or better, the persons in a certain moment in charge of a church. For what they decree is usually quite clear. Now it is never the self-understanding of a church that its decrees determine what is good. In the *ordo essendi,* God, and even scripture, plus tradition (in the Catholic case), come before the church. But regarding the *ordo cognoscendi,* churches often have claimed that they are the only way to access the will of God and that reason must submit to them.

There is a well-known circularity in wanting to found the legitimacy of a church on God and at the same time found the knowledge of God on the church. For in this manner, any church—and for an outside perspective there are many communities claiming to be churches—can find a way of justifying itself: it simply has to state that it has been founded by God and that one can understand this only by submitting to its authority. A self-justification may be possible for reason since any negation of it at the same time presupposes it; but this certainly does not hold for the various churches, whose authority can be denied without performative self-contradiction. But not only are there various competing churches; each individual church itself changes in its history. Tradition is far less homogeneous than it seems at first glance, and therefore the criticism of neo-scholasticism that led to the Second Vatican Council could be sincerely based on the authority of the Fathers. The variations in the concept of God that we find in the various books and strata of the Old Testament, as well as the different Christologies offered by the four Gospels, show us that, at least in the Christian tradition, scripture is not a monolithic bloc. Its doctrine varies, and it has evolved. And usually we can recognize moral progress—suffice it to compare the book of Joshua with the prophetic books.[37]

Since the criteria of identity for a doctrine are even fuzzier than those for personal identity, one may certainly defend the thesis that there has been only *a development* of a doctrine, without danger to its core contents and its identity. But even such a development inevitably triggers the question: why did a church evolve?[38] And the best answer one can hope for would be that new insights based on reason have led to a modification of the original position. The idea that the Holy Spirit guides the church is an expression of this trust, and no doubt Hegel's optimist philosophy of history is a legitimate unfolding of this idea. Needless to say, it would be an irresponsible optimism that believes that any accretion constitutes intellectual or moral progress; after all, even the spiritual world knows forms of increasing entropy. The reification of once novel ideas for the purpose of maintaining hierocratic power often leads to the loss of the truth originally present in them. A periodical return to beginnings is thus both wholesome and necessary. But one suffers from a profound self-deception if one believes that this attempt at reformation is a real return to the past. A grown-up cannot become a child again (only childish), and every sober analysis of the Christian Reformation will have to concede that it did not delay, but rather accelerated the transformation of Christianity that finally brought forth the modern world. Despite all the dangers and vices peculiar to modernity it seems obvious to me that a religious interpretation of it is obliged to acknowledge its function in the divine plan for human history. A tendency that has prevailed for almost three centuries now cannot be seen as purely negative.[39] And in fact it is obvious that the positive force of modernization is that it has destroyed the old hierarchical world and implemented moral universalism in new legal and economic institutions.[40] No doubt, a universalism that has become completely formal and detached from a religious interpretation of the world is not likely to be stable, and thus totalitarianism is a threat specific to modernity. Still, a church's right answer can never be the denial, but only the integration, of modernity, not only because of its efficiency, but also because of the moral principle that drives and ennobles it.

Let me return to my question: why does a rationalist need a church? The answer is relatively simple. Claims of truth are universal, and thus nobody can be satisfied with having found truth alone. It is certainly not the consensus that makes a proposition true, but given our own fallibility, we are well advised to check our convictions in discourse with other people. We even arrive at rational autonomy only after a long education during which we internalize the errors as well as the wisdom of the tradition. Through the appropriation of tradition we come to know arguments of an amazing intellectual force, which we would never have found on our own. Since it is good that a truth be known to finite minds, we have the natural desire to spread truth when we think we have discovered it. And in this process we may develop personal bonds with each other that go far beyond seeing each other only as tools for the growth of our individual knowledge (which is a form of reciprocal instrumentalization).[41] What I have said applies to all truths—even science is necessarily an intersubjective process. But it holds particularly for those basic truths on which a correct understanding of one's own place and task in the world depends, that is, for religious truths. They must enjoy a stronger stability than scientific opinions, the essence of which is to be challenged periodically. Thus it is of utmost importance that there be a respected institution that represents a long-standing consensus on basic metaphysical and moral issues and that renders people familiar with the arguments in their favor. In the religious cult, it must build up emotional support in favor of this consensus and forge a religious community. It is not at all an exaggeration to say that such an institution has a particularly high value and is therefore especially willed by God. Since even a child likely has metaphysical needs, and certainly has moral needs, this institution has the right and the duty to communicate its convictions to children, even if they cannot yet be based on arguments, as long as the end of the education process is that the adults may finally study the arguments and decide autonomously with regard to their validity. This includes their right to leave their church and choose another if they find that it expresses more adequately the demands of reason. The more a church is able to integrate the element of critical and intelligent reflection into its own institutional framework, the greater—ceteris paribus—its chance to endure under conditions of modernity.

Churches are, as we have seen, socially indispensable institutions, and the right and duty to contribute to the further development of their doctrine must be exerted in such a way that it does not endanger the moral stability of these institutions and of society at large. For one of the functions of religion is the achievement and maintenance of moral consensus. It runs against this purpose if every person who has a new idea founds her own church. As in a state people must submit to the final judgment of the supreme court, even if they think it a bad decision, so a certain self-discipline is essential to the maintenance of the unity of the church. A radical rationalist such as Johann Gottlieb Fichte recognizes that a scholar in theology must have the right to publish his critical opinions, but that he does not have the right to teach them from the pulpit: "It is right to forbid him to bring them to the pulpit, and it is unconscionable for him to do so, if only he is sufficiently enlightened."[42] The necessity of maintaining a certain stability as well as the desire to have only persons of high intelligence and integrity who are sufficiently familiar with the tradition contribute to the further development of doctrine justifies the limitation of democratic structures in the inner constitution of reasonable churches (as in, by the way, academic institutions). If one acknowledges that the modern constitutional state represents a complex balance between the two logically independent, but not incompatible, principles of liberalism and democracy, one can even argue that only the presence of nondemocratic organizational principles in nonpolitical institutions maintains a diversity vital for a liberal society.[43]

The desire for diversity may lead one to value positively the fact that there is a plurality of churches. It is much better that every religious tradition develop independently toward a greater standard of theoretical and practical rationality than achieve institutional unity without sound moral principles. On the other hand, the argument against the splitting of a church can easily be used in favor of the necessity to overcome religious divisions. The more humankind grows together, the more indispensable it becomes to add a common value system to a common market. Only the two together will allow the formation of effective global political structures. The most promising way to move in that direction is by promoting dialogue between religions. At the end of this process, there may be achieved one religion—as would befit one humankind created by one God.

IV.

The greatest challenge that Christianity presents to reason or reason to Christianity is not the doctrine of the Trinity. For Trinitarian ideas are already found in pagan neo-Platonism, and Hegel's peculiar version of Trinitarian thought shows that a more complex concept of reason that takes the failure of concept empiricism seriously is thoroughly compatible with the idea that our basic categories, and thus the basic structures of reality, are triadic. Even if tritheism must be avoided by all means, one of the most fascinating traits of the doctrine of the Trinity is that it aims at a compromise between subjectivity and intersubjectivity as basic principles of reality—a compromise whose philosophical articulation is truly difficult, but one of the worthiest tasks of reason. In general, the seeming paradoxes of Christianity have provoked intellectual efforts unmatched in the Islamic and Jewish traditions. And it might even be that the structures of the division of power built up in modern Western states, and which avoid granting sovereignty to one single state organ, are indirectly influenced by the Trinitarian model.

Not only the doctrine of the immanent, but also that of the economic Trinity, is rationally accessible: God must manifest himself in human history and overcome the alienation inherent in the status of natural man. The function of the church and its continuous development in this process has already been discussed; and there is no difficulty in seeing herein a manifestation of the Holy Spirit. The thorny issue is the correct interpretation of the nature of Jesus Christ. That he belongs to the series of mediators between God and man is obvious. But the prophets of the Old Testament count among them as well, and from Justin onward Christianity has recognized traces of the divine even beyond its own tradition, for example, in the Greek world. In the Enlightenment, the comparison of Socrates and Jesus became a commonplace. Few Christian theologians today would deny that even the founders of other religions were inspired by God. What, then, is unique about Christ?

There are at least three difficulties with orthodox Christology, as it is formulated in the ecumenical councils (the study of whose history is not always morally edifying). The first objection against the uniqueness of Christ is that its defenders often tend to regard those who do not share their interpretation of Christ as excluded from the community with God. This is morally unpalatable, and even the attempt to have Buddhists saved by declaring them "anonymous Christians" is often perceived as condescending (even if in his time Karl Rahner's theory was strategically smart in order to change the traditional understanding of *extra ecclesiam nulla salus*). Second, there is the problem of consistency. It is not at all clear whether the concept of a person who is both true man and true God makes sense logically. Is such a person both omniscient and non-omniscient? If he is simply omniscient, as the tradition assumes, can he still be regarded as a real man? If one defends the doctrine of *kenosis*[44] and denies Christ's omniscience (as he does himself in Matthew 24:36 and as the disappointment of the imminent expectation suggests), then the problem arises over what common elements guarantee the identity between the Second Person and Jesus of Nazareth. After all, "no entity without identity criteria" is an important principle of analytic ontology.

Perhaps even more intractable is, third, the problem of the historical reconstruction of Jesus. If we accept the usual historical methods, we come to a figure who is both an extraordinary moral innovator and who is deeply rooted in the Jewish culture of his time. We hardly come to an omniscient figure (according to the normal standards of reconstruction, Jesus does not even seem to have had a knowledge of contemporary Greek mathematics, which he probably, and rightly, did not regard as relevant for his mission). Of course, one may say that for dogmatic reasons we must ascribe to him all knowledge. But then there is the problem of justifying such a claim. The historical facts clearly do not provide such a justification; nor does there seem to be, despite remarkable attempts by the theological tradition, a cogent metaphysical argument for the existence of a God-man. (If there were, then the question would still remain how we can know that the God-man is Jesus.) A reasonable reduction of the Christological claim would be to say that Jesus' moral doctrine is the best possible and that he himself was morally perfect, and to add that, since the moral law is the core of God, the teaching and living of it may justify the doctrine of a (weak) identity of Jesus with God. This is certainly a reasonable approach, but there is no way of getting beyond mere probability with respect to Jesus' moral perfection (it is easier to come to a positive answer with regard to later saints, where the documentation is much ampler and historically more reliable).

More important is the fact that the normativity of a certain behavior cannot follow from the fact that Jesus has instantiated it.[45] The relation is inverted: Jesus is likely to have instantiated it because it is morally perfect. This not only follows from our criticism of voluntarism; it is also a result of the epistemological superiority of a priori claims, which we find in ethics, over a posteriori claims, which pertain to historical research. As the eighteenth century, in particular, Gotthold Ephraim Lessing and Immanuel Kant, already understood: the validity of ethics must never depend on historical research. But as long as narrative theology does not deny this point, it is based on a valuable insight. In order to train humans in moral behavior, stories are exceedingly important. One of the reasons the Bible is such an extraordinary book is that it offers many sublime stories about human experiences of the divine; and the historically trained reader of the Bible may extract particular pleasure from the fact that he is able to recognize a complex story at the meta-level, that is, regarding the development of the concept of the divine that unfolds in the various human authors of this Book of books.

In the introductory pages to his recent book on Jesus,[46] Benedict XVI has insisted on the limits of the historical method—fundamentally, it cannot answer the valuative question and thus the issue of the present appropriation of a past figure. This is doubtless a true and profound criticism of historicism. But the desire of appropriation, legitimate though it may be, cannot replace the historical work, nor should it influence it in such a way that the experiences of the successors are projected back into the source. History is full of examples of this very human tendency; and a universalist ethics cannot belittle them in other traditions and condone them in one's own. This said, there is no doubt that the vitality of Christianity depends on the ever-renewed attempts of imitation and succession of Jesus. The moral law should not only be grasped theoretically; it ought to be lived, and models are crucial for this purpose. Jesus is not only a teacher of how to live; the story of his passion is one of the most important sources of force in suffering and dying.[47] Recognizing the divine in this story is a far greater moral achievement than seeing it in the triumphs of a warrior prophet like Muhammad.

Christianity has a central social message, and there is no exaggeration in claiming that Christianity, from its beginnings to our day, has strongly contributed to the solution of social problems.[48] But it is of utmost importance to see that this message flows from both a metaphysical and an ethical basis. The redistribution mechanisms of the modern welfare society may be compatible with Christianity; but Christianity cannot be reduced to their support. The decisive point is that Christian ethics transcends the idea of reciprocity. Whoever supports the welfare state only because this is in his long-term interest does not act out of a specific Christian motive. Nor is the mere transfer of money to the poor a sufficient compliance with the demands of Christianity. The decisive point is the personal interest in the other and the willingness to be challenged in one's own habits, even if this entails the humiliation of feeling one's own failure in front of the demands of the moral law.[49] Not all forms of expression of this humiliation are morally or aesthetically attractive, but the experience of humiliation as such is indispensable given the weakness of human nature.

There is little doubt that the two major political problems of our time are the economic inequalities on an international scale and the ecological issue. Both are problems that can hardly be solved by appealing to an ethics of reciprocity. The quality of the Christian contribution to their solution will be a decisive indicator of Christendom's enduring vitality and the future that it will have.

CHAPTER 2

———•—·—•—·—•———

Why Teleological Principles
Are Inevitable for Reason

Natural Theology after Darwin

One of the most amiable characteristics of Charles Darwin is doubtless his modesty. In his *Autobiography,* which was begun in 1876 and continued to receive additions until 1882, he sincerely avers that his work has been "over and over again greatly overpraised"[1] and never claims to be particularly talented in metaphysical matters: "My power to follow a long and purely abstract train of thought is very limited; I should, moreover, never have succeeded with metaphysics or mathematics" (140). Needless to say, he understood that his revolution in biology had transformed the concept of species and lessened the gap between humans and other animals; for he showed in detail how the principle of natural selection could explain innumerable facts in the organic realm that had been previously regarded as irreducible, including the existence of species and human behavior in all its facets. Still, the enormous impact that *On the Origin of Species* of 1859 had immediately outside of the scientific community of biologists on the public at large and its quick spillover to religious and philosophical issues seem quite surprising.[2] Only one sentence at the end of the book hints about the origin of humankind,[3] dealt with in his later works of 1871 and 1872, and there are no explicitly antireligious consequences drawn in this or in any of Darwin's published books. Only at the end of *Variation of Animals and Plants under Domestication* of 1868 did Darwin ask, fully aware of transgressing the limits of his own discipline, some critical questions regarding the compatibility of the mechanism of natural selection with traditional theism. Darwin's intellectual self-restraint, which distinguishes him so strongly from some of the contemporary neo-Darwinists as, for example, Richard Dawkins,[4] was not simply a cautionary move, due to concern for his wife or fear of social ostracism: he had thought seriously about religious issues in the years immediately after his return from his voyage around the world and had come to the conclusion that his theory did not entail atheism. It is thus proper to start the following reflections with an analysis of his quite subtle religious ideas, which are certainly not inferior to those of most contemporary scientists addressing religious issues (I). I then put them into the context of a more general development of the concepts of God and nature and discuss the most important attempt of the nineteenth century to render Darwinism compatible with theism, namely, that by Asa Gray. The focus on Gray is due to the simple reason that progress in philosophy is, if it takes place at all, of a very different nature than in science; therefore, we can learn from philosophical reflections of past centuries far more than we can learn from scientific theories of the same time (II). Finally, I discuss in which sense even after the Darwinian revolution a teleological interpretation of nature remains not only a possibility, but a necessity (III).

I.

In the chapter of his *Autobiography* dedicated to "Religious belief"—pages published in complete form not earlier than 1958 since the first edition of 1887 had been subjected to family censorship—Darwin describes the reasons that led to the fading of the Anglican belief in which he had been educated. After all, he had for some time contemplated becoming an Anglican minister. He claims, and as far as we know his development, truthfully, that he had never had strongly developed religious sentiments (91); certainly he had never been an Evangelical. But at the same time he had imbibed traditional Anglican theology, and at the beginning of his voyage on the *Beagle,* during which his favorite book was John Milton's *Paradise Lost,* he was sometimes scorned by orthodox officers "for quoting the Bible as an unanswerable authority on some point of morality" (85). How did the slow evaporation of these beliefs, which he in vain tried to resist, come about? The reasons and causes Darwin mentioned have relatively little to do with his great scientific discovery. What are they? We can subdivide the chapter in question into three main sections. In the first (A), Darwin analyzes the arguments against the Bible being based on divine revelation; in the second (B), he moves from revealed to natural theology. Here he discusses both the arguments in favor of (B 1) and those speaking against (B 2) the existence of God, among which the theodicy problem figures; and he mentions also the logically independent issue of the immortality of the soul (B 3). In the third section (C), he reflects on his own development—one might say, on the evolution of his own religious beliefs and on their epistemological status. Such reflections are found at the end of the chapter, but they are also interspersed throughout B; I discuss them in the context of (C).

(A) With regard to the first point, Darwin deals separately with the Old and the New Testaments. Concerning the former, he mentions on the one hand historically false stories narrated in it, on the other hand the primitive feelings ascribed to God (like those "of a revengeful tyrant"). Concerning the second, he is disturbed by the connection of the New Testament with the discredited Old Testament. Additionally, the intrinsic incredibility of miracle stories, the credulity of the people living in those times, the impossibility of excluding that the Gospels were written later than the events narrated, as well as the contradictions among the evangelists, led him "to disbelieve in Christianity as a divine revelation" (86). He continues to recognize the beauty of the morality of the New Testament, but sees that it partly depends on later interpretations that did not capture the originally intended meaning. This original meaning comprehends, for example, the doctrine of everlasting punishments of nonbelievers, and he declares this doctrine "damnable" (87). Clearly, there is nothing in these arguments connected to natural science: they are based on ethical ideas and historical research; and even the general skepticism with regard to miracles is not so much a result of the scientific development as its presupposition. Most of the arguments mentioned as well as others directed against the *formal* idea of revelation had already gained currency in the eighteenth century, some in the seventeenth century (think only of Baruch Spinoza and Gotthold Ephraim Lessing), even if they had had more impact on the Continent than in England. But David Friedrich Strauss's *Das Leben Jesu, kritisch bearbeitet* of 1835–36 came out as *The Life of Jesus Critically Examined* already in 1846 in the translation of Marian Evans, later better known under her pen-name George Eliot, and clearly this book changed our relation to the New Testament as no other before or afterward.[5] Darwin himself recognizes that the arguments proposed do not have "the least novelty or value." By "value" he can only mean "value as original contributions," hardly "validity," for he insists that he has "never since doubted even for a single second that my conclusion was correct" (87)—one of the passages whose publication was prevented by Emma Darwin. The collapse of the naïve belief in revelation, by the way, does not exclude an understanding of the core Christian message, insofar as it is justifiable by reason, as a manifestation of the divine and of the whole of the Bible as a progressive revelation; and it certainly did not prevent the growth of natural theology in early modernity, but on the contrary stimulated it. It was only the latter's crisis that hastened the decline of theism. Let us see what Darwin contributed to this crisis.

(B 1) In the second section he begins by stating in a very concise manner the contribution of his theory to natural theology. "The old argument of design in nature, as given by Paley, which formerly seemed to me so conclusive, fails, now that the law of natural selection has been discovered." The sentence claims neither that the theory of natural selection[6] is *incompatible* with theism nor that it has *destroyed all proofs of God*. In the most natural, even if admittedly not the only grammatically possible, interpretation, it does not even state that the argument of design has been overthrown by the new theory; but it limits this claim to the argument of design *as exposed by Paley*. Darwin had thoroughly studied William Paley in Cambridge; he mentions that in order to pass his BA exams, he had to read his work *A View of the Evidences of Christianity* as well as *The Principles of Moral and Political Philosophy*, but obviously here Darwin has in mind Paley's last work, the *Natural Theology* of 1802 with the famous watchmaker comparison,[7] a book whose logic "gave me as much delight as did Euclid. The careful study of these works, without attempting to learn any part by rote, was the only part of the Academical Course which, as I then felt and as I still believe, was of the least use to me in the education of my mind" (59). Still, one could understand Darwin's earlier quoted sentence as implying that Paley's special creationism is the only valid form of the argument from design. But that this is not the case is proven by the context. For Darwin continues: "Everything in nature is the result of fixed laws" and then: "But passing over the endless beautiful adaptations which we everywhere meet with, it may be asked how can the generally beneficent arrangement of the world be accounted for?" (87f.). Here Darwin seems to recognize the point, both quite obvious and insisted upon by a friend like Asa Gray, that the set of the laws of nature within which natural selection alone can operate is not itself the result of natural selection. The mechanism of natural selection can explain the adaptation of single organisms and species only under the presupposition of a system of laws that render such an evolution possible. If no planet had water, for example, there would be no life, given the set of laws of our world; and it is easy to imagine other worlds in which natural selection could not lead to forms of life more complex than prokaryotes. Thus, the correct interpretation of Darwin's claim must be that it is directed only against a form of the physico-theological argument using special creationism. The causes for the development of the various species are immanent. But as long as we see ends *in the world as a whole,* not in the single species, we should still be allowed to ask why the world is such that in it awe-inspiring entities like organisms exist. In this form, so one could say, even if Darwin does not use this language, the cosmological and the physico-theological proofs merge: we are searching for a cause not simply of the world, as in the cosmological proof, nor of the adaptation of the single species, as in the traditional physico-theological proof, but of a world that allows for the evolution of organisms as we know them. And indeed Darwin does not reject this type of argument: "This follows from the extreme difficulty or rather impossibility of conceiving this immense and wonderful universe, including man with his capacity of looking far backwards and far into futurity, as the result of blind chance and necessity. When thus reflecting I feel compelled to look to a First Cause having an intelligent mind in some degree analogous to that of man; and I deserve to be called a Theist" (93). We will return to this passage since in a later addition to it Darwin weakened the statement.

(B 2) Darwin then addresses the classical theodicy issue, that is, the existence of evil as an argument *against* the existence of God. Of the various types of evil he mentions only suffering. At the beginning of his reflections, he does not seem to presuppose that the world has to be the best possible, or at least such that it could not be better, in order to justify the ways of God; he seems (but the appearance is deceiving) to be satisfied with the balance being in favor of happiness.[8] And this the sanguine Darwin clearly affirms, even if he is aware that the weighing of pleasure and suffering is very difficult.[9] But he sees in natural selection, which presupposes an overproduction, an argument for his belief. "According to my judgment happiness decidedly prevails, though this would be very difficult to prove. If the truth of this conclusion be granted, it harmonises well with the effects which we might expect from natural selection. If all the individuals of any species were habitually to suffer to an extreme degree they would neglect to propagate their kind; but we have no reason to believe that this has ever or at least often occurred. Some other considerations, moreover, lead to the belief that all sentient beings have been formed so as to enjoy, as a general rule, happiness" (88). Darwin then adds that if suffering lasts long it diminishes the power of action, while pleasurable sensations do not have this depressing effect; "on the contrary they stimulate the whole system to increased action." Thus it is reasonable that natural selection uses pleasure rather than pain as stimulus for action, even if the latter "is well adapted to make a creature guard itself against any great or sudden evil" (89). Darwin mentions various types of pleasure, as those from exertion of the body and mind and from sociability, and sums up: "The sum of such pleasures as these, which are habitual or frequently recurrent, give, as I can hardly doubt, to most sentient beings an excess of happiness over misery, although many occasionally suffer much. Such suffering is quite compatible with the belief in Natural Selection, which is not perfect in its action" (89f.). At the end of the third chapter of *The Origin* he consoles himself with the reflection "that the war of nature is not incessant, that no fear is felt, that death is generally prompt, and that the vigorous, the healthy, and the happy survive and multiply."[10] Nevertheless, the existence of any amount of suffering remains a disturbing problem, and this even more among animals than among humans since the latter, and only they, may benefit from suffering and improve morally.[11] "This very old argument from the existence of suffering against the existence of an intelligent first cause seems to me a strong one" (90). This sentence proves that Darwin did regard the problem of suffering as a serious challenge to theism. He did not believe, however, that his own theory had increased the difficulty of the problem. On the contrary, he thought that it had strengthened the idea that the balance is in favor of pleasure—an idea that is certainly not a sufficient, but a necessary presupposition of any solution to the problem.

There is one feature of his theory, however, that in Darwin's eyes did not simply destroy one of the *proofs* of God, but that might be directly *inconsistent* with God's existence. In our chapter of the *Autobiography*, he merely alludes to it and refers to the last pages of *Variation of Animals and Plants under Domestication*, affirming that "the argument there given has never . . . been answered." What is his argument? There Darwin compares the beneficial effect of natural selection based on variation to the use of stone fragments whose shape is the result of various accidents by an architect. As he generally does in his work, Darwin embraces determinism; that is, he insists on the existence of sufficient causes for the shape of the stones, even if they are not better known than the causes of variation were at his time. "And here we are led to face a grave difficulty, in alluding to which I am aware that I am travelling beyond my proper province. An omniscient Creator must have foreseen every consequence which results from the laws imposed by Him."[12] But is it plausible to assume that God has really intended all variations, even those that lead to particularly repellent behavior of animals? And if we deny this in one case, how can we maintain it in another? "However much we may wish it, we can hardly follow Professor Gray in his belief 'that variation has been led along certain beneficial lines,' like a stream 'along definite and useful lines of irrigation.'" Two things particularly worry Darwin: the plasticity of organization, which leads also to harmful deviations, and the redundant power of reproduction, which, according to the Malthusian basis of his theory, entails the struggle for existence. These "must appear to us superfluous laws of nature. On the other hand, an omnipotent and omniscient Creator ordains everything and foresees everything. Thus we are brought face to face with a difficulty as insoluble as is that of free will and predestination" (372). We will come back both to Gray's theory and to Darwin's argument that seems to challenge most directly theism since it states that the mechanism of natural selection, whose existence cannot be doubted, is somehow "superfluous" for an omnipotent and omniscient Creator.

(B 3) In the *Autobiography,* Darwin only briefly addresses the problem of immortality. He thinks that the belief in it is "strong and almost instinctive" since the thought seems intolerable that life will become extinct when the sun will grow too cold for life. "To those who fully admit the immortality of the human soul, the destruction of our world will not appear so dreadful" (92). Still, the reader does not have the impression that Darwin himself shares that belief.

(C) The passage just quoted shows that in Darwin's view the fact that a belief is almost instinctive does not prove that it is true. Indeed, one of the most amazing features of the chapter is the capacity of observing one's own beliefs, as it were, from outside. Darwin offers, so to speak, a "natural history" of his own religious views, as he had done with those of humankind in the second chapter of *The Descent of Man, and Selection in Relation to Sex* of 1871.[13] This stance is partly based on his work as a biologist, which included, particularly in *The Expression of the Emotions in Man and Animals* of 1872, unbiased observation not only of his children, but also of himself. Partly it presupposes the rejection of an intuitionist epistemology, that is, the position that there are indemonstrable and nevertheless legitimate basic convictions concerning religious matters. From at least Friedrich Heinrich Jacobi to Alvin Plantinga, philosophers of religion have used such an epistemology, which is indeed tempting; for it is not easy to see how without basic beliefs the whole idea of justification can begin to make any sense. And once this is granted, it is hard to deny our religious basic beliefs the same status that we grant to our nonreligious basic beliefs.

Darwin, however, pokes fun at this position by quoting the remark of an old lady directed against Darwin's notoriously skeptical father: "I know that sugar is sweet in my mouth, and I know that my Redeemer liveth" (96). His main objection against the epistemological position that such "inward convictions and feelings are of any weight as evidence of what really exists" is that different people often vary in their basic convictions, and that sometimes these are logically incompatible with each other. Among religions, for example, there is no consensus. "But it cannot be doubted that Hindoos, Mahomadans and others might argue in the same manner and with equal force in favour of the existence of one God, or of many Gods, or as with the Buddists of no God" (90f.; analogously with regard to moral beliefs *The Descent* . . . , I 99). What is even more, our own convictions change over time. Darwin describes the almost religious awe he felt as a young naturalist in the Brazilian forest, "but now the grandest scenes would not cause any such convictions and feelings to rise in my mind. It may be truly said that I am like a man who has become colour-blind." Darwin even thinks that his earlier quasi-religious feelings were in fact not of a religious nature, but more kindred to the sense of sublimity (92). He seems to suggest that the religious dimension was an *interpretation* of raw qualia that in themselves were not at all necessarily connected with the idea of God. In general, he reports an increase of skepticism in the development of his mind: "Nothing is more remarkable than the spread of skepticism or rationalism during the latter half of my life" (95). This self-distancing, however, is not applied to the moral feelings. "The highest satisfaction is derived from following certain impulses, namely the social instincts" (94). Sometimes we are allowed, even obliged, to act against the expectations of other people; then a person "will still have the solid satisfaction of knowing that he has followed his innermost guide or conscience" (95). But it is not clear why we should regard ourselves more bound by our conscience than by our religious feelings; after all, the demands of conscience vary among different people.

This self-distancing plays a central role in the already mentioned later addition to the passage in which Darwin declares himself to be a theist. He mentions that his conviction of the existence of a First Cause is based on a process of inference: "But then arises the doubt—can the mind of man, which has, as I fully believe, been developed from a mind as low as that possessed by the lowest animal, be trusted when it draws such grand conclusions?" (93). The belief in God was after all inculcated into children, and it could well be that the connection between cause and effect is not necessary, "but probably depends merely on inherited experience" (93). Therefore, Darwin declares himself no longer a theist, but an agnostic.[14]

II.

Darwin's religious ideas were not revolutionary, but were based on the development of science and philosophy in early modernity. There is little doubt nowadays among historians of science that the miracle of modern science was profoundly rooted in a religious vision of the world.[15] The latter offered both a moral justification to the novel enterprise of easing human life through the development of science and technology and a metaphysical foundation to the basic concept of universal natural laws that do not tolerate any exception, a concept still alien to the ancient world, which lacked its theological presuppositions.[16] It is true that several of the fathers of modern science were not orthodox Christians, that is, they rejected the doctrines of the Trinity and/or of the divinity of Christ, as Isaac Newton did; but most of them were committed theists or deists. The distinction between the latter two concepts, by the way, is fuzzy and often misleading. This is partly due to the fact that the various elements used to define "deism" are not equivalent logically and are not instantiated simultaneously empirically. Georg Wilhelm Friedrich Hegel, for example, like Matthew Tindal and John Toland, did not accept a revelation beyond reason, but took the doctrine of the Trinity more seriously than any other philosopher of modernity; Charles Dickens did not believe in the divinity of Christ, but regarded the morals of the Gospel as unsurpassed and unsurpassable. For historians of theology, a multidimensional continuum between traditional theism and natural or rational theology is more helpful than the strict opposition of the concepts.[17]

Another reason the distinction between deism and theism creates more problems than it solves is that one of the main dividing issues—whether God only created the world or continues to intervene in it—is amenable to an intermediate solution: God operates according to the laws created, but in the development of the world according to his laws, he himself is present, in certain axiologically relevant events more than in others. Immediately after the publication of *The Origin,* a famous and bestselling volume by liberal theologians, entitled *Essays and Reviews,* triggered disciplinary measures by the Church of England. (This did not prevent one of its authors, Frederick Temple, from becoming later the Archbishop of Canterbury, however.) In this book, the Reverend Baden Powell, who had rejected on theological grounds special creationism even before Darwin's book, argued that the belief in a world order without interruptions, that is, without miracles, shows more respect to God than the assumption that he has periodically to fix his creation by special interventions.[18]

Where did this conception originate? The idea that divine action is necessarily channeled according to the laws of nature was forcefully articulated by Spinoza. But the laws are not sufficient; every event must have also a secondary cause, none can be explained only by the eternal properties of God, that is, his natural laws.[19] The attractiveness of this idea is not limited to the pantheist context, within which Spinoza developed it; nor does the idea as such entail a theory of the substantial identity of body and mind or a rejection of any kind of physico-theology, even if Spinoza himself had only scorn for it as for any realist theory of value.[20] As is well known, the search for the ends of God in the creation of various natural objects was an important part of early science—think of the Boyle Lectures, which started in 1692. In England, this tradition lasted much longer than on the Continent, until the Bridgewater Treatises (1833–40). But already in the eighteenth century, the various "Theologies of Insects" and the like were widely made fun of, for example by Voltaire. In his masterful book *Natur ohne Sinn?* Matthias Schramm has shown how the research by Gottfried Wilhelm Leibniz, Leonhard Euler, and Pierre Louis Maupertuis that finally led to extremal principles, particularly the principle of least action, was already a reaction against the theological absurdities that found God in the most limited means-end relations, either between organs and their organisms or, worse, between other species and humans. A formal teleology was regarded as more promising than the traditional one oriented toward concrete contents.[21]

Leibniz is the most prominent among those thinkers who mediate between the Spinozian postulate that God necessarily acts through laws and a finalistic interpretation of the world, which no theist can give up. Leibniz accepts the principle of sufficient reason, and thus an all-pervasive system of efficient causes, but at the same time teaches that they do not logically exclude final causes. The world of consciousness cannot be grasped without finality, and even the system of the laws of nature, particularly the laws of movement, are not simple consequences from logic, but presuppose an axiological principle.[22] God chooses among all possible worlds the world with the maximal value: his wisdom is manifested in the choice of the whole, not in that of single ends.

Darwin's rejection of special creationism was nothing else than the application to species of Spinoza's idea that God acts only through antecedent conditions and general laws: species are not eternal features of the world, and thus also their existence has to be explained by antecedent conditions (earlier species) and general laws (among which the mechanism of natural selection is pre-eminent). Darwin had indeed a profound awe for universal laws, and this awe was one of the forces behind his discoveries. His son William wrote shortly after his death about Darwin: "As regards his respect for the laws of nature it might be called reverence if not a religious feeling. No man could feel more intensely the vastness or the inviolability of the laws of nature."[23]

The rationalist frame of seventeenth- and eighteenth-century philosophy was communicated to the early Darwin not by Spinoza or Leibniz, but by William Whewell[24] and John Frederick William Herschel, both of whom he personally met and neither of whom ever accepted his theory.[25] Among the great philosophers the most important influence was David Hume, which may explain the increasing skepticism of the aging Darwin with regard to religious issues. I already alluded to Hume's influence when I spoke about Darwin's offering a "natural history" of his own religious views, and indeed the early notebooks show a far-reaching impact of the Scottish thinker.[26] The works quoted are *A Treatise of Human Nature, An Enquiry Concerning Human Understanding, A Dissertation on the Passions, The Natural History of Religion,* and the *Dialogues Concerning Natural Religion.* The latter book must have been particularly fascinating for Darwin because it develops a powerful critique of the argument from design, even if long before Darwin's own theory—which, interestingly, is adumbrated in Part VIII of the book.[27] Hume's influence is also present in Darwin's rejection of free will;[28] and in the late *Autobiography* the main argument against the validity of the cosmological proof reflects Hume's criticism of the concept of cause. Also, Hume's idea of explaining the evolution of religion according to universal laws is mirrored in Darwin's criticism of a philosopher "who says the innate knowledge of creator <is> <<has been>> implanted in us . . . by a separate act of God, & not as a necessary integrant part of his most magnificent laws, of which we profane <<degnen>> in thinking not capable to <do> produce every effect, of every kind which surrounds us."[29] This passage is significant because it proves that the rejection of special creation or revelation in the early Darwin went together with a commitment to theism or deism. Indeed, Darwinism as such is compatible with both a Spinozian and a Leibnizian interpretation, and it is not science, but philosophy itself that has to decide which of the two interpretations is the more plausible one.

Most prominent among those of Darwin's contemporaries who understood this point and even tried to integrate the idea of natural selection into a theistic worldview was his friend and admirer, the great American botanist Asa Gray, one of the few persons to whom Darwin had communicated his theory before it was published.[30] (In fact, it was a letter written by Darwin to Gray in 1857 that was read on July 1, 1858, in the Linnean Society in order to prove that Darwin had developed his theory before he knew about Alfred Russel Wallace's analogous one.) Gray, who was an orthodox Protestant and had a remarkable philosophical intelligence, defends the central tenets of Darwinism with acumen against its critics (e.g., Louis Agassiz), but maintains that it is nothing other than an hypothesis—however, the best hypothesis available, which theologians are well advised to respect.[31] His reflections on the philosophical consequences of Darwinism impress the reader because of his complete grasp of the theory,[32] his awareness of the methodological and epistemological issues at stake, his elegant style, his sober religiosity, his impartiality and even respect for different opinions, and, last not least, his subtle humor.[33] It is thus not surprising that his various essays on Darwinism and religion were in 1876 collected in a volume (reissued in 1884) and that in 1880 he was invited to deliver two lectures on *Natural*

Science and Religion at the Theological School of Yale College.[34] His first text, published in March 1860 in the *American Journal of Science and Arts,* is a review of *The Origin,* which at the end addresses the philosophical and theological consequences of Darwin's intellectual breakthrough. Gray rightly states that the author is silent about how he "harmonizes his scientific theory with his philosophy and theology" (*Darwiniana,* 56) and tries to reconstruct its implicit philosophy. Alluding to Paley's watchmaker analogy, he wittily asks: "What is to hinder Mr. Darwin from giving Paley's argument a further *a-fortiori* extension to the supposed case of a watch which sometimes produces better watches, and contrivances adapted to successive conditions?" (57). Gray insists on the fact that God has to be conceived as non-temporal; and he says that every philosophical theist must adopt the idea that the Creator's intervention is done either from all time or through all time.[35] He sees dangers connected to both views, the first leading to atheism, the second to pantheism, and clearly prefers the second. "Natural law, upon this view, is the human conception of continued and orderly Divine action" (58). In order to undermine any distinction between initial creation and later interventions, Gray appeals, in my eyes ironically, to "profounder minds to establish, if they can, a rational distinction in kind between his [God's] working in Nature carrying on operations, and in initiating those operations" (59). Gray insists on a "continued directing intelligence," but this is compatible with a general plan. While at the end he grants that there may have been an independent origination of certain types and thus accepts "as much intervention as may be required," he insists "that Natural Selection, in explaining the facts, explains also many classes of facts which thousand-fold repeated independent acts of creation do not explain, but leave more mysterious than ever" (61). Only a few months later, he published in the same journal a dialogue "Design versus Necessity" on different ways of assessing the value of Darwin's book for natural theology.[36] Interesting is the note added at the end that the opponent to the theistic interpretation might have used the concept of contingency instead of necessity (86).

The third essay was also published in 1860 and has the programmatic title "Natural Selection not Inconsistent with Natural Theology." Gray mentions that Darwin's gradual evolutionary theory fits well with an old principle of natural philosophy—it "answers in a general way to the Law of Continuity in the inorganic world, or rather is so analogous to it that both may fairly be expressed by the Leibnitzian axiom, *Natura non agit saltatim.*" Gray insists that this principle cannot be presupposed a priori, but "naturalists of enlarged views will not fail to infer the principle from the phenomena they investigate—to perceive that the rule holds, under due qualifications and altered forms, throughout the realm of Nature" (123). (Needless to say, the later theory of punctuated equilibrium is also a form of gradualism.) Gray is aware that "the principle of gradation throughout organic Nature may . . . be interpreted upon other assumptions than those of Darwin's hypothesis" (126), but certainly the Darwinian theory offers an explanation of the phenomena that we observe. Gray exemplifies his theory with regard to individuality, which is connected to the loss of vegetative reproduction and was only slowly acquired in the course of evolution, even if it is the "very ground of *being* as distinguished from *thing.*" Gray calls only unicellular plants real units, not so the more complex ones. "In the ascending gradation of the vegetable kingdom individuality is, so to say, striven after, but never attained; in the lower animals it is striven after with greater though incomplete success; it is realized only in animals of so high a rank that vegetative multiplication of offshoots are out of the question, where all parts are strictly members and nothing else, and all subordinated to a common nervous centre—is fully realized only in a conscious person" (125). In the last section of the essay on "Darwin and his Reviewers," Gray insists on the very different quality of the reviews of *The Origin*; and he is particularly irritated by those who insinuate that Darwin's book is atheistic. Gray recognizes that Darwin has purposely been silent on theological issues, and in a witty application of the issue at stake to Darwin's behavior in proposing the issue comments: "This reticence, under the circumstances, argues design, and raises inquiry as to the final cause and reason why. Here, as in higher instances, confident as we are that there is a final cause, we must not be over-confident that we can infer the particular or true one" (144). One possible explanation may be that he is not familiar with philosophical inquiries and thus focuses only on secondary causes; another may be that he enjoys being attacked as atheist by inconsiderate people. In general, Gray writes, a theist is only committed to the idea that there are ends in nature, but not at all to a specific claim that a particular thing or event is intended by God. "Most people believe that some were designed and others were not, although they fall into a hopeless maze whenever they undertake to define their position" (138). Every intelligent person accepts general besides particular providence, that is, that many events are willed by God only insofar as they are the consequence of general laws, and no thoughtful theist ascribes design only to supernatural events (149). In one point, however, Gray treads upon dubious terrain, and that is his claim, forcefully denied by Darwin, that "variation has been led along certain beneficial lines" (148). It is true that the causes of variation were unknown at that time (and even today we do not know all of them), and it is also true, as he says, that Darwin's theory does not necessarily entail that there are more harmful deviations than were already known to exist. "Good-for-nothing monstrosities, failures of purpose rather than purposeless, indeed, sometimes occur; but these are just as anomalous and unlikely upon Darwin's theory as upon any other" (147). But in this passage he tends to play down the negative variations, and he somehow insinuates the direct presence of God when the secondary causes are not yet known. In any case, Gray does not claim that Darwinism leads to natural theology; in fact, he recognizes that the arguments from design may not convince everybody. "But we may insist, upon grounds already intimated, that, whatever they were good for before Darwin's book appeared, they are good for now" (152). Even if he does not use this language, Gray points to the fact that the *genesis* of an organism does not contribute at all to the question whether its astonishingly adapted structure is due to design (151f.; cf. 259).[37] Certainly, Darwinism can be interpreted in an atheistic way (159); but this interpretation does not follow from the theory. "If you import atheism into your conception of variation and natural selection, you can readily exhibit it in the result" (154). Gray recognizes the chance moment (which he rightly locates not in selection, but in variation) as the major stumbling block. A large number of these variations "are not improvements, but perhaps the contrary, and therefore useless or purposeless, and born to perish" (156). But Gray retorts by saying that nature abounds with analogous instances, not only in the inorganic world, but even among humans. "Some of our race are useless, or worse, as regards the improvement of mankind; yet the race may be designed to improve, and may be actually improving" (157).

Of particular interest is Gray's claim that Darwin brought back teleology to natural science, "so that, instead of Morphology *versus* Teleology, we shall have Morphology wedded to Teleology" (288). Teleology
(the term was coined by Christian Wolff) here means that one species is
useful to another. The reason for this return of teleology in Darwin is
that we owe ecology proper to the idea of the mutability of species.[38] If
species are not eternal, but survive only due to a constant struggle for
existence, then "the structure of every organic being is related, in the
most essential yet often hidden manner, to that of all other organic beings, with which it comes into competition for food or residence, or from
which it has to escape, or on which it preys."[39] It is this holistic approach
to nature that justifies analyses of causal interdependences between different species and leads to a "restoration of teleology" (357), as Gray
writes in the final essay of the volume, "Evolutionary Teleology." But
this is not only important for the natural science of biology; it makes the
argument from design more plausible to the objectors who always
pointed to the dysteleological structures in nature. "In the comprehensive and far-reaching teleology which may take the place of the former
narrow conceptions, organs and even faculties, useless to the individual,
find their explanation and reason of being. Either they have done service
in the past, or they may do service in the future" (375). The imperfections have the function of keeping the evolutionary process going on and
of producing better adaptations. "In this system the forms and species,
in all their variety, are not mere ends in themselves, but the whole a series
of means and ends, in the contemplation of which we may obtain higher
and more comprehensive, and perhaps worthier, as well as more consistent, views of design in Nature than heretofore" (378). Again, Gray does
not deny that the argument from design may be rejected: he is familiar
with both David Hume's and John Stuart Mill's well-known objections
(not, however, with Immanuel Kant's). But he reiterates his point that,
while the question of design in the world will be discussed by philosophers as long as that world lasts, there is nothing in Darwinism inimical
to that assumption. It only teaches us to look at nature as a whole and
find, or reject, design in her as a whole (379). But does not natural selection render final causes completely superfluous? Gray points to the fact
that selection operates only if there occurs variation toward new forms;
thus it cannot explain what in fact it presupposes (385f.).

In his Yale lectures, *Natural Science and Religion,* Gray makes this point more clearly. For him, not the whole theory of trans-specific evolution, but natural selection itself is not a simple hypothesis, but a truth (46), while the idea that variation is all-directional and accidental does not enjoy the same status. But whatever the exact causes of variation, at that time still unknown, natural selection cannot be one of them and thus it cannot *on its own* explain the slow evolution toward more and more complex forms (49). At the same time, together with variation, "the principle of natural selection, taken in its fullest sense, is the only one known to me which can be termed a real cause in the scientific sense of the term" (70f.). It is a cause only together with the laws of the living world, however, that remain as astonishing after Darwin as they were before him.

> Does it [natural selection] scientifically account for the formation of any organ, show that under given conditions sensitive eye-spot, initial hand or brain, or even a different hue or texture, must then and there be developed as the consequence of assignable conditions? Does it explain how and why so much, or any, sensitiveness, faculty of response by movement, perception, consciousness, intellect, is correlated with such and such an organism? I answer, Not at all! The hypothesis does none of these things. For my own part I can hardly conceive that any one should think that natural selection scientifically accounts for these phenomena. (73)

And thus the argument from design can be used as well, *if* one is already a theist (84f.).The conflict is "not between Darwinism and direct Creationism, but between design and fortuity, between any intention or intellectual cause and no intention nor predicable first cause" (89). Gray at the end mentions that explicit arguments for theism do not come from the study of nature—it only never bars them. His own reason for believing in a divine principle of the world is that it "gives us a workable conception of how 'the world of forms and means' is related to 'the world of worths and ends.' The negative hypothesis gives no mental or ethical satisfaction whatever" (91). Gray also gestures toward an epistemological argument by quoting a sentence ascribed to James Clerk Maxwell, "that he had scrutinized all the agnostic hypotheses he knew of, and found that they one and all needed a God to make them workable" (91). In any case,

Gray interprets evolution as the slow instantiation of the values willed by God. "As the forms and kinds rise gradually out of that which was well-nigh formless into a consummate form, so do biological ends rise and assert themselves in increasing distinctness, variety, and dignity. Vegetables and animals have paved the earth with intentions" (93). He then adds some (unsatisfying) reflections on the "insoluble" problem of the free will (97) and ends with some arguments for the immortality of the human soul.

We have seen that Darwin at the end of *Variation* remained skeptical with regard to Gray's attempt to reconcile natural theology with Darwinism. Partly this has to do with the fact that Gray looks at Darwinism from a theistic perspective, which for Darwin was not as evident.[40] But Darwin did not even regard as obvious the much weaker thesis that his theory was *compatible* with theism. As far as I can see, there are two main arguments against the compatibility claim. One of the arguments is not used by Darwin himself, but plays an important role in the usual accounts of the decline of physico-theology. According to it, the whole concept of evolution destroyed the idea of design.[41] For an absolute mind must be able to immediately get at its ends; why should there be a long way toward them? Already Leibniz, however, discusses this issue and accepts that progress toward perfection in finite beings may be compatible with the best possible world since change toward the better may be itself a perfection.[42] Indeed, one might argue, such a world may be more interesting and challenging than one that is absolutely stable.

The second argument is related, but more specific: Darwin points to the redundant power of reproduction and the harmful deviations that follow from the plasticity and extreme variability of organisms. Even if he does not say it, it seems to me that for him the Malthusian overproduction is somehow the opposite of the principle of the least action that so attracted natural theologians in the course of the eighteenth century. The negative variations and the overproduction with subsequent selection do not seem the quickest way to the results God might have in mind and thus are incompatible with providence.[43] How can these doubts be answered? With regard to the harmful variations, one can claim with Gray that the occurrence of such deviations was already known before Darwin; so his theory does not add anything negative to the old arguments of theodicy. On the contrary, natural selection *prevents* these harmful deviations from spreading; it thus limits the negative effects of chance and can even claim to be purposive with regard to adaptation.[44] Darwin himself indeed thought that one reason against special creationism was strictly theological: the latter ascribes quite ugly results to the direct will of God.[45] As he wrote to Gray on May 2, 1860: "I cannot persuade myself that a beneficent & omnipotent God would have designedly created the Ichneumonidae with the express intention of their feeding within the living bodies of caterpillars, or that a cat should play with mice."[46] The conceptual tool to deal with such ugly phenomena (which are easily surpassed by human suffering and cruelty) is old. Whoever interprets, in my eyes reasonably, divine omnipotence as God being the cause of everything, is well advised not to give up the normative difference between various states of affairs. Suffering is not willed by God in the same degree as pleasure, even if it is impossible to deny that both are willed by him, if they occur and if he is supposed to be omnipotent. The intellectual tool used by a theist such as Leibniz is to say that God accepts certain intrinsically negative states because they are necessarily connected with the positive states he aims at with his antecedent will, that is, in a strong sense of the term, yet independently of the consequences connected with them.[47]

But why did God accept a world in which suffering occurs at all, such as the mechanism of natural selection certainly entails? One classical answer is to say that one decisive criterion in the choice of the world that God created was the simplicity of the laws of nature, and that this again and again entails suffering, including that of innocent humans. Even if one rejects any "direction" of the variations, one may argue within a theistic worldview that the mechanism of natural selection has been chosen by God for four reasons: first, natural selection is an extremely simple mechanism with enormous causal power—Wallace in 1859 compared it with "the centrifugal governor of the steam engine."[48] Second, the overproduction which, together with the scarcity of the resources, variation, and inheritability of traits, entails natural selection as a logical consequence, is an expression of the principle of plenitude: all possible life forms are tried, even if only the compossible ones will last. The value of life is the reason it tries to spread as much as it can, even if the price it has to pay is the struggle for existence, which then leads to the development of more complex life forms. Third, paradoxically the over-production is the reason for the creation of scarcity, which obliges organisms to behave economically and to try to optimize resources: thus something analogous to the principle of the least action is imposed upon organisms by the redundant reproduction. And fourth, within a determinist universe, natural selection together with other natural laws and given antecedent conditions had to lead to the results that God wanted, such as the existence of morally responsible beings.

III.

Asa Gray's reflections, supported by the final considerations, have hopefully shown that Darwinism and theism are not logically incompatible. But, as Gray himself wrote, this does not prove that theism is true. Theism, the assumption that the world has been created by an absolute Mind, certainly entails a teleological interpretation of the world as a whole, for minds act according to ends. The inversion, however, does not seem to hold; for both Aristotle and Arthur Schopenhauer defend a teleological interpretation of nature even without belief in a Creator God: the ends are immanent in nature. What are the arguments for theism? The argument from design is indeed far from being cogent. *If* there is a divine principle of the world, then we have to interpret the world in terms of ends, but it is not the world as such that forces upon us a teleological interpretation. There is too much apparent dystelelogy in it. We may explain it away as necessary for desirable ends, but only if we already have independent arguments for a transcendent principle. Furthermore, Hume in the posthumous *Dialogues Concerning Natural Religion* of 1779 and Kant in *The Only Possible Argument in Support of a Demonstration of the Existence of God* of 1763 as well as in the *Critique of Pure Reason* of 1781 (B 648–58/A 620–30) have rightly individuated the main weaknesses of the argument.[49] Their lasting insight is that the argument cannot be grounded on an empiricist basis. To begin with Hume, he writes that we can infer causes from effects, when we have observed the two together in other cases; "but how this argument can have place, where the objects are

single, individual, without parallel, or specific resemblance, may be difficult to explain."[50] Furthermore, it is not clear why the cause of the world
does not itself need a cause (161). Since according to empiricism all our
knowledge is based on experiences of the world, we can only say that the
cause *of* the world must be analogous to one of the causes of order that
we find *within* the world, and all minds we know are finite. "This world . . .
is very faulty and imperfect, compared to a superior standard; and was
only the first rude essay of some infant Deity, who afterwards abandoned
it, ashamed of his lame performance" (169); it could also be the common
work of various deities (167). Beside reason as cause of artworks, instinct, vegetative reproduction, and sexual reproduction are also causes
of remarkable objects. Why then should we assume that one of these
causes is more likely to be the origin of the world than another? "Any one
of these four principles above mentioned (and a hundred others which
lie open to our conjecture) may afford us a theory, by which to judge of
the origin of the world; and it is a palpable and egregious partiality, to
confine our view entirely to that principle, by which our own minds operate" (178). One may deny the last sentence by embracing a Cartesian
theory of the epistemological priority of the first-person perspective;
but if one does not, then Hume's supposition "that the world arose by
vegetation from a seed shed by another world" is no less rational than
the belief in the creation of the world by a mind. Hume is aware of the
fact that there is also an a priori argument for theism, namely, the combination of the cosmological and ontological proof proposed by Demea,
but his interlocutors Cleanthes and Philo are unanimous in rejecting it
(188ff.).[51]

Already in the *Universal Natural History and Theory of Heaven* of 1755
(A XIVf.), and particularly in *The Only Possible Argument in Support of a
Demonstration of the Existence of God* of 1763, Kant had argued that the argument from design could only prove an architect, not a creator of the
world (A 116), and that it could not show that the cause of the world is
most perfect or even a single one (A 199ff.). The first criticism is repeated in the *First Critique* (B 655/A 627), where the general insight is
expressed that the cause inferred can only be proportional to the effect.
The empirical way can thus never lead to absolute totality (B 656/A
628).[52] Only by a surreptitious use of the cosmological argument, which

wants to demonstrate a necessary being and which itself presupposes the ontological argument, can the physico-theological argument lead to an absolute being. According to the later Kant, however, the cosmological and the ontological proofs are also irredeemably flawed, while the early Kant had still defended a new version of the ontological proof, which he later gave up. Still, as is well known, Kant's contribution to natural theology is not limited to the destructive work done in *The Only Possible Argument* and in the *First Critique*. The *Critique of Practical Reason* introduces God as a postulate of practical reason (A 223ff.), and even if the epistemological status of this postulate is unclear and controversial, clearly Kant can claim to have given the moral argument for the existence of God a new foundation. This is linked to Kant's radical break with eudaemonist ethics: the question of what our duty is cannot be reduced to the problem what makes us happy. But if the moral fact cannot be reduced to natural desires like that for happiness, then the moral Ought is not part of this world. But how can it operate in this world? How can we have a duty to act according to the moral law if the natural world is not in principle malleable by the demands of the Ought? These questions are dealt with in the *Critique of Judgment* of 1790, whose second part, the "Critique of Teleological Judgment," is the most impressive defense of teleological thinking in modernity after the collapse of traditional physico-theology. Kant's defense, however, insists on teleology being a regulative, not a constitutive principle (B 270): it is a subjective principle of judging the phenomena. Kant reiterates his opinion that physico-theology does not achieve what it promises. It does not have any potential to address the question of the ultimate end of nature (B 401); and it cannot infer a cause with absolute qualities: if it does so, practical reason is secretly supplementing what theoretical reason on its own cannot do (B 404).[53] Indeed, based on purely physico-theological arguments, the cause of the world might as well act with instinct as with reason (B 409). Only ethicotheology can lead to a true concept of God, physico-theology on its own might well lead to some form of demonology (B 414). The ultimate end that we, always aware of the subjective nature of this ascription, have to ascribe to God within ethico-theology is human beings under moral laws (B 415f.). On this ground, however, a teleological interpretation of nature, with which we humans remain inevitably connected, is legitimate (B 419).

Certainly no contemporary attempt to make sense of teleology in nature can ignore Kant.[54] The main reasons the naturalist worldview proposed nowadays by neo-Darwinians such as Dawkins is so unappealing are the two realms of normativity and of mentality. Naturalism does not render justice to the fact that as persons we inevitably have ultimate intellectual and moral ends that cannot be reduced to the execution of biological programs. One might try to explain causally, for example by socio-biological means, how our moral concepts developed, but even if these attempts at explanation have indeed shed light on the *genesis* of some of our ideas, for example, in the field of sexual morality, they are in principle unable to explain where the *validity* of our moral convictions comes from. This is the general problem of any *merely* evolutionary account: the space of reasons, in both the theoretical and the practical spheres, is irreducible to the realm of causes. Since thinking and arguing are actions, and action is inevitably oriented toward ends, we need a theory of finality in order to make sense of what we as thinking and acting beings are. This is, as Kant rightly understood, the starting point of any teleology. But why is it not sufficient to assume nature as a mere realm of causes on the one hand and rationality as an independent sphere on the other?

The answer is that the unity of nature that evolutionary biology has so powerfully pointed out is indeed inimical to any dualist theory of being. The only rational and moral agents that we know are, after all, complex animals, and if it is not plausible to assume that the categorical moral demands imposed upon humans are simply the result of a contingent evolution, then the idea is tempting that the development of moral beings was an end of nature. But are agents with moral ends the only end of nature? It seems a crude anthropocentrism to dismiss pre-human nature as having only instrumental value for humans. It is more plausible to see in the slow evolution of mentality and the capacity to have purposes another end of nature. Even if there are causal mechanisms for the development of species, and probably also for the origin of life, one can hardly deny that life with its marvelous adaptation of the organs to each other and the whole organism is characterized by a form of teleonomy distinct both from the inorganic realm and from the rational finality of humans. And there is nothing incompatible with modern science if one interprets the development from inorganic objects to organisms and self-conscious minds themselves as an unfolding of ever more complex ends: bringing forth entities that have increasingly complex ends is, so to speak, an end either of nature or of its creator; and the highest end is the generation of a being that can ask the question of what an ultimate end is.[55]

But not only are there practical ends for rational agents, such as justice; one theoretical end must be the recognition of truth, without which neither science nor philosophy makes sense. Now this end presupposes two things: first, there must be rational beings able to follow inferences, and, second, nature must be intelligible. This has implications for the way in which nature must be structured. If one rejects interactionism, that is, the idea that mental states can cause physical states, the argument from natural selection will fail to *explain* the development of mental states, for they are of no use. No doubt those err who aver that epiphenomenalism is inconsistent with Darwinism. For one may assume that there are laws of supervenience guaranteeing that there are certain mental states that accompany determinate physical states. But, as we already know, the existence of such laws is presupposed, and not explained, by Darwinism. There is an additional issue, however. If we want to take our own thoughts seriously, we have to assume that some of the physical states of brain are causally so interconnected that the corresponding mental states, for example in a logical deduction, are also logically connected. Such a presupposition is not simply wishful thinking; it is the transcendental presupposition of any rational investigation.[56] An analogous teleological explanation might be given for those constant parameters of nature without which life or intelligent life could not have developed. (Of course, it is not possible to justify *all* natural laws with such considerations.) It might be objected that it is a brute fact that such fine-tuning holds, but stopping at brute facts rarely helps either science or philosophy. Our philosophical curiosity is more satisfied if we can reduce laws to a principle of the world that is itself a mind and wants to be recognized by inner-worldly finite minds. Such a reduction is kindred in spirit to the satisfaction of the scientific curiosity, as when Darwinism no longer had to accept the different species as mere facts but could explain their existence. But, of course, in the case of metaphysical explanations *reasons,* and not *causes* as in scientific explanations, are at stake. Alternative, non-teleological explanations of those constant parameters can hardly convince. It is extraordinarily implausible that they and all the laws of nature are determined by logic, as Spinoza seems to have believed. The multiverse model, the idea that our world is only one among many other worlds that do not have such teleological features, on the other hand, is per definitionem empirically unverifiable; and there is nothing metaphysically attractive in the multiplication of actual worlds.[57] Furthermore, the argument can easily be mirrored to lessen the burden of theodicy: if we cherish the idea that there are many actual worlds, it could be that God has created all possible worlds in which good balances evil; we are in one such world, but not in one with maximal value.

But not only must nature according to this account be structured so as to bring forth minds; it must also be intelligible. And this means that we have reason to look for theories that are both simple and fertile. Needless to say, any good scientific theory must match the empirical facts; but matching them is a necessary, not a sufficient condition for the quality of a scientific theory. Already in the *Critique of Pure Reason* Kant insisted on such regulative principles as the continuous *scala naturae* of creatures (B 670ff./A 642ff., particularly B 696/A 668); in the *Critique of Judgment* (B XXVIIIff.), they are interpreted as an expression of the formal purposiveness of nature.

Darwin's theory is certainly one of the most powerful scientific theories. It enhances the consilience of the various biological disciplines, but also of biology and the sciences dealing with humans. Based on a very simple argument, it allows us to find causes for entities such as species that before him had resisted any explanation. It does not at all deny the beauty and complexity of the living world, but teaches us to see it as a complex and fragile web. It can easily be destroyed and for its preservation we humans maintain a moral responsibility. It increases our faith in the intelligibility, and thus in the formal purposiveness, of nature at the very modest price that we can no longer jump directly to the First Cause whenever we do not yet understand the relevant secondary causes.

CHAPTER 3

———— · + · ◆ · + · ◆ ————

Theodicy Strategies in Leibniz, Hegel, Jonas

Much has been written about the moral, political, and social import of religion; even critical intellectuals easily and quickly agree about that. But presumably the theoretical relevance of religion is not inferior to its practical significance. By advocating propositions that appear counterintuitive, it has forced the human mind to assume a perspective on reality that is different from the everyday view; indeed, it has provoked the human mind to achieve abstractions and justifications that are able to spellbind even those who cannot identify themselves with the content of these statements. This applies especially to theism, the existence of which has been called a "miracle" by an atheist like John L. Mackie, although not without a certain irony.[1] The idea that there exists an omnipotent, omniscient, and absolutely good God does not spontaneously suggest itself to the natural consciousness; and indeed, it has not been developed until relatively late in the history of humankind. It soon encountered resistances, which have their point of departure, among other things, in the theodicy problem, that is, in the question of how the existence of a God with those three attributes can be reconciled with the existence of evils.[2]

Among them one can count, first, physical imperfections, such as the occurrence of dysteleologies in the organic world that are not associated
with pain, but also, second, the suffering that we must attribute certainly
to human beings, but with good reasons to higher animals as well. The
causes of these evils can be of a physical nature (i.e., organic diseases),
but they can be of a directly psychic nature as well (as is the case with a
number of mental diseases). In some instances the cause of suffering has
a particularly high intrinsic unworth, namely, in the case of moral evil,
which constitutes the third category of evil, although in some theodicies
it is regarded as a smaller problem since it leads farther away from God
as the First Cause than the other forms of evil.

But it is by no means merely the case that different theodicy strategies result from different concepts of God; the failure of different
theodicy strategies has, rather, led to a modification of the concept of
God. There is apparently an interaction between the history of the concept of God and the history of the theodicy efforts; indeed, one can even
say that in our time the acknowledgment of the existence of evil, especially of moral evil, has much greater evidence than the belief in the existence of God in part because of a greater skepticism about a priori
doctrines of God, in part because of a heightened moral sensitivity, and
in part because of a strong sense of autonomy, which is sensitive to any
attempt of its instrumentalization, and be it for metaphysical purposes. It
is no longer classical theism within which the theodicy problem presents
itself; but vice versa: one begins with the objection from the existence of
evil and tries to find out which concept of God can best deal with it.

In the following I consider the capacity of the different concepts of
God to offer a solution to the theodicy problem, and I focus exclusively
on the abstract dimension of philosophy of religion. Nobody denies that
there is also an existential dimension to the theodicy problem—some
people became atheists due to individual blows of fate (others, however,
became theists due to analogous blows of fate); but from the perspective of the philosophy of religion, the suffering that affects the stranger
counts as much as the suffering that affects oneself; indeed, a religiosity
that is not disconcerted by the well-known extent of human suffering
as long as it only affects others, but starts losing faith when it suffers a
great loss itself, is understandable from a human perspective, but it is not

morally respectable on the basis of a universalist ethics. Just as it does not deal with the psychological dimension, this essay does not address the sociological dimension of the theodicy problem. Max Weber is certainly right—the different ways in which the individual religions deal with the problem of suffering have important consequences for the structure of a society;[3] but however interesting the social consequences of a theory might be, philosophy is primarily interested in the question of the truth or the falsehood of a theory—completely regardless of its consequences.

The original religious experience assumes the existence of a multiplicity of numinous powers that interfere with human life, and many of those powers are regarded as dangerous, indeed, as malicious and vicious: thus evil and moral evil do not exist despite, but because of, the gods. The dualism of the Avesta assumes a special God as the principle of moral evil. Likewise, the old monolatry of the people of Israel did not exclude the existence of other gods; it merely prohibited their worship, based on the assumption of a peculiar characteristic of Yahweh, which we would not always consider positive in human beings, namely, jealousy. The more this monolatry developed into henotheism and finally into monotheism, the more the existence of suffering became a problem. An obvious answer within a religion that was decisively characterized by the category of the covenant was that the suffering was a penalty for a breach of covenant; and indeed, this answer played a central role in the theology of history of the historic books of the Old Testament. The greatness of the book of Job consists in the fact that this answer, which Job's friends doggedly cling to, is given up—there can be human suffering that must under no conditions be interpreted as punishment. In my judgment the rejection of that false answer is the true achievement of the book, much more than the positive answer, which is alluded to toward the end and that probably breaks with the idea of a moral God since God appears as an ultimate power that is not bound to human ideas of justice.

After all, the theodicy problem is relatively easy to solve—or, better, it does not even appear—when one sacrifices the postulate that God is at least to a certain extent intelligible. But then the intellectual appeal of the theodicy problem disappears completely; for the position that God is omnipotent, omniscient, and perfectly good, but that his goodness is compatible with the existence of evil and moral evil in a way fundamentally unintelligible to us is a *sacrificium intellectus*. Such a sacrifice may have other appeals; intellectual appeal it does not have by definition. Philosophy can only take a theology seriously that strives for rationality; and a theology can only be rational if it imputes to its subject, that is, God, a rationality that is philosophically accessible—at least in principle, although not down to the last details. Of course, there are vast differences between finite and infinite rationality; but these differences do not establish an incommensurability, the necessary consequence of which would be the impossibility of a rational theology.

The theodicy problem does not present itself either if one defends a position that is related to though different from the one just mentioned, according to which the criterion for what is "good" lies in God's will only. For insofar as one interprets creation as a manifestation of the divine will and there is no evaluative criterion that transcends this will, one can hardly speak of a bad world—because what God has made is good per definition. Within the framework of voluntarism it could only be argued that there exists a contradiction between the moral norms that are determined by God through an arbitrary decision for the human being and the apparent principles of his creation; but the voluntaristic response to that is that God, like an absolute sovereign, is not bound by the norms that he issues for others. Of course this "solution" to the theodicy problem is even more dangerous than the first one, which is content with undermining any kind of clear and binding argumentation; for it destroys the sense of the absolute nature of morality and makes God indistinguishable from an omnipotent tyrant. As Immanuel Kant aptly remarks in "On the Failure of All Philosophical Attempts in Theodicy" concerning the opinion that "we err, when we regard that which is a law only relatively for human beings in this life as a law per se, and thus hold that which appears to be inappropriate according to our consideration of things from so low a perspective, to be so likewise, when considered from the highest point of view": "This apology, in which the defense is worse than the charge, requires no refutation, and may certainly be freely left to the detestation of every person who has the smallest sentiment of morality."[4]

Finally, the theodicy problem also dissolves when one—starting from completely different presuppositions but reaching a similar conclusion as voluntarism—takes "good" and "evil" for terms that make sense only in reference to finite beings. This is Baruch Spinoza's position, whose God is not a moral being. (One can, of course, ask whether it then still makes sense to speak of "God." But Spinoza unreservedly does so, and I would not have any problems referring to Spinoza's philosophy as a non-eschatological and amoral monotheism within a taxonomy of concepts of monotheism—but I would not have any problems either if others wanted to use the term "monotheism" more restrictively: one should not argue over names.) One could say that Spinoza denies God the predicate "perfectly good," but this interpretation would be misleading insofar as Spinoza, in Georg Wilhelm Friedrich Hegel's terminology, does not pass a negative, but a negatively infinite, judgment about the statement "God is perfectly good": God is for him not merely limitedly good or even evil, but he stands above the sphere of morality, the application of which to him leads to category mistakes (like the ascription of properties of color to numbers). But even if the theodicy problem dissolves in this approach (just like in the two preceding cases), since now a contradiction can no longer develop between a presupposed benevolence of God and the existence of evil, this solution can be compared to the curing of a headache by decapitation. Whoever considers the moral proof of God to be one of the two strongest proofs of God, cannot accept a philosophical theology according to which God is not a moral being anymore—at least with any meaning of the term "moral" that is still intelligible to us.

Nevertheless, it is possible to say that the theodicy problem in all its difficulty presupposes Spinoza's revolution of the concept of God. This statement may be surprising for two reasons—on the one hand, because I have earlier referred to the book of Job, which wrestles with a precursor of the theodicy problem, and on the other hand, because I have just said that Spinoza's God is beyond good and evil and thus escapes the theodicy problem. Indeed, this statement is in need of explanation. In answer to the first objection, the tension between the existence of good and powerful gods and the existence of evil was recognized quite early—even within polytheistic religions. In Aeschylus and Sophocles (but no longer in Euripides), Greek tragedy struggles for a balance between the experience of suffering and the belief in a divine power that, in my judgment, is not amoral; thus the final charge of Hyllus in Sophocles' *Women of Trachis* against the divine father of Heracles, who is suffering a terribly excruciating death, that he has fathered children and looks down on this suffering (V. 1266ff.), stands in an enigmatic tension with the final verse (V. 1278): "and none of these things which is not Zeus." In Greek philosophy the Sophist Thrasymachus concludes from the absence of justice among human beings that the gods do not care about human activities.[5] That Christianity has dealt with the theodicy problem from very early on is common knowledge; after all, Gottfried Wilhelm Leibniz himself uses elements of patristic and scholastic theories again and again in his *Théodicée.*[6]

And yet all this does not change the fact that Leibniz not only coined the term "theodicy"—he also radicalized the problem in a completely new way. Since Leibniz the problem is much more difficult to solve than before him; indeed, one can even say that it required an intelligence like his to attempt a solution. (I recall the well-known joke: if the defendant hires a very good lawyer, the audience assumes that his situation is quite desperate—but how desperate must have been God's situation in the seventeenth century, if he had to create an intelligence like Leibniz's for the purpose of writing a theodicy!) These difficulties are a consequence of the reshaping of the concept of God by Spinoza. But—and thus I come to the second objection—of course I am not referring to those modifications that turn God into an amoral being and thus do away with the theodicy problem; for Leibniz undid these modifications and only thereby recovered the theodicy problem. But he recovered it in a significantly sharper form because he took over the other modifications of Spinoza's concept of God. What do they consist in? The best way to interpret Spinoza's metaphysics is to read it as a rational theology of modern science.[7] Like René Descartes, Spinoza wants to establish a rational basis for modern science; like Descartes, he thinks that the absolute certainty that modern science strives for is unachievable without a concept of God. Three convictions, however, distinguish him from Descartes: first, that the self-certainty of the ego cannot be the first basis of philosophy, but has to be placed within the framework of a theory of being; second, that rationalism implies that all statements have to be justified and especially all events causally determined; third, that a real interaction between the physical and the mental is unthinkable. His system results largely from these three presuppositions. At the peak of being there is, according to Spinoza, a structure that founds itself in the manner of the ontological proof, the *causa sui,* that manifests itself in the different laws of nature having different degrees of generality; in addition to this vertical chain of dependency there is a horizontal chain of events, in which every event is fully determined by the antecedent conditions and the system of natural laws. Spinoza does not answer the question of how the laws of nature or the whole chain of antecedent conditions could be explained; but since he clearly attributes to them the modality of necessity, one could interpret him to think that the laws of nature are logically necessary—which they are evidently not.

I.

It is a sign of the quality of a solution that it solves two, or even more, problems that remained open in a prior theory in one blow. Leibniz, who was deeply influenced by Spinoza—he visited him personally in 1676— rejects his vague usage of the concept of necessity as well as his denial of God's moral attributes (and, furthermore, the absence of a satisfactory theory of subjective individuality). According to him, God is, first, a moral being, indeed, perfectly good; and it is, second, his perfect goodness—not formal logic—that explains why the world is as it is. The world is not based on a logical-mathematical but on a moral necessity. There are—in a continuation of Henry of Ghent's and Duns Scotus's revolution of the concepts of modality, which Spinoza does not seem to have absorbed—an infinite number of possible worlds, out of which only one is real, namely, ours. And this one is real because it is the best of all possible worlds and because God as a perfectly good, omniscient, and omnipotent being necessarily is the one who creates the best possible world (which does not imply, within Leibniz's modal logic, that God necessarily creates the best possible world). That God is perfectly good, omniscient, and omnipotent follows for Leibniz from the ontological proof of God, namely, the one via the perfections, according to which God has to be ascribed all positive properties to the highest degree. Now it was not only the common sense of Voltaire (whose *Candide* is a delightful novel, but not an important contribution to metaphysics) that could not come to terms with the thesis of the best of all possible worlds; it not only stands in an antithetical contrast with Arthur Schopenhauer's even more counterintuitive view that ours is the worst of all possible worlds;[8] it also contradicts the medieval understanding of the problem. In the sixth article of the twenty-fifth quaestio of the first part of the *Summa theologiae* Aquinas discusses the question "whether God can make the things better than He does," and affirms it emphatically.[9] It is true that he preliminarily mentions the arguments that seem to speak for a denial of the question. Two refer to the Christological dogmatics and can be neglected in our context. The other two are of a more general nature: God has done everything "in a most powerful and wise way,"[10] and thus could make nothing better than what he had made; and the world in its entirety is much better than the individual things, indeed, extraordinarily good, and could not become any better. But against this Aquinas objects God could not make something "better" (*melius*), if one understood the term in an adverbial sense, that is, implying "the maker" (*ex parte facientis*), but he could do so if one interpreted this term as an adjective, that is, implying "the thing done" (*ex parte facti*). It is true, he says, that there are some things that cannot be changed, and thus cannot be improved either, without losing their nature (e.g., numbers), but, generally speaking, one must distinguish between improvements with regard to the *essentialia,* which abolish a thing, and those with regard to the *accidentalia,* which are very well possible. Furthermore, although it is also true that in a given set of things the imperfections of this world contribute to the harmony of its order, that does not imply that no other and better order could exist, if one presupposes different things.

It is obvious that the last argument does not touch Leibniz at all. That a world that is different from the given is possible if one makes other presuppositions is his crucial point; but he thinks that a God who does not prefer the best world can no longer claim the predicate "perfectly good." And concerning the distinction between "the maker" (*ex parte facientis*) and "the thing done" (*ex parte facti*), it is not hard to see that it does not make sense for an omnipotent Creator-God; because the *factum* is a function of the *faciens* and has—insofar as one does not accept a principle of matter that is independent from God—no autonomy. One can say about an ordinary sculptor that he did the best thing possible with a given stone, but the stone could have been better. But if the sculptor is also the creator of the stone, he must face up to the question as to why he did not create a better stone. Indeed, it is easy to see which principle the Leibnizian commitment of God to the best of all possible worlds is based upon—it is the principle of sufficient reason. As a rational being, God must have a reason to prefer this world to another, and for a moral being this can only be the value of the world. It is true that Leibniz does not deny that the world is a kind of "fall" vis-à-vis God; but he wants to know why this "fall" has this and not another form.

Now one could try to argue against Leibniz that God would create the best of all possible worlds if it existed, but that it could not exist. The latter statement could be supported in two ways. On the one hand, one could argue that there is an infinite series of possible worlds of different value that cannot be brought to an end, just like the series of natural numbers. But this insight would have several consequences that would be most unpleasant, not to say disastrous, for the whole project of a rational theology. First, there would be almost nothing left of the basic structures of the world that could be explained. For if someone, for instance, claimed that God because of his benevolence had chosen at least a world with the value n, one could always reply that he could equally well have chosen a world with the value $n - 1$ since he passed up the world with the value $n + 1$. One could only claim that the overall value of the world should be larger than zero, and this is not very much if one is interested in discovering why the world is how it is. Second, one would have to admit that there could be a creator who is not omnipotent, who could have created a world that is better than the world created by the omnipotent, omniscient, and perfectly good God,[11] and this concession would put a monotheist in a difficult spot. As a result, all inductive proofs of God of the type of the cosmological and the teleological would collapse once and for all—but this is not a very strong objection, for they do not suffice anyway to get to the God of theism. On the other hand, one could defend the thesis that the aforementioned series comes to an end, but assume on the highest level a (possibly even infinite) plurality of worlds with the same value.[12] This possibility, which would bring God in the situation of Buridan's ass, is considerably less dangerous for the Leib-

nizian project. But Leibniz rejected it by pointing to the principle of sufficient reason, which would drop out with regard to the divine creation.[13]
But he must of course presuppose that the principle of sufficient reason
is a general condition for the theory of the possible worlds, and this is
anything but convincing. For even if one attributes an a priori status to
the principle of sufficient reason and assumes it would have to be valid in
all possible worlds,[14] this does not mean that it precedes the principle of
contradiction; but this would have to be the case if one world had to be
considered impossible only because it would have the same maximal
value as another world and would thus endanger the reasonableness of
the divine choice. At least this objection does not call into question the
Leibnizian thesis that a perfectly good, omniscient, and omnipotent God
could not prefer a worse world over a better one.

The Leibnizian universe is, like that of Spinoza, completely deterministic; but the laws of nature—which are in large part the laws of the
developmental tendencies of the individual monads—are fixed for moral
reasons, as are the antecedent conditions. It has to be emphasized, however, that for Leibniz "moral" means "axiological" and differs from the
modern concept of morality. In no way is it the primary criterion of the
Leibnizian God to reduce suffering, but other aspects play a greater
role, which Leibniz, however, does not exhaustively systematize and especially not hierarchize. Among the possible entities, those carry the day
"which, being united, produce most reality, most perfection, most intelligibility."[15] As one can see, to the axiological criteria belong also purely
ontological ones: ceteris paribus, a world with more entities is better than
one with fewer entities. According to Leibniz, the perfection of a world
is calculated according to two criteria that are in a certain tension with
each other—variety on the one hand, the order of the world on the
other hand.

"It follows from the supreme perfection of God that in producing
the universe he chose the best possible plan, in which there is the greatest
possible variety together with the greatest possible order: the most carefully used ground, place, and time: the greatest effect produced by the
simplest mean."[16]

There can be tensions between those two criteria, and an algorithm
of how to reach an optimum from both criteria is lacking. If simplicity

and fertility were inversely proportional to each other, even all combinations of both criteria would have the same value, provided that the two factors were weighed equally; but it is clear that Leibniz would have rejected this prerequisite, and for good reasons. Furthermore, he seems to have preferred variety over simplicity. To illustrate his thesis, Leibniz essentially makes do with the laws of conservation of physics and the principles of mechanics. Immediately after the passage just quoted, Leibniz mentions, besides these constructive principles, as further axiological criteria "the most power, the most knowledge, the most happiness, and the most goodness in created things that the universe could allow."[17] What is of concern here are thus the concrete entities that can result from those laws; and here what counts is their power, knowledge, happiness, and goodness. Leibniz certainly takes power to be the radius of action of monads; knowledge corresponds to the intelligibility of the universe. For the best of all possible worlds must be both cognizable and contain beings that can cognize it. God is thus not only the architect of the world; he is also the legislator of the "City of God." It is only with the creation of intelligent and moral beings that God's benevolence truly comes to bear; now we finally have—just like with happiness, which, however, appears only in passing—an axiological criterion that most likely corresponds to our moral intuitions:

> This City of God, this truly universal monarchy, is a moral world within the natural world, and is the most exalted and the most divine of the works of God. And it is in it that the glory of God truly consists, for there would be none at all if his grandeur and goodness were not known and admired by the spirits: It is also in relation to this divine city that he in a proper sense has goodness, whereas his wisdom and power are manifested everywhere.[18]

Yet rational monads are not the only beings with intrinsic worth, and if God prefers a human being over a lion that does not mean for Leibniz that he would prefer a man over the whole species of lions.[19]

It has already been suggested that—if it is permitted to associate Sigmund Freud with Leibniz—happiness does not play a central role in the conception of the best of all possible worlds.[20] But it is one criterion among others, and the inevitable question is how this is compatible with the existence of suffering. In response Leibniz offers an argument that basically undercuts his revolutionary accomplishment with regard to the theodicy problem. He says, again and again, that the good in the world surpasses and compensates for the moral evil. Our delusion is based on the fact "that the evil arouses our attention rather than the good: but this same reason proves that the evil is more rare."[21] Now this statement is quite controversial from an empirical perspective, and its empirical basis is quite thin even when one follows Leibniz in assuming other, non-human rational beings[22] because we have even less empirical knowledge about them; indeed, the inclusion of the eschatological dimension, which Leibniz retains, cannot be empirically justified either. Kant's vote with regard to the question of the predominance of the good in this world is well known:

> But the answer to this sophistry may surely be left to the decision of every person of a sound understanding, who has lived and reflected long enough on the value of life to be able to pronounce a judgment on this, when the question is proposed to him: Whether, I will not say on the same, but on any other conditions he pleases (only not of a fairy, but of this our terrestrial, world), he would not wish to act the play of life all over again.[23]

It could be replied to this, however, that we would not live in the best of all possible worlds if all of us wanted to live our lives again and were not able to do it; insofar as one preferred the only one life above the mere nothingness, Leibniz's theory would be sufficiently justified. But the problem is that Leibniz thereby falls back into that old theodicy concept that he actually wanted to overcome. For the existence of an omniscient, omnipotent, and perfectly good God not only entails that the value of the world is positive, but that it is maximal. Obviously this thesis goes further than the first, which is yet not necessarily implied by it: after all, it is conceivable that the best possible world has a negative value. Only if we accept the empty set as a possible world, the choice of the best possible world implies that it has a positive value, insofar as it does not lead to the empty set. And just this optimality of the world is far from proven by the predominance of the good.

Now of course Leibniz does not want to prove the optimality of the world inductively. For him it follows from the concept of God, whose existence is established through five proofs of God—the ontological in its modal-logical version and in its version via the perfections, the cosmological, the teleological (in the new form of the doctrine of pre-established harmony), and the proof via the eternal truths. The ontological proof via the perfections is the one that is required if the doctrine of the best possible world is to be an analytic truth that follows from the concept of God; for the modal-logically proven God certainly does not have the attribute of perfect goodness. What Leibniz wants to show is rather that the a priori established proposition that our world is the best of all possible worlds is not in contradiction with the empirical facts. In order to do this it is not sufficient to point out that, for instance, certain evils are necessary for the sake of greater goods if one presupposes our system of natural laws; for just the necessity of this system of natural laws is in question. It is, however, misguided to object like Schopenhauer: "Even if the Leibnizian demonstration that among the possible worlds this one is still the best was correct, it still would not constitute a theodicy. For, after all, the Creator has not only created the world but also the possibility itself: thus he should have designed it so that it admitted a better world."[24]

This criticism is bizarre because the possibilia, even though according to Leibniz they presuppose the existence of God, are still given to his reason just like the axiological criteria of the creation. Thus Leibniz can make do with showing that some evils are necessary for the sake of higher goods for logical reasons.

How can he do this? Perhaps one can say that Leibniz's achievement consists in the fact that he reduces the three most important theodicy considerations of the tradition to this concept of functionalization. The tradition—Augustine, for instance—had tried to make the existence of evil compatible with the existence of God in part through the privation theory,[25] in part through a rudimentary dialectic theory,[26] in part eventually through reference to the free decision for moral evil on behalf of some angels, respectively on behalf of the first human being, and to its consequences.[27] Insofar as the privation theory is concerned, it is significantly reinterpreted by Leibniz compared with the tradition, although he remains verbally committed to it. For Leibniz, every finite being, not just the inferior being, is characterized by a privation. This has to do in part with the Spinozian replacement of the Platonic-Aristotelian system of *eide* with the absolute, in part with Leibniz's theory of individual substance: compared with the absolute, one can speak about a privation not only with regard to a sick horse, but with regard to any horse; and there exist individual concepts of the healthy horse and of the sick horse as well. "Characterized by privation is that which expresses negation," it reads in a strong break with the tradition.[28] In this context belongs the concept of the "metaphysical evil," which, according to Leibniz, consists in a simple imperfection.[29] It is true that Leibniz, like the tradition, maintains that, due to the privative nature of evil, it does not have an efficient, but merely a deficient cause; but he is too concerned with the principle of sufficient reason that he could be satisfied with this. The suggestion that evil *is* not truly does not play a role in Leibniz (and it is not hard to see that it solves the problem only terminologically; because even though evil *is* not, it still exists, and its existence remains something to be explained); and even the old idea that evil partly destroys itself, partly depends on the good, in order to have any effect at all, does not answer the question why God has not created a world consisting only of good things or states. Leibniz holds on to the idea that in the realm of eternal truths there has to be an ideal cause of evil, and this is the fact that, due to God's uniqueness, which follows from the *principium identitatis indiscernibilium,* everything that is outside of God has to have an ontic defect.[30] This entails an amount of entities as large as possible because of the principle of plenitude, that is, an ontic variety as far-reaching as possible. Evil in all its forms is a function of finitude, and the latter serves God's manifestation in a creation as manifold as possible. In this idea the theory of privation converges with the dialectic theory: the negative (in a more than the formal sense in which the positive is also the negative of the negative) is necessary so that the positive can stand out. "Do men relish health enough, or thank God enough for it, without having ever been sick?"[31] Apparently, Leibniz would have to assume that this reciprocal dependence is not only grounded in natural laws but also logically; but he lacks any elaboration of such a dialectic logic. Also, he merely alludes to the argument that only the existence of evils makes the development of especially valuable virtues possible,[32] evidently because Leibniz subscribed to a pre-Kantian eudaimonistic ethics.

Now such a functionalization of evil with regard to the best possible world also applies to the appeal to the freedom of the will. It is true that Leibniz has a complex theory of the freedom of the individual human being; but this theory is absolutely compatible with a thorough determinism. Freedom originates from the autonomy of the monad, the idea of which exists independently of God; but the monad was created in correspondence with the system of the laws of nature of the best possible world, and all its movements are determined by this system and the antecedent conditions. In God freedom coincides with a maximum of rationality; the concept of a freedom to act against reason is an absurdity for Leibniz. From this perspective, the *malum morale* is nothing else but the consequence of the peculiar limitation of a monad with regard to rationality. It is true that the spiritual being can be called to account for its actions; for they are *her* actions, even though they are simultaneously consequences of the world-entirety. But this exoneration of God is not sufficient since, as an omnipotent and omniscient being, he foresaw those actions and should have created a better world with other monads—of course: *if* such a world could have existed. Thus for Leibniz the insertion of human freedom changes nothing of import with regard to the theodicy problem. Even a non-compatibilist generally will have to admit that the suffering that arises for human beings from sickness is hardly less than that which they experience through the malice of their fellow human beings, and that it thus hardly leads any further to base the theodicy discussion primarily upon a non-compatibilist concept of freedom.

Of course, all this does not explain the concrete forms of evil that exist in the world. According to Leibniz, such an attempt is on principle beyond the power of the finite intellect because it presupposes a comparison of all possible worlds. The finite spirit, however, can sooth herself with the certainty that she lives in the best of all possible worlds, even if this must not prevent her from fighting for what she has to hold as better due to her finitude, although she then has to reconcile herself with what eventually prevails and what is better in the context of the whole world and from the perspective of an infinite intellect maximizing total utility (who, as an infinite mind, has alone the right to put up with certain evils). That the theory of the best of all possible worlds can hardly be refuted empirically is something that even David Hume, the most intelligent critic of rational theology, admits. In the *Dialogues Concerning Natural Religion* toward the beginning of the eleventh part Philo declares that, even though the evils of the world are an argument of strong plausibility against theism, it is still possible to develop a theory that makes God's existence compatible with the existence of evil. But from the world as it is, nobody without a prejudiced opinion would derive an omnipotent and perfectly good God.

"The consistence is not absolutely denied, only the inference. Conjectures, especially where infinity is excluded from the divine attributes, may, perhaps, be sufficient to prove a consistence; but can never be foundations for any inference."[33]

Of course, Hume's doubts hinge on his contestation of the ontological proof in the ninth part of his *Dialogues,* which must indeed be the basis of all rational theology, in whichever of its many forms.

II.

The context within which the theodicy problem presents itself to Hegel differs significantly from the Leibnizian one. On the one hand, this is due to reasons that have to do with the history of philosophy—Hume and Kant, whose criticism of the inductive proofs of God is still unsurpassed, even though I do not think one can say this about their analysis of the ontological proof of God, mediate between early modern rationalism and the systems of German idealism. Kant is here more constructive than Hume since he works out a new ethico-theological proof of God, based on his novel conception of morality for which there is no equivalent in Hume, a proof that could—as one, going beyond Kant, may conjecture—be combined with the ontological, cosmological, and teleological proof. On the other hand, the structure of their systems is considerably different, even though both thinkers are the greatest rationalists of the tradition. But Hegel knew Leibniz only superficially and in particular never accepted his metaphysics of the possible worlds, whereas Spinoza's influence on him can hardly be exaggerated. But, one may ask, does he thereby not stand outside of the history of the theodicy problem, like we have established for Spinoza? This question is perfectly justified, and especially Hegel's unjustified criticism of Kant's dualism of Is and Ought almost suggests an affirmative answer. Recall the following passage from Hegel, which is, however, taken from the chapter about the Jewish religion from his *Lectures on the Philosophy of Religion* and thus only partly reflective of his own theological convictions: "Goodness consists in the fact that the world is. Being does not belong to it, as Being is here reduced to the condition of a moment, and is only a being posited or created . . . The manifestation of the nothingness, the ideality of this finite existence, that Being is not true independence, this manifestation in the form of power is justice, and therein justice is done to the finite things."[34]

It is true that this sounds very pious—it reminds one of Job 1:21: "The Lord gives and the Lord takes away; blessed be the name of the Lord"—but the Spinozism behind it cannot be overlooked, despite the moral predicates: according to this conception, every world with finite things, which come to an end, proves God's justice and benevolence.

Yet appearances are deceptive in this case. In contrast to Spinoza, Hegel has a theory of *eide;* indeed, one can say that his *Encyclopedia* is the greatest attempt to realize the Platonic-Aristotelian program of a system of *eide.* In one respect Hegel is much more ambitious than Leibniz: he wants to understand in detail why the world is as it is; he is not content with the generic assumption that it is simply the best possible world. His indifference vis-à-vis Leibniz's alternative possible worlds[35] results from the conviction that the world analyzed by him is the most rational, indeed, the only rational one. The guarantor of this rationality is the concept, for Hegel a normative authority, out of whose dialectical development ought to result the basic structures of the world. But—and as far as that goes the appearances are not completely deceptive—the normativity of the concept is not specifically moral: the concept of the organism is just as normative as the concept of the state and has the function of differentiating successful instantiations from unsuccessful ones. Obviously I cannot extensively comment here on the method of the Hegelian development of concepts and the results that he achieves partly through it—and partly without it.[36] Only a few fundamental remarks are necessary.

First, the method that Hegel applies is dialectic: a positive concept is followed by a negative one, which is combined, or synthesized, with the first one to a third. According to him, this triple step is the basic structure of reality and its principle, God, who is the epitome of the uncircumventible categories of reality (to which the category of the good also belongs, which is, however, understood purely formally as a formation of the object through the subject). This has, second, the consequence that Hegel, like Jakob Böhme and Friedrich Wilhelm Joseph Schelling in his essay on freedom, who subjects the privation theory of moral evil to an impressive phenomenological critique, and in contrast to Leibniz, integrates the negative into the absolute. God is the unity of positive and negative categories, not just the bearer of positive properties. Hegel integrates in a complex manner speculative theology, ontology, logic, and transcendental philosophy, partly because he wants to prove the absolute idea, the highest step of the logic, indirectly—through the proof of the inconsistency of the preceding categories. This means, third, that the negative originates from God—even though it can assume concrete shapes like the moral evil only outside of God. For in God the negative is, as Hegel says, ideal or a moment, that is, it cannot break free and is thus not threatening. The latter happens only in nature and spirit, which are to logic as antithesis and synthesis are to the thesis, with nature being understood as the idea external to itself, the first expression of which is space, and spirit as the return from nature to logic. From this it follows, fourth, that for Hegel the task of understanding the rationality of the world predominantly relates to the realm of spirit, whereas Leibniz does not derive much more than the existence of rational beings and draws mainly upon the laws of physical nature when he gets concrete. Hegel is interested in them as well, but much less than in the determinations of the spirit. Within the philosophy of spirit it is paradoxically the philosophy of history for which Hegel reserves the term "theodicy." It is true that toward the end of his lectures about the history of philosophy he says: "Philosophy is the true theodicy, as against art and religion and their sensations";[37] but within the individual disciplines of philosophy, the philosophy of history is clearly privileged from the perspective of theodicy: "Our investigation is insofar a theodicy, a justification of God, which Leibniz has attempted in his manner in still undetermined, abstract categories, so that the evil in the world had to be understood, and the thinking spirit had to be reconciled with moral evil. Indeed, nowhere lies a greater challenge to such a reconciling insight than in world history."[38]

This is paradoxical for two reasons. First, it is not easy to explain, within the framework of a theory according to which the world is supposed to be rational or the best possible, why it is not like this from the beginning, why there is supposed to be a development toward rationality. Leibniz has wrestled with this question. In the short text "An mundus perfectione crescat" (written between 1694 and 1696) he initially emphasizes that he believes that the world always retains the same perfection, even though parts of the world exchange their perfection among each other. But toward the end he writes that since the souls do not forget the past, they would have to work themselves up to ever more explicit thoughts, and the world would have to perfect itself ever more, "if it cannot happen that a perfection be given that cannot be increased"[39]—a condition that by the way endangers his theory of the best of all possible worlds. Evidently the thesis of progress can be made consistent with that of the best of all possible worlds only if one assumes that the fact of progress in itself and the mental experience related to it have a higher value than what could be achieved if the later condition was given from the beginning. For Hegel of course things are easier: since for him the idea of development is centrally integrated into his metaphysics, and particularly since the spirit originates in nature, it is easy to understand why the consciousness of freedom and its institutionalization within the modern constitutional state can only be the result of a slow development. The first step of creation is the complete externality of space, out of which, only after many intermediate steps—especially the world of the organic—emerges the spirit. If one opts for an evolution instead of an emanation, the further development is easy to explain—toward the goal, from which, however, the later Being according to the model of emanation becomes estranged. Problematic in Hegel is that he begins with space, but claims to explain it with the dialectic method—concretely: with the self-application of the absolute idea to itself.[40]

The second problem with the choice of the philosophy of history as the real place of the theodicy concerns of course the fact that history has not always been the place of interpersonal kindness. Hegel, whose phenomenological eye for reality, even for the abysses of reality, is considerably sharper than that of Leibniz, who, even as an adult, always retained something of a child about him, and of course of the quite remarkable child that he had already been in the first years of his life, namely, a good-natured wunderkind,[41] Hegel knows about the brutality of history:

> When we watch this spectacle of the passions and see the consequences of their violence, of the ignorance, which consorts not only with them but even and indeed especially with what are good intentions, legitimate ends; when from this we see the evil, the moral evil, the decline of the most thriving empires which the human spirit has produced; then we can only be imbued with sorrow about this general transitoriness, and end up in moral distress, in an indignation of the good spirit, provided such a spirit exists in us, over such a spectacle, as this decline is not only a work of nature but of the will of human beings.[42]

And still, even if history appears to be a shambles, "upon which the happiness of the people, the wisdom of states, and the virtue of individuals have been sacrificed,"[43] even if the periods of happiness are only empty pages in it,[44] that does not change anything about Hegel's triumphant verdict that all this serves the final purpose of progress in the consciousness and the reality of freedom. Even world-historic individuals are merely tools to approach the final purpose.

That Hegel still holds on to the theodicy (and even though in his case any eschatological compensation for the victims of history is lacking) is due to the fact that, on the one hand, for him, even more than for the late Leibniz, happiness is not a crucial criterion of the perfection or rationality of the world. In the heroic sacrifice of happiness lies a specific dignity of the human being; indeed, for Hegel even the generating principle of the modern constitutional state is not the idea of happiness, but the idea of freedom. On the other hand, Hegel regards the complaint about the world itself as a moral evil that is directly punished through the suffering that is connected with this complaint:

> The celebrated question as to the origin of evil in the world, so far at least as evil initially is understood to mean what is disagreeable and painful merely, arises on this stage of the formal practical feeling.

Evil is nothing but the incompatibility between what is and what ought to be. This Ought has many meanings, indeed, an infinite number of them, since the arbitrary ends may also have the form of Ought. But with regard to the arbitrary ends, evil only executes what is rightfully due to the vanity and nullity of their planning: for they themselves are already evil.[45]

One cannot dispute that with regard to some suffering from the world, this suffering, and not the world, is the true problem (one recalls Schopenhauer's pessimism, which is more a function of his character than of the world). But since the subjective suffering itself is a part of the world, this only shifts the problem.[46] And even if one may come to terms with the suffering of a culprit, one will not be able to subsume all suffering under it—and Hegel does not do this. In the further course of this *Anmerkung,* in which he explicitly refers to Böhme, he declares that evil and pain are still alien to unorganic nature because it has not yet come to the contrast between concept and existence within it, and thus not to the Ought. But Hegel leaves no doubt that evil and pain are not too high of a price for the higher level of being characteristic of life and spirit.[47] His conception recalls the well-known dictum of Augustine: "But as the sentient nature, even when it feels pain, is superior to the stone, which can feel none, so the rational nature, even when wretched, is more excellent than that which lacks reason or feeling, and can therefore experience no misery."[48] In a quite similar vein Hegel interprets moral evil, the highest enhancement of evil. It is for him the necessary consequence of the emancipation of subjectivity, "the innermost reflection of subjectivity in itself as against the objective and general, which it regards as mere appearance."[49]

As pain is the necessary accompanying phenomenon of life, moral evil is the other side of conscience:

The origin of evil in general lies in the mystery of freedom, i.e., in the speculative aspect of freedom, its necessity to emancipate itself from the naturalness of the will and be internal against it . . . The human being is thus simultaneously as such or by nature and through his reflection in itself morally evil, so that neither nature as such, i.e., if it were not naturalness of the will remaining in its special content, nor the reflection that turns in itself, cognition as such, if it did not maintain itself in this contrast, is evil in itself.[50]

Moral evil is the absolutization of natural desires against the universal represented by the good through reflection, that is, something that ought not to be. According to Hegel, the responsibility for this falls exclusively on the individual subject. But the moral evil is necessary insofar as this standpoint of rupture has to emerge—"it constitutes . . . the separation of the irrational animals and the human being." "So-called primitive, innocent people—worse than wicked," we read in the handwritten addendum to this paragraph.[51] It is evident how Hegel must interpret the myth of the fall on the basis of these prerequisites—not as a tale of decay, but as a necessary transitory stage on the way to full humanity. "Paradise is a park where only the animals and not the human beings can remain . . . The fall is thus the eternal myth of the human being, through which he only becomes a human being."[52]

The two above-mentioned paragraphs of the *Encyclopedia* (with the more detailed version of the second one in the *Philosophy of Right*) are Hegel's most important contribution to the theodicy problem: evil and moral evil have their place in the necessary self-development of the concept. Yet Hegel differs from Leibniz in one point: apparently he assumes real ontological contingency, namely, in a double sense that has to be strictly distinguished. On the one hand, he appears to regard the laws of nature not as deterministic and possibly to believe in human freedom of the will in a non-compatibilist sense. On the other hand, it is obvious to him that, with the externalization to nature, the idea hands itself over to a sphere of contingency, which neither finite reason nor the absolute itself can catch up with. Thus the theodicy problem is in a certain sense defused since for Hegel the concrete extent of evil and moral evil—but not the existence of the corresponding structures—is no longer the responsibility of the absolute, but a consequence of its self-externalization to nature. With this view Hegel is more Platonic than Leibniz, and thus we can find in him a return to the old doctrine of privation: the irrational in the world is a mere appearance, distinguishable from reality in an emphatic sense of the term.[53] Connected with this position is an exhortation to, as it were, a Stoic view vis-à-vis the adversities of being—it is important to discern the rose in the cross.[54]

III.

Hans Jonas, to whom we owe one of the most forceful contributions to the theodicy discussion of our century, can identify himself neither with this privation-theoretical "de-substantiation of evils, which reconciles itself with God behind the back of the sufferers,"[55] nor with the functionalization of the atrocities of history *ad majorem gloriam* of the modern constitutional state. His new approach is explained, on the one hand, by the crisis of rational theology since the middle of the nineteenth century, on the other hand, by the excess in the experience of moral evil in the twentieth century. It is not a coincidence that Jonas is Jewish—as it is no coincidence that the rejection of the optimistic philosophy of history of Hegelianism by Walter Benjamin, Max Horkheimer/Theodor W. Adorno, and Karl Löwith originated from men who had to experience the genocide of their own people. In *Der Gottesbegriff nach Auschwitz*,[56] Jonas starts with this experience, which, as he says, compels us to let go the master of history.[57] Indeed, the modern spirit compels us to conceive the world as left to itself and its laws as not tolerating any interference. God—so it is told in a mythical story with allusions to the Kabbalah— has opened himself up to the contingency of becoming, and in the evolution first of life and then of spirit, the deity comes to the experience of itself. "With the appearance of the human being, transcendence awoke to itself and henceforth accompanies his actions with bated breath, hoping and beckoning, with joy and with pain, with satisfaction and disappointment."[58] Jonas's God is a suffering God, he is an evolving God, whose relation to the creation constantly changes; he is a caring God. And—he is not an omnipotent God.

Jonas even thinks that there is a contradiction in the idea of omnipotence—because power presupposes a resistance that is to be surmounted, which cannot exist under the condition of omnipotence. Furthermore, omnipotence and perfect goodness (Jonas does not speak of omniscience, maybe because he interprets it as a factor of omnipotence) are not both simultaneously compatible with the existence of evil, at least if one wants to hold on to the intelligibility of God. Even the assumption of a mere restraint of omnipotence does not bring us any further: "For in view of the enormity of what, among the bearers of his image in creation, some of them time and again, and wholly unilaterally, inflict on innocent others, one would expect the good God at times to break his own, however stringent, rule of restraint of power and intervene with a saving miracle."[59]

God, so we must assume according to Jonas, has divested himself of any power to intervene in the physical course of things. "It is the human being's now to give to him. And he may give by seeing to it in the ways of his life that it does not happen or happen too often, and not on his account, that God must regret that he let the world become."[60]

The reason Jonas is one of the great philosophers of the twentieth century is also evident in this text—all theoretical reflections are backed up by personal experience, not merely by hermeneutical reference to others' opinions. Yet one should not agree with Jonas too quickly. The God in Wolfgang Borchert's *Draußen vor der Tür* (*The Man Outside*) is a rather embarrassing figure, and Jonas's God approaches him alarmingly, despite his indisputable dignity. Also, his logical criticism of the concept of omnipotence is insufficient: for a timeless being, omnipotence can only be constructed as omnicausality, and this is exactly how Spinoza and Leibniz understand it, for whom God does not interfere with the laws of nature and does not have to do so since he has created them. That Jonas does not discuss the concept of omnicausality has of course to do with his rejection of determinism, which is entailed by this concept. Furthermore, even though his triumphant passing over of history's victims is unacceptable, one should not dismiss Hegel's philosophical conception that the Western constitutional state is the end of history too quickly—it experienced another partial confirmation at the end of the twentieth century, and it is, even though it cannot erase the suffering of the victims of totalitarianism, at least more consoling than, for example, a pessimistic philosophy of history, which easily becomes a self-fulfilling expectation.

But Jonas is completely right about one thing: if one has to choose between omnipotence and perfect goodness, then the second attribute is preferable. If one wants to find the way back to God after Auschwitz, then this has to be a God who does not desire these crimes. Indeed, the terrible tragedy of that morally justified atheism, which gives up the idea of God out of indignation about the injustice in this world, lies in the fact that sooner or later it transforms the foundation of its own indignation into a subjective feeling of discomfort or even accepts moral evil: the path from Arthur Schopenhauer to Friedrich Nietzsche is amazingly straight. The moral law must have a dignity independent from the whims of the subject and the malice of history if it is to bind the human will. Indeed, the Kantian moral law has some of God's attributes: it is unconditionally valid, that is, it is absolute, it stands outside of space and time, it is the source of all value. But if the moral law cannot be reduced to factual existence—whence comes the possibility (because a possibility it certainly is, even though it is perhaps more than a mere possibility) that existence corresponds with it? Evidently Being cannot be completely independent from the moral law, if it is supposed to be open toward it in its historical development. A possible solution would be that empirical Being has the moral law as its only principle—and even if it is counterintuitive in the face of evil, it is certainly more economic than the other solution, which assumes a second (or third, etc.) principle besides the moral law to explain Being or which is content with the factuality of the laws of nature. Maybe it is possible to show why only a multiplicity of beings that are capable of suffering, even capable of malice, can realize the moral law in its whole entirety in a world accessible to experience, but in its future development unpredictable for those beings; and maybe it is also possible to show why, among other things, the principles of Darwinian theory, which explains a good deal of the evils that worry us, count among the laws of this world.[61] But this is only a suggestion. Thank God the moral human being does not need complex theory to regard the evils in the world as an occasion for their active defeat.

Translated by Benjamin Fairbrother

CHAPTER 4

—•—•—•—•—

Rationalism, Determinism, Freedom

An excellent book about determinism ends with the following advice: "As a practical 'solution' I recommend the ostrich tactic: don't think too closely or too long on the issues raised here, and in daily life continue with the presumption that the 'I' that chooses and the self to which we attach value judgments are autonomous. Let those who want to call themselves philosophers bear the risk to their mental health that comes from thinking too much about free will."[1]

Belonging unfortunately to the high-risk group called "philosophers," I want to dedicate at least some time and energy to reflecting upon the relation of freedom and determinism. I do not claim in this essay the truth of determinism, but I want to make as strong as possible a case for it, and I certainly want to defend compatibilism, that is, the idea that determinism does not exclude a meaningful concept of freedom. At least I want to reject some gross misrepresentations existing about determinism that have led to exaggerated expectations with regard to quantum mechanics—as if only this theory could free us from a horrible and ultimately immoral vision of the world. There is no doubt about the fact that quantum theory signifies a profound challenge for ontology; but its philosophical importance would remain great enough, if, for example, it enforced a revolution in mereology (the doctrine of the relation between parts and the whole) and in relation to the locality principle without, at the same time, undermining determinism or even realism. In any case, quantum theory is not the only way to overcome determinism, and perhaps there is no urgent need to overcome determinism.

Max Planck's and Albert Einstein's seemingly stubborn refusal to embrace a non-deterministic interpretation of quantum mechanics is explained by psychological categories of a reductionistic nature only by those persons who are not acquainted with the arguments in favor of determinism. Such arguments played a role already in ancient philosophy; it is, however, not difficult to see why in Late Antiquity and in the Middle Ages determinism became a more concrete position, attractive to philosophers of all three monotheistic religions. The doctrines of divine prescience and, even more, of divine omnipotence are, to say the least, more easily compatible with a deterministic universe than with a non-deterministic one, even if much effort was dedicated to various attempts to show that free will was not excluded by those two doctrines. In early modernity, finally, a determinist view of the world was largely accepted, partly on theological grounds—albeit the changes in the concept of God that took place in this time were profound—and partly also by agnostic or even atheistic positions. It is significant that one of the classics of determinism—perhaps the best known—antedates Isaac Newton's *Philosophiae Naturalis Principia Mathematica* of 1686: Baruch Spinoza's *Ethica* appeared (posthumously) in 1677. This shows that the triumph of determinism did not presuppose the emergence of classical mechanics, even if it would be misleading to deny that it was favored by it.

And yet there are philosophical arguments for determinism that do not depend on the state of the art of physics; and because determinism did not need Newtonian physics in order to be articulated as a philosophical position, it cannot be confuted either by the replacement of Newtonian physics by other paradigms. I do presuppose here, for the argument's sake, that Newtonian mechanics is a deterministic theory. This is, however, a position not shared by everybody. John Earman denies it explicitly—even if by introducing solutions of the relevant mathematical equations that could be considered as not genuinely possible physically.[2] He regards special relativistic physics as more friendly toward determinism. But I will not discuss these issues in this essay. (I have to ignore the problem of statistical laws as well.)

I must restrict myself in this context to a very rough concept of determinism. By "determinism" I understand an ontological, not an epistemological, position; predictability is therefore not a necessary moment in the concept here presupposed, even if it played an enormous role in its history.[3] The universe should be called deterministic if whatever will happen is already implicit in what has happened earlier and in the natural laws, if—to be more precise—the present is compatible with only one future development. In order to understand this definition it is not necessary to analyze in detail the difficult concept of causation. There are, however, obvious links between determinism and the principle of sufficient reason, even if it is wrong to regard the statement "every event has a cause" as the equivalent of determinism. This principle is only implied by determinism since an earlier state of the world can be regarded as the cause of the later one, but the mere statement in itself does not yet imply determinism. This is at least true as long as we do not add something like "the same causes always have the same effects." One could imagine a world in which every event had a cause, but the same causes always produced different effects, and it would be absurd to call such a universe "deterministic."

Yet one could counter that this addition was already implicit in our proposition. In fact, this proposition, well understood, and even more determinism, is not as much an assertion about "causes" as an assertion about the universal character of certain relations. It presupposes a metaphysics of natural laws, another point that unfortunately has to be ignored in this essay. Here I want only to draw attention to the fact that the idea that the same causes must have the same effects is formally similar to the basic principle of ethics and law that equal cases have to be treated equally. It suggests some more general principle in the architectonics of our reason, a principle prior to the split between theoretical and practical reason. I am not presupposing in my approximate definition of determinism that natural laws are coextensive with physical laws—in fact, such an assumption would obviously be false. It can rightly be doubted whether the laws of chemistry can be reduced to those of physics;[4] and it is manifest that the psycho-physical laws will never be reduced to the laws of physics, which do not contain concepts about the life of the mind.

The problem of determinism and freedom is not only, and perhaps not even mainly, a problem of the philosophy of physics. It is linked to various fields of philosophy—one could even risk the statement that there are few philosophical issues so tightly connected with so many other philosophical disciplines. As we will see, epistemological options influence strongly the rationality or irrationality of deterministic assumptions; and the ancient, Diodorean form of determinism shows that questions of logic (particularly of modal logic) are also at stake.[5] Whether the world is deterministic or not is an important metaphysical issue. There are few features that characterize the structure of the world as profoundly as this one—the very concepts of being, substance, and time change if we accept determinism. But the general interest in determinism is not limited to nature in the narrower sense of the word; the existentially relevant question is whether it also applies to human actions. Their relation to nature and consciousness, along with the whole mind-body problem, is at the core of the determinism-freedom controversy. This controversy has important consequences for ethics, particularly for the doctrine of sanctions, and since decisive fundaments of our conceptions of law and state consist in questions of criminal law and of punishment, it is also of grave concern for legal and political philosophy. The links with philosophical theology concern in part eschatology (a topic related to the last one, but ignored in this essay), in part the relation of freedom and necessity in God.

In the following pages I first develop some classical arguments in favor of determinism (I); second, I name the most important objections against it and the main strategies used to avoid it, and suggest why these strategies remain problematic (II); finally, I explain why, after all, certain concerns of the critics of determinism can be dealt with in a subtler form of determinism (III). In fact, one of the purposes of this essay is to distinguish different forms of determinism and to show that, while some forms are morally repugnant and even self-contradictory, others are more interesting and challenging. The conception proposed here of a non-materialistic determinism is very close to Gottfried Wilhelm Leibniz's philosophy. It is something the truth of which I do not wish to assert but simply to discuss with people who perhaps are too prone to deduce from the unacceptability of some forms of determinism the impossibility of all forms. In the course of my essay, I briefly sketch the positions of several philosophers of the past, for I have never been able to convince myself that the later positions in the history of philosophy are always the better ones.

I.

One of the determining features of early modern philosophy is its rationalism. By "rationalism" we mean a strong trust in reason as the ultimate intellectual capacity. In a broader sense of the word, rationalism can be ascribed to those early modern authors who insist on the importance of experience. Therefore, one may regard even the empiricists, John Locke, George Berkeley, and David Hume, as belonging to the larger family of rationalists; for they regard it as rational to ground knowledge on experience. The central idea common to both rationalists (in the narrower sense) and empiricists is their opposition against authority and tradition as last justifications of validity claims. But the Latin word *ratio* from which "rationalism" stems means not only "reason"; it also means "cause" and "ground." Therefore, rationalism usually is committed to the acceptance of some form of the principle of sufficient reason. The application of this multifaceted principle to events leads (with the above-mentioned addition) to determinism, and therefore determinism can be regarded as implied by rationalism in the broader sense of the word. The two forms of rationalism, however, are merely connected, not logically equivalent. René Descartes is a rationalist in the epistemological sense of the word, but denies a determination of human actions, as he also rejects necessity in God. Hume is not a rationalist in the narrower sense of the epistemological term, but he defends some form of methodological determinism with regard to events (actions included). And yet, despite the logical independence of the two forms of rationalism, a certain connection between the two is obvious, and this renders it reasonable to begin with some general reflections in favor of epistemological rationalism.

The main reason for early modern rationalism was the profound de-sire for freedom. The powerful traditions of the Middle Ages were felt as limitations of intellectual and political freedom, whose vindication is the main purpose of a work as seminal as Spinoza's *Tractatus theologico-politicus*. Traditional beliefs ought to be justified, and their reasons should be clarified; this is one aspect of modern rationalism. At the same time the project emerged to liberate humankind from seemingly perennial problems such as hunger, plagues, and wars, which clearly limit the free-dom of human actions. It was soon understood that only an unbiased analysis of nature and society could help to bring about this aim, and therefore an appeal to reason or to experience had to replace the tradi-tional philosophies of nature, the human, and the state. One had to ex-plain, to find the causes of such problems, in order to gain the chance to overcome them. But why are the projects of justification and explanation connected with "reason"? In a very rude approximation one may say that reason is the human capacity that asks the original question "why?" This capacity is already present in children, and the rejection of the corre-sponding question by the educators, although sometimes important and even inevitable for the stability of a society, is often detrimental to a philosophical development of the individual concerned. The question "why?" is indeed the link between rationalism in the epistemological sense and determinism, and the intermediate ring in the chain is the prin-ciple of sufficient reason.

The idea that every process presupposes a cause is found already in Plato,[6] and in Boethius we find the explicit argument that for something to happen without a cause would contradict the (Eleatic) principle that nothing comes from nothing.[7] In Spinoza's *Ethica* something like the principle of sufficient reason is stated as the third axiom of the first book, and even if he does not distinguish terminologically between causes and reasons, in his vision of the ontological structure of the world a clear distinction is made between things or events on the one hand and natural laws (the laws of the divine nature) on the other. Both are "caused," but in different ways: single events only by other events on the basis of general laws, general laws by other, more general laws culminat-ing in the *causa sui* (which can be best understood in terms of the onto-logical proof). One could speak of horizontal and of vertical levels of "causality." We would say today that only events could have causes; laws, on the other hand, have reasons—if such reasons are conceivable at all. In fact, Spinoza's attempt to ground the general laws is utterly dissatisfying; it is not even clear whether he would like to defend the position of panlogicism, according to which the propositions about natural laws are analytical.

More elaborated are his assertions about the horizontal level of "causality." It is on this level that one can speak of determinism, even if the principle of sufficient reason encompasses both the horizontal and the vertical levels. Spinoza explicitly applies determinism to the two intelligible attributes of substance, to thought as well as to extension; every human action, every thought, is caused and predetermined. As a consequence of this determinism, Spinoza denies the character of substantiality to all but God—God is the only substance. This signifies an unutterably profound break with Aristotelian ontology, which has as its starting point the assumption of different, sensible substances (the Spinozian conception, however, has certain traits in common with Eleatic metaphysics). For Aristotle as well as for his ancient and medieval followers, this plant, this cat, this man are entities within their own rights. For Spinoza they are only modi of a general extension, which itself is but one attribute of a more universal structure, which alone can cause itself: the divine substance. As caused, the single modi manifest only natural laws, but they do not subsist on their own and must therefore not be called "substances,"[8] even if there are pragmatic reasons for the observer to isolate single "slices" of the *res extensa*.

Spinoza's physics is the strongest challenge to atomistic thinking one can conceive—it is a form of "field ontology."[9] Time does not create anything new; to understand the world as necessary means to understand it "sub specie aeternitatis" (II p. 44 cor. II). While God can be called "free" insofar as he exists based only on the necessity of his own nature (I p. 17), a freedom of the will is impossible (I p. 32, II p. 48). Teleological arguments, which had been so important for ancient and medieval philosophy and science, are rejected in the appendix to the first book. With regard to the four traditional causes, Spinoza is interested mainly in the *causa efficiens*. Assertions about the teleological behavior of organisms or human beings have to be translated into a language in terms of efficient causes. If something appears as accidental, that is, as undetermined, this is due only to our own ignorance (I p. 33); and in fact one has to concede to Spinoza that it is difficult, if not impossible, to exclude the possibility of hidden parameters determining a process.

The profound influence that Spinoza exerted on Leibniz is manifest. Despite major differences between the personalities, careers, methods, and styles of the two thinkers, one cannot deny that they share a similar program of rational theology and that, for both, rationalism in the epistemological sense implies determinism. Yet at least the two following aspects distinguish the contents of their philosophies. First, even if Leibniz shares Spinoza's rejection of atomism, he insists on the substantial character of the monads, the subjective centers acknowledged also by Spinoza, but immersed in the one attribute of thought.[10] There are no atoms since matter can always be divided, but there are individual unities that serve as the basis of the different streams of consciousness and that are ontologically different from each other. Second, Leibniz is much more interested in the "vertical" series than is Spinoza, and he understands that the panlogical program cannot be fulfilled. The world as a whole is contingent, not per se necessary; therefore not logical, but only moral reasons that were rejected by Spinoza can explain why the world is as it is.

But all this does not deny the principle of sufficient reason—on the contrary, it presupposes it. Leibniz is the first to bestow on it an importance equal to that of the principle of contradiction: "Our reasonings are founded on two great principles, the one of contradiction . . . and that of sufficient reason, thanks to which we consider that no fact can be found true or existent, no assertion true if there is not a sufficient reason why it is so and not otherwise, even if these reasons most often cannot be known to us."[11] As arguments in *favor* of this principle (which to him does not yet entail that the same causes must have the same effects) Leibniz gives the following: "Without this great principle, we could never prove the existence of God, and we would lose an infinite amount of very correct and very useful reasonings, of which it is the principle: and it does not allow for any exception, otherwise its force would be weakened. Thus there is nothing as weak as those systems where everything vacillates and is full of exceptions."[12] Leibniz fears that even a single exception to this principle would endanger the work of reason—for if we grant that there are facts without causes or reasons, then we can never exclude that the search for causes or reasons in a given case is meaningless and that those are right who are satisfied with simple facticity. In particular, he is afraid that his arguments for the existence of God would fail, if the principle lost its absolute validity.

The persuasive force of determinism must have been powerful indeed if not only the majority of the great philosophers of the seventeenth and eighteenth centuries were convinced of it, but if even the thinker to whom we owe the greatest revolution in our concept of causality remains committed to some form of determinism, at least as a form of thought of the human mind, without any ontological commitment. I must ignore here the difficult question of whether the epistemological projects of *A Treatise of Human Nature* and of *An Enquiry Concerning Human Understanding* are similar or at least compatible with each other; but it can be stated safely that Hume regards in both works the idea of a free act of the will not determined by anything as an empty idea. Our whole social intercourse presupposes regularities in the behavior of our fellow human beings that are not significantly different from the regularities of natural bodies. "There is no philosopher, whose judgment is so riveted to this fantastical system of liberty, as not to acknowledge the force of moral evidence, and both in speculation and practice proceed upon it as upon a reasonable foundation. Now, moral evidence is nothing but a conclusion concerning the actions of men, derived from the consideration of their motives, temper, and situation" (*Treatise,* II.III.I). Hume acknowledges liberty as "a power of acting or not acting according to the determinations of the will" (*Enquiry,* par. VIII, Part I). But this liberty shared by everybody who is not a prisoner and in chains is compatible with factors determining the will, being themselves functions of character and the situation. As Locke put it, freedom implies the existence of the will; therefore, the will itself cannot be called "free" (Locke, *An Essay Concerning Human Understanding,* II 21, particularly 16).

Hume is not the only philosopher who simplifies Spinoza's and Leibniz's subtle and complex conception of determinism by eliminating the ontological and the cosmological proof originally connected with the program of rationalism and by taking interest merely in the horizontal series of events. The atheistic and materialist philosophers of the eighteenth and the nineteenth centuries pursue a similar project, although on the basis of a dogmatic epistemology. Even if Arthur Schopenhauer can be regarded only in a superficial way as a materialist, it makes sense to focus on his position as paradigmatic for this alternative type of determinism since he has dedicated more explicit reflections to the principle of sufficient reason than all old materialist philosophers I know of. Furthermore, Schopenhauer has elaborated determinism in its application to human actions in a way which, even if it is not really original, is more concrete than all the earlier applications. I do not claim in the least to render justice to Schopenhauer's philosophy as a whole—I must ignore both its core, the metaphysics of the will, and the strange mixture of transcendental idealism and realism—but I will try to name the main features of his peculiar type of determinism. In fact, his dissertation, *Über die vierfache Wurzel des Satzes vom zureichenden Grunde* (*On the Fourfold Root of the Principle of Sufficient Reason*), as well as his *Über die Freiheit des menschlichen Willens* (*On the Freedom of the Will*) signify important steps in the history of our problem. When in popular discussions the ghost of determinism appears, one often associates with it fragments of argumentations developed by Schopenhauer.[13] He was influential also because he developed, as before him Thomas Hobbes and Baruch Spinoza, an immanentistic ethics that is built on merely descriptive sentences. The project of a justification of ethics was integrated into the "horizontal" deterministic worldview.

The main intent of Schopenhauer's dissertation was the distinction of four classes of objects to which the principle of sufficient reason is applied, assuming different forms. Schopenhauer recognized that these forms have a common feature; all four forms guarantee a unity of our conceptions, "due to which nothing which subsists for itself and is independent, nor anything single and detached can become object for us."[14] The first class is formed by empirical representations; for this class the principle of sufficient reason appears as the law of causality, as the *principium rationis sufficientis fiendi*. It states that every change is caused by another; there can be no first cause, but only an infinite series of events. Corollaries of this principle are the principle of inertia and the law of the conservation of substance. The changes presuppose something stable, namely, matter, but also the forces of nature. The laws determining the actions of these forces are eternal and cannot be explained; the cosmological proof is rejected as strongly as the ontological one. Causality manifests itself in three forms: in the inorganic world as a cause in the narrower sense of the word, in plants as a stimulus, and in animals (including humans) as a motive. Motives presuppose cognition and therefore a process of mediation that in humans is more complex than in other animals, but this does not change the deterministic character of the world. Given the character and the motive, the actions of a person follow with the same necessity as the fall of a body in a gravitational field. Only the principle of causality can transform the amorphous mass of sensations into a structured whole, into an objective world—through the assumption that the sensations have an external cause. With this reflection Schopenhauer wants to ground the a priori nature of the principle of causality, while he rejects Immanuel Kant's demonstration in the first *Critique,* which had insisted on the causal relation as the only way to guarantee an objective time order (*Kritik der reinen Vernunft,* A189ff./B232ff.). Schopenhauer, it should be noted, does not aim at grounding the validity of the principle of sufficient reason. Such an attempt he regards even as absurd since it would presuppose the principle it tried to prove.[15]

The second class of applications for the principle of sufficient reason dealt with by Schopenhauer consists of concepts; in this realm the principle becomes the *principium rationis sufficientis cognoscendi.* Judgments have to be justified, and Schopenhauer acknowledges four types of reasons for the truth of propositions, according to whether they are logical, empirical, transcendental, or metalogical truths. It is, however, clear that the justification soon comes to an end—either with an empirical fact or with a transcendental principle such as the principle of causality (V 172, par. 50). The third class consists of the a priori forms of intuitions; here Schopenhauer treats the demonstration of mathematical truths (*principium rationis sufficientis essendi*). Of special interest is his idea that a cogent demonstration may nevertheless fail to grasp the ontological reason for a mathematical theorem. The fourth class finally consists of one's own subjectivity, that is, of the subject of one's own will. As the *principium rationis sufficientis agendi,* the principle for this class becomes the law of motivation already discussed within the first class, but now based on introspection. For Schopenhauer the will is the essential feature of a person; intellect and reason are only its tools. In *Über die Freiheit des menschlichen Willens,* Schopenhauer explains with the peculiar character of introspection the illusion of the free will, an illusion favored furthermore by the theological desire to find an exoneration of God in the free will, as far as it can be made responsible for evils.[16] It remains remarkable, however, that Schopenhauer's work ends, surprisingly, with an invocation of Kant's transcendental freedom, which he regards as necessary in order to allow for the possibility of moral imputation.

II.

This is indeed the first, if not the main, objection against determinism: that it seems impossible to regard persons as "responsible" for their actions if whatever they have done and will do is predetermined by an earlier state of the world. Punishment and even weaker forms of social sanctions seem to presuppose that the person could have acted otherwise and therefore are not applied when the person was, for example, forced to commit the reproachable deed; but in a certain sense of the expression this cannot have been the case if the universe is a deterministic system.[17] It is always safe to state that the person would have acted otherwise if he or she had made another decision; but the problem is that he or she did not make the decision and could not have done so, given the laws of nature and an earlier state of the universe.[18] One can readily grant Leibniz that the necessity at stake is not a logical one, but it is still a necessity, given the factual world in which we happen to live.

Now "compatibilism" has always taught that our system of sanctions can survive even if we accept the truth of determinism—we should only interpret it in a different way, related to the future and not to the past. The so-called hard determinists, on the other hand, recognize an incompatibility between determinism and our practice of social sanctions; but while they deduce from it that our practices are not appropriate, the indeterminists, on the contrary, see in our practices a proof of the absurdity of determinism. It is not only the love for habits inherited from times immemorial that prevents the indeterminists from reforming our practice of sanctions. They argue that the wrongdoer must deserve the punishment (which is not the case if the main justification for punishment is its deterrent effect) and that he is honored by being regarded as responsible. Even if Peter Strawson belongs to the large family of compatibilists, one could try to find material against determinism in his brilliant essay "Freedom and Resentment."[19] In fact, the change from the reactive to the objective attitude that takes place when we come to the conviction that a certain person is a psychotic individual and that has the consequence that we no longer resent his behavior but regard it as some calamity that simply has to be brought under control is not necessarily in the interest of the wrongdoer. Certainly a world would be poorer emotionally in which individuals would know only objective attitudes toward each other because they believed that reactive attitudes made no sense in a determinist universe.

But not only does our practice of sanctions seem to contradict deterministic beliefs—our self-understanding does so as well. We regard ourselves as free and react angrily against those who pretend to anticipate our decisions. The conviction of our own freedom is perhaps even a presupposition of our acting. Therefore, some critics of determinism argue that this position must lead to fatalism, namely, to the refusal to act because whatever will happen will happen also without our own contribution. Particularly a physiological determinism that denies the causal power of mental states could invite quietism: people should simply attend to how their neurons will behave. In any case one cannot deny that the belief in our own freedom is one of the strongest intuitions we have. If we accept an intuitionistic epistemology, we should take such an intuition very seriously.

In general, an intuitionistic epistemology has to reject central tenets of rationalism in the epistemological sense of the word. On its basis, it is utterly impossible to ask, as Leibniz did, for a justification for every assertion because this would lead to an infinite regress. There are final certitudes that cannot and need not be grounded. Even Schopenhauer defends such a position with regard to reasons, while at the same time he thinks that every change has a cause. Can the principle of causality itself be grounded? Schopenhauer denies this question; he tries to justify only its a priori status, not its validity. But if the principle of causality is not justified in a cogent way, why should we accept it? Nobody will deny that it is important and useful—yet this does not imply that we should sacrifice to it one of our most cherished intuitions, namely, the intuition of our freedom. This is all the more convincing, as determinism is nothing more than a general program, not realized completely even for the domain of physics. We are very far from understanding all the factors determining human behavior—even if one can hardly deny that, for example, criminology has shown us several causes of criminality, individual as well as social ones. It is, however, always possible to regard these causes as merely rendering a certain behavior more probable, not as sufficient causes since nobody will, at least in the near future, be able to name all the factors that together could be a sufficient condition for a certain action.

This way of thinking, however, shows only that we need not accept determinism—not that we must reject it. Furthermore, it shares the general weaknesses of intuitionism: first of all, that my intuitions are not necessarily also the intuitions of other persons (a point that endangers their claim of truth since truth is necessarily intersubjective, and even elicits the suspicion that certainties may be variables dependent upon social factors, as power in its various forms, including education[20]); second, that even in my own set of intuitions there may be some that contradict each other—in this case, which one should I prefer? Intuitionism usually does not include a criterion for solving conflicts between contradicting intuitions. If we are frank, we must confess that most of us accept both some version of the principle of sufficient reason and the belief in our own freedom (perhaps also in the freedom of other human beings); and therefore the insistence on the second intuition can easily be countered by pointing to the first one.

It is in this context that one type of solution has been proposed that could be called "perspectivistic." According to this conception, which exists in diverse variants, both determinism and indeterminism are necessary perspectives of our mind, but they are valid on different levels. The most famous version comes from Kant, whose subtle and even astute argument has the following form: the principle of causality is necessary for science, for physics as well as for psychology. But this necessity cannot be grounded on experience, which already presupposes the prin-

ciple; therefore it stems from reason. Since Kant conceives reason fundamentally as a subjective faculty, the causal determination concerns only
the phenomena, that is, the world as it appears to us, not the noumena,
the world in itself. Therefore, it is possible to assume that in the real
world entities exist that are not determined by the past but still have the
capacity to begin anew a causal series. This assumption—which in the
domain of theoretical reason is only a possibility—becomes a necessity
in the domain of practical reason. We must believe for moral reasons in
the transcendental freedom of moral agents. Kant's subjective-idealist
limitation of the claims of experience and science has been very influential, even in our century, and it is sufficient to liberate us from the threat
of determinism. Those philosophers of quantum mechanics who interpret it in a non-realistic and in a non-deterministic way may have good
reasons to do so, but they go too far if their only aim is to overcome determinism. A non-deterministic and realistic interpretation of the theory
is sufficient for this purpose as well as a deterministic and phenomenal-
istic interpretation.

Kant's solution has a great merit lacking in many other "perspectiv-
ist" solutions (which after the "linguistic turn" and the late Ludwig Wittgenstein now prefer to speak of different "language games"). Kant offers
a clear hierarchy of the two positions. He presupposes—perhaps with a
certain naiveté—the superiority of the point of view of practical reason
because he does not regard the moral law as something merely subjective, while he does so with natural science. If one does not share this
presupposition, one would be at a loss; for we would have no criterion to
decide which perspective is, in the last instance, the right one. In fact,
nothing is achieved by granting that there are different legitimate perspectives. As long as they cannot be simultaneously true, one has to
choose between them.

In his famous lecture *Vom Wesen der Willensfreiheit* (*On the Essence of the
Freedom of the Will*), Planck proposed a solution to our dilemma that insisted on the deterministic character of the laws of physics (also of quantum mechanics) and of nature in general while granting at the same time
the irreducible freedom of the subjective will from the point of view of
introspection. "Considered from outside, objectively, the will is causally
bound; considered from inside, subjectively, the will is free."[21] This is

supposed not to lead to a contradiction; Planck even appeals to relativity theory to explain why from different systems different statements can be made with exactly the same right. But the comparison is grossly misleading—for movement is a relative category, while determination is not. Planck himself seems to recognize this when he states that the acting individual only feels free (312)—which, of course, is compatible with his or her being determined. One cannot be at the same time determined and not determined—one can only say that there are two different positions with regard to this issue. But then the question unavoidably arises: which position is the right one? Kant tries to answer this question, Planck does not.

While compatibilism aims at showing that determinism does not endanger our common intuitions and while perspectivism wants to demonstrate that determinism and the belief in free will are positions appropriate to different levels of our thought, there are also attempts to confute determinism, to show that it is wrong and perhaps even self-contradictory. It is the achievement of Ulrich Pothast to have categorized the great number of such arguments, that is, to have reduced them to some few elementary types. It is further to his credit that he has shown that none of these arguments is really cogent. His book, *Die Unzulänglichkeit der Freiheitsbeweise*,[22] deserves particular praise because of the remarkable capacity of treating with equal competence both analytical and "continental" arguments; he succeeds in showing a common logical structure wrapped in very different languages. What are the elementary types?

One group of authors insists on the impossibility of predicting the future with absolute certainty. Such an impossibility is, by the way, an immediate consequence of one physical theory of recent decades, namely, chaos theory: infinitesimal deviations from a given value can lead to a very different behavior of the relevant physical system. Since there are limits to our approximation of physical values in measurement, humans will never be able to anticipate which course such a system will take. But it is very easy to object against this argument that no reasonable person has ever defended epistemological determinism and that epistemological indeterminism does not entail ontological indeterminism. Quantum mechanics might lead to a destruction of ontological determinism; chaos theory, on its own, certainly does not.

More interesting are those arguments that do not make use of concrete physical theories, but are more general. So Karl Popper claims to dispose of an argument valid also within classical mechanics against determinism, an argument based on the impossibility of a complete description of the world by a system that always must leave itself out, at least in some aspect.[23] Furthermore, one encounters the argument that one cannot know today how one will decide in ten days—otherwise either the decision would be made today and not in ten days, or the categorical difference between prognosis and decision would be undermined.[24] The argument does make questionable presuppositions; but even if we grant them, it will show as little as Popper's that my decision is not predetermined, but only that I cannot know it before I make it. Nobody denies that the I-perspective that for so many aspects is indeed a unique privilege also implies certain restraints: one cannot objectify oneself as other persons. But it remains unintelligible why this should prove freedom in an ontological sense of the word.

The second group of authors works with the distinction between reasons and causes.[25] To understand an action, it is argued, we must recognize the intentional character of psychic acts; but the logic of intentionality is completely different from the logic of causes. The merit of these authors is that they clearly recognize that indeterminism is in the best of cases a necessary, but never a sufficient presupposition of freedom. To act in an utterly unpredictable way is not yet to act freely; an action can be regarded as my action only if it is willed and caused by me. Some philosophers have tried to deduce from this fact that free will even involves determination.[26] But even if this claim is too far-reaching, it is clear that a model of self-determination is needed if we want to have more than hazardous behavior. If this self-determination is to transcend determinism, it must have certain further qualifications which, however, are hard to specify and to conceive because we have given up the categorical thread of causality.[27] We have to express ourselves in the following way: the action is caused by the person, and the person itself is utterly free in causing the action (a quality several philosophers and theologians would ascribe only to God); a causal explanation of the relevant act is therefore inconceivable.

I will not discuss such attempts,[28] but return to the clear distinction between causes and reasons. Our authors analyze the peculiar nature of responsible decisions in which arguments *pro* and *con* for a possible action always play a role. They are completely right to reject a naturalistic ontology that knows only causes and ignores reasons. Not only could such an ontology never be justified because justifications presuppose reasons; such an ontology would deny the difference between humans and the other animals—for humans are animals able to grasp reasons. But the difference between reasons and causes, as important as it is, does not imply indeterministic consequences. Reasons as such cannot cause anything; but it is the understanding of reasons, that is, a mental act (or its physical pendant), which, together with a series of other factors, may cause human behavior. The free person, according to a profound concept of freedom, is not the person whose actions cannot be accounted for. The free person is the person who follows the strongest reasons. The capacity to follow reasons, however, may well be caused by different factors, such as education, features of personal character, intelligence, and the like. In any case the essential distinction between reasons and causes can be easily integrated into a deterministic system.[29]

In order to confute a position one may try to show that it contradicts some assumptions regarded as true by the opponent, who, however, might be willing to give up these assumptions if this is the price he has to pay for sticking to that position. It is therefore better if the critic can show that a position is immediately self-contradictory. The contradiction may subsist on the propositional level, or it may be a contradiction between the position itself and the presuppositions necessary for its performance. Arguments showing a contradiction of the last type have been called "transcendental," and they are a powerful tool for grounding fundamental principles of epistemology and of metaphysics. It is therefore no surprise that such a transcendental argument for freedom has been elaborated in the discussion about determinism, and—what is particularly interesting—both by pre-analytical and by analytical philosophers.[30]

The argument has the following structure: in order to claim the truth of determinism, one has to appeal to a norm of rationality. Therefore, one must in principle be able to judge according to this norm. But this presupposes freedom: if our mental acts and our behavior were only functions of a blind causal process, we could not determine ourselves according to truth and rationality. The argument is indeed sufficient to reject a naturalistic determinism, which can never arrive at justifying truth claims. It is impossible to say, "I am determined by a blind series of causes, and I state this as true"—for the statement can be taken seriously only if it is more than the result of a causal process. But does anything exclude that it is both the result of a causal process and something else? Could it not be that I am determined to argue well and to accept the best argument that I can find? And would not such a determination be a better reason to trust me than a *liberum arbitrium indifferentiae,* which would still grant me the possibility of contradicting the insights of reason?

I am even willing to go a step further and concede that the fact that I am able to argue and that there are in general persons able to follow reasons cannot be a contingent truth. This has important consequences with regard to the understanding of modalities that cannot be analyzed here; the task of bridging the gap between the formal and the transcendental concept of necessity has yet to be well understood. But if I accept the idea that the world must contain persons able to follow reasons and to discuss rationally truth claims with regard to questions such as determinism, then nothing prevents us from believing that the existence of such persons is brought about by a causal process. Indeterminism is not the only possible consequence that can be drawn from our argument; a conceivable solution is also a non-materialistic determinism that accepts teleological restraints to the whole system of the world, without, however, violating the causal order by the concrete interference of ends. The ends determine the laws of nature and the initial conditions—but with this their task is fulfilled.

III.

This corresponds quite thoroughly to the complex deterministic conception of Leibniz, to which I will return after my further discussion of the indeterministic strategies will have shown that their arguments are not cogent. Not even the Kantian strategy is really convincing. On the one hand, the price Kant has to pay for his transcendental idealism is high; he has to assume a separate world of unintelligible entities, the things in themselves, about which he nevertheless has to make statements. On the other hand, it remains dubious whether indeterminism is really necessary for the general traits of our practice of sanctions (and it cannot be accepted as a valid argument for indeterminism that without it our more cruel ways of punishing could no longer be justified[31]). It may be true that the criminal could not act otherwise, given the person he or she is; but it still remains true that this is the person he or she is. Therefore, criminals cannot complain about their punishment, for they could do so only in the name of a metaphysics that denies the substantiality of their own selves, and then it would no longer be they who complained about it, and scarcely could they claim to have any rights. In a statement like "I believe that my actions are the product of causes existing already long before my birth," there is a complete abstraction from *one's own* actions; but as even an author such as Pothast writes: "With the same right, or with the same lack of right, with which someone, using this description, distances himself from his own actions, he could distance himself from himself."[32]

I would go even further: such persons could not even distance themselves from themselves, for such an act of distancing presupposes, on the performative level, a subjective act of the I. The I cannot be eluded; in this unavoidability there is a hint of the absolute, which justifies the peculiar rights of the I and which may claim substantiality even if the concept in this use has a meaning very different from that in Aristotelian metaphysics. A society would collapse not only empirically, but in its own claim to be taken seriously under a moral perspective if it would accept a distancing from one's own actions such as the one suggested. Nevertheless, Strawson is right when he writes that the decision for an objective behavior rather than a reactive one has nothing to do with the problem of determinism. There is something in the essence of a person that determines whether we resent his or her actions or begin to objectify his or her behavior, and it may well be that this something is determined in both cases. Therefore, we can at the same time in which we resent the behavior of wrongdoers have a certain compassion for them; and this compassion should prevent us from applying sanctions that destroy them. I believe that the last aim of punishment is the future prevention of evils, even if this aim can be achieved only if we act as if the criminal had been free in the past. True freedom is moral rationality, but we have a chance to raise wrongdoers to it only if we presume that they are also free in evil acts.[33] As compassion for the wrongdoer, also a certain modesty with regard to oneself and even a sense of gratitude toward the creator will be peculiar to the moral person who is convinced of this kind of determinism—qualities that should, I think, recommend the more considered forms of determinism.[34]

Furthermore, it is clear that epistemological indeterminism is indeed a presupposition of our actions—but this does not yet prove ontological determinism. Precisely because we do not know what will happen, we have a duty to do our utmost to realize the good. Fatalism is not at all implied by ontological determinism, but only by epistemological determinism. Leibniz dedicated much of the energy of his subtle and noble mind to confute *la raison paresseuse,* which sees in determinism an invitation to laziness. Yet determinism does not teach that something will happen as such, but only that something will happen if something else happens, for example, if our action takes place; and ontological determinism does not claim to anticipate our actions. Leibniz rightly asserts that the argument—or, better, sophism—proves too much: Not even the defenders of fatalism will drink a poison, saying, "If I have to die, I'll die, if not, I won't." "It is false that the event will occur whatever one does; it will happen because one does what leads to it; and if the event is predetermined, also the cause that brings it about is. Thus the connection between effects and causes, far from establishing the doctrine of a necessity that harms practice, serves to destroy it."[35]

Every person should concede that the belief not to be determined in one's own actions and decisions is at least a necessary and healthy illusion. When I have to make a decision, a reflection on the causes determining me is utterly useless because I have to concentrate on the relevant reasons. But this does not signify that the causes no longer exist. As psychoanalysis teaches us, even unconscious causes may continue to operate. Therefore, I should try to become conscious of the unconscious motives of my behavior; this may even lead to an alteration of my motivational structure. In fact, those determinists err who teach that we can only act as we will but that we cannot will what we will—one can try to change one's desires, even if this is a long and tortuous process. Yet even if higher-order volitions do exist, I do not want to contradict those determinists who insist on the fact that there are causes for the existence of such a capacity in certain human beings and its nonexistence in others.

The arguments against determinism may all seem weak; but if there are not positive arguments for it, why should we take it so seriously? One cannot agree with Schopenhauer that the principle of sufficient reason simply need not be proved—it would be awkward if the principle asked for something that it itself would not satisfy. Schopenhauer sees something important when he states that a proof for it would be circular, but he does not grasp that the impossibility of grounding a principle otherwise than in a circular way may be a mark of its being a first principle. This circle has to be distinguished from the vicious circle, however, because this trait also has to be accompanied by the further one that the principle cannot be denied without being simultaneously presupposed.[36] This applies, for example, to the principle of contradiction. One has to concede, however, that the principle of sufficient reason does not enjoy the same logical status, for it is not contradictory to deny it, even if every attempt to deny it with the help of an argument will presuppose some form of it.[37] Leibniz in any case does not offer satisfying reflections on the foundation of principles, and certainly one of the greatest lacks in his metaphysics is his complete inability to ground (and even name in a satisfying way) the moral criteria that allow God to choose between the possible worlds. The idea of a transcendental foundation of ethics is completely alien to Leibniz, even if ethics or, better, axiology in the framework of Leibniz's metaphysics acquires the status of First Philosophy.

Nevertheless, Leibniz has some important arguments that explain why he sticks so stubbornly to this principle, also and particularly in the context of his philosophical theology. It may sound paradoxical, but it is ultimately an ethical argument that leads Leibniz to embrace determinism. For perhaps even greater than in the *ordo cognoscendi* is the function of this principle in the *ordo essendi* of Leibniz's rational theology: God himself has to apply it in the creation of the world. Leibniz rejects the idea that God could have created another world as well as the real one, that there was no sufficient reason to prefer the existing one to possible alter-

natives. He concedes, as I have already said, that there are no logical reasons for the necessity of the actual world, but he insists on the existence
of moral reasons determining the choice of the real world. God must
create the best possible world,[38] although this necessity is obviously not
anything external to God, but God's own self-determination. Leibniz regards as particularly repellent the voluntaristic conception according to
which not only the structure of the world but also the moral duties depend on an arbitrary act of will of God. Such a position—as it was
defended by Descartes and Hobbes—would render God indistinguishable from an almighty tyrant, for no moral criterion beyond the divine
power would exist in order to evaluate it.[39] Leibniz regards as even more
repugnant the conception that there are objective criteria of good and
evil, but that the capacity to violate the moral norms is the true expression of freedom and something higher than obedience toward them—be
it God or the human who owns this "freedom." This conception is familiar to the friends of German literature from Eberward Schleppfuß's
lectures, described in the thirteenth (!) chapter of Thomas Mann's *Doktor
Faustus*. Schleppfuß is Privatdozent of theology at Halle, but his lectures
even more than his name and appearance suggest that he is one of the
manifestations of the devil in Mann's sublime novel.

According to Leibniz, freedom and moral necessity coincide not
only in God, but also in moral human beings. Leibniz rejects passionately
the idea that the irrational and immoral person could claim to have more
freedom than the person dedicated to reason. In the *Nouveaux Essais,*
Philalèthe states "that God himself could not choose what is not good
and that the freedom of this omnipotent being does not prevent him
from being determined by the best."[40] And he adds: "To be determined
by reason in an optimal way, that is to be maximally free. Would anyone
want to be an idiot for the reason that an idiot is less determined by wise
reflections than a man of common sense? If freedom consists in shaking
off the yoke of reason, the madmen and the stupid ones will be the only
free ones, but I do not believe that for love of such a freedom a person
would like to be mad, with the exception of those who already are mad."[41]
Like Spinoza, Leibniz cannot take the idea of the *liberum arbitrium indifferentiae* seriously: the determinant factors are unknown to us, but this
does not mean that they do not exist. Even when one commits an act

contrary to one's own interest in order to show one's freedom, one is in fact determined by the will to demonstrate one's freedom.[42] The good person cannot act otherwise than morally, as even Schelling will acknowledge in *Über das Wesen der menschlichen Freiheit* (*On the Essence of Human Freedom*), which in many aspects breaks with the earlier tradition of rational theology. But Schelling agrees with regard to the finite individual: "Already according to the meaning of the word, religiosity does not allow for a choice between opposite positions, not for an *aequilibrium arbitrii* (the pest of all morals), but only for the utmost determinacy to do what is right, without any choice."[43] At the same time, Schelling's work constitutes an important step forward in the phenomenology of evil—an advance that in principle can be integrated into a deterministic system.

The challenge of Leibniz's determinism is all the greater, as he rejects—again with Spinoza—any form of "interactionism." Since Descartes' lasting discovery that mental states and physical states cannot be reduced to each other but have to be characterized by two different, mutually exclusive classes of predicates, the mind-body problem has been vexing philosophers. If we accept such a dualism (which I regard as unavoidable, even if I readily grant that it, alas!, creates many problems happily alien to ancient and medieval philosophy), there are fundamentally four possible combinations for determining the relation between mental and physical states. Either there are causal interactions between the two domains (this position will be called here "interactionism"; sometimes this specific possibility is meant when one speaks of "dualism" in a narrower sense of the word), or the mental states are functions of the physical states (epiphenomenalism), or the physical states are projections of the mental acts (subjective idealism), or there exist causal connections within the two domains, but not directly from one to the other (parallelism).

While interactionism seems the most natural position and has been reworked in the last decades by several philosophers,[44] the objections against it, as they were understood already in the seventeenth century, are powerful. First of all, it is not clear how a causal relation between two domains so different could be conceived without undermining the ontological difference between them.[45] And second, the assumption that a physical movement could be caused by something immaterial endangers the physical laws of conservation (and even opens the door to magical beliefs[46]). Even if Descartes is one of the earliest philosophers who sees in the conservation laws of physics an expression of God's immutability and even if he adduces as an example the conservation of momentum,[47] he still regards momentum as a scalar magnitude, not as a vector. Therefore, he can believe that the *res cogitans* may influence the mere direction of the *spiritus animales* without altering the quantity of momentum. But already in the seventeenth century the vectorial nature of momentum was discovered, and therefore the Cartesian belief in a possible change of direction without a violation of the corresponding conservation law had to be abandoned.[48] Occasionalism was one of the attempts to cope with the new situation, and there can hardly be a doubt that, compared with it, Leibniz's doctrine of the pre-established harmony represents a considerable progress.[49]

According to Leibniz, no physical event—no action either—is caused by anything mental, but only by antecedent physical states. The world is structured in such a way, however, that simultaneously with certain mental events the corresponding physical events take place, and vice versa. When I want to lift my arm, it is not my will that lifts it, for my will cannot cause anything physical, but only other mental states, such as, for example, a feeling of satisfaction or frustration; the cause of the lifting is a physical state (e.g., the state of my brain). But it is not by chance that I usually lift my arm when I want to lift it—God guarantees such a correspondence between the mental and the physical states. The development of the mental states follows a special logic grounded in the peculiar nature of the single monad: this distinguishes Leibniz's position distinctly from the epiphenomenalist one. While epiphenomenalism must deny even the ontological continuity of mental life (every mental state is caused by a physical one and is unable to produce another mental state) and must deny even more forcefully its power to act in the physical world, Leibniz strongly defends the first quality—even to the point that all propositions about mental acts of a monad are ultimately analytical propositions. And even if with regard to the monad's power to act Leibniz denies a direct impact on physical states, he certainly recognizes that the creation of the physical world by God was done with the intention of guaranteeing a correspondence with the mental states of the different monads. This means that the essences of the created monads—not, however, the concrete acts of the existing monads—do determine physical events, via the choice of the best possible world by God. It would go beyond the task of this essay to analyze Leibniz's conception in greater detail—its main problems are that it is not easy to justify on its basis the assumption of an external world (which Leibniz in fact seems to interpret merely as intersubjectively shared phenomena); and it is even more difficult to imagine sufficient reasons for the correspondence of physical and mental states. But I think that parallelism deserves a revival in our time, for which the mind-body problem has regained an importance comparable to the relevance it had in the seventeenth century.

I repeat that it is not the purpose of this essay to argue for the truth of determinism. I regard a theory that assumes a plurality of entities capable of beginning a causal series on their own as a very serious philosophical alternative, and I am often tempted by it (even if I do not believe that it really solves the theodicy problem with any greater ease, also because the pain inflicted by nature on sentient organisms is still huge). I think, however, that it then becomes quite natural to deny God's omnipotence,[50] as Hans Jonas, one of the great philosophical theologians of our time, had the courage to do. The price for this step is high, for example, in terms of the philosophy of history. But it is certainly worth trying to develop the strongest possible arguments for such a theory. What I wanted to show in this essay is that there are different types of determinism, and that a determinism of the Leibnizian type copes remarkably well with some of the questions other determinisms are unable to answer. It will not be surprising if I finish with the wish that this type of philosophy, too, might be made as cogent as is possible and needed in our time, so that the competition between the two systems might be both fair and interesting.

CHAPTER 5

—•—•—•—•—

Encephalius

A Conversation about the Mind-Body Problem

Philonous: Theophilus, what are you thinking about? To be sure, I can tell by your facial expression that you are concentrating intently and meditating on something difficult, but I cannot discover the content of your thoughts. Only you have immediate access to that content, and it is up to your free will alone whether you want to share it with us.

Encephalius: The inability to infer the content of thoughts from a facial expression may be unsettling to behaviorists. Indeed, behaviorism is passé. More subtle are those materialists who have begun to make their way inside. Here one does not mean the so-called inner realm (this term bespeaks the inability of even dualists to transcend spatiality, from which the mental is supposed to have escaped), but rather something quite physical, even if it is something hidden beneath the skull—namely, the brain. These more subtle materialists make up for their inability to infer the content of thoughts by claiming, first, that propositional attitudes— doubtless the most significant mental states—do not have that qualitative determinateness which, according to the persistent opinion of some, characterizes a toothache or a red perception, for example, and which is vexing for anyone who would like to reduce the mental to the physical. Here it is convenient that at least the thought that π is a transcendental number and, hence, that a circle cannot be squared with ruler and compass feels no differently, according to the admission of even the wildest idealists, than the conviction, let's say, that there are only five regular polyhedrons. Whoever focuses on propositional attitudes as the decisive class of mental states or events is thus rid of the problem of qualia.

Philonous: Really?

Encephalius: And, second, it can certainly be explained by evolutionary biology why the inability to read off intentions was an advantage: whoever was able to disguise himself could survive longer and leave behind more offspring (perhaps with many women, each of whom he led to believe that she was his only lover). But this does not change the fact that one will soon be able to find out what a human being is thinking even if the latter is unwilling to reveal it—if, that is, the neurosciences continue to make such great advances. It will not even be necessary to crack open the skull but only to admit tiny sensors—cerebroscopes—into someone's brain, and the determination of any given brain state will answer all questions that are legitimately raised concerning another human being. But since we are not—unfortunately!—there yet, I too must ask you, Theophilus, to reveal to us what you were thinking just now.

Theophilus: What a coincidence—or should I rather say: what pre-established harmony! I was reflecting on the mind-body problem for some time before I saw you two coming, and now both of you are raising it yourselves. Perhaps, however, it was not pre-established harmony, but rather that you recognized, by something in my facial expression, what I was thinking; this is entirely possible even if you were not conscious of it. I remember once being on an airline flight with a friend whom I abruptly asked about a passing acquaintance, and my friend replied to me that he was sitting five rows in front of us. I was completely surprised, for his presence had not entered my consciousness until then; but the fact that I had suddenly thought of him is most easily explained by my having somehow perceived him.

Encephalius: Like all investigations into subception, your anecdote shows that cognitive tasks of human beings can be achieved even without consciousness; a good part of the human brain seems to function not much differently than an apparatus that achieves tasks of differenti- ation—for instance, the magical eye in an elevator that reopens the clos- ing doors whenever one sticks an object between them at the right height. It is possible that brains are the realization of complex Turing machines and their algorithms, and the master algorithm that forms the basis for the development of these algorithms is called natural selection.

Philonous: Perhaps part of our brain does work like an apparatus; but the other part, which operates in a different way because it operates in a conscious way, is doubtless more interesting. Indeed, we are *interested* in those unconscious functions only because we *are* also—or better said, because we are centrally—conscious beings with the capacity even to raise unconscious thoughts to consciousness. We are *we*—that is, "I's"— thanks only to our consciousness.

Your explanation, Theophilus, that we unconsciously perceived in your facial expression that about which you were thinking, is certainly not to be excluded a priori; whenever people think that they are being met with sympathy, they usually do not consciously notice the dilation of another's pupils, which often correlates with sympathy for a conversation partner, and from which such sympathy is inferred. But I share Encepha- lius's skepticism about whether individual thoughts are always correlated with something in one's facial expression; there are simply too many thoughts and too few variables in facial expression (even if there are surely more than we normally perceive consciously). Moreover, one does not need to assume telepathy in order to have a much easier explanation for this convergence. When we saw you, we both thought about our last conversation with you and Hylas, which after touching upon many moral and political questions finally came to rest on the mind-body problem, whose clarification is indispensable if one wants to understand how actions—and thus also moral actions—are at all possible. Recollection of this conclusion from our last discussion may have awakened in us— whether consciously or unconsciously—thoughts regarding the mind- body problem. Something mental—a recollection, combined perhaps with an expectation—elicited something mental.

Theophilus: This is indeed a plausible explanation; and it may also be true of me that the desire that arose a while ago to reflect just then on the mind-body problem was also caused by the expectation of your impend- ing visit. Incidentally, I agree with the view shared by the two of you that concrete propositional attitudes cannot be correlated with individual facial expressions. My remark referred not to the *content* of my thoughts but to the *feeling* of perplexity that was perhaps reflected in my face—and to the fact that no other philosophical problem provokes the kind of deep puzzlement that the question regarding the relation of mind and body does. And this feeling of standing before a mystery has a tormenting quality; indeed, it is a quale before I quail.[1]

Encephalius: I do not recognize this in myself. Or, to be precise with language, which likes so much to tempt us into hypostatizing words—a fact that has allowed a Blackforest sorcerer[2] to spin an entire metaphysics out of the seven letters "nothing" and more enlightened minds[3] to spin an entire metaphysics out of the single letter "I"—*my brain* does not recognize this in *itself.*

Philonous: Should I say "you fortunate one" or "you poor thing"? Have you solved the problem? Or is there perhaps wandering among us in this world an actual zombie—that is, a being lacking in subjectivity that on the outside acts just like a subject? Until now I had supposed such beings to exist only in wholly other worlds; but our world seems to be more replete with wonders than I had thought. Are you unfamiliar with even those simpler qualia that are not attached to propositional attitudes, such as the taste of a mango fruit? Answer me honestly, Encephalius, if our discussion is to be crowned with success.

Encephalius: What is this moralizing all about? This brain is concerned with the truth and nothing else.

Philonous: Truthfulness is certainly no sufficient condition for the discovery of truth, but it could by all means be a necessary one—at least when the mental is concerned.

Encephalius: Truthfulness refers to an internal state, and that is what my brain does not want to allow.

Philonous: That goes for untruthfulness as well. So my request can be restricted to this: please do not be untruthful.

Encephalius: I can also not deny, if I wish not to be dishonest, that I had believed in my youth that I had sensed the taste of mango fruit and the smell of rotten eggs. But because I neither know whether the three of us understand the same thing by the term "qualia," nor can be certain whether in the enjoyment of mangos you do not perhaps sense the same thing that I sense when I eat kiwis, and vice versa; and because there is nothing more important to me than intersubjectively grounded science and nothing more dubious than wallowing in something purely subjective, my brain has developed a mechanism for shooting down concepts of that kind.

Theophilus: My dear Encephalius, that you are not a narcissist is something we already knew, and this fact makes you, at least in this age, not unlikable. But do tell me, is not what distinguishes a cognition for you just this: that it should be intersubjectively verifiable?

Encephalius: What I am concerned about is indeed intersubjectivity! And for this reason I categorically reject introspection as a scientific method, for introspection brings with it the primacy of first-person access, which some even designate as infallible: if we believe something about our mental states, then it supposedly must be just as we believe. This purported infallibility of our judgments regarding our own mental states and its fantastic converse—if we have mental states, then we should also know that we have them—together constitute the doctrine of the transparency of the "I." It is a doctrine that no one who is familiar with the fallibilism that is a result of modern epistemology can even for a moment take seriously. One easily recognizes it as a descendent of the old belief in an all-knowing God—at bottom it is only a secularized instance of theism. The "I" that is transparent to itself as the idealist legacy of God! I can smell that rat!

Philonous: Given that you have no qualia, I dare not cast judgment regarding the way things otherwise are with your sense of smell; but that your scent for connections in the history of ideas is keen is infallibly evident—even from a third-person perspective. Or should I say, from a second-person perspective?

Theophilus: Does your question suggest that along with first- and third-person access to the mental there is also second-person access to it? An interesting suggestion, about which I would like to hear more from you at another time. Only two things are to be noted about Encephalius's concerns. First, privileged access to one's own mental acts is restricted to present mental acts; and the latter make up a tiny fraction of our mental life, which constantly seeks to understand itself as a whole and thus must span forward and backward—with all the risk of error.

One's own identity can be built up only by spanning across time; and my memory of my earlier mental acts may very well be deceptive. We write down in our diaries what we have sensed, for example, just so that later we can perceive those things anew, as it were, in the third person.

Philonous: Clearly it is extension in time that makes ourselves become again and again, for ourselves, third persons; somehow the punctuality of the pure "I" is particularly well suited to the punctuality of the now. In any case it is precisely through acts of retension and protension, which presuppose this extension, that the present temporality of the "I" gains a particular intensity.

Theophilus: Where nothing is written down, I may very well bow to the authority of a friend—to Philonous, for instance—who claims to remember very well my once being angry about something, even if I myself am no longer able to remember it—at least if the memory of Philonous has proven to be as good as, or even better than, mine. If furthermore I can find a cause for why it was natural, given my psychology, to forget that anger or even actively to suppress it, and if analogous causes are not to be found with Philonous, then I would without question believe him and not me when it comes to those past mental states of mine. Whoever really wants to know oneself must thus objectify oneself—indeed, one needs the help of others; intelligent self-knowledge must combine first-person with third-person modes of access. Whoever practices only introspection is not only a solipsist and hence a monster morally; he is also unable to comprehend himself.

Encephalius: Finally, a reasonable remark!

Philonous: But I would have been able to see only the manifestation of your anger, or to hear your expressions regarding this matter; I would not have been able to perceive your anger itself. Even with an excellent memory, my authority extends no further than to the *expression* of your anger. You could have perhaps disguised yourself.

Theophilus: If I recognize the authority of your memories, then I also presuppose, along with this quality, your honesty in your expression regarding this matter; we are thus, in this matter, even. And this mutual presupposition is natural, indeed, transcendentally necessary, such that prima facie it must be constantly made. Only concrete doubts permit any reveling in suspicion. You have never awakened such suspicion in me; I hope it is also the case that I have not awakened it in you.

Encephalius: Moralizing seems to be a habitual function of the brain with you idealists!

Theophilus: And a fortiori there is no infallibility with regard to one's own future mental states. A good psychologist can predict that the manic-depressive who just experienced a manic phase will soon fall into depression, and with much more certainty than the patient in question.

Encephalius: Was this the second point you raised before?

Theophilus: What a noteworthy memory, which, if I am ever interested later in a reconstruction of our discussion, I will duly take into account! Did my first point before not restrict the transparence of the mental to the present? And does not the non-present mental include the past as well as the future mental? Then I will carry on as if my second point concerned something else. And, indeed, the following occurs to me—from wherever it is that new ideas strike us. Your striving for intersubjectivity is honorable, and I understand one's misgivings about a culture that teaches one to raise the drawbridge around one's own subjectivity, a culture that revels in the inexpressibility of an individual's inner depth while it at the same time pridefully suffers from it. The belief that one stands there lost in the universe with one's own qualia and unable to share them with any other human being is accompanied by a particular quale—which by the way shows that some propositional attitudes, and perhaps the most interesting of the philosophical ones, are at least connected with qualia. (It feels differently when one believes that there is a moral world order than when one does not—indeed, supposedly even the physical pain of religious human beings that is caused by the same inflammation has different qualities from that of the nonreligious.) In any case, what continually bothers me about the condition I have just described is that it has become quite universal. Hugo von Hofmannsthal's Lord Chandos[4] has evidently been understood by many readers, and the literary technique of the inner monologue, which is supposed to open up a sphere of inwardness that remains hidden because it is not being shared, was very successful. It articulated emotions in language and by doing so made them intersubjectively accessible—emotions in which many recognize themselves, and which indeed perhaps are felt by some more intensely now after having been fashioned into language for them. The closed inner world of the heroines of Virginia Woolf becomes more accessible to the intelligent female readers of this author than to the partners of her heroines; on the one hand this is tragic, but on the other it shows that such a state of being closed is not absolute, that an exceptionally gifted author can pry it open. Complex intersubjectivity requires toilsome work, but every intelligent portrayal of its difficulties must somehow have mastered them; and such portrayal shows others how one might invite the drawbridge to be lowered.

The business of the subtle writer is hard and full of risks because one can understand someone else for the most part only when one seeks to understand oneself; and this search is not always flattering. But perhaps it promises more insights into subjectivity than rummaging around in other persons' brains with the help of cerebroscopes.

Encephalius: I'd like to do that in my own brain as well!

Theophilus: You have always been marked by a great sense of fairness. In any case, as much as you profess yourself to be a fallibilist, you do not want to take the risks of those writers; and thus you reject introspection and the psychological insights that come along with this mode of access (this mode of access cannot, as I said, be the only one). You want to observe only the hard facts—that is, what is given in the external world—for we all have the same access to them. But whence comes this assumption? You yourself even assume that it is possible for us to sense wholly differently what we both call "green"—what I sense as green, you sense as red (in my language).

Encephalius: Of course! And for just this reason I want to get rid of the beetles in the box: whatever you sense does not matter; the main thing is that we agree in our expressions!

Theophilus: But is it really an agreement when terms refer to different contents of consciousness? Indeed, are we then at all speaking the same language?

Encephalius: Language does not refer to beetles in closed boxes but to public objects; and it is irrelevant how the beetles feel, or whether they even exist, as long as reference to objects functions reliably.

Philonous: Can an apparatus—I mean, an apparatus that is not a brain—not do the same thing? And I suppose often more reliably, given that the interference of other brain functions, which mistake themselves to be qualia, would fortunately be absent?

Encephalius: But of course!

Philonous: This means that the "inter" in intersubjectivity, to which you aspire, signifies precisely the elimination of the subject? Indeed, your cognitive procedure, which does away with introspection, seems to come to this, and I am not sure if ethics fares better upon this foundation than it does in the case of solipsism.

Theophilus: You raised the question at which I was aiming. I always thought that the concept of intersubjectivity involved more than subjectivity, but Encephalius seems to think that what is common to all subjects in true intersubjectivity is just this: that the subjectivity of each has been eliminated.

Encephalius: True intersubjectivity just is true objectivity. Despite your siren songs about mango fruit and sensitive female authors, the following remains the case: because I have more than one reason to fear that a conceptual framework artfully introduced by dualistic philosophers would force me, like a cuckoo bird's egg laid in my nest, to make concessions that I would regret, I will—that is, my brain will—simply deny having any familiarity with qualia. For to identify qualia with brain states is admittedly not easy; they would really feel differently—if they were to exist. Physical states are, however, the sole reality; hence, there are no qualia.

Theophilus: Welcome, Hylas—I was hoping the entire time that you, too, would come and enrich our conversation.

Hylas: Forgive me, friends, if I have come too late; but since I know you and had been thinking about our last discussion, I had already bet on the way here—with myself, and hence admittedly without much risk—that I would come across you while you were discussing the mind-body problem. How exactly you arrived at this topic I cannot know; there are too many paths leading to this intellectual Rome, which magnetically attracts all who call themselves philosophers. Even without having crept into Encephalius's brain, I suspect that his decisive utterance, "physical states are, however, the sole reality; hence, there are no qualia"—which is the only thing I heard—was preceded by another premise, something like, "qualia cannot be identified with physical states or brain states."

Encephalius: Even if you had agreed to a bet with someone else regarding this matter, it would have involved just as little risk. You have done nothing else but impute elementary standards of rationality to my brain.

Hylas: Perhaps not to your brain, but rather to mental properties belonging to it—to that which occurs in it. This imputation does not yet, of course, mean that I share your position. Indeed, we will still see that it does not at all allow me to affiliate myself with your position. Fortunately, one can defend materialist intuitions without having to advocate an identity of mental and physical properties, as you so often do; for at least qualia powerfully block themselves from such identification. Further arguments have led me away from identifying mental and physical properties. First, the same mental states can be realized in our world in different ways—in different species anyway, and perhaps even in different inorganic entities like future computers. Even beings without brains, or with brains built wholly differently, may sense pain; to dispute this on the grounds that consciousness is coupled with the brain would clearly be a circular claim. And in human beings the same states of consciousness can be connected to very different brain structures; we all know the reports of persons in whom a part of the brain was destroyed and yet who afterward thought similarly to the way they had before. The brain seems to have tremendous plasticity.

Encephalius: Unfortunately, not with Alzheimer patients!

Hylas: I have in no way claimed that all changes in the brain are irrelevant to consciousness because my argument against an identification did not require it. And second, as a famous man[5] has shown, there are no contingent identities in the case of rigid designators; but neither "pain" nor "C-fiber firings" is a non-rigid designator. Such identities would of course be contingent—hence, they are not identities; for certainly there can be worlds in which there are beings with self-consciousness in which pain is excited through wholly different fibers, or through something wholly other than fibers.

Philonous: I have never even heard a convincing argument that would rule out, as logically impossible, bodiless beings that have mental life.

Encephalius: Not every bit of nonsense is worthy of an explicit refutation; and at least the world in which we actually live is not a world in which bodiless spiritual substances exist. Similarly, I will never concede that, in our world, mental states or events that are not identical to physical ones can be the cause of physical changes. The law of conservation of momentum cannot be challenged, and only because René Descartes mis-

interpreted momentum as a scalar magnitude instead of correctly understanding it as a vector was he able to offer his laughable myth about
interactions in the pineal gland. This myth fails, independently of any
particular law of physics, due to the fact that the physical world is causally
closed; to believe that a physical event can be caused by something non-
physical is animism, and this we really should have overcome in the age
of science.

Hylas: I agree with that last part, even if I take the art that belongs to
animistic epochs to be more interesting than the art of our time, and for
this reason I do not employ the concept "animism" only negatively.

Theophilus: That both of you defend the fundamental status of the
laws of conservation in any theory of nature is hardly to blame; but it
surprises me that someone who professes himself to be an empiricist
when it comes to epistemology, as Encephalius otherwise does, wants to
hold on to a universal principle at any price—even if elementary experiences seem to contradict it. An empiricist should rather give up a principle before reinterpreting experiences in idiosyncratic ways—indeed,
before denying them. And it is a universal experience that one says something because one has *thought* it to oneself and *wants* to say it; thus,
thoughts and willful acts seem to be able to move lips.

Hylas: What is so fascinating about the position I advocate is that
one can hold on to the nonidentity of mental and physical properties
without having to give up the causal closure of the physical world or the
causal power of mental events.

Philonous: You must let us, too, share in this ingenious find—we
who even suffer from that feeling of puzzlement in the face of our problem and who thus, in this context, can distinguish between multiple qualia in us; for to suffer from puzzlement is more than to be merely puzzled.

Hylas: Anomalous monism is the answer to our question.[6] This
theory is so elegant and original that it could have been found only late in
the history of philosophy; and it proves you wrong, Theophilus, who
provocatively declared in our last discussion that all essential options for
the solution of the mind-body problem had basically been thought out
between the mid-seventeenth and eighteenth centuries, and that the only
accomplishments of the second half of the twentieth century were the
several clarifications that were made as a result of the philosophy of

science and modal logic. You declared that Descartes had discovered the problem, and that the tremendous innovativeness of his discovery had propelled his contemporaries and the generations immediately following him to their most creative achievements.

Theophilus: In making that claim I was in no way disparaging those clarifications; I merely hold the view that interesting clarifications presuppose antecedent, smart ideas, and that with a shortage of ideas eagerness for clarity seldom advances philosophy. Looking back to the classics may by contrast unearth ideas that have wrongfully been forgotten today. Incidentally, I praised analytic philosophers of recent decades for having turned their attention to this problem—an attention that doubtless was both deserved and demanded—in such excellent writings as those by the acute man from the land of the morning calm,[7] by the Briton who likewise immigrated to the United States and holds high the torch that burns with the mysterious flame of subjectivity,[8] and by the most comprehensive and best analytic philosopher of continental Europe, who works in the city of the Perpetual Imperial Diet.[9] It is in any case regrettable that the turn to language and the social world in the nineteenth century, and after the "linguistic turn," removed the mind-body problem from its central place in philosophy; making it out to be nothing but a pseudo-problem was an act of philosophical barbarism.

Philonous: It would be better to say that it can legitimately be declared a pseudo-problem only if one is a subjective idealist. In George Berkeley's philosophy it is actually no longer a problem—or rather, Berkeley's philosophy arises from the readiness to dispose of the problem at *any* price. But the problem inevitably forces itself upon whomever shares realist intuitions; and only he who declares himself blind to that which is given to him immediately and in the first person can act as if the problem no longer exists for him. I am, otherwise than my namesake in Berkeley's fictional universe, first, a real person and, second, not a subjective idealist; but I hold subjective idealism to be much more difficult to refute and less absurd than the form of materialism that refuses the act of introspection.

Theophilus: Enough of the sidelong glances into history! Let us concentrate on the question at hand! Hylas, explain to us how anomalous monism solves the problem.

Hylas: Anomalous monism is a monism; that is, it defends the view that mental and physical *events* are identical. But the *properties* that we attribute to them are not identical with one another; and some properties are of a mental nature and some of a physical nature. There is thus no type-identity but only a token-identity. The same event has the property of being pain and a C-fiber firing.

Philonous: The pain/C-fiber firing correlation comes up so often in the literature that, as a layperson, one does not exactly come away with the impression that neuroscience has advanced very far in the discovery of psychophysical laws. Or perhaps materialist authors are seldom up to date with neuroscientific research. But, however this may be, how is this theory to be consistent? I can easily understand that there are different tokens of one and the same type; but how can there be different types of one and the same token?

Hylas: Just like the same object can be elliptical and green.

Philonous: But events are actually characterized by a particular object instantiating a particular property at a particular point in time; if different properties are instantiated at the same point in time, then we are precisely not dealing with the same event.

Hylas: You are presupposing that events must be characterized in that way; anomalous monism, in contrast, treats events as unanalyzable—just like objects.

Theophilus: In making such a move, anomalous monism is doubtless a consistent theory, but it is not, on that account, already justified. Ceteris paribus, a theory that ends up with fewer basic entities is certainly superior, and this speaks for Philonous's understanding of events. But we want to hear what advantages the new theory of events has for the solution to the mind-body problem. We can happily accept a more complicated ontology if it simplifies philosophy in other places; the standard of simplicity cannot be valid for individual philosophical disciplines but rather is valid for philosophy as a whole. For one of the most fascinating attractions of philosophy is that it is a unified whole and thus that it can be pursued only as a unified whole, at least as far as our powers will allow.

Encephalius, Hylas, Philonous: This is true.

Hylas: Anomalous monism makes compatible what seems to be irreconcilable—the nonidentity of mental and physical properties, the causal power of events that have mental properties, and the causal clo-sure of the physical world (by which I understand that everything physical is caused by the physical and *only* by the physical). It is these three as-sumptions that appear so natural to all of us and yet, when one begins to reflect on them, also appear to be incompatible with one another. If the physical world is causally closed and the mental is not reducible to the physical, then the mental cannot cause the physical; if the physical world is causally closed and the mental causes the physical, then it must be identical with the physical; if by contrast the mental is not identical with the physical but is nonetheless capable of causing the physical, then the physical world is not causally closed. How is anomalous monism able to escape this trilemma? If I want now to raise my hand, then this is an event that has an irreducible mental property—namely, being an act of wanting to raise my hand; but it is at the same time a physical event, and as such it can cause something physical without putting in question the causal closure of the physical. See, I have really raised my hand!

Philonous: It remains a miracle, even if our sense of it is dulled by its everydayness—or should I rather say, "everysecondness"? What distinguishes this position of yours from epiphenomenalism? Accord-ing to the latter, it is also indeed the case that the mental cannot cause anything—neither anything physical nor anything mental; mental phe-nomena are only epiphenomena of physical states or events, which alone have causal power. Some, but not all, physical states or events, then, have corresponding mental states or events.

Hylas: You forget that in anomalous monism causal power is as-signed to events, which have both mental and physical properties! It is precisely here that the point of this approach lies, for it combines mo-nism on the level of the token with dualism on the level of the type; in doing so, it succeeds in fulfilling those three demands simultaneously.

Theophilus: And what do the causal laws that anomalous monism assumes connect?

Hylas: That is perhaps the best part about this theory: its ingenious author assumed that there were causal laws only for the physical—at least in the original version of the theory—and expressly disputed the existence of psychophysical laws that bind together the physical and the mental as well as the existence of laws that connect only the mental.

Philonous: Anomalous monism, then, is just a type epiphenomenalism. Nothing about mental properties—like the property of being an act of wanting to raise my hand—can explain why I raise my hand; what figures in the explanation are only the physical properties of the former event, which—coincidentally—has the aforementioned mental property as well. For if I understand it correctly, according to anomalous monism it can very well be the case—the position cannot, at any rate, exclude it—that tied to the event that has the physical property of being an act of firing neurons, which elicits the corresponding movement of muscles, in different human beings or in the same human being on different occasions, is the mental property of thinking about the Goldbach conjecture, of hearing the Lilliburlero, or of *not* wanting to raise one's hand under any circumstances. Elliptical objects can just as well be yellow, blue, red, and so on, as they can be green. With this form of causal power of the mental I can, frankly speaking, thankfully dispense.

Encephalius: And my brain can thankfully dispense with this form of materialism! Of what help is it to my brain if ultimately its sensor can be inserted into your brain and is still unable to tap into your thoughts?

Hylas: That wouldn't be so bad; for whatever the mental properties of the events you are investigating are, the complete analysis of the physical properties that are accessible to you would allow you—should we be living in a deterministic universe—to predict the behavior of the organism that was outfitted with that brain; and in the case that our world is not deterministic, the knowledge of mental properties would similarly be of no help to you.

Encephalius: That is correct; but that there should be something in the world that escapes the laws of the physical and enjoys an autonomy, however powerless—a realm of the mental that is at any rate not bound to matter with an iron chain—this is something that my brain is not willing to allow under any circumstances.

Theophilus: Denying psychophysical laws is something that clearly does not satisfy either Encephalius or Philonous; on this matter they are in agreement. And even if Encephalius is presumably more interested in laws that determine the mental through the physical, whereas Philonous is more interested in laws that fix the physical through the mental, this agreement between two such very different philosophers—one of whom understands himself as an "I" and the other as a brain—is such a seldom and propitious event that it could be counted as an indicator of the truth. Thus, I too do not want to conceal my doubts regarding anomalous monism, a theory that is striking for its formal brilliance, which has found a consistent middle way between monism and dualism, no less than for the little plausibility of its base assumption—namely, its denial of psychophysical laws. But because we want to impute rationality to its advocates no less than we impute it to Encephalius, I would like to know from Hylas what his teacher's argument is for the denial of psychophysical laws; for he must certainly have had a weighty one.

Hylas: It is the following. My teacher, like all significant philosophers, did not confine himself to a single philosophical discipline. Besides working on the mind-body problem and action theory, he also worked on hermeneutics. He was concerned with how it is possible for us to infer from linguistic expressions the opinions of speakers whose language is wholly unfamiliar to us. In this context he developed the principle of charity as a transcendental principle: we have a chance at inferring the meaning of sentences of a language only when we assume that a good part of the statements asserted by the speakers of a language is true, and that speakers generally proceed rationally—that they do not, for instance, hold opinions that are inconsistent with each other, or at least do not know that they hold inconsistent opinions. This assumption of rationality makes sense, however, only with regard to the mental; in the case of physical states it is clearly absurd. Precisely because in the reconstruction of mental states we are necessarily guided by a presupposition that does not correspond to anything in the investigation of the physical, there can be no psychophysical laws (at least in the strong sense of the term).

Philonous: This argument is significant; but the following objection immediately occurs to me: not everything mental is characterized by rationality.

Theophilus: But is not our human mind determined essentially by rationality? Even if we, for instance, sense intense pain, we categorize it—or we at least can do this, indeed, we should do this, if we want to make it understandable to others (as a dull pain, etc.). Moreover, such pain is often accompanied by reflection. Depending upon one's natural disposition, it might be accompanied by a feeling of indignation at the fact that we are at all exposed to pain, or by the consideration of what had caused it and how we might avoid it the next time, or by its acceptance due to the conviction that it perhaps possesses a hidden meaning. And the perception of an object by a rational being is always accompanied by its being placed in a network of connections: was it to be expected, was it at least compatible with the known laws of nature, that just now this object was perceived by us as having thus and such properties?

Philonous: For one thing, this rational musical accompaniment does not change anything about the fact that pain is something different from its rational analysis. For another thing, small children and nonhuman animals doubtless have sensations that are not rationally transformed. In the history of mental life, rational mental life is a very young offshoot, and it seems to me out of place to elevate it to paradigmatic status and to deny psychophysical laws given the exceptional position of rationality.

Theophilus: A later offspring may be the secret *telos* of a development; only from its standpoint may that which came before it become transparent. Equating consciousness and rational mental life, as done by Descartes, is a mistake. Whoever denies sensations to mammals, for instance, is dishonest in another and less laughable way than the eliminativist materialist, who denies qualia even in himself; but he is still dishonest— like those who deny their poor relatives. Still, it is an argument that forces him into such dishonesty. The Greeks had discovered something unique about reason; whoever then found the ontologically decisive break in the existence of consciousness easily succumbed at first to the temptation of letting both breaks collapse into one. Indeed, even if consciousness and reason—and here I now mean conscious reason—are not coextensive, it is entirely true of reason and the highest form of consciousness, self-consciousness, that they are coextensive. The ability to refer all mental acts, and thereby their contents, to a subjective center, to perceive them as one's own, is something quite special that presupposes introspection but that also goes beyond introspection; such an ability alters in a subtle way the quality of all mental acts. Rage is something with which even provoked animals are familiar; but simmering with rage is something else—indeed, it feels differently when I know that it is my rage, and that it is connected to other traits of my person. And clearly it is this ability to refer all of my mental acts to a subjective center, and only thereby to one another, that generates that need for consistency without which there would be no rationality—that is, the raising of validity claims in the form of inferentially connected propositions. We presuppose this rationality, in fact, wherever we suppose rational beings.

Philonous: I do not exactly understand the point of your contribution.

Theophilus: I am trying to awaken an appreciation for those theoreticians who see in self-conscious reason not the antagonist of the soul but rather the truth of the soul. If self-consciousness is somehow characterized by the further doubling of a reality that was already split into the physical and mental because it, so to speak, opposes a subject to mental objectivity, and if rationality is, so to speak, the other side of self-consciousness, then rational mental life is not a contingent subspecies of the mental but rather the *telos* of the mental.

Encephalius: That is too elevated for me.

Philonous: The inner life of a jellyfish, if it has one, is certainly less interesting than ours (even if our inner life shrank to our sensations while observing fluorescent jellyfish); but the arguments against psychophysical laws do not hold for its inner life.

Theophilus: There could be eidetic laws of the soul—and thus of pre-propositional mental life—with respect to which a similar argument to that of anomalous monism could be formulated.

Encephalius: What do you mean by that? Eidetic laws are almost as repugnant to my brain as immaterial substances.

Theophilus: One could, for instance, think of it in this way—that for sentient beings the lessening of pain is a positive quale, or that there is a hierarchy of qualia according to which evolution cannot achieve higher levels before lower levels have been passed through. Naturally we cannot really know when subjectivity appeared for the first time, but in whichever organism this was the case . . .

Encephalius: At least you are speaking of organisms! I had already feared that you would reveal yourself to be a panpsychist—that is the last trick that remains for those who do not want to recognize the primacy of matter.

Theophilus: Not everyone who does not want to recognize the primacy of matter is in need of this trick. Panpsychism fails, among other reasons, by either endowing electrons with a mental life like ours—but then one wonders why an evolution of brains should have taken place at all.

Encephalius: Exactly!

Theophilus: I am pleased with your assent, but be attentive to the fact that, with regard to the evolution of the universe, the argument has a teleological premise. I do not have any problem with this, but perhaps you do. Since we both, however, seem to be in a teleological mood today, allow me a second argument against the attribution of full consciousness to electrons: what would they do with it? To perceive the injustices of the world and not to be able to do anything—I mean anything—at all about it! Consciousness that is situated within a material world should have the possibility of acting upon it; perception and action should somehow be correlated if object-subject and subject-object relations—thus percep-tual and volitional acts—constitute a decisive division within the mental. Attributing to a plant that cannot run away the perception of an animal eating it would be an unnecessary cruelty.

Hylas: As if the world were not full of such things!

Theophilus: We have the duty to perceive them wherever they are manifest and to combat them whenever possible, but we should not im-pute to the world as a whole cruelties that need not be assumed. Such a principle of charity is valid at least in our dealings with fellow human beings.

Philonous: You are on the best path for joining in Nicolas Male-branche's defense of the Cartesian thesis that animals are machines—a defense that is helped by his new argument that with this Cartesian thesis the argument from evil is rendered less acute.

Encephalius: In the meantime, I have prepared myself for anything; after the mention of eidetic laws, the urge to ascend to the deity is most likely no longer to be checked.

Theophilus: I was interrupted when I supposed that subjectivity began with organisms; with which ones I do not know, but it may even be that it began with the first organisms. There is hardly another material structure suited for having subjectivity than the kind that sustains itself through metabolism and that is concerned with itself in its feedback structures. I attempted, furthermore, to correlate the mental states that we attribute to organisms with their actions or functions; that seemed to me to be an argument against panpsychism, and it is also an argument against exaggerated attributions of mental states to nonhuman organisms. I do not know whether plants can sense; but I do think that if they sense something when there is a lack of water, their thirst cannot have the qualia that Antoine de Saint-Exupéry so vividly described;[10] for they cannot set out on their way to a source of water. "Thirst," when the word refers not to the metabolic state of lacking water but rather to the quale that is correlated to this state, is a homonymous term. Perhaps the so-called thirst of plants, if it exists, is comparable to the weak feeling of thirst that we sometimes experience in fleeting dreams, and that lacks the intensity of our wakeful thirst. I do not use flypaper, but Robert Musil's fly is decisively too human for me in its inner life.[11]

Panpsychism, as I wanted still to add, can adopt the alternative strategy of attributing to electrons not the kind of mental states that are familiar to us but rather something completely different, something that is in principle inaccessible to us. But then its claims are meaningless. I can understand only those mental states that are familiar to me or that are somehow analogous to those familiar to me, such as, for example, perceptions had by senses that I do not possess—like the electric sense. If I am to think of something when regarding the inner life of a jellyfish, then I have to retreat to my own inner life. We all, with the possible exception of Encephalius, know the peculiar quale of waking up in the morning from a deep sleep and not yet knowing where, indeed who, we are—imputing such a quale to a jellyfish[12] may be admissible.

Hylas: If your teleological rapture continues, you will soon claim that our dreams have the function of treating us to the qualia of the whole world and making out of our mental world—not, as the ancients thought, out of our body—a kind of microcosm that contains in itself the macrocosm of mental evolution.

Encephalius: Friends, I have lost the thread of our discussion. Not that all of these mental leaps and associations are not interesting, but our conversation is gradually taking on a dreamlike quality. Where did we begin, and how did we get to where we are now? Where do we want to go?

Philonous: Is that not the charm of a living conversation, that its course cannot be told ahead of time? Even when we are alone, our individual streams of consciousness are clearly not determined. And when several streams of consciousness flow together, it goes without saying that surprising currents will develop that were not able to be anticipated. After all, we are not writing an essay—not even a dialogue—we are talking to one another; and we need not worry if our discussion should, so to speak, overflow as long as we are taking pleasure in it. No one is thinking about its transformation into written form, which, because such a form cannot be further developed but is, as it were, dead, seeks to compensate for its lack of life by having an artificial order.

Theophilus: Flight from the stream of subjectivity into the world of artifacts, to which art also belongs, is not always a betrayal of life; perhaps life finds in this temporary flight from itself a special source of power, and perhaps the combination of order and multiple paths of association is a special appeal of the artwork. Conversely, however, one could also say that a living discussion requires special concentration; with something written down one may page back and reread; with a shifting conversation a good memory is required. My memory suggests to me that behind our backs something like an order has thoroughly imposed itself upon our discussion—or is this only my construction? We began with the relations between facial expressions and the mental; indeed, Encephalius had soon captivated us with the thesis that the true inner realm is the brain and that the method of introspection is to be banned from science—that is, from the intersubjectively valid investigations of science. Qualia are to be denied if this serves the establishment of the truth—that is, the reinforcement of the thesis that mental states are identical to brain states. Neither were our considerations regarding the fruitfulness of combining first-person access with third-person access successful in changing Encephalius's mind; nor were we entirely brought by him to give up our subjectivity for the sake of true intersubjectivity. The gods know how our discussion would have continued had Hylas not suddenly appeared and offered us a ship that, as he promised, would safely pass us between the Charybdis of dualism and the Scylla of monism, and that would allow us to understand how mental states can be causally efficacious without being identified with physical states and without breaching the causal closure of the physical world. The ship was baptized "anomalous monism." But two towering waves endangered it—the one was type epiphenomenalism, which is entailed by anomalous monism, and the other was the denial of psychophysical laws, a denial that emerged from the logical relations between the elements of an especially interesting class of mental acts, propositional attitudes. In the intensity of the storm I did not even take notice whether our ship was wrecked or whether the water that we saw all around was confined to the deck. What does one do in such an emergency? One climbs a ladder—even if one does not see exactly where it leads—and we have found such a ladder in the *scala naturae* of qualia.

Philonous: Because such a mental *scala naturae* should correspond to the *scala naturae* of physical states—not so much of the brain but of the functions and actions of organisms—your discussion of questions concerning natural philosophy, after the debate about epistemological and formal metaphysical problems, seemed to imply a recognition of psychophysical laws. But you had defended focusing on this point against my objection that the denial of such laws is valid only because anomalous monism has rational-mindedness exclusively in view; thus, I initially thought that you wanted to defend such a denial even though you had affirmed Encephalius's and my—seldom shared—misgivings immediately before Hylas had offered the decisive argument. Frankly speaking, I do not understand your vacillation. But if it suits you to reflect upon this matter further, allow me to strengthen the other wave for the time being. That is, let me strengthen the objection that anomalous monism amounts to an epiphenomenalism—a type epiphenomenalism, but an epiphenomenalism all the same. Such a position collapses, as is well known, for two reasons. If mental events—or in our case, mental properties of events—have no causal power, then nothing can be argued any longer that makes claims to the truth. For everything that I say would be an effect of brain states; it would not follow its own logic, and it would not have the power to bring about other mental states. But how something dependent like this could claim that it follows only the best argument is utterly mysterious. Epiphenomenalism can make plausible one's claims to the truth just as little as determinism can. A transcendental argument of this kind is especially strong because it reflects only the truth claim that is necessarily presupposed in every theory and, unlike the argument that I will present in a moment, does not make any external presuppositions.

Hylas: You seem to overlook the fact that it is precisely this logical connection of mental states that anomalous monism takes as its point of departure!

Philonous: Not at all. I spoke of "saying," not "thinking." According to your theory, logical relations must be imputed to mental, not physical, events; speaking is, however, a physical event.

Hylas: I still don't understand you.

Philonous: The sequence of sounds I hear, the sequence of visual signs I see, are results of physical events; according to your position, when explaining their properties, I have to recur exclusively to the physical properties of the causal events; what one says is thus not determined by mental properties and, hence, I need not impute any logical relations to what is said.

Hylas: Only as something interpreted is the production of sounds capable of the truth, and your interpretation is itself a mental act that is subject to the demands of logic.

Philonous: Without a doubt. But even the most constructive interpretation is bound by the signs that it encounters because, after it has found an initial way into the language, it cannot ignore the fact that certain interpretations simply are not compatible with these signs. Either we wholly set aside the expressions of a person and impute truth and rationality to everyone (and this, of course, means what we ourselves take to be rational); or we take seriously what the person said—that is, as I see it, what the person has transferred from the mental world into the physical one. This is how the exchange between subjects functions in our world, at least in the normal case. One subject encounters another subject through the physical—if we want to prescind from the possibility of telepathy; and while some qualia manifest themselves in facial expressions, linguistic expression is most often needed in the case of propositional attitudes so that the latter can be made accessible to others. Language is the becoming physical, so to speak, of the mental; and if the mental acts of others become accessible to us through language, then there can be no absolute dualism between the physical and the mental, as anomalous monism assumes.

Hylas: What are you talking about? It is rather the case that this theory attempts to be as monistic as possible and only as dualistic as is necessary!

Philonous: Certainly that is the intention of its advocates. By assuming laws for the physical while excluding them for the mental and especially for the relation between the physical and the mental, however, they make a distinction between both spheres that could scarcely be more radical; and the consequence, in turn, is windowless monads that can individually follow their own logic but whose insights do not have the power to be reflected in external reality, not even in the external reality of language. Actual intersubjectivity is not to be had in such a way.

Hylas: This is food for thought, as they say, using an insightful idiom that unconcernedly mixes the mental with the physical. What was the second objection to epiphenomenalism?

Philonous: It is precisely with Darwinism, a truly naturalistic theory, that epiphenomenalism is not compatible; for without the causal power of the mental the genesis of the mental cannot be explained—namely, it would be completely functionless. If the same behavior could result without pain, why would there be pain?

Hylas: And may I ask what inference you are drawing from these objections to anomalous monism and to all other forms of epiphenomenalism?

Philonous: That an identity of the mental with the physical is not admissible is beyond a doubt for three of us. If even anomalous monism does not succeed in making compatible with this first and unshakeable premise the two other principles whose conjunction contradicts the first, and if the causal power of the mental cannot be contested, then we must abandon the causal closure of the physical.

Encephalius: I knew it! This amounts to animism, a position that by itself is bad enough, but that is even worse when miserable arguments are offered for it. The argument for the supposed incompatibility of epiphenomenalism with Darwinism was brought into the world by an otherwise meritorious man after his brain had become old and after he had carried out too many old-crock conversations with a Catholic neuroscientist.[13] But it is clearly invalid—even if I would not like in any way to defend epiphenomenalism, which has in fact several problems that the identity theory deftly avoids. For mental states do not have to have any function at all; what is selected for are ways of behaving that are elicited from corresponding brain states, and if natural laws should determine that a mental state is correlated with brain states, then this accompaniment is, to be sure, a functionless luxury, but nothing in Darwinism excludes this.

Philonous: Luxury is certainly a problem for Darwinism; consider the debate over sexual selection.

Encephalius: But only when energy is invested in this luxury that could be used in some other way! This is, however, not at all the issue with the epiphenomenon of the mental—if there is such a thing.

Philonous: It is in any case idiosyncratic that in this theory a phenomenon is caused that has absolutely no effect; that does not seem to comply with Isaac Newton's third law.

Encephalius: Indeed, intelligent epiphenomenalists should not name epiphenomena "effects"; and, since that which is neither a cause nor an effect is nothing at all, they should, if they are even more intelligent, become eliminativists or identity theorists.

Hylas: Perhaps they should become supervenience theorists; they have several similar intuitions to the epiphenomenalists, yet they formulate their theory with a more subtle conceptual apparatus. They, too, do not recognize causal power of mental states, not even with regard to other mental states; it is always only a physical state P1 that causes a physical state P2, while on P1 and P2 mental states M1 and M2, respectively, may supervene. And, if one wants, one can call the relation between M1 and M2 "supervenient causation," which, however, is to be sharply distinguished from normal causation.

Theophilus: Encephalius, you are speaking to me from the heart.

Philonous: Are you serious?

Encephalius: *Timeo Danaos et dona ferentes*—that is the only thing that I retained from Latin class, and it teaches me to have a healthy mistrust of the words of Theophilus.

Theophilus: Philonous, Encephalius is right—wherever he is right. Epiphenomenalism is in fact not incompatible with Darwinism; and if something cannot itself be a cause, one should best also not call it an effect.

Philonous: But at least you will accept my first counterargument to epiphenomenalism—you who like so much to appeal to transcendental arguments?

Theophilus: Precisely because I like to employ them so much, it is important to me to use them as carefully as possible; and I am not at all certain that every form of determinism, for example, can be countered by transcendental arguments.

Philonous: I am speechless.

Theophilus: I was seized with the desire to hold on to the causal closure of the physical world as a premise and to see how far one can go with it—even if this should mean denying the causal power of the mental.

Philonous: What the devil has gotten into you? Clearly we presuppose in every discussion, even in the one transpiring now, that we and our conversation partners are able in principle to find expressions that fall under logical relations. No one who would claim that what he said was nothing but the effect of neurons firing or some other determining factor could be taken seriously for even a single instant, and someone who seeks to refute the argument of another by remarking that it is just his neurons forcing him to speak in a certain way deserves for his brain to be fiddled around in by his conversation partner with all the cerebroscopes in the world.

Theophilus: I do not disagree with you.

Philonous: Theophilus, what is the matter with you—or should I say, with your brain? First you advocate something absurd, and now you are even contradicting yourself. In such cases where the capacity to think is obfuscated, the cause may be sought indeed in deficiencies in the brain.

Theophilus: Do you assume only in those cases a covariance between the brain and consciousness? And the entire work of evolution on the development of complex brains is to have been in vain?

Philonous: What exactly are you trying to say?

Theophilus: That it seems to me unfair to assume that our states of consciousness correlate with brain states only if they do not satisfy logic. Certainly the best thing about the brain is that it serves us inconspicuously; normally one attends to it only in cases of impaired consciousness. But this does not mean that it does not have an instrumental role on other occasions. Tell me, Philonous, do you suppose that reflection on the mind-body problem can be attributed to the ganglia brain of a tick?

Philonous: Certainly not.

Theophilus: Why not?

Philonous: That is certainly more difficult to answer.

Encephalius: Indeed! This is the price that you idealists must pay. You invent a world behind the things that alone are accessible to all, and even if you supposedly each have for yourselves secure access to your most highly individual inner lives, you get caught up in a mess or wholly in fantasy when you have to speak about the inner life of others, and, above all, of the beings of other species. For how does Philonous know that what is lurking inside a tick is not the soul of his departed grandmother?

Theophilus: Is it not then a plausible principle that for at least every individual species brain, consciousness, and behavior co-vary in at least some rough sense? And even if it does not seem compelling at first glance that mental states must supervene on physical states—thus that there must be some other brain state corresponding to the thought that π is a transcendental number than the one that corresponds to the thought that there are only five Platonic bodies—it still seems that a strange consequence results from the thesis that both thoughts could be grounded by a single brain state. If, namely, we add to each of these ideas the wish to write down what was just thought, and if there is for such a wish one and only one brain state (which is at least more plausible than in the earlier case), then the same brain state could lead to wholly different actions, at least as long as one accepts the causal closure of the physical.

Philonous: But that is precisely what I am not doing.

Theophilus: I want rather to see how far one can go with that principle. In any case, if it is true, it can be grounded only a priori; and if it is not easy for materialism to make a priori knowledge plausible, then a justification of that principle could precisely not be construed as a triumph of materialism.

Philonous: Before you proceed further, you still owe me an explanation of what constitutes the supposed irrefutability of determinism by transcendental arguments.

Theophilus: When you argue, do you obey logic?

Philonous: As is generally known, interesting arguments cannot be found through logic alone; but you presumably mean to ask whether I properly draw conclusions from admitted premises and seek to avoid inconsistencies. This I affirm.

Theophilus: Taking you seriously thus means assuming that you argue properly. Could you deviate from the valid rules if you wanted?

Philonous: Of course I could; for that there is free will. But I do not do this.

Theophilus: And that you do not do this allows me to follow you better than if you were deliberately to produce inconsistencies.

Philonous: Certainly. But what does this have to do with our question?

Theophilus: It is supposed to show that the presupposition of any rational discussion is that the conversation partners argue unimpeded; but this absence of any impedance is something different from an indeterminateness that can opt for irrationality. Such an opting for irrationality would rather itself be an impeding factor.

Philonous: That may be; but even then it remains the case that I always have the option of deviating from reason.

Theophilus: And the others always have the option to look for the causes that explain why you are deviating from a straightforward analysis of reasons. Such deviation may be motivated by the desire for a quick victory; or it may perhaps legitimately result from the wish to become acquainted with, or to provoke, certain reactions of others. I at least prefer those conversation partners who do not engage in such deviations without good reason.

Philonous: It is difficult to deny that the formal possibility of deviating from that which is rational and good is not a worthwhile good; and I presume that you blame, and not unjustly, that vanity for which the mere power to say no to reason is more important than the calm acquiescence in reason. Hence, I understand why you said that rational argumentation does not exclude determination; clearly you had in mind determination through the striving for reason and through the capacity corresponding to it. But this striving varies according to one's natural disposition, and thus every successful conversation involves unforeseeable turns.

Theophilus: That is indisputable; however, being unforeseeable and being indeterminate are two different things. And I likewise concede to you that, in addition to offering new insights that could not have been gained single-handedly, those unforeseeable turns offer to conversation partners a wealth of qualia that would be denied even to a perfect reason.

Philonous: I am relieved. But even if being unimpeded is, as a transcendental presupposition of every conversation, not incompatible with a determinism of reason, I still do not understand why something analogous should be valid for epiphenomenalism and supervenience theory as well—whichever you choose.

Theophilus: Without hesitation, the latter, even if I would like to leave open here the kind of supervenience—strong or weak, global or local. It could well be that our brain functions in such a way that its states are normally—that is, when no impedance occurs—the functioning basis upon which rational acts of consciousness supervene: there is nothing inconsistent in this assumption.

Philonous: Yes, but it is not merely such that this could be the case. It must be the case if we are to trust thoughts and expressions that are supervenient on, or effects of, brain states.

Theophilus: "A word momentous calmly hast thou spoken."[14] Logic is certainly nothing psychological—but this fact does not exclude logic from imposing itself upon a mental world that is structured in such a way that it is again and again capable of representing logical relations. Logical relations can supervene on mental acts or on interpreted sequences of signs just as in general the normative dimension—whether it is of an epistemological, moral, or aesthetic nature—supervenes on facts to which it is certainly not reducible. Analogously it is true that the physical is certainly nothing mental, but this does not in turn exclude it from being able to serve as the basis for mental states, the most significant of which are capable of representing logical relations.

Philonous: I am still hesitant. For supervenience—if I understand it correctly—does imply dependence. If someone or something has a supervenient property, then he, she, or it has this property only on account of a base property; and the possession of this property is sufficient for the possession of the corresponding supervenient property.

Hylas: Correct; but the supervenience relation is only reflexive and transitive; it is neither symmetrical nor asymmetrical. It does not make any claims about dependence, but rather only about covariance. It, however, does not exclude relations of dependence either.

Theophilus: Relations of dependence can moreover be mutual. It is thus correct that, if one rejects panpsychism—as we all have agreed to do—then, according to the theory of supervenience, while there are no mental states without physical states, there are in fact physical states without supervening mental states. It is also correct that, if one assumes the thesis of the multiple realization of the mental in the physical, the possession of certain physical properties is sufficient for the possession of the corresponding supervenient mental properties, but not the other way around. But all of this is compatible with a teleological interpretation— there exist precisely those physical properties on which the required mental properties supervene. Hence, the original given, in the transcendental meaning of the term, is *the logical.* When we argue with one another, we presuppose first a sphere of pure validity; we presuppose further that our subjectivity can in principle grasp these logical relations and that we are therefore capable of the corresponding mental acts; and we presuppose, third, that, *if* those mental acts supervene on neurophysiological states, then the latter, or the corresponding psychophysical laws, are subject to a priori restrictions that explain why those supervenient acts achieve what they must achieve. Logic establishes a framework for the doctrine of the mental, and the latter establishes a framework for the doctrine of the physical. Precisely as long as the mental supervenes on the physical, the physical must be oriented toward the mental; the supervenience relation thus affords us insights into the nature of the physical based on the nature of the mental—insights that would remain closed off to us if the mental and the material were without a relation to one another.

Encephalius: As if that were not the old neo-Platonic metaphysics, according to which mind, soul, and matter are the three emanating hypostases! At some point we will also see the One merrily popping up.

Theophilus: Perhaps not the One; but its functional equivalent— namely, a principle of the logical—may be somewhere to be found.

Encephalius: This mixing of modern supervenience theory and old metaphysics is nothing less than *unconscionable.* Do you not grasp that the point of Darwinism, which you at first seemed to presuppose, is the radical randomness of the mental? Everything could be wholly different, even our logic.

Theophilus: Really? It seems to me that this relation between logic, subjectivity, and matter is necessary.

Hylas: What necessity is it that you are speaking of here? Analytical or nomological?

Theophilus: I am speaking of a third necessity—the transcendental. Certainly not everything that is nomologically necessary is transcendentally necessary; our laws of nature, for example, our psychophysical laws, could be wholly different without this transcendentally necessary structure being put into question. But also not everything that is transcendentally necessary is analytically necessary, if everything is analytically possible that does not involve a semantic contradiction—even if the ability to cognize the corresponding possible world is not given from within that possible world.

Hylas: I would like to hear more about that.

Encephalius: What is the point of dissecting these concepts when Darwinism has long since dispensed with them? Has not Theophilus himself just confessed to Darwinism?

Theophilus: Have I done that? Perhaps I have expressed my admiration elsewhere for this great—that is, simple and far-reaching—scientific theory, which, however, is not easy to interpret philosophically; but that I had done this in our conversation I had forgotten.

Encephalius: You did agree with me against Philonous that epiphenomenalism in no way stands in contradiction to Darwinism!

Theophilus: Oh, you mean *that*. I do stand behind that claim. A causally powerless domain of the mental is not indeed excluded by Darwinism.

Philonous: But it would likewise be compatible with Darwinism if only the physical existed! You at least have to concede this claim—namely, that Darwinism cannot explain this domain of the mental.

Encephalius: Once the existence of this domain is hypothetically conceded, then its existence follows from the fact that there are psychophysical laws that correlate the physical with the mental. What is selected for is the physical—that is, behavior; but along with it there exists, as a musical accompaniment, this peculiar sphere of consciousness.

Philonous: That may be, but at least psychophysical laws will not even begin to be explained by Darwinism, rather they will be presupposed by it.

Theophilus: If you were to create a work of art, Encephalius, would you invest more thought in what is important to you or in what is unimportant to you?

Encephalius: In the former, of course.

Theophilus: What will the ultimate scientific theory of the physical look like?

Encephalius: From a few elegant axioms a wealth of theorems will be derived.

Theophilus: What form does a law of nature normally have?

Encephalius: The form of a function—think of the law of gravitation. The same relation is universally valid for an indeterminate number of arguments and values.

Theophilus: Let us assume for now that qualia exist. What would the psychophysical laws look like that tie the physical to the mental?

Encephalius: If the brain is in state Z_1 after the eye of an organism has been stimulated by the light of wavelength A_1, then it has a red sensation, etc.

Theophilus: Often the little word "etc." masks more problems than it may seem. I can imagine how it continues, but it still seems obvious to me that you will not be able to find a general function that will allow you to determine the value of a given argument. The Weber-Fechner law will presumably remain a rare exception.

Encephalius: What is that supposed to mean?

Theophilus: In order to precisely describe our world, you will thus need, when more brilliant physicists appear, perhaps a few dozen physical laws, but an incalculable wealth of psychophysical laws. In the construction of this world the mental thus seems to have an incomparably greater significance.

Encephalius: What a crude anthropomorphism to speak of "construction"! And what is the point of bringing up the relation between physical and psychophysical laws when faced with the obvious fact that the mental has not even existed for many billions of years in the evolution of the cosmos and exists even now only in a tiny fraction of the cosmos. Now more than ever do I know that qualia do not exist!

Philonous: Encephalius, it may really be that you do not have qualia. But the three of us are familiar with them, and we will be satisfied only with a philosophy that knows how to incorporate this fact. Do you, Theophilus, then exclude the possibility that there can exist connections between individual psychophysical laws?

Theophilus: Why should I? They will, however, not be simple to find, although one could suspect that, for instance, different sensations of an individual sense—say, color sensations—are processed in the same region of the brain, or that more complex mental states require a more complex brain. We will learn much more about this from brain research, and insofar as brain research confines itself to removing obstacles to the correct functioning of the brain, our gratitude will be owed to it.

Philonous: But only an empirical psychology that does not eschew introspection will teach us to treasure the richness of our inner life; and only a philosophical psychology that has command of the method of conceptual analysis will make clear the necessary connection between different types of mental acts—like perception, memory, fantasy, thinking, willing, feeling. These tasks seem to me to be more essential than finding out on what these mental properties supervene—just as it is more important to interpret a poem than to investigate on what kind of paper it has been written.

Theophilus: In no way am I contradicting you. Indeed, for individual human beings a significant life task lies in constituting an internal coherence among the wealth of different mental acts that belong to one; and one can happily go about this task even if one knows nothing about one's brain.

Philonous: The word "constituting" displeases me. Is not the unity of every self-consciousness something given, as your phrase "that belong to one" implies?

Theophilus: It is a formal foundation, the point of reference for all self-attribution of mental acts, which, however, gains content only when individual mental acts are interpreted and combined by higher acts as moments of a meaningful process. Johann Wolfgang von Goethe's *Poetry and Truth* is perhaps the highest form in which a human being has managed to interpret the greatest possible multiplicity in the life of the "I" as being at the same time a unity. But this kind of interpretive work, which is quite properly called "spirit," constitutes, on very different levels, the *conditio humana*.

Hylas: You initially said that it is perhaps possible to establish a connection between individual psychophysical laws. But even in that case the following still holds true: the fact that there are psychophysical laws at all is a puzzle because it is a mystery that there is such a thing as the mental at all.

Philonous: It is a mystery, yet one that lies so close to us that at a certain level of reflection it is the existence of the non-mental that begins to present itself as the genuine puzzle.

Theophilus: If the physical world is interpreted as genuine being, then the mental is indeed something puzzling. Even understanding it as "irreducible" is not correct; for the mental is something new in an entirely different sense than an electrical charge is, to name one of the irreducible quantities of physics. What the first psychophysical law is that came into effect in our world we do not know; perhaps cognitive science will at some point find this out. Philosophy can, however, say that the presence of the mental, indeed, of conscious reason in the world—by whatever physical basis it was brought into being—is alone that for which puzzles can exist; it is thus not only the object of the puzzle, but even more its presupposition. Thus the puzzle is in a certain sense solved: the mental exists because otherwise the world would not be intelligible; that it is intelligible in principle is presupposed by anyone who broods over puzzles. The intelligibility of the world also has consequences (such as laws of conservation, for example) for the domain of the purely physical; and it implies a fortiori that the world is oriented toward something intelligent, that this is a *telos* of its development. A world without the mental would be a far greater puzzle—only no one would reflect on this fact.

Philonous: It remains unclear to me how you see the problem of mental causation. Can the mental at least cause the mental, a thought another thought?

Theophilus: In a supervenient way. The relation between two states of consciousness nowhere implies a transfer of energy; it is thus not a normal causal relation, like the kind that can occur only between physical states. But it is not for this reason any less real. Perhaps one can put it as its own self-standing form between the ground-consequence relation of logic and physical causation. The unity of our stream of consciousness, about which we do not know at all whether in deep sleep it really is wholly interrupted, is not an illusion. No one who seriously thinks or speaks about anything can deny that he has it. But one need not dispute the fact that it supervenes on a firing of neurons so long as it is clear that this firing is aimed at the production of this stream of consciousness.

Hylas: Philonous thought first that among the psychophysical laws of which one must assume an enormous quantity there is not a single one that could be explained by Darwinism as soon as one assigns no causal power, in the usual sense, to the mental. Where then do these laws come from? Are they simply a fact of this actual world?

Theophilus: One can always deny the reduction of plurality to unity. But whoever feels the need for unity will be inclined to suppose that it was most likely in regard for a hierarchical order of consciousnesses embodied in organic bodies and for a community of self-conscious beings that those laws were established. And such a person will not deny subjectivity—in whatever form—to the principle of these laws since the production of subjectivity in the world clearly is its main end.

Philonous: The firing of neurons can, as we all know, suddenly be subject to disturbances, such as a stroke; and at the end of life it becomes extinguished, sometimes gradually, and in that case an increasing reduction of consciousness can often be observed from the outside. Can the "I," then, outlast the end of its basis?

Theophilus: We do not know, and it is best that way. The mental is not identical with the physical, and a world that consists in pure consciousnesses is in no way impossible.

Hylas: But our world is no such world, if in it the mental supervenes on the physical.

Theophilus: For this reason one speaks of the world beyond; but this term has been unfittingly chosen, for if there is a continuing existence of subjectivity after the decay of the brain, the same subjects will remain. And even if one cannot grasp ahead of time this possible phase of consciousness, presumably memories of mental states from earlier phases would be present in it. Thus it would be a matter of one and the same world, in which, of course, everyone passes through a great divide—beforehand one's mental life supervenes on the physical, but afterward no longer, and communication between subjects that belong to different phases is not possible.

Hylas: I admit that it cannot be logically excluded that our actual world is structured in this way; and, trivially, experience can likewise not exclude it. But is such a supposition rational?

Theophilus: We also do not know the answer to this question because otherwise we could know the answer to our first question. That we are not only mortal animals, but also living beings who know about our mortality, is closely connected to the fact that we are self-conscious beings; fear of death, which is marked by an unmistakable quale, motivates us in very particular ways to live our lives rationally and responsibly. And the development of a universal ethics that justly demands more from human beings than what is to be found in their biological nature has certainly been promoted, on the one hand, by belief in an afterlife; but the moral attitude achieved special purity the moment it became clear that our duties exist entirely independently of their possible consequences for us here or in some beyond. An agnosticism regarding our own future lives may be more moral, and may even be more religious, than the desire for a guaranteed immortality. I will gladly let myself be surprised—in this life as well as perhaps in another.

Philonous: And why should I not place a bet where it is not at all possible for me to lose it? Moreover, an agnosticism regarding our own future lives may perhaps be more moral, especially in the case of us friends, who were blessed with conversations like the one we just had. But not every rational being reaches its *telos* in this world, and the injustices that we see are scandalous. If the principle of the world has itself implemented that universal ethics that we demand from ourselves, then it remains impossible to give up the hope that behind the curtain of death more justice will be provided for than what we behold in front of it.

Hylas: Notice how triumphantly Encephalius looks about! He has kept silent long enough, and he has—this really can be read off of his face—something gigantic to say. Let him have the floor and, with it, the last word of this conversation.

Encephalius: Did I not smell and surmise that old rat in disguise?

Translated by James Hebbeler

CHAPTER 6

———◆·▪◆▪·◆———

Religion, Theology, Philosophy

In our age, a fresh contemplation of the relation between theology and philosophy is perhaps more urgent than ever. The manifest crisis Christian theology has been laboring under for several decades now is partly a result of the upheavals that the concept of philosophy underwent in the late nineteenth century, which have exerted not always an immediate and direct but subliminally all the more effective influence on all disciplines and thus on theology as well; partly it is itself a cause of the stagnation, even the decline of philosophy. The crisis of theology and philosophy is all the more distressing, as the intensity of religious needs has not diminished at all; on the contrary, the human being remains incurably religious, and these religious needs inevitably seek for forms of satisfaction— forms that can become the more bizarre and irrational, even dangerous, the more they set themselves off against that at least partially rational penetration of religious experiences that was achieved within theology.

RELIGION

A plausible determination of the relation between religion, theology, and philosophy presupposes a clear conception of each of the three phenomena in question. If one simplifies matters, the following definitions may serve as a starting point. Religion is of course notoriously hard to define,[1] if only because there have existed so many different religions that have very little in common with regard to the content of their belief. But what is no doubt an essential part of religion in all cases is the sense of commitment to a power that is recognized as the last criterion of the conduct of one's own life, a power that is worshiped through religious activities, through a cult, even though it cannot be regarded as a part of the world that can be scientifically experienced. (This does not imply that all religions acknowledge a principle that transcends the world—to cross the immanence within which the gods of polytheism are situated presupposes a capacity to perform complex intellectual operations, a capacity that humanity has acquired only late and not in all places.) This sense of commitment is a mental reality that can interlock with other aspects of the human mind, for example, emotions of a completely different nature, but volitive and intellectual acts as well. Not for all, but for many religious people, it has priority over other human interests, for example, of an economic nature, but also over the ordinary everyday morality (cf. John 12:1ff.). Of course, from the fact that the motivational power of religion is considerable, it does not yet follow that its influence is laudable from a moral perspective. There is no doubt that Mother Teresa's acts of charity were religiously motivated, but religious motives, among those of other origin, also formed the basis for the Crusades. For the follower of a religion, religious conduct is morally sanctioned per definition; but it is possible to view this kind of conduct from outside and subject it to an evaluative critique that differs widely from the internal perspective. Of course, this evaluation must also appeal to an ultimate criterion of validity if it wants to be taken seriously—thus it remains itself within the framework of religion in the broadest sense of the term.

What complicates the situation is the fact that religious belief and religious practice both strive for intersubjective recognition due to the inevitable sociability of the human being. The human being is born into religious traditions that confront her with an authoritative claim. Usually social entities are stable and capable of forming decisions only as corporate groups; thus religions frequently organize as hierocratic corporate groups within which a clergy plays an outstanding role. The sphere of activity that the particular religions aim at differs according to epoch and culture: only the universal religions want to convert the entire humankind to their own convictions (partially for altruistic reasons), whereas the traditional national religions have their recognized boundaries in their own people; only with regard to the universal religions can the hierocratic corporate group be called "church." Of course, the individual does not have to be content with participating in a religious tradition; she may feel the urge, which she will interpret as a vocation, to change the traditional religion or even replace it with a new one. In such cases there almost inevitably develops a conflict between the bequeathed religion and its representative hierocratic corporate groups on the one hand and the innovator and her disciples on the other. Certainly from the inescapability of the pursuit of consensus—may this be a criterion for truth, may it be an end that follows from the grasping of the truth as a moral necessity—results the impossibility of a religious solipsism; and this means that even the innovator will try to institutionalize her new faith and make it intersubjective.

THEOLOGY

The term "theology" cannot be reduced to the concept of religion: although there is no theology without religion, not every religion has yielded a theology. Of course, it is possible to employ the term in such a broad sense that every discussion about the subject of religion, that is, about God and the gods, is referred to as "theology," and then any kind of myth is theology per definition. Even Aristotle occasionally employs the concept of theology in such a manner, for example, when he calls Hesiod and other mythological writers "theologians" in his *Metaphysics* (1000a9). Hesiod's theogonical systematization is certainly impressive, but it would be inappropriate to ascribe a scientific quality to his work, whereas theological philosophy, which, according to Aristotle (*Metaphysics* 1026a19), constitutes the third and supreme part of theoretical philosophy, deserves such a predicate. In a similar way, Plato ascribes a scientific status to *theologia* (*Republic* 379a), a concept that was minted by him for the first time: theology is not the mere discussion of God but the science of God, and one of the main tasks of the theology conceived by Plato is to criticize the notions of the gods that had been handed down by the ancient poets and that cannot stand up to philosophically trained reason. In the Stoic conception of the tripartite theology, the philosophic, that is, the so-called natural theology, is set against the poetic theology of the poet-mythologists and the political theology of the civil cult; thus here "theology" is any kind of discourse about God, both in a scientific and in a pre-scientific form. In the following I want to adhere to Plato's definition and refer to "theology" exclusively as the science of God (or the gods). It goes without saying that a theology in this sense presupposes that a culture has risen to the level of scientific thinking, from which it immediately follows that not all religions can have a theology: whereas religion is a universal anthropological constant, this certainly does not hold true for science. Science in the narrow sense of the term has developed only in Greece, and therefore only the Greek culture and those cultures that absorbed it possess an explicit theology. Thus there is a Jewish theology certainly at least since Philo of Alexandria, and Islam can also claim to have worked out a theology, although not with Muhammad, but relatively soon after its encounter with Greek science. But one can hardly speak of a theology of the Maya.

The theologies of the three monotheistic religions differ from theology in the sense used by Plato and Aristotle, that is, from philosophical or natural theology, because they have been developed within the framework of a religion of revelation. For them a central point of reference is a text that they regard as revealed and that serves as the ultimate guiding principle of their theological efforts. Surely theology as a science cannot be content with the recitation of the sacred texts—it must try to interpret them, it must try to apply them to new situations that were not yet foreseen in the sacred texts. But however often the text is transcended in this interpretation, however much things are read *into* it that were quite alien to the *mens auctoris* (*auctor* here refers to the finite, historically located

writer of the corresponding text), the religious consciousness of the
naïve theologian of revelation assumes that she has read her interpretations *out* of the text, and even if she does not stay away from developing
far-ranging implications of the text, she will always shrink from explicitly
contradicting the sacred text. This, however, applies to a lesser extent in
cases where the sacred text itself contains contradictions, for instance,
because it does not stem from a single author and was perhaps even developed over the course of many centuries; in such a case, the theologian
cannot avoid taking a stance against a passage in the sacred text, although
she will try to buttress it with a formal hermeneutic criterion (e.g., the
later text annuls the earlier one). The task of the theologian can be compared with the task of the jurist, who also orients herself by the accepted
texts without questioning the legitimacy of their validity, but still employs
scientific methods, especially logic and hermeneutic means, to apply
these texts to contemporary problems. What distinguishes Christian theology from the theologies of the other monotheistic religions is the relation between this theology and the church, for the simple reason that, for
example, Islam does not have a church that could be compared to the
Christian church. Christian and especially Catholic theology is not only
bound to the revealed scripture but also to the magisterium of the church,
if it wants to claim authoritative validity. Not all interpretations of the
Bible count as legitimate theology, only the one that is accepted by the
respective church. A striking difference between Catholic theology and
Protestant theologies consists in the fact that Catholic theology, besides
the Holy Scripture, ascribes an authoritative status also to the patristic
and scholastic tradition; furthermore, Catholic theology can also be subjected to greater control due to the more hierarchic and monocratic
structure of the Catholic Church. The first aspect guarantees a greater
reservoir of legitimate intellectual approaches because it extends the
number of authoritative texts; the second aspect sets limits to individual
freedom, but also to the license of the individual theologian.

But what most radically distinguishes contemporary Christian theology from its earlier theology and that of contemporary Islam is the
adoption of the *modern* conception of science through modern theology
(on a broad scale since the nineteenth and twentieth centuries). Although
the Greeks, and thus also the medieval Arabs, were already familiar with

the methods of science in general, it is of the utmost importance to understand that the world witnessed *two* scientific revolutions—one in the fifth century BC and another one in the seventeenth century AD. Although the products of both revolutions can be called science, the differences between the two types of science are considerable: the far-reaching transformation of reality over the last centuries could only be triggered by *modern* science.[2] Much has been said about the modifications in the concept of the natural sciences, and although they have brought about a significant modification in the nature of philosophic theology, they will be left out of account here. Of much greater importance for a theology that refers to a revealed scripture are the transformations in the humanities, for example, in historiography, that have been much neglected by the contemporary history of science—which, and especially in Germany, often focuses exclusively on mathematics and the natural sciences. The development, for example, of source criticism or the differentiation of layers within a text created a consciousness of the great historical divide between the different epochs. Somebody who is familiar with the historical approach can no longer without any bother take a text from an earlier age at historic face value, let alone apply it to present times; she must assume that its author was guided by categories of thought that are fundamentally different from those we adhere to today. Paradoxically, humanism collapsed precisely because classical philology developed into the modern humanities, because it was discovered that there existed not a *single* antiquity, but a multitude of divergent moral conceptions that had changed over the course of history. In a similar way the application of the categories, developed by literary criticism, to the sacred texts and particularly the adoption of the comparative method according to the model of cultural studies that regard themselves as value-free and are concerned with the abundance of the positively given (e.g., comparative religious studies), has led historical theology into a crisis that still remains to be overcome. When renowned exegetes, who are legitimated by the church, are teaching that the historical Jesus had no thoughts about the Trinity and that he probably would have been surprised about the second part of the Creed, that his (unfulfilled) imminent eschatology makes the foundation of a church by him at least very unlikely if it does not rule it out completely, then not only the traditional self-understanding of Christian religion but also and especially that of Christian theology is in danger. A theology that wants to be more than a descriptive science of religion and lays claim to revelation can hardly give up the authoritative character of the sacred texts, which is, however, initially threatened by the historical analysis. But it is clear that the condemnation of such exegetic findings after the fashion of the decree of the Holy Office *Lamentabili* of July 3, 1907, or the anti-modernist oath does not solve the problem because those exegetes argue, although always only with greater or smaller probability, on the basis of the modern humanities, and one can hardly recede from their method.

Since the development of a method that renders the discovery of the *mens auctoris* possible, the modern theologian can avoid no less than the scholar of religion observing that the sacred texts are not free of mistakes; at the very least, that the ideas of its authors were subject to historic change. Pre-modern hermeneutics (e.g., the doctrine of the fourfold meaning of the text) allowed allegorical interpretation of the text if it contradicted what the interpreter deemed to be right. As one out of numerous examples I want to mention Meister Eckhart's sermon "Intravit Jesus in quoddam castellum, et mulier quaedam, Martha nomine except ilium" (on Luke 10:38; Pfeiffer IX), in which Eckhart tries to prove that Jesus chose Martha over Mary. The sermon is certainly splendid and contains a wealth of important ideas—but it would be bizarre to deny that it does not exactly capture Luke's *mens auctoris*. There is probably no work that has expressed the basic ideas of modern hermeneutics with greater clarity and innovativeness than Baruch Spinoza's *Tractatus theologico-politicus*. Especially the dispute with Moses Maimonides at the end of the seventh chapter, "De Interpretatione Scripturae," is important. Whereas Maimonides, in this sense a classical proponent of pre-modern hermeneutics, teaches a correspondence of all authors of the Old Testament both among themselves and with reason, Spinoza rejects both assumptions. He holds that the meaning of the Holy Scripture can only be extracted from itself, and that there is no reason to ascribe to the authors of the Old Testament, who clearly contradict each other, a familiarity with the philosophy of Maimonides that they could not have had. "He supposes finally that we are allowed to explain and torture the words of Scripture according to our own preconceived opinions, to deny the literal meaning, even if it is most obvious and explicit, and to change it into whatever different meaning we like."[3] Spinoza's new hermeneutics allows for two reactions: on the one hand the distinctly modern fundamentalist return to the sacred text together with a rejection of all later developments, even if they are supported by strong arguments; on the other hand a depreciation of the sacred text as the expression of an earlier stage of the development of reason, as Spinoza himself intends. What is lost with Spinoza is one of the secrets of the success of pre-modern cultures—the advancement of tradition while maintaining a certain feeling of attachment to it, which is central for the collective identity of the respective culture. The assertion of this new hermeneutics in the theological realm took a long time; David Hume still had to remove some remarks from the galley proofs of *The Natural History of Religion,* which nowadays belong to the standard repertoire of every theological introductory course about the Old Testament, for example, about the gradual transformation of Israel's early monolatry into a pure monotheism.[4]

PHILOSOPHY

Due to the development of historicism that has to a large extent undermined one of the two foundations of theology, the other basis of theology, the philosophical, becomes more important. But what is philosophy? A definition of philosophy according to its content is awkward—what distinguishes philosophy from other sciences is precisely the fact that it does not have a narrowly demarcated subject area: there is a philosophy of the organic and of music, but no biology of music or musicology of the organic. Especially the definition to be found in the Middle Ages, which opposed philosophy as the science of the *ens creatum* to theology as the science of God, has to be rejected. According to this conception, the concept of a theological philosophy that was already developed by Aristotle, and analogously that of a philosophical theology, would be contradictory; the project of a philosophy of religion would lose its meaning to a great extent. Rather, one has to define philosophy as the science of the principles of being and knowing that is entirely based on reason.

But this makes the question of God the focal point of philosophy be-cause God is the principle of all being and all knowing. The method of philosophical (or rational or natural) theology, however, is distinct from the method of the theology of revealed religions. Philosophy must not substitute authorities for arguments; texts, even sacred texts, must not as-sume the function of justification. Whereas the jurist does not question the validity of the constitution but tries to answer contentious questions on its basis, the philosopher of law tries to address the issue of whether the constitution is just. Likewise, theology accepts the sacred texts and the magisterium of the church as a starting point for its own inquiries, whereas philosophy of religion searches for arguments for the truth of the fundamental tenets of religion that do not depend on revelation.

But there are at least as many philosophies as there are religions; and especially with regard to the question of the evaluation of religion there exist manifold differences among philosophers. Some philosophies re-ject religion's claim to truth and its social function completely; others teach the social benefit of religion, independent from its indefensible claim to truth; yet others hold that the fundamental content of their reli-gion can be established through reason; finally, there is the position that there are rational arguments to accept the truth of religion even if there are no rational reasons for its substantive statements. The last position refers, on the one hand, to the deficiency of human reason; on the other hand, it usually relies on historical arguments in favor of revelation. Those kinds of arguments, which play an important role in Blaise Pascal's apologetic work, can of course never be more than arguments of plausi-bility; and especially since the development of the modern historical the-ology they have lost a lot of their appeal. Thus a philosophical theology that takes religion seriously will strive for a substantive justification of its claims and will regard these efforts themselves as a work of God or the Holy Spirit. From this perspective, the process of rational penetration of religion appears to be a continuation of the process of revelation in which God makes himself known to human beings. Gotthold Ephraim Lessing in *The Education of Humankind* regarded this intellectual pene-tration of religion as its perfection, and simultaneously defended the the-sis that in the beginning there must be positive revelation. "The transfor-mation of revealed truths into truths of reason is absolutely necessary, if they shall be useful for humankind. When they were revealed, they were not yet truths of reason; but they were revealed in order to become truths of reason."[5] This position may sound radical, but it is not too far away from Anselm's program of *fides quaerens intellectum,* which dominates medieval theology to a large extent, even though already Thomas Aquinas turns his back on the rationalism of the eleventh and twelfth centuries and develops a conception that assumes a middle ground between rationalism and fideism and subsequently became canonical for the self-understanding of Catholic theology. According to Aquinas, it is possible to prove some but not all articles of faith (the first being the preambles to the articles of faith proper). But at least Aquinas's partial rationalism has protected Catholic theology from the kind of fideism and positivism of revelation that has come to dominate large parts of Protestant theology especially in the twentieth century.

RELATIONS

After this attempt to define the concepts of the three relata we can ask again: what is the relationship between religion, theology, and philosophy? This question can be answered on a descriptive and a normative level. To start with the descriptive, it goes without saying that there can be tensions among the three intellectual powers. There are many religions without a theology and a fortiori without a philosophy; there are atheistic and antireligious philosophies; there are fideistic theologies, which exhibit hostility toward any kind of philosophy; there are even areligious theologies. The last claim may be surprising since it has been stated above that a theology presupposes a factual religion. But if religion is not merely a social subsystem but an internal disposition that governs the emotional life of a human being, then it is at least possible that there are areligious theologians—administrators of a religion's magisterium (or of an academic position) who pursue their profession for external considerations but do not share in the vital power that is the source of religiousness. But it is equally clear that a unity of religion, theology, and philosophy is possible as well, and it is also quite obvious that it is this unity that is normatively distinguished: since there is only one God, the different ways to experience and get to know him must eventually be compatible with each other. The doctrine of the twofold truth is patently absurd. Thus it is difficult to do without the motivational power of religious impulses. Someone who has no sense of the absolute may be able to design interesting systems of thought; but it is very unlikely that she will succeed in leading a life that is agreeable to God, that she will succeed in letting her insights govern the conduct of her life. One cannot, for example, want to become a priest on the basis of a decision that is based exclusively on abstract considerations. A true vocation has to be based on an enthusiasm for that what one *feels* to be the truth. But even though as a starting point the religious experience is indispensable, it cannot be the end. The education of a religious person who desires to become a priest rightfully includes a study of theology in which the religious sentiment is disciplined and familiarized with concrete dogmatic and moral content that transcends the indeterminateness of feeling. Certainly the control of religion through the church, namely, through a church that possesses a theological tradition, can bring about the suppression of great religious experiences; but it derives its legitimacy from the necessity to control anarchic and immoral religious impulses. Theology is an attempt to rationalize religion, and even if intelligence cannot replace the purity of the heart, it is indispensable in order to distinguish pure from less pure hearts.

But theology should not only join together with religion but with philosophy as well. Why? I have already mentioned that the historic arguments for the truth of the Christian religion have increasingly lost their credibility since the development of historicism, up to the point where a study of exegesis frequently leads to a total collapse of naïve religious beliefs, which would not have to be a tragedy in and of itself if they were replaced by more reflective ones, but becomes appalling if this collapse results in an atheism that wants to remain within the church for purely economic reasons. The motivational power of a historically legitimated faith is small, if only because this faith has abated very strongly. This makes it all the more important to develop all rational arguments in favor of the central dogmas of Christianity and the fundamental principles of its ethics, also and especially in theological education. Although it is not the intent of this essay to elaborate on this, I want to suggest confidently that the proofs of God's existence are by all means more powerful than many non-theologians and unfortunately theologians as well nowadays believe. It is true that popular versions of the teleological argument have lost their attractiveness since Charles Darwin; but the cosmological proof would be cogent in a universe à la Stephen Hawking without initial conditions as well, because—if one accepts the principle of sufficient reason—the system of the laws of nature itself needs a reason that transcends the world. But what could this justification look like? It cannot be of a logical nature, as Spinozism presupposes; acceptable are only teleological arguments, which of course do not override the immanent causality of the world. The world is as it is because beings that make moral decisions can exist only in this world or in one that is similar to it. Such an argumentation is of course implicative: *if* there should be moral beings, then the world should have a certain structure. But philosophy can only reach an end if it grounds categorical and not implicative propositions; it must answer the question of why moral beings should exist, namely, absolutely and in themselves, without consideration of any further ends. The categorical nature of the moral law is indeed the basis of the moral proof of God's existence that can and ought to be interlocked with the cosmological version. According to the moral proof of God's existence, which exists in different varieties, the moral law cannot be an immanent fact of the world: even if the most abominable social systems of the world had prevailed, the values that they would have established as socially valid should not be regarded as just. If, however, it is not possible to ground ethical claims in descriptive claims, then the moral law has to be something that transcends the world. But if it is not contingent that the moral law can have an effect in the world, then the moral law and the world cannot be two completely independent spheres, and since it is unthinkable for the above-mentioned reason to anchor the moral law in the empirical world, the empirical world has to be—at least partially— principled by the cause that transcends it. But how can the categorical nature of the moral law be justified and what is its content? In this respect Karl-Otto Apel's ideas concerning an ultimate foundation of ethics should not be underestimated in terms of their importance for contemporary rational theology. Through a reflection upon the conditions of the possibility of any rational dialogue we discover something that cannot be challenged because without it no questioning or criticizing would be possible. Such transcendental arguments are indeed an alternative to both an intuitionistic theory of knowledge that has to be content with the bare assurance of one's own intuitions and a deductive-hypothetical model of foundation that inevitably leads into an infinite regress. It is rather absurd that our time thinks a great deal of its culture of rationality and always demands reasons, but discards the idea of an ultimate foundation because without an ultimate foundation, every argument in the non-empirical realms, such as ethics and the theory of knowledge, can be countered with another argument that deduces other conclusions from different premises with the same right. Early modern rationalism has with much greater insight established the ontological proof of God as a correlate to the principle of sufficient reason because the latter makes sense only if there is a final structure that can ground itself. Immanuel Kant (in the third chapter of the second book of the Transcendental Dialectic in the *Critique of Pure Reason*) rightly wanted to trace back the cosmological to the ontological proof of God—the question of the former proof is reasonable only if the latter is valid. But Kant and Hume err when they reject the ontological proof of God, which is surely the king among all proofs of God, on the basis of their empiricist theory of knowledge, which is unable to provide a foundation for itself and even contradicts itself.[6] Even today the reader of Anselm's *Proslogion* still feels the blissful gratitude of its discoverer, who can indeed lay claim to having achieved one of the most important intellectual accomplishments of humanity. Anselm has provided a new foundation for the program of rational theology that leaves behind all the efforts of the Greeks that were themselves important enough. (If a very personal remark is permitted: I would unhesitatingly choose the *Proslogion* if the last library were aflame and I had the chance to save only one work of medieval philosophy.) But it can be conceded to Kant that the concept of the necessary being remains curiously empty—and it is here where I think a linking of the ontological and the moral proof of God is indispensable. But this is not the place to elaborate on this idea.[7]

It goes without saying that a rational penetration of Christianity has to start primarily with the concept of God. God's existence and his attributes are the main subjects of a rational theology. A concentration on these questions will facilitate the dialogue with other monotheistic religions considerably, and especially in a multicultural society like ours, the interdenominational dialogue must be supplemented by an interreligious one. That does not mean that the two specific dogmas that distinguish Christianity from the two other monotheistic religions, the doctrine of the Trinity and Christology, are incapable of justification. If the doctrine of the Trinity is interpreted to point to a triadic structure of the principle of the world, and thus of the world itself, then it can indeed be made intelligible; and an interpretation in terms of self-love can found the central importance of intersubjectivity for ethics. A philosophical engagement with Christology should on the one hand emphasize the central moral aspects of the revolution of Jewish ethics that was started by Jesus Christ; on the other hand it should underscore the connection between metaphysics, ethics, and philosophy of history that distinguishes Christianity, say, from Islam and has been a central contribution to the dynamic of Occidental culture. That the moral law determines reality and history and that the sacrifice of one's own life for the truth represents the highest manifestation of the divine in the world, these are fundamental insights, to the rational penetration of which Immanuel Kant and Georg Wilhelm Friedrich Hegel have made major contributions. This judgment remains valid even if one does not approve of Hegel's rejection of eschatology and regards the incorporation of eschatology into the process of history that started off after him as tremendously dangerous because it is based on a misconception of human nature. The dogma of original sin contains anthropological insights that are much more apt than all Rousseauism, whose occasionally downright malicious naiveté is responsible for some of the catastrophes of the twentieth century. By the way, it does not matter that much whether certain moral or metaphysical insights can be attributed to the persona of the historical Jesus or whether they stem from the apostles or the Church Fathers, if Christology has its foundation in pneumatology.

And presumably one will come to the conclusion that the Holy Spirit, as the principle that renders the grasping of truth possible, operates beyond the time of the Church Fathers and the scholastics in the history of the church, even of mankind. Indeed, Christianity must regard the epoch-making cataclysms that underlie the project of modernity not only as threatening—although there is certainly something that is threatening about them, against which the reservoirs of pre-modern patterns of thought can sometimes be a useful antidote. The genius of Aquinas articulated itself in the fact that he transformed the insecurity of Christianity that resulted from the discovery of the Aristotelian corpus, a store of knowledge that in many aspects surpassed its own, into a positive development and, despite many hostilities that culminated in suspecting him of heresy, conceived a great synthesis of Christianity and Aristotelianism that satisfied both the religious need and the need for knowledge of the empirical reality. In the face of this stunning achievement it is understandable why neo-scholasticism essentially went back to Aquinas. Yet it cannot be denied that the discovery of the complete Aristotle was not the last intellectual crisis of Christianity; the development of the modern natural sciences and the humanities are further crises to which Thomism and the neo-scholastic currents referring to him usually did not have a satisfying answer that "sublated" the new currents. Maybe it is possible to detect in the philosophies of Gottfried Wilhelm Leibniz and G. W. F. Hegel attempts analogous to Thomism to take seriously the new intellectual challenges of their times and simultaneously to integrate them into a Christian tradition of thought. In any case the Catholic Church should not too lopsidedly privilege Thomistic neo-scholasticism as its philosophic interlocutor; the wealth of philosophic positions that was present, for example, in the French Catholicism of the seventeenth century (traditional scholasticism, the Atomist Pierre Gassendi, the intellectual revolutionary René Descartes, the anti-interactionist Cartesian Nicolas Malebranche, the Jansenist Antoine Arnauld, and the critic of rationalism Blaise Pascal) was a sign of its intellectual vitality. It is at any rate beyond doubt that the additional legitimacy that the church can derive from close contacts with philosophy presupposes that philosophy inquires freely and is committed only to the authority of the best argument.

Conversely, cooperation with theology is decisive for philosophy as well. First, the better argumentative training that the philosopher has often enjoyed is not always accompanied by a sufficient knowledge of the tradition. Of course, reference to the tradition as such is not an argument, but there is a wealth of arguments belonging to the tradition that deserves to be taken as seriously as the ones that are circulating today. A historic education cannot replace a systematic endeavor; but it can enable one to discern the limits of one's own time. Second, no honest person can deny that even in a democratic market society discourses are controlled by subtle forms of exercise of power that are not always present in the consciousness of those who are subjected to them. For example, it is obvious that classical metaphysical questions and especially the question of God in the present academic subsystem that calls itself "philosophy" are widely put under taboo. Now in principle it would be possible that these questions have been identified as meaningless; but the most important theory on the basis of which such a claim can be made, logical positivism, has collapsed completely. There are no sufficient arguments left to bracket such questions from the realm of legitimate research; moreover, as I have said above, the concept of philosophy, and especially that of a rationalistic philosophy, peremptorily provokes such questions. The contact with a discipline that has to hold on to such questions, even though the method of its treatment is not that of pure reflection on validity, is healthy and even indispensable for philosophy. By virtue of its basic willingness to question everything, philosophy cannot perform the regulatory function that is necessary for every society, a function that appertains to the church and its theology even within the framework of a society in which it has become only one regulatory institution among many. The church will be able to perform its regulatory function the better the more it appeals to the most important source of legitimate validity claims that has been given to the human being— philosophically enlightened reason.

Translated by Benjamin Fairbrother

A RATIONALIST'S TRADITION:
INTERPRETATIONS OF CLASSICAL TEXTS

CHAPTER 7

◆ · ι · ◆ · ι · ◆ ·

Philosophy and the Interpretation of the Bible

One can hardly deny that hermeneutics is one of the basic disciplines of philosophy. Philosophers deal not only (or at least ought not to deal only) with texts and other entities in need of interpretation, such as lectures or discussions at conferences, but certainly they dedicate to them a very great amount of their time. Partly they are the direct object of their efforts, as, for example, in philosophy of literature or in history of philosophy; partly they are a necessary medium and tool in order to develop a theory of something that is in itself not an *interpretandum:* the philosophical theologian has to think about God and his attributes, but he will make progress probably only if he is willing to study what *other* philosophical theologians have written on the subject, and therefore even he needs to engage in hermeneutical activities. Hermeneutics may well claim to be the sister discipline of logic, insofar as every philosopher should have studied it at the beginning of his career *before* any specialization. This, though, would grant hermeneutics only the honorary title of "organon," enjoyed in the Aristotelian tradition by Aristotle's logical works—it would not show that it is an end in itself and even less that philosophy

155

might be reduced to it. Nevertheless, to be an indispensable tool is something of considerable importance, and thus it must be complained that in the Anglo-American world hermeneutics often enough is not even regarded as a normal discipline of philosophy.[1] The exaggerated expectations connected with hermeneutics in parts of contemporary continental philosophy, however, are also misleading: hermeneutics does not answer the fundamental questions of metaphysics, epistemology, and ethics, as little or even less than logic does. It is therefore not their legitimate heir, not a modern form of First Philosophy. Furthermore, Martin Heidegger's and, to a lesser degree, Hans-Georg Gadamer's hermeneutics stand in opposition to classical rationalism, insofar as they suggest that the dependence on traditions inherent in human nature confutes the pretensions of an autonomous reason. But the recognition of the basic character of our hermeneutical activity does not entail any rejection of rationalism whatsoever; it is in fact compatible with a host of different epistemological and ethical positions. There may be good arguments against rationalism, or there may not; the fact that humans are necessarily interpreting beings is in any case not such an argument. There is a rationalist hermeneutics, as well as a conception of hermeneutics directed against rationalism, and particularly if we take Heidegger's and Gadamer's claim of an existential historicity seriously, it should be worthwhile to analyze the historical development of hermeneutics in order to see how different forms of hermeneutics have emerged. Perhaps one might even succeed in the anti-Heideggerian activity of finding a logic of development in the history of hermeneutics; in any case it is extremely important to recognize that not only historicist hermeneutics, as Gadamer rightly insisted upon, but also Heidegger's and Gadamer's hermeneutics are only different historical realizations of what hermeneutics can be. For new reflections on hermeneutics it may well be useful to consider also the oldest form of hermeneutics, which existed before the rise of historicism.

In the history of the West there has been no text that has been regarded as a worthier object of interpretation than the Bible. Therefore, ideas about the history of hermeneutics can best be exemplified by some reflections on the development of the interpretation of the Bible. Obviously, an analysis of the philosophical presuppositions in the various historical interpretations of the Bible is interesting not only for the philosophy of hermeneutics, but also for the philosophy of religion and theology. The existence of a text with authoritative claims is a challenge for any rationalist philosophy, and there is no doubt that the revolution in the hermeneutics of the Bible is due not only to an improvement of the tools of historical analysis, but also to profound changes in the concept of reason (also, but not only insofar as these changes are at the basis of the just-mentioned improvement of the historical method). There is little doubt that due to these changes our approach to the Bible has become somehow disenchanted and that this price we had to pay is a very high one. One can argue that there have been very few (if any) changes in the history of religions as far-reaching as those that transformed particularly the more intellectual branches of Protestantism at the end of the nineteenth century, after the general reception of modern hermeneutics by official theology, and one has the impression that Catholicism, a century later, is in a similar process of transformation, due to analogous causes. (An important difference, however, lies in the fact that scripture in Protestantism played a far more central role than in Catholicism, so that a paradigm change in exegesis within a Protestant framework entails more radical theological consequences.)

Despite all feeling of loss that probably most readers of the Bible have experienced when they became for the first time familiar with the work of critical exegesis, it is quite manifest that these changes were intellectually necessary and that we can only hope to go beyond them, not to fall behind them. In the following I first describe in very general terms the mode of Bible interpretation that was in force from the beginning of Christianity until its eclipse in the eighteenth century and, second, the reasons for and consequences of the great revolution in biblical hermeneutics. Third, I discuss the question whether Gadamer's criticism of historicist hermeneutics can be of significance for the theological study of the Bible and sketch how, on the basis of rational theology, a hermeneutics of the Bible may be conceived that renders justice to the greatness and even holiness of this book without betraying the demands of rational autonomy. Being a philosopher and not a historically trained theologian, my quotations rarely come from theological Bible commentaries, but mainly from philosophical works dealing with the Bible. I do, however, also consider those philosopher-theologians who deal explicitly with classical metaphysical issues, such as Augustine, Thomas Aquinas, and Nicholas of Cusa, and those exegetes who were influenced in their work by philosophical ideas, such as David Friedrich Strauss. Obviously, neither my competence nor the space allows for an exhaustive account; the names I select could be easily complemented by many others whose neglect has to do with my ignorance and not at all with any objective value judgment about their importance.

I.

In his study *The Eclipse of Biblical Narrative: A Study in Eighteenth and Nineteenth Century Hermeneutics,*[2] Hans W. Frei characterizes the interpretation of the Bible before the use of historicism by the following three features. First, an acknowledgment of the literary sense of the Bible implied immediately its historical truth. One could, as we will see, certainly deny that a literary interpretation was appropriate, but one could not accept the literary interpretation as capturing the true sense of the text and simultaneously refuse the conclusion that the facts described had really occurred. Second, the interpretation of the Bible presupposed an encompassing unity of the histories narrated. Not only were the stories of the Old Testament supposed to depict a unitary historical process beginning with creation; in typological interpretation they were thought to refer to persons and events in the New Testament. Third, the encompassing character of the biblical narrative entailed that the reader would find all his real and even possible experiences anticipated in the Holy Book. Not only was it possible for him, it was also his duty to fit himself into that world in which he was in any case a member, and he too did so in part by figural interpretation and in part of course by his mode of life.[3] The Bible was the Book of books, thought to contain at least implicitly all the knowledge of the world, and much more than merely theoretical knowledge—it pointed the only way toward salvation.

Nothing shows in a more obvious way the break with the ancient ideal of education than the manner in which Augustine conceived his program of Christian education as focusing on the study of the Bible. He succeeded, however, in saving the traditional arts by recognizing their importance for an appropriate interpretation of the Bible.[4] Nevertheless, their function is only a subservient one—one may be a saint without any education in the liberal arts, as it is possible to know them well without being a decent human being. In his famous autobiography he recalls in a witty pun the studies of his youth when he was forced to learn Aeneas's odyssey (*errores*), while forgetting his own moral faults (*errores*).[5] The *Confessions* may be interpreted as the long and tortuous path of an educated pagan toward the recognition of the Bible as God's own word— one could even call the *Confessions* a sublime love story, namely, the narration of a complex relationship of Augustine with God and with the Bible as his manifestation. The presupposition for writing the text is a stable bond with God and a recognition of the Bible's authority, as the innumerable quotations from the Bible show; but the text has as one of its main contents the description of Augustine's manifold resistance against the formation of this bond and against this recognition. It was also his classical education that prevented him at the beginning from embracing the Bible: compared with the dignity of Cicero's eloquence, it seemed unworthy of his attention when he first began to study it.[6] Augustine needed a change in his hermeneutics of the Bible in order to acknowledge its authority. In Milan, he learned from Ambrose a spiritual and non-literal interpretation of those passages of the Bible that had repelled him.[7] Ambrose liked to quote 2 Corinthians 3:6 about the letter killing and the Spirit giving life, and Augustine saw that through such an interpretation it could at least be shown that the relevant passages were not manifestly wrong.[8] This did not yet prove their truth, however, and the belief in God was not sufficient to do so either. Augustine's answer is partly that one has simply to believe in the authority of the Bible, as we believe in many other things, as historical facts, the assertions of friends, and the like, rejecting the critical question of how we can know that the Bible is inspired by God. Partly, however, he adds some rational arguments for the necessity of believing: on the one hand, the weakness of our reason renders authority indispensable; on the other hand, God hardly would have allowed the almost universal recognition of the Bible's authority if he had not wanted to be known via the Bible. The fact that the Bible can be read by everybody and at the same time contains a profound meaning understandable only by few persons was a further argument in favor of the trustworthiness of its authority.[9] It was the study of (neo-)Platonism that enabled Augustine to find a spiritual meaning in the Bible, even if he repeats again and again that the truth of Christianity transcends the insights of Platonism by far: only in the Bible did he find charity based on humility.[10] But the intellectual and moral recognition of the Bible was not the last act in Augustine's relation to it: even more important was the existential conversion, that is, the change of his form of life, motivated by a passage in the Bible (Rom. 13:13f.), which he had found by chance when he opened the Bible after hearing a voice, probably of a child, saying "Take and read," and after remembering that Anthony had also found his monastic vocation after reading by chance another passage of the Bible (Matt. 19:21).[11] Yet neither the narration of Augustine's final conversion nor that of the death of his mother Monica, preceded by a mystical experience shared by mother and son, concludes the work. The first nine autobiographical books are followed by one book dealing with philosophical psychology, which forms an apt transition to the last three, which consist of a detailed philosophical commentary on the beginning of Genesis, including important hermeneutical reflections—Augustine proves by this act of interpretation that he indeed achieved the aim of his development, namely, to become a philosophical exegete of the Bible.

Even in the Late Middle Ages almost all research had to be justified by the fact that either it was enlightened by the study of the Bible or it helped to foster the correct understanding of the Bible. "Henry of Langenstein found it helpful to arrange a series of studies on scientific problems (in physics, optics, zoology, and so on) in an order dictated by the six days of creation as they are described in Genesis. It must of course have been the case that a number of scholars were drawn to these subsidiary subjects for their own sake, and secretly had little use for their theological application. But the study of such matters continued to be justified by the need to understand the Bible better."[12] Nevertheless, within this general framework there are remarkable differences in interpretative approach, and it is possible to discover a slow progress toward the emergence of modern critical thought during the Middle Ages. Although in "every surviving library catalogue of the early medieval centuries . . . books of the Bible, glossed and unglossed, outnumber every other kind of book, even the liturgical in many cases,"[13] and although the number of extant medieval commentaries on the Bible is huge,[14] surprisingly enough the study of medieval Bible hermeneutics began quite late: the first explicit monograph is Beryl Smalley's amazing work, *The Study of the Bible in the Middle Ages,* which recognizes the need for a thorough analysis of medieval Bible hermeneutics in order to understand medieval culture, even if she does not deny the enormous difference between it and the modern art of interpretation. It is to her book and to the studies of her pupil Gillian Evans that I am indebted most for the following information about the methodology of patristic and medieval hermeneutics (even if I am primarily interested in the common traits of pre-modern hermeneutics).

One of the main differences between pre-modern and modern hermeneutics is, as we have already seen, the devaluation of the "literal" approach contrasted with the "spiritual." What does this exactly mean, and how did this hermeneutical position manifest itself? Certainly one of the most striking features of pre-critical hermeneutics is its extended use of allegorical interpretation. This assertion is valid not only for Christian access to the Bible; it is valid for every culture that possesses authoritative texts belonging to an era with a less refined intellectual or moral taste. Allegorical interpretations allow two things that under the presuppositions of modern hermeneutics are almost impossible to reconcile: one may reject the more primitive meaning of the text without having to challenge its authority—for the text is now supposed to mean in truth something very different from its face value. The Stoic allegorizations of traditional myths—which only to a limited extent were also applied to poetry, for example, to Homer—are a good example of the procedure I have in mind; and already before the beginning of Christianity, Hellenized Jews, beginning at least with Aristobulus, had developed an analogous method of interpreting the Bible. The greatest of them is Philo of Alexandria. Philo does not deny that there was such a historical person as Samuel; he thinks, however, that the fact of his existence is only probable and in any case of much less importance than its allegorical significance, namely, of a mind worshiping God.[15] Smalley comments: "The abstraction which Samuel signifies is more real to him than the historical Samuel.

Scripture has become a mirror which he studies only for its reflections. Then, as he watches them, the distinction between reality and imagery is melted. Reading Philo one has the sensation of stepping through the looking glass. One finds, as did Alice, a country governed by queer laws which the inhabitants oddly regard as rational. In order to understand medieval Bible study one must live there long enough to slip into their ways and appreciate the logic of their strict, elaborately fantastic conceptions."[16] While commenting on Genesis, Philo introduces again and again philosophical and scientific ideas that every historically trained person today recognizes immediately as incompatible with the worldview of the authors of the corresponding texts. One can certainly revere the Priestly source because of its non-anthropomorphic concept of God without being able to assume that the six days of God's creation are an allusion to the number 6's property of being a perfect number (i.e., the sum of its factors), as Philo maintains.[17] Such properties of numbers were analyzed by Greek mathematicians, but nothing suggests that they were present to the mind of a Jewish priest not familiar with Greek mathematics. Not less extravagant are Philo's etymologies from the point of view of our modern knowledge, even abstracting from the fact that Philo, whose knowledge of Hebrew was poor, usually refers to the text of the Septuagint, which he regarded as equally inspired.

Philo's impact on Christian exegetes was strong, as later Rashi's and Moses Maimonides'. Obviously, only Christian exegetes tried to show that figures and events of the Old Testament foreshadowed those of the Gospel, but despite this important difference the Jewish and the Christian approaches to the Bible were structurally similar. Origen, also born in Alexandria, distinguishes literal, moral, and allegorical senses, corresponding to body, soul, and spirit (the latter two, however, often flow together), in order to make sense of theoretical assertions of the Bible that seem absurd, such as about God walking in the Garden (Gen. 3:8), as well as of moral precepts, both in the Old Testament (Gen. 17:14) and in the New Testament (Matt. 5:29). Every passage of the Holy Scripture, he thought, had a spiritual, but not every passage a corporeal, literal meaning, which often enough seems simply impossible.[18] In opposition to the Alexandrian school, the Antiochene school insisted more on the literal meaning, in which the spiritual sense was inherent, but also here the typological interpretation of the Old Testament was practiced. On the other hand, Origen himself was an excellent philologist aiming at a solid textual basis for the Bible. As a Platonist with a profound consciousness of historical developments, Augustine combines a predominant interest in the spiritual meaning with a recognition of the historical truth of the letter, at least in most cases. He does not object to and even demands a spiritual reading, as long as this does not entail a negation of the truth of the literal meaning.[19] He defends thus the possibility of a plurality of different, but equally valid interpretations; wanting to address various persons with quite different intellectual capacities, God will have given several senses to his word.[20] Two things, however, are according to Augustine undoubtable: first, God's word is true, and, second, the human writer of the text had this truth in his mind.[21] Moses, for example, must have had in his mind all the different meanings of the beginning of the Genesis that are possible.[22] Since the *mens auctoris* fundamentally does not differ from the objective meaning of the text envisaged by God himself, for the pre-modern hermeneutics there is no need to find out something about the mental states of the author—they coincide with the objective meaning of the text. In a certain sense the whole human author is superfluous because the real author is the Holy Spirit.[23]

In the later development of biblical exegesis, the pneumatic, allegorical sense was further subdivided into two: the allegorical and the anagogical. The literal meaning was thus reduced to only a quarter of all meanings, and in the Early Middle Ages it lost increasingly its importance. In the twelfth century, however, important changes take place. The consciousness of possible contradictions within the Bible grows, and different methods are proposed to deal with them.[24] Furthermore, a strong interest in history develops, and in this context the Victorines re-evaluate the literal meaning.[25] This tendency continues in the thirteenth century with the appropriation of Aristotle and a new attitude toward empirical reality. Aquinas is a good example. On the one hand, he recognizes the fourfold sense of scripture, the literal or historical, the allegorical, the tropological or moral, and the anagogical. The three spiritual senses refer to events in the New Testament, alluded to by events of the Old Testament, to our moral duties, and to the coming glory.[26] Metaphors are necessarily used in the Bible, and we should raise our minds from the sensible veils to their intellectual content.[27] On the other hand, Aquinas insists on the literal sense as the basis of the others; everything that is necessary for faith is also said in a literal manner, never solely in a spiritual one.[28] In the literal meaning—which contains also the aetiological, analogical, and parabolical and which is what the author has in mind—sounds signify things; in the spiritual meaning, things signify other things. The latter presupposes the former and is founded on it.[29] Two examples will show how Aquinas's hermeneutics is applied to concrete cases. The question whether the paradise described in Genesis is a physical place is answered by Aquinas in the affirmative: there may be a spiritual sense, but the historical truth has to be taken as foundation.[30] Aquinas, however, regards it as necessary to give up the literal meaning when it contradicts known facts. The truth of scripture has always to be defended, but since there are different interpretations of it, one must choose the one that avoids false statements and never stick stubbornly to one that may be confuted by reality; otherwise scripture will be derided by the infidels and their access to faith will be precluded.[31] These remarks are in the context of a discussion of the apparent contradiction between Genesis 1:1 and 1:9; Aquinas proposes various interpretations in order to avoid a conflict with Aristotelian cosmology and metaphysics, whose truth he defends.

In the Later Middle Ages progress was achieved with regard to textual criticism, to information about the historical background, and to the study of the original languages. Nicholas of Lyre, interested in the rehabilitation of the literal meaning, was a good Hebrew scholar.[32] At the same time efforts spread to translate the Bible into the vernacular languages. These efforts were regarded as dangerous: "In the case of the Dominicans, whose *Chapter General* of 1242 forbade the friars themselves to make translations to help in their preaching, the reason may lie in the practice of the Waldensians. The Waldensians seem to have been the earliest sect to set out to master the Bible in their own language and the result of their efforts was that many of them were able to match text for text with those who sought to convert them. There was, then, a danger of heresy in putting the Bible into the hands of laymen, which the missionary preachers were the first to feel in its practical results. They insisted that the 'naked text' at any rate could not be put into their hands; they needed interpreters to guide them as to its meaning."[33] In the Reformation, however, the idea becomes triumphant that scripture is its own interpreter—only the Holy Spirit mediates between the reader and the text, no longer the hermeneutical authority of the church. The new principle *sola scriptura* goes hand in hand with Martin Luther's philological work on the Bible and his superb translation into German. Luther insists strongly on the literal meaning, although he, too, is unable to dispose of the spiritual meaning completely and maintains the typological interpretation.[34] But certainly with early Protestantism's focus on the literal meaning (later challenged by Pietism), the philosophical interpretation of the Bible so masterfully represented by Origen comes to a halt. Nicholas of Cusa—one of the great medieval philosophers and theologians who did not write exegetical books (at least not on the Bible—he authored, however, the *Cribratio Alkorani* [*Sifting the Koran*])—in his *De Genesi* (*On Genesis*) could defend the idea that the world had no beginning in time: Moses had spoken to the people according to their understanding, not intending literally what he wrote in Genesis.[35] But this idea, with which Origen could have agreed, would have appeared nefarious to early Protestant orthodoxy; only in the course of the eighteenth century was the biblical chronology of creation and of human history rejected by the intellectuals of the time.

II.

Early Protestant biblical interpretation is the stage of transition between pre-modern and modern hermeneutics. The interest in the original languages, the awareness of philological problems (shared with humanism, despite the strong differences content-wise), the rejection of the patristic and scholastic hermeneutical tradition are steps toward the modern "scientific" reconstruction of the *mens auctoris* as the aim of the hermeneutical process. Nevertheless, three very important differences remain. First, early Protestantism is convinced of the absolute truth of the Bible: the reconstruction of its meaning regardless of the question of truth would have appeared idle to it. Since now the literal meaning is what mainly counts, the way of escape open to earlier allegorizations is closed: if the Bible contradicts scientific or philosophical opinions, these must be

wrong (or, one would say later, the Bible cannot be right); the reconciliation of tradition and progress has become far more difficult. Fundamentalism is therefore a product of modernity and its revolution in
hermeneutics; it is not a phenomenon conceivable in traditional societies.
Second, despite all subjective seriousness in the determination of the literal meaning of the Bible, certain dogmatic boundaries must not be
crossed: John Calvin had Michael Servetus executed for his important
discovery that the doctrine of the Trinity is not present in the New Testament. It seems difficult to us to assume that the Calvinist fathers of modern capitalism could really believe that their new rationalization of
economic behavior breathed the spirit of Jesus—to us, the contrast between Matthew 6:19ff. and their maxims seems strident; but since they
regarded Christianity as the final criterion of morality and felt (probably
rightly) that their revolution of the spirit of economy was necessary for
moral reasons, they simply had to overlook that contradiction. Third, the
early Protestant approach to the Bible is, although philological, not yet
permeated by the spirit of historicism. The idea that the way of thinking
of the authors of the Old and even of the New Testament could be radically different from their own would not have occurred to them—
although awareness of the break between the two Testaments certainly
facilitated the development of a historical consciousness. What are the
factors that contributed to the triumph of the modern historicist approach to the Bible?

In the first place one has obviously to mention the revolution in
natural sciences, which broke forever with the cosmologies of pre-
modern times (which despite all differences among them had a lot of
traits in common, but stand in marked contrast to modern science). The
trial against Galileo Galilei is the most famous example of the conflict
emerging, but far more important than a contradiction on a finally minor
point is the idea, shared by most modern metaphysicians, that God acts
through natural laws. The concept of natural law begins to emerge in
the Late Middle Ages and is alien to the ancient world. If one accepts this
concept, miracles become a problem. Baruch Spinoza's *Ethics* is the
grand attempt to propose a new philosophical theology that eliminates
traditional teleology and regards natural laws as the proper way in which
the manifestation of God is structured. Spinoza distinguishes between

that which follows from God's absolute nature and the finite and individual, that is, between natural laws and singular events, and he teaches that the latter can be explained only on the basis of natural laws and other singular events (I p. 28). Spinoza thus anticipates the Carl G. Hempel–Paul Oppenheim scheme of causal explanation, and that is not compatible with the idea that God could act against or even past natural laws (which according to Spinoza are strictly deterministic). Every event is lastly performed by God, and it is not possible to regard a certain class of events as acted in a higher degree by God than another. Yet this is not the only contribution of Spinoza to a new interpretation of the Bible. On this basis, he could—so at least it seems at first glance— still have tried to show that the Bible, rightly understood, pointed toward his conception.

But in fact his hermeneutics (which is not integrated into the systematic structure of the *Ethics*, but developed separately in the *Tractatus theologico-politicus* [*Theological-political Treatise*]) criticizes in an acute way the traditional attempts to find metaphysical truths in the Bible. When he declares it as ridiculous to try to find the Aristotelian absurdities in the Bible,[36] he seems to voice concerns similar to those of Luther. But the central difference—and here we come to the second point—is that for Spinoza the Bible not only does not contain these absurdities, but even less the true metaphysics he himself has elaborated, for the simple reason that the Bible did not achieve the level of rationality philosophers aim at. The phenomenon of prophecy as well as the writing of the Bible has to be explained on the basis of the metaphysical structure sketched above, that is, by finding their immediate, secondary causes—which does not exclude the existence of a First Cause, as long as it is not assumed that it acts directly, without mediation through immediate causes. According to Spinoza, the prophets did not possess more perfect minds, but more vivacious imaginations (therefore they spoke in riddles);[37] the biblical explanation of events by miracles simply has to do with lack of knowledge of the relevant secondary causes;[38] the differences in style between the courtier Isaiah and the peasant Amos show that God adapts his style to the person he is speaking to (i.e., that God manifests himself through the personal peculiarities of those humans with a strong imagination whom we call prophets).[39] Spinoza regards it as obvious that

Joshua and perhaps also the author of the text (10:12–14) had a false geocentric cosmology, and he thinks that to deny that destroys any, however limited, usefulness the Bible has because it allows the most arbitrary way of interpretation.[40] In general, the Jews knew little about God, and their religious representations were the only ones a people of their level could have had; therefore Moses—who was a moral legislator and insofar indeed legitimized by God, but had no philosophical insights himself—addressed them as children.[41] (Spinoza maintains, however, that Jesus did not believe in demons, but spoke of them only in order to communicate with his contemporaries; for he regards Christ not as prophet, but as God's mouth.[42]) The Hebrews were not the only nation endowed with prophets, as they are not in any special sense a chosen nation—the augurs of the gentiles can also be regarded as prophets.[43] In the seventh chapter, Spinoza develops his hermeneutical rules. Essential to them is his postulate that the method of the explanation of scripture must be the same as the method of the explanation of nature.[44] The rules state, first, that one has to study the language of the books of the Bible and its history; second, that one should group the different statements of the single books in order to understand on their basis the difficult passages, not confounding the sense of a text with its truth; third, that one should try to write, as far as possible, the history of the authors of the books, of the fate of the text, and of its canonization.[45] These maxims are opposed to Maimonides' pre-modern hermeneutics,[46] and on their basis, in the eighth and ninth chapters, Spinoza can doubt, as shortly afterward the Catholic priest Richard Simon, Moses' authorship of the Pentateuch (whose final redaction he ascribes to Ezra), thereby endangering the unity of the Bible. Moreover, biblical chronology loses its reliability;[47] the literal meaning no longer has historical truth attached to it. Nevertheless, Spinoza defends with conviction the divine truth of most moral precepts contained in the Bible, particularly in the Gospels.

With Spinoza modern hermeneutics has definitely overcome the pre-critical way of interpreting holy texts. Something is still missing, however. Perhaps because he regards time as finally an illusion, Spinoza lacks any consciousness of a real change in the human mind over the course of history. He certainly recognizes that prophecy belongs to an earlier epoch; but he would never have stated that archaic men thought in a completely different way than modern ones. This discovery we owe, third, to Giambattista Vico, whose contribution to the understanding of the Bible is deeply ambiguous. On the one hand, Vico proposes in his main work, *Scienza nuova* (*New Science*), a theory of the evolution of culture which, if applied to the Bible, leads to far more radical consequences than those developed by Spinoza. For according to Vico human nature is not ahistorical, but changes profoundly in the three ages into which he subdivides history: the age of gods, the age of heroes, the age of men. The men in the age of gods are dominated by fantasy and passions and think according to a poetic logic that is fundamentally animistic. It is absurd to assume that their myths, the only way they can express their historical experiences, hide metaphysical insights;[48] and it is no less erroneous to believe that fraud played a role in the formation of their religions.[49] Based on the assumption that the three ages, due to a collapse of the age of men, recur again and again, Vico interprets in the first two chapters of the fifth book of his main work the Middle Ages as analogous to early Roman and Greek history and compares not only social and political institutions, but also religious beliefs of the three epochs. He recognizes thereby several connections between social and religious systems. With the concept of the fantastic universal, Vico tries to explain why premodern societies ascribe to certain individuals, such as the seven Roman kings,[50] a series of innovations, even if in fact it is historically not true that they authored all of them. Such a fantastic universal is Homer, whose poems in the third book are taught to have developed over centuries, being the product of the collective poetic force of the Greek nation. Even if Vico does not take historical accounts of mythical sources as literally true, he is a master in discovering which historical facts are indeed implied by the text, for example, by the form of the narrative or by incidental allusions. On the other hand, not only this account of human history is founded in a complex metaphysics that borrows much from Spinoza, but even more from Leibniz and Plato—the devout Catholic Vico refuses furthermore to apply the principles of his new science to sacred history and defends biblical chronology (something Isaac Newton had also done in his last decades). Symptomatically, the comparisons between Moses and Homer in the first edition of the *Scienza nuova* are reduced in the larger second edition, in which Vico for the first time proposed his theory according to which the Homeric poems had evolved over centuries.[51] It is not clear whether the motive was fear of sanctions or the sincere conviction that the comparison now could be misleading, but it is obvious that the application of Vichian categories to the interpretation of the Bible could have led already in the eighteenth century to a mythical interpretation even of the New Testament.

David Hume's *The Natural History of Religion* continues the program of finding the secondary causes of religious beliefs, but radicalizes it to a new degree since he rejects any search for a First Cause. Hume is indeed an absolute naturalist—something that can be maintained of Spinoza only with several caveats and not at all of Vico. Besides this theoretical aspect, his book is important in our context for two reasons. On the one hand, Hume reflects explicitly about the Bible—in passages that he had to eliminate in the galley proofs he remarks, for example, that the eldest Jewish religion was not, to use modern terms, a monotheism, but only a monolatry.[52] On the other hand, he compares ancient polytheism and Christian monotheism with regard to values and makes clear that the two religious systems foster different moral principles and virtues, showing a certain nostalgia for the pagan world. We have now named the fourth reason for the demise of the traditional authority of the Bible—the conviction that the belief in it contradicts not natural laws, sound hermeneutical rules, or historical facts, but moral principles. But Hume is certainly not the most important author to use this objection; since his own conception of ethics lacks any absolute basis and its content differs explicitly from some of the traditional Christian norms, his criticism cannot surprise. Much more weight is carried by the criticism brought forth by that moral philosophy that claims to offer a solid basis for our religious beliefs and to have conceptualized the universalism present in Christianity—I have in mind, of course, Immanuel Kant's ethics.

Kant is an enlightener insofar as he strenuously defends an autonomous conception of morality—something is moral because my practical reason recognizes it, not because it has been mandated by God. At the same time the absolute, that is, unconditioned, character of the categorical imperative and particularly the relation between the moral Ought and the physical world leads to the idea of ethico-theology, an idea completely foreign to Hume, whose forceful criticism of traditional onto-

and cosmo-theology Kant shares and deepens. It is on the basis of this idea that the biblical representations have to be evaluated, and not vice versa. But what, then, is the function of the Bible? Obviously, no statement of the Bible that contradicts practical reason can be accepted as valid—Kant rejects forcefully the conception that God could have ordered Abraham to slaughter Isaac. We can never be sure that God is speaking, but we can at least be sure that it is not he who is speaking if something immoral is imposed upon us.[53] In his work on religion he tends—as the young Georg Wilhelm Friedrich Hegel and later in the most extreme form Arthur Schopenhauer—to see mainly the morally problematic aspects of the Old Testament; he does not search for any moral evolution within the Old Testament. (Only in the essay *Mutmaßlicher Anfang der Menschengeschichte* [*Conjectural Beginning of Human History*] he refers respectfully to Genesis 2–6, using it, however, as a historical, not as a moral source, and accepting its authority only insofar as it corresponds structurally, not literally, to the conceptual reconstruction of human history by philosophy.) The commands given in the Old Testament are not of moral, and therefore of religious, but merely of a political nature: the Ten Commandments are the basis of every commonwealth; the threat and the promise with regard to future generations (Exod. 20:5f.) are not compatible with moral justice; the notion of a chosen people contradicts the notion of a universal church. Even the monotheism of the Old Testament deserves less credit than a polytheism whose gods are believed to help only the virtuous persons since the god of the Old Testament is more interested in rites than in moral improvements.[54] With Christianity, however, suddenly, although not without preparation, a moral revolution transpires that replaces the old statutes for a single nation with a new moral spirit for the whole world.[55] The apparent continuity with Judaism was preserved only for strategic reasons. Kant is very critical of the history of real Christianity, but he regards it as possible that its founder corresponded indeed to the ideal of humankind pleasing God, an idea necessary to practical reason. He insists, however, that such a belief could be justified only by historical documents, while the religion of reason does not need any such accreditation. True religion, therefore, cannot consist in professing a belief in God's acts for our salvation, but in moral actions.[56] In his late work, *Der Streit der Fakultäten*

(*The Conflict of the Faculties*), Kant elaborates hermeneutical maxims for dealing with the Bible that are based on his philosophy of religion. His hermeneutics falls behind that of Spinoza, as he does not aim at capturing the *mens auctoris*. Kant wants to make sense of the Bible, even if he has to contradict the convictions of its finite authors. Kant seems to adopt here the hermeneutical rule that one has to understand an author better than he understood himself.[57] (Since one can say that the Bible has both a finite author and an infinite author, however, perhaps Kant would have claimed that he tries indeed to capture the *mens auctoris, auctor* intended here as God himself.) Of particular importance is the first rule, according to which we may interpret certain passages of scripture containing theoretical doctrines that transcend reason (as the doctrine of the Trinity or that of resurrection) in a way that is advantageous to practical reason and must do so in case of those doctrines that contradict practical reason. An example of the latter is the doctrine of predestination, which Kant regards as Paul's private opinion and as incompatible with the belief in our freedom. Even in the case that a passage in the Bible contradicts not our practical reason, but only necessary maxims of theoretical reason, as in the case of the stories about persons possessed by demons, a reasonable interpretation is to be recommended in order not to facilitate superstition and fraud, although it is difficult to doubt that the authors of the Gospels believed literally in the stories told.[58] (Kant does not note that the Gospel of John has eliminated all exorcisms.) Kant discusses several objections against his hermeneutics, one being that it is neither a biblical nor a philosophical but an allegorical-mystical one. His answer is that his way of interpreting the Bible is opposed to the traditional typological one and that only the acceptance of a solid conceptual framework as that of moral concepts avoids mysticism. But does not the reduction of revelation to practical reason destroy its divine character? No, because compatibility with the doctrines of reason about God is a *conditio sine qua non* for assuming that we really have to do with revelation and because a historical fact never can be proven definitely to be divine revelation.[59]

It is this last point that was urged with energy by Johann Gottlieb Fichte in his first book, *Versuch einer Kritik aller Offenbarung* (*Attempt at a Critique of All Revelation*), which, published anonymously in 1792, was regarded as Kant's long-expected work on religion. The book need not be analyzed here because it deals with the Bible almost not at all, but only with the formal criteria that allow one to recognize something as being possibly a divine revelation (which type of acknowledgment is never cogent and furthermore useful only for persons who are not morally perfect). In accordance with Kant's ethico-theology, compatibility both of the content and of the means of communication of the alleged revelation with the demands of practical reason is a necessary condition for regarding something as revelation. (A set of sufficient conditions does not exist.) For A to be a revelation, it is, by the way, not a necessary condition that God intervened in the causal order immediately before—there may be an infinite series of intermediate causes between God's will to communicate himself and the act of revelation itself, Fichte writes in a passage reminiscent of Spinoza's basic theorem discussed above.[60] Fichte's rationalist impetus becomes particularly manifest when he discusses Matthew 5:39ff. and denies that this passage, certainly one of the most sublime of the whole Bible and the core of Jesus' moral revolution, can have the status of divine revelation because these precepts do not follow from the moral principle, but are merely prudential rules, valid under certain conditions only.[61] Now, it is as manifest that Fichte misses completely the prophetic power of this central part of the Sermon on the Mount as it is true that from the beginning Christians have not obeyed, and could not obey, these rules in every situation. One can recognize a certain honesty in Fichte's criticism, which tries to make sense of the behavior of us all; but one can rightly object that Fichte does not take the provocation of what we regard as reason seriously enough and therefore misses the opportunity of giving a more profound interpretation of that passage.

While Fichte is not really interested in the historical figure of Jesus, it is Hegel's merit to have applied Kant's ethico-theology to a reconstruction of Jesus. Hegel's *Das Leben Jesu (The Life of Jesus)*, written in 1795 but published completely only in 1907, is on the one hand the attempt to show that Jesus was a perfect moral teacher who enhanced practical reason and was willing to die for his beliefs. Miracles and exorcisms are eliminated in this reconstruction, and the work ends with Jesus' burial, not his resurrection, already rejected by Kant and Fichte, who saw in it only a form of expressing the immortality of the soul. On the other hand, the work can claim a certain philological accuracy. It is based on schemes trying to bring order into the facts narrated, partly in contrasting manner, in the different Gospels,[62] mentions, for example, the contradiction between John's and the Synoptics' account of the place of Peter's denial,[63] and takes into account the historical knowledge of the late eighteenth century about Jesus' time, for example, when it says that probably only the hands but not the feet were nailed to the cross.[64] One may well say that Hegel is the only great philosopher who has dedicated so much energy to the search for the historical Jesus—with the possible exception of Friedrich Nietzsche. Nevertheless, Hegel's interpretation of Jesus as a moral teacher is not really original—it follows almost necessarily from the first and fourth above-mentioned reasons. Therefore, first, Hegel was not alone in his endeavor to make moral sense, and moral sense only, of Jesus' life and doctrine. About a decade later, Thomas Jefferson began with a similar work—a miracle-free account of Jesus' morals and life (also ending with his burial), which was for the first time published in 1904 (in a limited edition distributed only to the members of the House of Representatives and of the Senate of the United States).[65] Second, in Hegel's mature philosophy of religion Jesus plays a limited role because Hegel came to see the moral interpretation of religion in the manner of Kant and Fichte as extremely reductive. His own speculative philosophy of religion is much closer to the Alexandrinian theology of, for example, Origen than to Kant's and Fichte's ethico-theology, not to speak of the biblicism of Lutheran orthodoxy, even if he, as a distinctively modern thinker, manages to combine with his theological metaphysics a philosophy of history, in which the history of religious consciousness has a prominent place. From his point of view, the spiritual interpretation of the Bible is what counts, not the literal, this being a postulate of the Bible itself (2 Cor. 3:6).[66] Every exegetical effort shows not so much what is written in the Bible as what the presuppositions and categories of the interpreter are—almost everything can be proved with the Bible, even heretics and the devil like to quote the Bible, tradition is as such necessarily a transformation of older concepts into new ones.[67] A good example of Hegel's Bible interpretation is his analysis of the story of the fall in Genesis 2–3. He does not take the story literally and not even historically as Kant had done, but as a mythical expression of a general truth about the human spirit. As myth, the story necessarily entails inconsistencies; only its philosophical reconstruction in the medium of the concept avoids them. The truth of the story is that the human spirit has to leave the immediate unity with nature, that by doing so it becomes free, and that freedom, even if it means openness also to the possibility of evil, contains the principle of healing.[68] Paradise is a park in which animals but not men may stay.[69] On the one hand, by his positive appraisal of the fall, Hegel seems to contradict the meaning of the story, to deconstruct it. On the other hand, also tradition had spoken of *felix culpa,* and even if for Hegel the redeeming event is no longer as much Jesus' death on the cross as its philosophical interpretation and the institutionalization of the constitutional state based on the rule of law, both conceptions share a dialectical pattern. Hegel believed, and could rightly believe, that his new interpretation of Christianity was only a further step within the realm of the spirit, the third stage in his philosophy of Christianity; and even if he was conscious that his conceptions were a provocation to many contemporary Lutheran theologians, he continued to regard himself as a faithful Lutheran,[70] particularly because of the consequences of the Reformation in the sphere of objective spirit, showing simultaneously sympathy to contemporary Catholic thinkers such as Franz von Baader because of their original speculations and rejection of Protestant subjectivism and biblicism.[71]

The later Hegel's idea that philosophy translated religion from the medium of representation to the medium of concept had to have an impact on the interpretation not only of the Old Testament, but also of the New Testament. Hegel had ignored the stories about Jesus' miracles in *Das Leben Jesu*—stories that at the end of the eighteenth century had become a problem to many Protestant theologians. While the so-called supranaturalists continued to defend the historical reality of the miracles, the rationalists denied that something incompatible with the known laws of nature could have occurred. Hegel's former friend and later enemy Heinrich Eberhard Gottlob Paulus—to name only one—in his *Das Leben Jesu als Grundlage einer reinen Geschichte des Urchristentums (The Life of Jesus as Foundation of a Pure History of Early Christianity)* did not doubt the truthfulness of the biblical account of Jesus' deeds; but he proposed an interpretation of them that eliminated their miraculous character. The stories about persons resurrected by Jesus, according to him, prove that Jesus was a person with a remarkable capacity to recognize apparent death, as he himself did not die on the cross, but was taken only half-dead from it and recovered in the cool sepulcher.[72] Obviously, neither the supranaturalist nor the rationalist solution is coherent with Hegel's philosophy; however, Hegelian in its spirit is that book which, despite all its errors (e.g., on behalf of the chronological position of the Gospel of Mark), can claim to have founded modern New Testament scholarship—David Friedrich Strauss's *Das Leben Jesu* (*The Life of Jesus*). The central idea of this work is to apply the category of myth to the stories of the New Testament, as had already tentatively been done with regard to the Old Testament. This seems to be a rehabilitation of the old allegorical interpretation, but the difference is manifest: while allegorization believes to have unveiled the true intention of the author of the holy text, Strauss wants to prove that the authors of the Gospels themselves thought in a mythical manner and were unable to write history in a modern sense. In contrast to Hermann Samuel Reimarus, who assumed a conscious fraud from the side of the pupils, Strauss thinks that the evangelists saw reality as they described it. One could say that Strauss applies Vico's theory of the age of gods to the analysis of the Gospels, although he apparently did not know Vico. Strauss's sensibility for the contradictions between the Synoptics and John, whose value as historical source he regards as small just because of his profound theological conception, his reversion of the typological interpretation (the stories of the Gospels are woven out of allusions to the Old Testament instead of this being an anticipation of them), his awareness of the historical context in which Jesus acted, finally the elegance of his style and the clarity of his philosophical categories, explain the impact of the book. Schweitzer lists sixty works published in reaction to it in the course of four years.[73] It is of extreme importance to recognize that Strauss at the beginning did not want to attack Christianity; even if he recognized that his historical research would have an impact on Christian dogmatics, he ends his book by proposing a Hegelian interpretation of Christ as compatible with his discoveries. Christ cannot be only a moral ideal, as Kant had suggested; the ideal must be real in history, as Hegel had taught. Its reality is not that of a concrete individual, however, as the conservative Hegelians Philipp Marheineke and Karl Rosenkranz had maintained, but the whole historical process of mankind.[74] This idea is radicalized in the later edition of the book, *Das Leben Jesu für das deutsche Volk bearbeitet* (*The Life of Jesus for the German People*).[75] Here Strauss ends by saying that we know very little about the historical Jesus—less than about Socrates—and that it can never be necessary for our salvation to believe in facts whose historical ascertainment is extremely difficult, if not impossible. Only the belief in the moral ideal represented by Christ can have this function, he teaches with Spinoza[76] and Kant. The historical Jesus has a high rank within the series of the persons realizing the moral ideal, but he is not the only one—he has had predecessors in Israel, Greece, and elsewhere, and he himself did not succeed in elaborating the consequences of his moral principle for such spheres as economics and politics. Furthermore, there are morally reproachable ideas already among his pupils and the canonical works of the New Testament—Strauss mentions the Apocalypse of John, but not the doctrine of eternal damnation for nonbelievers. It was this doctrine which, among other problems, motivated Charles Darwin's break with Christianity.[77]

Darwin's ideas form an ingredient of the utterly unsatisfying philosophy, no longer regarded as Christian by himself, which Strauss exposed in his last book, *Der alte und der neue Glaube* (*The Old and the New Faith*). The most merciless critic of this book was the young Friedrich Nietzsche. The fact that he dedicated his first *Unzeitgemäße Betrachtung* (*Untimely Consideration*) to an invective against Strauss at first seems surprising because Nietzsche, a professor of classical philology, had himself absorbed the philological criticism of the Bible in his youth. But just because of that, Strauss's ideas, which in the 1830s had appeared revolutionary, in the 1870s seemed almost trivial to him,[78] and furthermore he disliked the awkward compromise philosophy of the late Strauss, which continued to maintain a lot of Christian elements, for example, in ethics. In our context, Nietzsche's general attack against Christianity is not of interest—it is an attack that is profoundly ambivalent because Nietzsche never ceased to identify in an existential manner with Jesus, the model of his childhood and adolescence.[79] He continues to regard respect for the authority of the Bible as the best piece of discipline Europe owes Christianity,[80] and he praises Luther's translation of the Bible as the best

German book.[81] What is important here is something more circum-
scribed, namely, his radical opposition to any attempt to find a double
meaning in the Bible that transcends the literal one. Already in *Menschliches, Allzumenschliches* (*Human, All Too Human*) he compares the metaphysical explanation of nature and the self-interpretation of the saint
with the pneumatical interpretation of the Bible.[82] In *Morgenröte* (*The
Dawn*) he writes that people read their own desires and needs into the
Bible—"kurz, man liest sich hinein und sich heraus."[83] With particular
aggression he attacks the typological interpretation of the Old Testament
(not surprising, given his preference for the Old Testament[84]); and he
doubts the sincerity of those old interpreters: "Has anyone who averred
this ever believed it?" Nietzsche suggests that Christian philology lacks
any sense of justice and honesty, as Christian additions to the Septuagint
prove.[85] Through his own philological art he wants to discover other
moral depravations in Christianity—particularly in Paul, whom he regards as the real founder of Christianity and whose talk about love hides
the most profound hatred and desire of revenge.[86] Paul's born enemies
are physicians and philologists, in general science—which is therefore
forbidden by God in Genesis 2f., claims Nietzsche in an anti-Hegelian
interpretation of the story.[87]

Nietzsche is the last great philosopher to deal extensively with the
Bible. There are two reasons for this. First, after his extreme attacks the
question of a divine inspiration of the Bible seems settled—philosophers
no longer regard themselves as threatened by the authority of the book
and no longer have to try to limit it. They can simply ignore it, as do
many, if not the majority, of their contemporaries. Second, the work of
concrete interpretation has been taken over by a highly specialized discipline, biblical exegesis, with which philosophy does not dare to compete.
What should a philosopher add to the studies in textual criticism, literary
criticism, form criticism, and redaction criticism that structure the modern exegete's work?[88] Nevertheless, one can doubt that the relation between philosophers and the Bible can end simply in parting company.
Modern exegesis participates in the procedures peculiar to science—it
tries to discover the *mens auctoris* and to find the causes that led to the
upholding of certain beliefs and the formulation of certain texts. But
with these means alone it cannot answer the question of what the text

means for us, that is, whether what it says is true or not. Nor do the attempts to leave the philological interpretations behind and to give meaning to the Bible by relating it to contemporary concerns—the exodus story, for example, to the liberation struggle of oppressed classes or an oppressed gender—seem to be the right solution because they are too obviously a modern, politicized equivalent of the old allegorizations: one reads into the text one's own ideas. Exegesis also cannot appeal to the authority of the text as to something that is warranted by the church. By analyzing its causes it deprives it of the unconditional authority it had for pre-modern hermeneutics; and furthermore, the circle that consists in grounding the authority of the canon on the church and the authority of the church on the events narrated by the Bible is too patent to be ignored. A similar circle is present if one founds the truth of the Bible in the miracles narrated by the Bible itself—already St. Peter alerts Dante to this circle in their talk in canto XXIV of the *Divina Commedia:* "Tell me, who assures you that those works really occurred? The same thing that needs proof, nothing else, attests this to you." Dante's answer is famous: if Christianity triumphed over the ancient world without miracles, then this is a miracle worth more than hundred times all miracles narrated.[89] Perhaps one should take Dante's suggestion seriously and see the greatest miracle in a miracle-free account of the Bible's greatness.

III.

The fascination Hans-Georg Gadamer's hermeneutics has exerted on so many scholars and philosophers has its main reason in a singular awareness of the limits of modern hermeneutics—in a certain sense Gadamer aims at a rehabilitation of some features of pre-modern hermeneutics, but on the basis of an immanent demonstration of the shortcomings of the modern *Geisteswissenschaften.* While before Gadamer most scholars regarded the methods they used as something obvious and not in need of any justification whatsoever, Gadamer showed, by applying the principle of historicism to itself, the complex historical genesis of historicist hermeneutics. Obviously, it is not the task of this essay to render justice to the whole of *Wahrheit und Methode;* of interest are only some ideas of the largest, the second part, dedicated to the problem of understanding in the humanities, even if an appropriate interpretation of the book would have to respect the holistic maxim of hermeneutics and consider also the peculiar position of the second part between the first on the artistic experience and the third on language. The second part consists of two sections, of a historical analysis of the evolution of modern hermeneutics from the beginnings to Wilhelm Dilthey and Martin Heidegger, in which Gadamer can demonstrate his remarkable hermeneutical competences, and of a systematic theory of hermeneutical experience. Gadamer's aim in the first section is to unveil the aporias of an understanding that objectifies the *interpretandum* in a manner comparable to the approach of modern natural sciences toward nature and to show how phenomenology—particularly Heidegger's—overcomes the epistemological concerns of the founding fathers of the *Geisteswissenschaften*.[90] To isolate the search for sense from the search for truth is the peculiar feature of modern hermeneutics and the methods it elaborates. Gadamer sees this critically. The "and" in the title of his book stands for "instead": in order to grasp philosophical truth one has to get rid of the obsession with scientific methods. He exposes convincingly the loss this new hermeneutics entails: "But a reference to the truth which is hidden in the text and shall be brought to light is indirectly present whenever one aims at understanding, for example, Scripture or the classics. What shall be understood, is in reality not a thought as a moment of life, but as a truth."[91] In his constructive part, Gadamer begins with a defense of prejudices, rejected by historicism only because it continues to stand on the ground of the enlightenment movement. He rehabilitates tradition and authority as essentially kindred to the well-understood humanities: "At least understanding in the humanities shares a basic presupposition with the continued life of traditions, namely regarding oneself as being addressed by the tradition. Is it not true for the objects of research—as well as for the contents of tradition—that only then their significance can be grasped?"[92] In this context Gadamer develops his famous concept of the "anticipation of completeness" (*Vorgriff der Vollkommenheit*): in principle we have to assume that we can learn from the *interpretandum,* and only when this attempt fails are we allowed to look at the mental acts of its author instead of at what he was trying to say.[93] The understanding of a text cannot be reduced to the discovery of the *mens auctoris*. "Not only occasionally, but always the meaning of a text transcends its author."[94] The process of interpretation can therefore never come to a completion; and the historical tradition of which the interpreter is himself a part guarantees that the interpretation does not become arbitrary. Essential is the concept of application: understanding is applying, and one must conceive the humanities after the model of jurisprudence and theology. Gadamer recognizes the difference between the procedure of a jurist and of a historian of law. But he tends to play it down: the judge must also know something about the original meaning of the law, and the historian of law must be able to find a legal meaning in the text. In a similar way the theologian has to apply the Bible to the concrete situation, without, however, denying the priority of the text with regard to all interpretations: "Scripture is the Word of God, and this means that Scripture maintains an absolute priority with regard to the doctrine of those who interpret it."[95] The task of the historian is different only in degree from the task of the philologist: in contrast to the latter, the historian tries to see what is only implied by the text, but he, too, must connect the text with other sources to a unity, the unity of world history of which he himself is a part. "If the philologist understands the given text, that is, if he understands himself in his text according to the sense mentioned, the historian understands also the great text of world history itself, which he guesses at and in which every text passed down is only a fragment of sense, a letter, and he, too, understands himself in this great text . . . It is the historically effected consciousness, in which both meet as in their true foundation."[96] After an utterly unconvincing criticism of Hegel, Gadamer ends his second part with an analysis of the fusion of horizons inherent in the process of questioning and answering. "For it is certainly true that compared with the real hermeneutical experience that understands the meaning of the text the reconstruction of what the author had in his mind is merely a reduced task. It is the seduction of historicism to see in such a reduction the virtue of being truly scientific and to consider understanding as a sort of reconstruction that somehow repeats the genesis of the text."[97]

This is not the place for a thorough criticism of Gadamer; therefore, I cannot argue here sufficiently for the following assertions. Gadamer's historic achievement is the insight that understanding is more than the unveiling of the *mens auctoris*. In Edmund Husserl's language one can say that hermeneutics cannot deal only with the *noesis* of the author of a text, but must consider its *noema,* and that only by doing so can it respect the author who is not taken seriously if he is psychologized. If I try to understand a person, I try to understand what he says. To learn from a text has a higher dignity than to learn about it; therefore, the operation called *Verstehen* cannot be reduced to explanation. It is also true that history cannot be conceived only as a place of errors discovered finally by the interpreter—being a part of history himself, he must interpret history as a place of the possible manifestation of truth. But these insights must not conceal the ambivalent sides of Gadamer's grand theory. Its main problem is the Heideggerian rejection of any transcendental reflection on the *quaestio iuris*.[98] We need a method to distinguish good from bad interpretations, both of the *noesis* and of the *noema,* and Gadamer has little to offer in this respect. Therefore, one cannot deny that, for example, the deconstructionist hermeneutics with its appalling lack of sense for the *mens auctoris* has its roots partly in Gadamer. The "objectivity" of modern hermeneutics is certainly not everything, but it is something that must not be given up.[99] Gadamer confuses genesis and validity when he insinuates that the complex prehistory of modern hermeneutics impairs its claims.[100] Only if modern hermeneutics is integrated into a broader concept of hermeneutics may Gadamer's conservative revolution convince. And in order to develop a plausible theory of how to understand *noemata,* we need a recognition of an autonomous reason and of a dimension of validity that cannot be offered by the radical historicism to which Gadamer continues to belong. It is true that he leads beyond historicism by pointing to the contradiction inherent in its naïve belief in "objective" understanding—one cannot historicize everything except one's historic interpretation. But he brings historicism only to an explosion, he does not overcome it. In order to do so, he would have to allow more room to Husserl than to Dilthey and Heidegger, and he would have to recognize that the facticity of history is not the final criterion of validity, even if it remains true that history is not a meaningless place, alien to the ideal sphere. But it is the ideal sphere that constitutes history, and not vice versa.[101]

And it is only the recognition of such an ideal sphere that permits us to make sense of religion, and therefore of the Bible. I can only sketch how such a post-Gadamerian hermeneutics of the Bible might look. First, it seems hopeless to me to justify the authority of the Bible by the miracles narrated in it or assumed to have led to its revelation. Even if we assume that certain miracles have taken place (and, given the darkness that encloses the mind-body problem, we certainly should not exclude healings based on the power of spirit, even if it is misleading to believe that such events are in contradiction to the laws of nature—we only do not know how to explain them), this could never prove their divine origin; for some malicious spirit might be their cause (whose existence is hard to exclude, if we accept supranatural interventions in the course of nature). Besides that, miracles are not necessary to defend the idea of divine revelation, as Fichte was right in pointing out: it suits an omnipotent and omniscient being far better to have organized the world in such a way that his purposes can be achieved without any concrete intervention, simply by the normal course of nature and history. Second, the divine manifests itself in what has a particular affinity to its central values and truths, whatever its genesis may be. Obviously, as Kant and Hegel taught, we already need some a priori knowledge of them in order to find out whether a text can claim to manifest these values particularly intensely—it can be only reason that justifies the authority of the Bible, not the Bible that justifies the validity of certain rational or moral convictions. But does this not imply that any revelation beyond reason is superfluous? Not at all. On the one hand, the autonomy of reason is a late result of history and presupposes genetically both pre-rational experiences without which it could never have understood itself and the power of traditions in which it is embedded, as Gadamer rightly recognized.[102] On the other hand, even if the examen by a subjective reason is the necessary presupposition for the justified acknowledgment of a text, nothing excludes that the subjective reason can learn from a text innumerable things that were not known to it before. Third, a rationalist framework entails that there can be many inspired texts, even in different cultures and traditions.[103] Christians should certainly not deny that, for example, Muhammad achieved for his time and his culture what could be reasonably expected, and one should therefore not shrink from calling him an inspired prophet.

Nevertheless, there are—fourth—good reasons for regarding the Bible as a very special book. Compared with the Qur'an, its most striking features are the richness of the literary genres present in it and the range of time during which it was written.[104] This abundance explains the numerous contradictions one finds in it—contradictions which, by the way, favored the development of hermeneutics within Christian culture and contributed to the rise of modernity. It is senseless to downplay these contradictions, if one accepts the principles of modern hermeneutics; and on the basis of a universalist ethics it would be profoundly immoral to accept the application of these principles to other religions, but not to one's own. Furthermore, it is not necessary to downplay those contradictions in order to defend the authority of the text. That the concept of God of the Priestly source and already of the Elohist is less anthropomorphic than that of the Jahwist, that John eliminates exorcisms from his account of Jesus' acts, is a sign of religious progress that should not disturb even if it entails that the more primitive concepts of God are not the definitive ones and makes it plausible that also the later concepts may become more subtle. The *telos* of the theological concepts of the Bible is in any case the rational *noema* of God—this is what gives meaning to the historical reconstruction of the earlier *noeseis*. One could defend the thesis that the story of the fall says something about a necessary step the human mind has to take, even if we came to the conclusion that the Jahwist saw in it only something negative—but the story has its own weight, transcending the intentions of its author. In some cases one can even recognize in a story different strata representing contradictory intentions, and here the modern interpreter has in any case to break with at least one of the interpretations given by the authors of the story.

Even less problematic are the contradictions between the Bible and our modern scientific knowledge—one can and has to demythologize the Bible,[105] as long as one recognizes that it is monotheism, as it was first conceived within the Bible, which is a necessary presupposition for the genesis, and perhaps also the validity, of modern science. It is also impossible to deny that several passages particularly, but not only, of the Old Testament manifest moral ideas that are unacceptable to us—as long as one recognizes that the ideas of justice and of love have hardly ever been articulated as powerfully as in the Bible, particularly by the prophets. And has not the Bible itself shown the weaknesses of its heroes, so that we need not be surprised at some weaknesses of its authors (as well as, later, of the Fathers of the Church)? One need only to think of Peter's denial, certainly one of the most powerful scenes of the Gospels and one of the most innovative texts of world literature.[106] Besides the dignity of its theological and moral ideas, the Bible excels indeed because of its literary qualities. It is significant that it not only teaches moral precepts (as in the book of Proverbs), but that it shows morality in action—it thus allows, particularly, but not only, in the Gospels, for a personal identification that abstract ethical treatises do not offer. This effect does not depend on the historicity of the stories told, even if the books of Samuel and of Kings can claim to have given origin as few other texts to historical thinking. It has to do with its art of narrative, which is in many cases superb— I name only the Joseph novella.[107] A person with such a vast and profound knowledge of the classics as Harold Bloom writes, without reference to religious motives, that if on a desert island he could have one book, it would be a complete Shakespeare, if two, that and a Bible.[108]

But of course, literature cannot be the central criterion for valuing the Bible—it can only add to the weight of its theological and moral ideas. Their truth cannot be proven with exegetical tools—this is the task of systematic philosophy. And this means that exegetical studies, even after they have found their own method, are well advised not to part with philosophy. Only a philosophically enlightened exegesis can avoid the Scylla of fundamentalism and the Charybdis of historic relativism.

CHAPTER 8

———— ·•··•··•·· ————

To What Extent Is the Concept of Spirit (*Geist*) in German Idealism a Legitimate Heir to the Concept of Spirit (*Pneuma*) in the New Testament?

Theology has a peculiar status within the theory of science. On the one hand it is, as its name says, not just a human science (*Geisteswissenschaft*) dealing with the reconstruction of beliefs, for its theme is God himself. Its concern is not primarily of a hermeneutic-historical kind: it cannot, in contrast to the scientific study of religion, be satisfied with an investigation of what kinds of religious concepts exist today, be it in its own culture, or be it elsewhere, or be it in earlier times. A reconstruction of the views of other people that is intersubjectively valid and unbiased by one's own projections is, particularly when those views are expressed in other languages and in contexts that are markedly different from one's own, notoriously difficult. The methods required for this inquiry were developed first in the eighteenth and then particularly in the nineteenth century—later than those of the modern natural sciences in the seventeenth century. For this reason it cannot come as a surprise that many important scholars who have dedicated themselves to studies in the human sciences have in fact stuck with their studies in these sciences—they were complex and demanding enough. And one can only speak with greatest reverence of each of the pioneering exegetes and historians of dogma and church—for example, of Heinrich Holtzmann, Julius Wellhausen, Adolf von Harnack, and Ernst Troeltsch—whom we have dearly to thank for our contemporary picture of the genesis of the New and Old Testaments, of the history of Christian dogma, and of the development of Protestantism, even if we are of the opinion that some of them occasionally tended to reduce theology to historical theology (in a broad sense, including the exegetical disciplines). This admittedly would transform theology into one of the humanities; it would be a discipline of the products of the human mind directed toward God, but it would not itself speak in the first person of God. *Assuredly, however, the humanities are spiritless and gutted if they speak only intentione obliqua of the most important objects of the human spirit.*

Against this it must be insisted that systematic theology be the center of theology. Nevertheless, its nature is different from that of a pure systematic discipline like mathematics or philosophy. Even if every mathematician or philosopher is well advised to study the work of his predecessors, the validity of a mathematical or philosophical theory still does not depend on its correct rendering of other perspectives. Something analogous is true perhaps also of fundamental theology, traditionally the first and most fundamental part of systematic theology. But it certainly is not true of dogmatics and theological ethics, which constitute its center. For both of these disciplines are in their own self-conception tied to given texts like Holy Scripture, works of the tradition, and articles of faith: whoever contradicts these is undermining his own claim of truth. That explains why the historical-hermeneutic disciplines in theology are much more important than those in philosophy: one needs them in order to be sure of the presuppositions on which dogmatics and theological ethics can be constructed. *Systematic theology, like philosophy, doubtless speaks in the first person, but it cannot, one could say with a little exaggeration, speak in the first-person singular:* it must subject itself to the received "We" of the authoritative texts. So it occupies an intermediary position between a pure descriptive science like religious psychology and a pure normative discipline like philosophical ethics: it is doubtless normative, but the starting points of this normative stance are givens—mostly, but not exclusively, texts whose normative relevance is presupposed and may not thereafter be questioned.

This connects theology to jurisprudence, its twin sister from the point of view of the theory of science.[1] Four differences, however, are striking. The first is that it is only the law of the state, at least under the conditions of modernity, that legitimizes the exercise of violence—violations of dogmas and also of church law have no such dramatic legal consequences. For this reason, second, the dogmas of theology can afford to be less clear than those of the law, whose social effectiveness would be endangered if the exact meaning of article 65 of the Basic Law of the Federal Republic of Germany were just as controversial as that of the Chalcedonian Formula. Third, church dogmas have no explicit mechanisms of continuing development, in the way that most modern legal systems do. That goes well with the idea that theological dogmas are not a product of human agreements. But naturally the status of dogma has changed over time and, even more, the interpretation of dogmas. This happens partly in an explicit way at councils, partly as an unavoidable consequence of the general changes of history, and above all of methods of correct textual interpretation. Since in the modern world valid law is seldom very old, the development of the historical-critical method has revolutionized legal history, but not legal dogmatics: exegetical jurisprudence seldom needs that method. But exegesis of scriptures that are as old as the Old and New Testaments is dependent upon it if it wants to be taken scientifically seriously, and precisely in this lies one of the two problems of theology as a science that have remained unsolved since the nineteenth century.

The problem is in a simplified way just this: that the validity of dogmatics presupposes the kerygma of Jesus Christ. This conditional relationship explains why, particularly since the Protestant turn to the principle of *sola scriptura,* the fundamental investigation of the actual meaning of the Bible became a religious task—contrary to the interpretations of the scholastics. Without this particular religious sense of mission the historical-critical method would hardly have been so quickly developed—one should not forget that the hypothesis that the Pentateuch goes back to four different versions was developed by Jean Astruc in order to safeguard the authorship

of Moses, which had been doubted: all four versions, for Astruc, stem
from Moses. The development of this method later led to dissections of
the New Testament and critical questions regarding its historical worth.
Soon it was grasped that the differences and even the inconsistencies
between the evangelists and occasionally inside of the same Gospel go
back to different editorial sources and redactions respectively. (See John
13:23–26 and 18:15f., which evidently are later insertions. It is undoubtedly correct that with such hypotheses the inconsistencies of the texts
remain and are only ascribed to the last editor. But that is psychologically
much more plausible than to ascribe them to the original author, who in
truth is honored if one does not attribute inconsistencies to him.) And
the different uses of the same sources by the evangelists point to different Christologies. Thus John's Gospel not only eliminated all exorcism
histories, probably because it felt them to be embarrassing; but the Gospels of Luke and Matthew likewise eliminated all of the actions that in
the Gospel of Mark (7:31–37; 8:22–26) have magical traits and accompany two healings. At any rate, it is plausible that the oldest and the theoretically least-burdened Gospel comes closer to historical truth: Jesus
was undoubtedly an exorcist, who perhaps also used magic practices.
Whoever in accordance with the widespread and validated contemporary
historical method seeks to peel away the interpretive layers of the Gospels from the historical Jesus will consider probable a picture of Jesus
such as is sketched by Ed Parish Sanders.[2] Much remains undetermined,
but a figure does shine through, who undoubtedly in his moral teachings
belongs to the most fascinating men in human history, but who hardly
can claim to have all of the characteristics that were attributed to him by
later dogmatics. Jesus himself does not appear at all to claim omnipotence or indeed even godlike goodness (Mark 10:40 and 10:18 respectively). It does not help at all to object that the "true" historic Jesus, in
contrast to the historical Jesus, is the one that the church teaches or that
is grasped by faith—at least to the extent that the church and faith want
to ground their legitimacy in Jesus. For then the foundational circle becomes too obvious.

To make even more problematic the idea that theology has a scientific status, it must be added, second, that the great tradition of philosophical theology and its core, the doctrine of the proofs of God, has
been in a major crisis since the nineteenth century. Doubtless there are

very good grounds against the old dualistic model, according to which reason should prove the being of God and historical probability arguments prove the existence of a revelation that is finally articulated by dogmatics. In particular, it is absurd, as was clearly grasped by Gotthold Ephraim Lessing and Immanuel Kant, to ground the validity of moral norms on probability considerations. *But it is a still more absurd circle to attempt the grounding of the being of God in a revelation that can be recognized as divine only if there are already independent arguments for the being of God.* Certainly dialectical theology derived its legitimacy from a polemic against the culture-Protestant inclusion of the religious in the social world, an inclusion that robs it of every critical transcendence, which constitutes the essence of the New Testament. But theology can hardly be helped by an anti-philosophical affect since in an era of religious plurality theology needs a foundation that goes beyond appealing to revelation and dogma. Nevertheless, theology occasionally fears that a self-grounding philosophy—like especially the Hegelian—would make it superfluous in the end, or at least would steal its epistemic autonomy. And it is sometimes more willing to do without such a foundation than without its autonomy, to which the study of its holy texts inevitably belongs.

In the following I briefly sketch a model that perhaps makes it possible to include the best from the Christian tradition in a philosophical conception that radiates outward from the self-grounding of reason and that at the same time recognizes that one of its central concepts takes its genetic starting point from an idea that is articulated with special force in the New Testament. I refer to the concepts of *pneuma* and *Geist.* I first identify some facets of the concept of spirit in the New Testament (I) and second name some central moments of the concept of spirit in German idealism (II). Comprehensiveness is not at all being sought, but my selections of passages with *pneuma* from the Gospels should be fairly representative.

I.

In the Septuagint *pneuma* appears almost always as a translation of the Hebrew word *ruach,* which, however, in other contexts is also translated as *anemos*.[3] The basic meaning of the Hebrew word is "wind" and "breath." In matters that concern God the translation that is appropriate is "active energy" or also "spirit," such as when "the spirit of God" comes on a prophet (2 Chron. 15:1) or rests on the Messiah (Isa. 11:2), thus inspiring people to extraordinary, divinely inspired speech and action. From the sinful the spirit can be withdrawn (Ps. 51:13), and in eschatological expectations it plays an important role (Isa. 32:15; Ezek. 36:26f.; Joel 3:1ff.). Doubtless the post-Cartesian separation of the concept of spirit from the physical world is alien to the Old Testament, but the translation into a foreign language must correspond to its conceptual world, even when this unavoidably entails that a one-to-one correspondence between the terms of both languages is unsustainable. *Furthermore, Jewish monotheism has been a necessary presupposition of the Cartesian conceptual picture: first one must think God as pure spirit before one can sharply separate in humans the mental from the physical.*

The Greek word also has a physical meaning besides its mental one: John 3:8 plays with it, and in Matthew 27:50 just as probably also in Luke 23:46, Acts 7:59, John 19:30, and James 2:26 "life breath" is intended. But in the New Testament the spiritual meaning is undoubtedly the dominant one.[4] *Pneuma* can be ascribed to God just as also to human beings; in the latter case it can be a link to God, but can also designate the psychic inner world (John 11:33; 13:21). Very often the holy spirit is mentioned; however, there are also unclean (Mark 1:23, 26; 5:13; 6:7; 7:25), dumb (Mark 9:17), and evil spirits (Matt. 12:45; Luke 7:21; 8:2; 11:26). Note that *pneuma* can be qualified with adjectives of contrary normative meaning. Even plural *pneumata* without any adjective can indicate "demons" (Matt. 8:16; compare to the usage of the singular in Acts 16:18, where, however, previously an adjective was used); but angels are also named *pneumata* (Heb. 1:14). One should consider furthermore that *pneuma* can designate a quality of God and of humans as well as independent spiritual substances. The "spirit of God" oscillates between both meanings, for it sometimes appears to designate a property, sometimes something self-sufficient.

Fascinating is the "immanentization" that occurs in Luke in contrast to the two other Synoptics in the pericope on the temptation of Jesus. After Jesus' baptism, when the spirit, the spirit of God, and the holy spirit, respectively, have come down in the form of a dove on Jesus (Mark 1:10; Matt. 3:16; Luke 3:22), the spirit drives Jesus into the desert (Mark 1:12; Matt. 4:1); in Luke, however, Jesus is himself described as *plērēs pneumatos hagiou,* "full of the holy spirit" (4:1). In passages like these, it is the evangelists who speak of *pneuma* (just as in the birth legends: Matt. 1:18, 20; Luke 1:35). The contrast of baptism with water and baptism with the holy spirit (and with fire) is ascribed to the Baptist (Mark 1:8; Matt. 3:11; Luke 3:16; John 1:33). *In authentic Jesus logia the concept appears to play no significant role.*[5] Maybe Jesus actually taught that David was in his composition of Psalm 110 inspired by the holy spirit (Mark 12:36; Matt. 22:43), and that his disciples should themselves, if delivered up, trust in the holy spirit or in the spirit of the Father, respectively, who will speak through them (Mark 13:11; Matt. 10:20; Luke 12:12). Probably he spoke of an unforgivable blasphemy against the holy spirit, when it was said of him that he himself had an unclean spirit and that he used Beelzebub to drive out the demons in his exorcisms (Mark 3:22ff.; Matt. 12:22ff.). That he drives out the demons in the spirit of God[6] means that the kingdom of God has come to his hearers (Matt. 12:28); here in a fascinating way the concept of the kingdom of God, which is so central for Jesus, is linked with the concept of spirit, and the kingdom is described as already arrived (*ephthasen*)—one of those passages in which the eschatological expectation, which would otherwise relate to something imminent in the future, is brought into the present.

The concept of spirit is more significant in Luke than it is in Mark and Matthew. The proximity of Luke 1:80 and 2:40 indicates that *pneuma* can almost be a synonym of *sophia* (cf. also Acts 6:3, 10). At any rate, the risen Christ is decidedly distinguished from a mere spirit, for he has flesh and bones (Luke 24:37, 39)—here the word stands for a non-bodily appearance. *In the book of Acts, which takes as its starting point the Pentecost event, the term is used more frequently than in all of the other writings in the New Testament.* The baptism with the holy spirit announced by the Baptist is promised by Jesus immediately before his ascension; it takes place on Pentecost in the form of the filling with the holy spirit (Acts 2:4). Again and again, the spirit inspires the apostles, especially in the context of the diffusion of Christian faith (8:29; 10:19; 13:4); indeed, the spirit of the Lord works wonders among them (8:39). Occasionally the spirit prevents preaching

(16:6). The appearance of Christ on the road to Damascus has the purpose of filling Saul with the holy spirit (9:17; cf. 13:9). The holy spirit also falls on the audience of the apostles, and indeed on the pagans no less than on the Jews (10:44ff.; 15:8). In the face of this experience, which reminds him of the word of Jesus in Acts 1:5 (see 11:16), Peter decides upon the baptism of the first pagan, the centurion Cornelius: whoever has received the holy spirit cannot be refused the baptism of water (10:47). Even the Apostolic Decree, so crucial in the history of Christianity, explicitly refers to the holy spirit (15:28).

The philosophical value of the Gospel of John is inversely proportional to its worth as a historical source. The fact that the Gospel is teaching a spiritual pathway to Christ makes it interested only casually in historical facts. The birth by the spirit, Jesus teaches the slow-witted Nicodemus, is a precondition of the access to the kingdom of God; that which is born of spirit is itself spirit, *pneuma* functioning as a counterpart concept to *sarx* (3:5f.). Jesus declares to the Samaritan woman that the time is coming, and indeed that it has already arrived, when the true worshipers will worship the Father in spirit and in truth. The Father wants such worshipers, for God is himself spirit: *pneuma ho theos* (4:24). *This can be regarded as an assertion regarding the essence of God that has changed history, just as has been done by the competing statement from the Johannine circle (1 John 4:8): ho theos agapē estin, God is love.* To the spirit belongs the property of enlivening (6:63). But the disciples, who in John are just as uncomprehending as in Mark, cannot grasp it; the spirit becomes reality in them only with the transfiguration, that is, the death and the resurrection of Jesus (cf. 7:39 and 20:22). In his farewell speeches, Jesus promises that the Father will send an advocate, the spirit of truth, whom the world cannot grasp because it does not see or know him, but who nevertheless will remain with the disciples in eternity (14:17). This Paraclete or holy spirit, who proceeds from the Father (15:26), will teach the disciples everything (14:26) and lead them to all truth (16:13). The fact that the Paraclete can only come after the death of Jesus makes this death even valuable for the disciples (16:7). Ernst Haenchen writes in his commentary, which combines philological precision with spiritual appropriation, that "In this first half of the verse it is clearly implied that what the spirit will teach will go beyond the message of the earthly Jesus; one could perhaps say: will go beyond it as much as the corrections and additions of the gospel writer go beyond the tradition that was accessible to him in the form of his source. Here we find a clear awareness that between that which the earthly Jesus said and did, and the message of the spirit, there is a gap . . . John has radicalized the eschatological expectation that for Mark still lay as a cosmic event in an undetermined future, in such a way that chronological time is eliminated and with it that change inside the world that Mark and early Christianity were waiting for."[7]

The first letter of John—to quickly characterize the New Testament letters—distinguishes the spirit of truth from the spirit of error (4:6) and requires that there be differentiation between the two. The relevant criterion is whether the spirit recognizes that Christ has come in the flesh; then, and only then, does the spirit originate from God (4:1f.). That explains why the Vulgate writes "Christus est veritas," while the Greek text identifies the *spirit* with the truth (5:6). Already in the Pauline letters the concept of the spirit, as is well known, plays a decisive role. Paul's theology is certainly Christocentric, but some of his statements on Christ correspond to those on *pneuma,* also because the risen Christ has become a *pneuma zōopoioun,* a life-giving spirit (1 Cor. 15:45; 2 Cor. 3:17). Thus Paul can likewise maintain that we are one body in Christ (Rom. 12:5), just as we are one in the one spirit (1 Cor. 12:12). This one spirit, or Christ respectively, overcomes the division between Jews and Greeks, slaves and free people (1 Cor. 12:13; Gal. 3:28). Certainly Paul has bound "more fundamentally than his tradition Pneumatology to Christology."[8] Faith in the redeeming work of Christ should replace the works of the law. But just in this faith the spirit shows itself (Gal. 3:2; 5:18). Paul speaks of *pneuma tēs pisteōs* (2 Cor. 4:13); at the same time the promise of the spirit is the *object* of belief (Gal. 3:14). *The spirit is thus equally subject and object of faith.* The spirit of God is in this way distinguished from the spirit of the world (1 Cor. 2:12); it lives in humans (3:16; 6:19). It is important that the pneumatic Paul, who ascribes to the spirit the different charisms (1 Cor. 12:4ff.), moralized the concept of *pneuma:* the spirit shows itself not only in extraordinary deeds and events, but also in a form of life inspired by faith (Gal. 5:22ff.).[9] Influential is Paul's opposition of spirit and flesh (*sarx*) as well as of spirit and letter (*gramma*). The first contrast[10] has of course nothing to do with the Cartesian: being fleshly is an attitude.

The flesh cannot obey the law of God at all. While the law leads to the knowledge of sin and inevitably to sin, the human being is freed from the law of sin and of death through the law of the spirit of life in Christ, which leads to life and peace (Rom. 8:2ff.). The spirit, which is not a spirit of servitude, makes us into children of God; it is the divine spirit that exhibits the corresponding witness to our spirit (8:14ff.; cf. Gal. 4:6). In it is freedom (2 Cor. 3:17). Analogous is the contrast between spirit and letter: he only is a true Jew with whom a circumcision of the heart in the spirit and not in the letter has taken place (Rom. 2:29). The novelty of the spirit is placed in contrast to the old age of the letter (7:6); the latter kills, the former enlivens (2 Cor. 3:6). With two metaphors and a polyptoton Paul explains in one of his most beautiful passages that whoever sows to the spirit will reap from the spirit eternal life (Gal. 6:8).

II.

The long way from the pneumatology of the New Testament, past the old church formulation of the Trinitarian dogmas,[11] and through to the medieval doctrines of the holy spirit,[12] cannot here be followed, even if Joachim of Fiore's theology of history already manifests the desire to go beyond the New Covenant. I must immediately jump into the fifth paradigm of Christendom, that of the Enlightenment, after the early Christian, Hellenistic, medieval, and Protestant paradigms.[13] Inside the context of this paradigm German idealism is particularly fascinating because it holds on one side to the rationalism of the Enlightenment, on the other side on the basis of a more complex conception of reason it seeks to transform more of the Christian tradition into conceptual form than other representatives of Enlightenment were able to do: one should not forget that Johann Gottlieb Fichte, Friedrich Wilhelm Joseph Schelling, and Georg Wilhelm Friedrich Hegel were all educated as Lutheran theologians. All three knew the Bible very well, and it was the Pauline opposition of spirit and letter that enabled Fichte to understand his philosophical innovations as a legitimate continuation of the Kantian philosophy— which understandably irritated Kant, who, against the claim that "the *Kantian* letter killed the spirit just as much as the Aristotelian," insisted "that the Critique is to be understood according to the letter."[14] Yet still the young Hegel stressed in 1801: "The *Kantian* philosophy needs for the spirit to be separated . . . from the letter."[15] But obviously it was not only the Kantian philosophy. Christendom is also subjected by Hegel to a new interpretation, which can be conceptualized in the following simplified form: *Christology is absorbed by pneumatology.* Why has this philosophical program been so plausible?

The two most important breaks in the history of modern philosophy are defined by the names of Descartes and Kant. The one discovers that the mental is not reducible to the physical; the other that the moral law belongs to another order than the natural world (to which the mental also belongs). While Descartes and Kant are dualists, their successors—Baruch Spinoza, Gottfried Wilhelm Leibniz, and the German idealists, respectively—try to draw up philosophies that overcome these dualisms. If the mental cannot be reduced to the physical, idealistic consequences are tempting, of either a subjective- or objective-idealistic kind: one starts either from one's own consciousness or from a general reason in which the finite consciousness partakes. *If the sense of the normative cannot be derived from descriptive mental conditions and one believes in a single principle of the world, then it is plausible to interpret the openness for the moral law, which one can name "spirit," as the true principle of reality.* The "I" of the early Fichte, the "absolute" of the early Schelling, and the "spirit" of Hegel are the respective principles of their philosophies. With Kant already that ethical insight is paramount that holds that the moral law must be grounded on the principle of autonomy: what is at stake is a legislation of practical reason itself. In this regard the traditional Christian ethics is felt to be heteronomous, insofar as it traces the validity of moral norms to revelation. It is certainly no coincidence that the turn to the ethics of autonomy is driven by Protestants. The turn admittedly means that they at the same time stand in stark opposition to the literal scriptural beliefs of the Lutheran orthodoxy of their time. Even the old Schelling, who limits the idea of the self-justification of reason, stresses that the Reformation, which "proceeded more out of a profoundly religious and moral excitement than a scientific spirit, had let the old metaphysics stay untouched, and thus remained uncompleted" and complains about the "belief in revelation as a merely external authority, into which the Reformation undeniably degenerated at the end."[16]

There are multiple reasons that in the seventeenth and eighteenth centuries led to a decline in faith among many intellectuals in the literal truth of the Bible.[17] First of all a new metaphysics of the laws of nature made the concept of the miraculous appear problematic in a very different way than it was in Antiquity (Porphyry does not challenge the possibility, but rather the *singularity* of the miraculous deeds of Jesus and points to Apollonius of Tyana). Second, the development of a hermeneutic method that with Spinoza strictly separates the question of sense from the question of truth made it possible to bring the questionable statements of the Bible into sharper relief, whereas earlier they had been interpreted away. Third, the development of historicism led to the idea that a different, namely, mythical way of thinking can be ascribed to older cultures. And fourth, the thought that people who do not know of Christ could be excluded from salvation came to be felt as morally unbearable. Indeed, ethical universalism, which was undoubtedly enlivened by Christendom, inspired in the eighteenth century a completely new interest in other cultures. *Johann Gottfried Herder exemplifies a new type of humanities, which for him has evident theological roots: God's energy is manifested in all meaningful works of the mind.* Close to Herder is Johann Wolfgang von Goethe's epic fragment, *Die Geheimnisse (The Mysteries)*, which sketches out the idea of an integrative universal religion. Without doubt the combination of the new humanities with a complex metaphysics and epistemology, a synthesis that was not achieved by Herder himself, is one of the most important matters of concern for Schelling and Hegel.

Even though Fichte's fundamental concept is "I," the concept of "spirit" already plays an important role for him. We saw how he called on the spirit in his transformation of the Kantian philosophy. In the summer semester of 1794 and in the winter semester of 1794–95 Fichte lectured in Jena "de officiis eruditorum," "on the duties of the intellectuals"; the main emphasis of the second half of the course was on the difference between the spirit and the letter in philosophy. In the first relevant lecture Fichte starts by declaring that spirit is "that which one otherwise also names *productive imaginative power*."[18] In this sense all humans have spirit. But if we differentiate spirited from spiritless humans, we refer to the fact that only the former have ideas and ideals, which are concerned with the "unification of everyone to the kingdom of truth and of virtue . . . whoever gets to the latter region, is a spirit and has spirit in a higher meaning of the word" (60). To have spirit does not mean that it is possible to scientifically describe it. For a spirit cannot immediately affect other spirits, but must represent itself in a body and this external representation is a "representation of the spirit merely for him who himself has spirit" (62). History consists of a "struggle of the spirits with each other" (63). Spirit, so summarizes Fichte, is in its essence autonomous: "The spirit acts in accordance with its own rule; he needs no law, but is a law unto himself" (64). And in the corresponding essay we read: "The spirit leaves the borders of reality behind itself . . . The drive to which it is given over proceeds on toward infinity" (162).

Of the three greatest representatives of German idealism, Hegel is the one who most thoroughly studied the historical Jesus—one thinks of *Das Leben Jesu* (*The Life of Jesus*), written in 1795 in Bern, in which all of the Gospel miracle reports are cut out. The manuscripts written in Frankfurt on the so-called *Geist des Christentums* (*Spirit of Christianity*) offer a philosophical interpretation of the material investigated earlier. Jesus is set off in stark relief from his Jewish surroundings, which was characterized by a heteronomous belief in a merely transcendent God. Hegel's anti-Judaism is striking; he speaks of the "old covenant of hate" (1:293; cf. 287). Jesus steps forward in a time of radical change. Hegel uses, apparently following Montesquieu, the term *Geist* first in a general sociological sense: "At the time that Jesus stepped forward in the Jewish nation, they found themselves in a position that is the condition of revolution, which has to occur earlier or later, and that always has the same general characters. Whenever spirit has vanished from a constitution, from the laws, and through its change the spirit no longer agrees with these, a search, a striving after something else develops" (297). The "sublime spirit of Jesus"—here, second, the term designates something individual—particularly in the Sermon on the Mount turns against the law (324). Hegel's interpretation of Jesus surely is influenced by his own critique of the "self-forcing of Kantian virtue" (359); Jesus' moral and religious ideas are far more anchored in Judaism than Hegel, who ignored the contemporaneous Jewish tradition and willfully appropriated the construction of the Gospels (cf. 355 on John 2:24f.), could know (even if I as a complete layman do not rule out that today Jesus' originality is sometimes underestimated—out of the all too understandable desire to break with the dreadful tradition of Christian anti-Judaism). For Hegel, Jesus' central message is something living and spiritual (here, third, in a normative sense), namely, love: "That love has triumphed does not mean, as when duty has triumphed, that it has subjugated the enemy, but rather that it has overcome hostility. It is for love a kind of dishonor, if it is commanded, if it, a living thing, a spirit, is called by a name" (363). Hegel especially latches on to the speeches of Jesus in the Gospel of John:[19] the foundation of a real community in the "same spirit of love," not the mere satisfaction by the sacrifice, is what Jesus was aiming at (367). The consubstantiation must as it were be doubled: "Not only is wine blood, but blood is also spirit" (366). Whoever grasps "the spiritual with spirit" will also grasp that the "sequence of thetic sentences" at the beginning of the prologue to John has "only the deceptive appearance of judgments" (373). The divinity of Christ points to the connection of the infinite and the finite, which is life itself (378). *Only one who feels the divine in himself can recognize it also in Christ (383); whoever is unable to feel it is by this fact itself now already damned, not just in the future (379 with reference to John 3:18).* At the same time Jesus is a dividing wall between the disciples and God (384); Hegel explicitly cites John 16:7. "Only after the separation of his individuality could their dependence on him cease and their own spirit or the divine subsist in them" (388). Hegel interprets in John's spirit the logion of Jesus (Matt. 12:22ff.): "Whoever separates himself from the divine, and blasphemes nature herself and the spirit in her, his spirit has destroyed the holy in himself" (389). Certainly for Hegel the history of early Christendom ends tragically: even if belief could have become a self-fulfilling expectation (397f.), the disciples failed and externalized their image of Jesus into a transcendent world rather than appropriate it. "The shroud of reality, wiped off in the grave, has again stepped out of the grave and adheres to the person risen as a God. This need of something real, sad for the community, is deeply connected with its spirit and its fate" (410). Especially fascinating is the end of the treatise, where Hegel defends the typological interpretation of the Old Testament that can be found in the authors of the Gospels. Hegel does not dispute that the prophets themselves did not think of Jesus, but he distinguishes between historical *reality* and the *truth* of the appropriation, whose legitimacy does not depend on the former. Hegel can even refer to John 16:51, where the evangelist recognizes in the sentence of Caiaphas a prophetic, though, as he knows well, for him unintended sense. In this ability to recognize the spirit even where it works *à contrecœur,* lies "the highest belief in spirit: . . . he speaks of Caiaphas as himself being filled with the spirit, in which the necessity of the fate of Jesus lay" (416f.).

If one wants, one can see an equivalent of this highest belief in spirit in the changes that led finally to the very different Berlin *Vorlesungen über die Philosophie der Religion* (*Lectures on the Philosophy of Religion*). *The historical unfolding of the Christian religion appears to the mature Hegel to be no longer a history of decline, but rather to be willed by God.* The space that is available to me does not allow me to develop Hegel's mature philosophy of religion, which integrates much more strongly the old Church's Trinitarian dogmatics.[20] Only three points are in order. First, Hegel's philosophy of religion is not primarily concerned with God, but with human conceptions of God. In contrast to Schelling,[21] "absolute spirit" for Hegel does not refer to God, but rather to art, religion, philosophy. God in himself is thematic for Hegel in the *Wissenschaft der Logik* (*Science of Logic*). But God manifests himself also in the development of the world, particularly of the spirit; for this reason Hegel can, probably with John 4:24 in mind, write in §384 of the *Berlin Encyclopedia*: "*The absolute is the spirit;* this is the highest definition of the absolute" (10.29). Since manifestation belongs to Hegel's concept of spirit, this means that the absolute must reveal itself: "Or, to express it more theologically, God is essentially Spirit, insofar as he is in his community. One has said that the world, the sensory universe, must have spectators and be for the Spirit, so must God be much more for the Spirit" (16.53). God manifests himself in all religions, but most of all in that which conceives of him explicitly as spirit—namely, the Christian religion. Second, the mature Hegel, too, sees pneumatology as the truth of Christology: Christ must die to make possible a more complex relationship with God. "The relationship to a mere human being becomes a relationship that is changed and transformed by the spirit" (17.296). Third, Hegel follows the further development of Christianity on the one hand through to the modern nation-state, on the other hand to a philosophy that conceptualizes Christianity (17.330ff.).

To what extent is the Hegelian philosophy of spirit, probably the pinnacle of German idealism, a legitimate heir of the New Testament concept of *pneuma?* The answer to this question naturally depends upon the nature of the criteria for legitimate inheritance. If the criteria are of a philosophical nature, the only question at stake is to determine whether the Hegelian philosophy is better grounded than all possible alternatives. If this is the case, it may certainly integrate earlier forms of the spirit into its own prehistory. If contrariwise the criteria are of a theological nature, one must ask which significant ideas of Jesus are lost in the Hegelian philosophy. So far as I can tell, three ideas have been highlighted in the criticism of Hegel. The determination of what is significant is itself led by concerns that transcend the texts and does not simply result from the frequency of the idea in the New Testament; for otherwise one would have to highlight the exorcisms, too. First, one can argue that in the mature Hegel the concept of spirit has driven out and replaced the concept of love. The existential appropriation of the command of love is more than philosophically grounded humanities—this insight of Søren Kierkegaard is attractive and becomes even more so when it is uncoupled from his return to the old Lutheran orthodoxy, which promises to all who do not believe in the unicity of Christ eternal damnation. Second, it is possible to criticize the notion that the experience of one's own sinfulness is impeded when one points as strongly as Hegel does to the divinity of the human spirit; whoever suffers can find comfort in the picture of the crucified that the Hegelian philosophy of spirit does not convey to him. And third, one may refuse to come to terms with the immanentization of eschatology in Hegel. But Hegel could reply that all three peculiarities of his interpretation are at least rudimentarily found in the Gospel of John;[22] and that whatever lies beyond that owes itself to the forcefulness of the spirit that John proclaims. One can only successfully reply to him when one tries to show why each of the three limits misses something essential and in fact tries to show this with philosophical arguments. *For the living spirit is only at work where spiritual traditions are studied as well as subjected to argumentative examination.*

Translated by Jeremy Neill

CHAPTER 9

---·—·—◆—·—◆—·—·---

Reasons, Emotions, and
God's Presence in Anselm of
Canterbury's Dialogue *Cur Deus homo*

with Bernd Goebel

One of the most important results of the historiography of medieval philosophy in the twentieth century was the rejection of the monolithic image that the neo-scholastic revival of medieval thought had favored in the late nineteenth century. One of the reasons medieval philosophy is an important epoch in the history of philosophy is precisely that it contains such a wide array of different positions on a great variety of issues. The exact determination of the relation between faith and reason, for one, is a crucial issue for both philosophy of religion and epistemology. With regard to this question we find, besides Thomas Aquinas's influential delineation of faith and reason with its distinction between natural and supernatural truths, medieval thinkers who believe that not even the existence of God can be proven by reason, while other philosophers and theologians maintain that the main doctrines of the true religion can and must be demonstrated rationally. All medieval Christian philosophers view Christianity as the true religion. The rationalists among them are thus above all committed to the program of justifying by reason alone those two dogmas of Christianity that more than all others distinguish it from the two other great monotheistic religions—the Trinity and the incarnation. Despite this apologetic character, however, their rationalism tacitly implies that those dogmas that cannot at all be proven rationally can hardly be regarded as true, or must at any rate be interpreted in a way accessible to rational demonstration. And this is one of the reasons their project was regarded with suspicion by many church officials.

After Aquinas, if not earlier, the majority of medieval theologians and philosophers abandoned the rationalist project, the most notable exceptions being Ramon Llull and his followers.[1] But up to the twelfth century, rationalism, usually mitigated by some version of negative theology, was a widespread position among the most original philosophers. Eriugena, Anselm, and the Victorines—as well as, albeit to a significantly lesser extent, Peter Abelard—are nowadays mostly regarded as rationalists, even if still in 1931 Karl Barth defended a radically fideistic interpretation of Anselm's ontological proof (which definitely says more about his own dialectical theology than about Anselm's argument).[2] In the following, we support the modern rationalist reading of Anselm, showing in particular that his recurrent appeals to God's help do not endanger the autonomy of reason. At the same time, however, faith indeed plays an important role for Anselm's program of *fides quaerens intellectum*—although it does so only with regard to rendering the discovery of truth possible or more probable, not with regard to justifying what has been discovered. Still, the emotional support given by faith to the activity of the intellect is indispensable, and an account of Anselm's rationalism that fails to render justice to this aspect would be incomplete.

In order to make our point, we focus on Anselm's *Cur Deus homo* (*Why God Became Man*). This is for two reasons. On the one hand, this work contains the most extensive discussion of the thorniest issue for a rationalist interpretation of Christianity, namely, the incarnation. On the other hand, *Cur Deus homo* is the only work by Anselm that is a full-fledged, living dialogue. No doubt, *De grammatico, De veritate, De libertate arbitri,* and *De casu diaboli* are dialogues, too; but there the interlocutors remain anonymous—they are simply called *magister* and *discipulus;* and while the teacher may of course be identified with Anselm, the disciple neither seems to correspond to a real person nor displays any individuality as a literary fiction. This situation is reminiscent of that in Cicero's *Tusculanae disputationes,* probably Cicero's least accomplished philosophical dialogue as far as its qualities as a dialogue are concerned. His experimentation with the existentially more profound forms of the meditation-based treatise and the direct address of God in his *Monologion* and *Proslogion* respectively, his composition of prayers, meditations, and hundreds of personal letters, his spiritual life, and almost thirty years of teaching in the school of Bec all helped Anselm to acquire the capacity of writing a dialogue in which the interlocutors are real individuals. We mean this not only in the sense that there are historical persons whom the literary universe of *Cur Deus homo* conjures up—Anselm is explicitly named, as well as his real-life pupil Boso of Montivilliers (ca. 1065/66–1136).[3] "Real individuals" wants to convey more: the two interlocutors, that is, no longer appear as abstractions, but as concrete human beings with different emotional structures no less than with different intellectual capacities, standing in a deep and personal relationship to each other.[4]

In fact, apart from the innovative use of literary forms, the experience of an intense friendship seems to have been one of the main reasons *Cur Deus homo* became the liveliest dialogue to be written since Late Antiquity in the Latin world. Whoever reads the letters Anselm wrote to his pupil Boso (who was to become his second successor as abbot of Bec) cannot help realizing how very affectionate their relationship was. It is indeed impossible to account for the affection Anselm and Boso showed for one another simply with reference to the mores of the time. There is a certain exclusivity in their friendship, even an almost erotic quality, as long as this does not suggest anything physical.[5] In one letter, Anselm writes that he knows that Boso does not love anybody more than him, and he adds that he himself does not know whom he would love more than Boso;[6] in another he adds that he knows that Boso desires him more than anything worldly. "The kindness of your love for me knows the kindness of my love for you, and my affection for you knows your affection for me"; and this mutual and true love has its principle in God.[7]

Two times Anselm, now archbishop of Canterbury, had Boso come to England. When he returned from his second exile, he asked his former monastery to send him Boso "because he would rather live with him in solitude than without him in great riches," as Boso's biographer Milo Crispinus puts it.[8] Eadmer of Canterbury, in his *De vita et conversatione sancti Anselmi,* tells us that Boso had first come to Bec because his mind had been vexed by intricate questions (*perplexis quaestionibus*) that nobody had been able to resolve, and that he had opened his heart to Anselm and had received from him all the answers he required. "As a result, he was moved to admiration and captivated by a profound love for Anselm."[9] Shortly afterward (probably around 1088), Boso, together with his two brothers, took the monastic habit at Bec. Eadmer, following Milo, narrates that the devil later tempted Boso for several days and that Anselm put an end to his troubles by listening to him and saying no more than "Consulat tibi Deus"—"Let God provide for you."[10] Obviously, the anecdote, wrought by Milo into a miracle-story, has to be interpreted with the help of modern psychological and historical categories. Boso must have had—as did other monks and nuns in the eleventh and early twelfth centuries (such as Otloh of St. Emmeram, Peter the Venerable, and Elizabeth of Schoenau)[11]—serious intellectual and emotional problems with his Christian faith, and Anselm must have been able to deal with both orders of problems in the right way. *Cur Deus homo* expresses this mixture of emotional and intellectual issues in a complex, artistically subtle way that very likely has its roots in the old abbot's experiences with his pupil and friend more than thirty years his junior. While most philosophical dialogues of our tradition are pure fiction, we may assume that many of the questions asked by Boso in *Cur Deus homo* were indeed asked by him in real life. In a certain sense, the dialogue occupies an intermediate position between an artwork devised by a single mind, as philosophical dialogues usually are, and a real exchange between two persons, like the one between Anselm and Gaunilo of Marmoutiers, which Anselm decreed to be included as an appendix to his *Proslogion.*[12] (This may partly justify our neglect of the distinction between Anselm the author and Anselm the interlocutor of *Cur Deus homo.* Even if this distinction must be taken seriously in discussing certain questions, it need not for the issues discussed in this essay.) This interpretation is not contradicted

by the fact that Anselm at the beginning of the work explicitly defends
the use of the dialogue form as pleasing and thus pedagogically helpful;
for he hastens to add that it is Boso who has most insistently asked him
to write this work.[13] One of the arguments Boso uses in *Cur Deus homo* to
lure Anselm into the discussion with him is that in the process of conversation the interlocutors may discover something new; God may reward
the person who is willing to communicate his knowledge with new insights.[14] And Anselm reacts by saying that he does not so much want to
teach as to embark on a joint inquiry.[15]

Cur Deus homo is fascinating not only because it links the issue of the
relation between faith and reason to Boso's personal problems as well as
to the both loving and tense relationship between Anselm and his favorite pupil (to whom he later dedicated his *De conceptu virginali et de originali
peccato*). Our dialogue is also exceptional because it occupies a middle
position between the two main types of philosophical dialogues we encounter in the Middle Ages—the teacher-pupil dialogue and the interreligious dialogue.[16] It is a dialogue between a teacher and his pupil, though
a far more individualized and independent pupil than usual; and one aspect of this independence is his being able to represent eloquently the
non-Christian viewpoint. In a medieval Christian setting Jews and Muslims could hardly make their objections more forcefully than Boso does,
who, as a professed and committed Christian, does not risk anything in
attacking Christian dogmas for the argument's sake.

In what follows we first analyze Anselm's rationalism in *Cur Deus
homo* (I), then consider the function of Boso's emotions in the rational
inquiry of this dialogue (II), and finally look into Anselm's account of
the nature of God's presence in the intellectual search (III). While the
first of these issues has been fairly thoroughly dealt with in the literature[17] and the third has also been touched upon by a number of scholars,[18] the second has been almost entirely neglected so far.

I.

Anselm does not deny and even states forcefully that faith is the privileged starting point for any attempt to understand one's own religion.

The *rectus ordo,* remarks Boso in his very first utterance, demands that we first believe the tenets of Christianity before we presume to discuss them rationally. He continues, however, that it would be negligent not to try to understand what we believe—that is, we have a moral duty to try.[19] In his letter to Urban II recommending *Cur Deus homo* to the pope, Anselm goes so far as to place the understanding of the faith in the middle between an unreflective faith and the beatific vision (*species*).[20] He certainly insists on the fact that the *veritatis ratio* (the "logic" of the truth) cannot be exhausted by mortals; but, interestingly, in the context of the letter this is meant to suggest that it cannot be excluded that Anselm's book offers new insights that were still hidden to the Fathers. Anselm wants to render the following two claims compatible: that neither he nor future theologians are equal to the Fathers; and that it is nevertheless possible to have theological insights absent from them. The twelfth century would express exactly this position with the famous metaphor of the giants and the dwarfs.

The fact that, from a genetic point of view, and from this point of view even necessarily, faith is the starting-point of understanding is something that even a rationalist like Gotthold Ephraim Lessing grants (albeit under very different historical and intellectual conditions) in his *Die Erziehung des Menschengeschlechts* (*The Education of the Human Race*). A quite analogous thesis also seems to apply to large parts of mathematics; for often, before one tries to prove a theorem, one must already have the conviction that it be true in order to know in which direction to search.[21] We discuss later whether Anselm assigns to faith a still more important role in intellectual inquiry than this uncontroversial stance. What is clear, however, is that an interpretation of Anselm's position to the effect that his arguments are valid only if the truth of the Christian faith is already presupposed[22] is at odds with the whole nature of his program. The sarcasm with which the skeptic Senamus, in the fourth book of Jean Bodin's interreligious dialogue *Colloquium heptaplomeres* (*Colloquium of the Seven*), treats the logical circles with which every faith tries to justify itself[23] would have been quite alien to the kind of sober and pious person Anselm was; but he certainly would have shared Senamus's opinion that such alleged proofs do not have any worth.

In the preface to his work (which he urges always to be copied with
the whole text) Anselm states with unequivocal clarity that he wants to
prove *rationibus necessariis* ("by necessary reasons") in the *first* book that
without a God-man nobody could be saved, and in the *second* book that
humans must in principle be redeemable; from these two premises the
existence of a God-man is then inferred. This program is certainly more
than the mere refutation of the objections of the *infideles*. Both books
pretend to proceed *remoto Christo, quasi numquam aliquid fuerit de illo* ("leaving Christ out of the case, as if there had never existed anything to do
with him") and *quasi nihil sciatur de Christo* ("as if nothing were known
about Christ").[24] There is little doubt that the argument for incarnation
is, to put it in a language not yet that of Anselm, an a priori argument for
the necessity, on moral and metaphysical grounds, of the existence of a
God-man. Anselm, or at least his Boso, seems to lack any clear consciousness (to be found later in Llull) that such an argument is not yet
sufficient to establish the identity of Jesus with this God-man; Boso naïvely presupposes this identity from II, 10 on,[25] and it is on its basis that
at the end of the work he justifies the authority of both the Old and the
New Testaments.[26] In the last chapter Boso assesses that Anselm's argument ought to satisfy both Jews and the *"pagani" sola ratione* ("by *reason
alone*"), once some allusions to the doctrine of the Trinity and to Adam
(which, it is implied, are no necessary presuppositions of his argument)
have been removed.[27] In fact, throughout the dialogue, Boso represents
the position of these *infideles* or, as it is put elsewhere, of those "who are
unwilling to believe anything without a prior demonstration of its reason."[28] Again and again, Boso insists that he wants to hear reasons for
the tenets of his faith.[29] This is not to say that Boso would give up his
faith were he unable to find a reason for it;[30] his refusal to do so distinguishes him indeed from the infidels, and we will see that in Anselm's
eyes this is very important. But the fact that Boso is willing to remain
committed to his faith even if it cannot be justified to his satisfaction is
more of psychological and existential than of justificatory significance.
His problem, insofar as it is envisaged as an ideal entity in the sense of
Frege's third realm, and that of the infidels are identical: "I grant that
they are in search of the reason [for faith] because they do not believe,

whereas we are seeking it because we do believe. Nevertheless, the object of our quest is one and the same."[31]

But *Cur Deus homo* not only proposes rational arguments for the necessity of the incarnation; the demands for the rationality of an argument are quite high. Anselm's first rejection of the infidels' objections is not well received by Boso because it is not based on anything solid; indeed, he likens the "arguments of convenience" in I, 3 to painting on water or in the air: "Therefore, when we offer to unbelievers these notions which you say are convenient, like pictorial presentations of an actual past event, they think we are, as it were, painting in a cloud, since they think that what we believe in is not a past event, but a fiction. What has to be demonstrated, therefore, is the rational soundness of the truth, that is: the necessity which proves that God ought to have, or could have, humbled himself for the purposes which we proclaim. Then, in order that the physical reality of the truth, so to speak, may shine forth all the more, these conveniences may be set out as pictorial representations of this physical reality."[32] Anselm thus is forced to offer more than *convenientiae;* Boso asks explicitly for *necessitas.*[33] In our eyes it is not plausible to claim that in chapter 10 of the first book Anselm rehabilitates the concept of *convenientia;*[34] rather, he proposes only the methodological principle that nothing inappropriate whatsoever be ascribed to God and that, where God is concerned, a reason be regarded as necessary, unless it is overturned by a stronger one: "for just as, in the case of God, from any inappropriateness—however small—follows impossibility, correspondingly with the smallest reason, if it is not defeated by a larger one, goes necessity."[35] Indeed this twofold principle—which Boso accepts in form of a pact—is itself a necessary principle; its negative part by no means states that *convenientiae* are sufficient, but rejects whatever is inappropriate for God; its positive part, significantly enough, speaks about *ratio,* not about *convenientia,* and amounts to something like "Whatever increases the value of God's actions, needs to be ascribed to him." It is clearly related to Gottfried Wilhelm Leibniz's later, more famous claim that, given God's nature, his deeds (including his creation) must constitute an axiological maximum.

Nevertheless, Anselm is a rationalist in a qualified sense. First, it is a reasonable form of rationalism—that is, Anselm is aware of the limits of human reason in general and of his own in particular. One of the reasons he hesitates to discuss the problem of incarnation is that he knows perfectly well that it is intimately connected with a series of other questions.[36] It is this holistic dimension of human knowledge that renders the inevitable limitation of our research to some determinate issue inherently problematic. In addition, Anselm states several times that, being fallible, all his arguments may be replaced by better ones; "it is to be accepted with only this degree of certainty: that it seems to be so provisionally, until God shall in some way reveal to me something better."[37] Even if *Cur Deus homo* does not show us Anselm committing an error, Boso explicitly withdraws an argument, which he initially thought cogent but gives up after Anselm's clarification.[38] At the end of the work Anselm asserts that a mind superior to his might satisfy Boso better than he did and that there are more and greater reasons than he or any other mortal mind could grasp.[39] Indeed, Anselm never claims that he has exhausted all possible reasons; even if he thinks that one (necessary) reason is sufficient to validate a position,[40] there may well be more reasons, which remained unknown to him.[41] Humans may not be able to grasp them, but they are still reasons. Thus, it is crucial that the rejection of an argument must itself be based on a better argument: reasons are confuted by greater or, as he writes at the beginning of the dialogue, deeper reasons (*altiores rationes*), which, however, may transcend human understanding.[42] Even the appeal to the divine will is not sufficient. On the one hand, God wills something because it is reasonable, and not the other way around;[43] and in a similar way we humans cannot withhold our assent from a cogent argument, even if we wanted to do so.[44] On the other hand, even if we can trust that something is reasonable if it is willed by God—since God's will is never irrational—it is not easy to know, as Boso remarks, whether a certain thing is really willed by God.[45] Therefore, the generic appeal to God's will can never be a substitute for an argument. Anselm insists, however, that even if we may understand *why* God wants something to happen we do not know *how* he achieves it.[46] This reflects what Anselm had said in chapter 64 of the *Monologion* concerning the incomprehensibility of the divine Trinity's *quomodo* after having proven its existence with arguments conveying "certitude."[47]

It is revealing that in the discussion of the issue of the intelligibility of the divine, Boso is the driving force. Even if he recognizes in strong (perhaps ironic?) words his intellectual inferiority with regard to Anselm,[48] it is his insistence that makes Anselm speak up and develop his strongest arguments. Boso often asks the questions the reader already had in mind, and in the stubborn honesty of his rationalism there is even something reminiscent of Socrates, despite Boso's role of a pupil:[49] both function like gadflies for their interlocutors—their questions oblige them to make their ideas clearer, although Anselm is never brought to confess an aporia. A passage that sheds light on the nature of their relationship is found in chapter 16 of the second book. The two friends are discussing the question of how the God-man could be assumed from the mass of sinners without being contaminated by original sin. Since Anselm rejects the idea of an immaculate conception of Mary,[50] he has particular difficulties with this issue and tries to avoid a clear answer. "Now, if we cannot understand the reason whereby the Wisdom of God did this, we ought not to express astonishment, but reverently bear with the fact that in the hidden recesses of so surpassingly great an actuality there is something, which we do not know . . . Who may presume even to think that a human intellect might be capable of fathoming how it is that such an act has been performed so wisely and so wonderfully?"[51] Boso's reaction is significant. "I agree that no human being can in this life disclose the innermost depths of such a great mystery, and I am not asking you to do what no human can do, only as much as you can do. For you will be making a more persuasive case for there being deeper reasons for this action if you show that you discern some reason for it, than if, by saying nothing, you make it self-evident that you understand no reason at all."[52] Anselm recognizes that he cannot free himself from Boso's "importunity,"[53] which Boso does not feel sorry for,[54] and develops his theory according to which Mary was purified from sins before Jesus' birth. This, then, leads to the further problem of determining in which sense the death of Jesus (which alone could guarantee that purification) is necessary.

Second, Anselm's rationalism is limited by the authority of the church (in particular of the pope[55]) and the Bible. Since, however, he does not regard it as possible that there is a conflict between reason and authority, this limitation does not amount to very much: it only forces us to track down the fault in our argument and to look for better reasons instead. Anselm clearly states that in all questions left open by the Bible, reason is allowed to proceed on its own;[56] and even if immediately before he says that he will recognize his own conclusions as false, should they be shown to contradict the Bible *without any doubt,* the qualification is important. Now, if one follows the Anselmian method of biblical interpretation, it is not easy to adduce a contradiction with a passage in the Bible that could not be interpreted away. Thus, in I, 9 and 10 he deals with the doctrine that God ordered Jesus to die and that he was exalted because of his death. Anselm regards the doctrine as incompatible with divine justice and denies it by use of a creative interpretation of the relevant passages. Anselm operates with *ac si* ("as if") and *quasi* ("as it were") in order to mitigate passages of the Bible that appear to be at loggerheads with his philosophical teaching.[57] In this, Anselm takes up a method that he already employed in his earlier works. Thus, in *De casu diaboli* he explicitly writes: "Take care not to think, since we read in Sacred Scripture (or say in quoting it) that God causes evil or non-being, that I am criticizing or denying what is said there. But, in reading Scripture, we ought not to attend so much to the impropriety of the words that covers truth as pay attention to the propriety of the truth that is hidden under various kinds of verbal expression."[58] With regard to the authority of the church, Anselm's submission to it is connected with the awareness of his own fallibility. His formula of submission (for as such we interpret the penultimate sentence of the work), however, is remarkable: "If we have said anything that ought to be corrected, I do not refuse correction, if it is done in a rational way."[59] The correction of his work must itself be based on reason.

Third, it must be insisted that a defense of Anselm's rationalism obviously does not entail that his argument in *Cur Deus homo* is convincing. Like every argument, it has premises that may be denied even if one grants that the conclusion follows from them; validity, not soundness, is implied when one ascribes a rational structure to Anselm's argument. Its strength resides mainly in the relentless rejection of the archaic idea that due to original sin man is justly the property of the devil.[60] Among the many criticisms that have been raised against Anselm's argument in *Cur Deus homo,* a frequent but invalid one is to object that Anselm in the dialogue presupposes the existence of God. Anselm could counter this critique not only by pointing out that the opponents whom he is concerned with are themselves monotheists, but also by claiming that he had proven the existence of God in the *Monologion* and *Proslogion*. Far more problematic are the axiological premises of his argument. Sometimes he even refuses to discuss them; thus it is evident for him and his fellow monk Boso that, for example, the God-man ought not to be conceived in an intercourse, but must be born from a virgin.[61] But this is only a minor issue. Crucial for his argument, however, is the idea that only a God-man can make up for the insult that God has suffered from man's sin. This idea is, as has often been remarked,[62] somehow reminiscent of the feudal value system according to which the higher the position of a person, the more severe the punishment of an insult against his or her honor must be. But for modern people, it is impossible to accept this as a truth of moral reason. In general, Anselm does not possess a method by which he could justify all his axiological statements and presuppositions, even if he tries to offer a complex ontological justification for the human race's debt toward God.[63] Second, it remains mysterious how someone may satisfy for someone else, if one thinks that guilt is individually imputable. Anselm, who in *Cur Deus homo* comes close to the intentionalism of Abelard,[64] sympathizes with an individualist account of guilt even when trying to find a rationale for the view that an infant is already affected by original sin,[65] and it is by no means clear how such a theory may be compatible with the doctrine of vicarious satisfaction. True enough, there are passages in the dialogue where Anselm teaches that Christ's self-sacrifice functions as a model to be imitated by humans,[66] but they are incidental and not the core of his argument. Third, it remains implausible that Christ's death may satisfy also for the deeds committed after his death. If every sin is such a violation of the divine majesty that not even infinite worlds could compensate for it,[67] those sins that have been committed after the God-man's self-sacrifice would seem even more atrocious because ingratitude is added to the violation of God's will. Fourth, Anselm's argument is based on some form of an unacceptable "speciesism," as becomes obvious when he justifies his belief that the fallen angels cannot be saved with the argument that even a God-angel could not satisfy for them since there are not two angels belonging to the same species.[68] Thus, according to Anselm's principles, for rational organisms belonging to a species different from the human a new incarnation would be necessary. Fifth, since the insight that leads

out of the despair experienced in the first part of the book is the idea
that God's ends with man cannot be thwarted,[69] the reader asks herself
whether God must not want and be able to bring about a universal salvation. To another order belongs the sixth objection that one easily may
harbor reasonable doubts whether the idea of a God-man is a consistent
one or at least whether the interpretation of this idea by Anselm relates
in any plausible way to the historical facts. Thus Anselm is committed to
the belief that Jesus, at the very moment when God became incarnate in
him, that is, already as an embryo, was omniscient[70]—a belief not easily
acceptable for a person versed in modern biblical criticism. There are no
doubt good philosophical reasons for ascribing divine attributes to Reason incarnate, but the danger of all logos theology (beginning with the
Gospel of John) is that it leads quite far away from the historical figure of
Jesus of Nazareth who remains strangely absent from *Cur Deus homo*.

Several of the arguments just developed already play important roles
in the last two books of Bodin's *Colloquium heptaplomeres* and are widespread in the Enlightenment criticism of Christianity. Whoever thinks
that Anselm's theory does not work, but is still interested in a rational
interpretation of the dogma of incarnation, is well advised to have a look
at an alternative strand of philosophical Christology in the Middle Ages,
developed already in the twelfth century. According to this "cosmological" theory, the incarnation would also have occurred without original sin
in order to complete the creation. Rupert of Deutz, Duns Scotus, and
Ramon Llull are defenders of this position. Georg Wilhelm Friedrich
Hegel transformed it later into a complex philosophy of the place of the
human mind in the structure of being and of its necessary historical development, in which the Christian belief in the incarnation of God plays
a decisive role. But as unsatisfying as Anselm's argument is, he deserves
respect for having been the first to envisage a rationalist theory of incarnation: while his theory may have failed, his methodology is exemplary
for any philosophy of religion committed to reason.

II.

One of the reasons for the choice of the dialogue form in *Cur Deus homo*
is that Anselm can show the emotional impact of the various steps of his

argument upon the sensitive Boso—something that in a treatise would be impossible. At the same time Boso's emotional upheaval is checked by the fact that, in contrast to the infidels he pretends to represent, he already has the faith he desires to understand. As we will see, the emotional shock connected with Anselm's argument is still strong enough; but there are good reasons to say that Boso is not lacerated by it because his faith gives him an emotional support that fends off the worst aspects of that shock. As we have shown, the truth of the Christian faith is not presupposed by Anselm's argument; it remains to be seen whether it is a presupposition of a medieval Christian's emotional capacity to work through Anselm's argument. From chapters 11 to 24 of the first book Anselm offers a true crescendo of emotional unrest in Boso's reactions to his almost juridical argument. After Anselm's first introduction of the idea that the sinner owes God a satisfaction, Boso answers that he has no objections since they had agreed to follow reason; but he confesses feeling a growing uneasiness: "although you frighten me a little."[71] At the beginning of chapter 16 the vague possibility of a *taedium* (disgust) in the continuation of the discussion appears on the horizon;[72] but it is at the end of chapter 20 that Boso first expresses his anxiety in clear terms. Since penitence, contrition, abstinence, and physical work have been shown to be something that we owe God in any case and that therefore cannot constitute a satisfaction of the violation of God's honor through sin, Boso has to respond negatively to Anselm's question how he could be saved: "If I take account of your reasons, I do not see how it can be. But supposing I return to my faith: In the Christian faith, 'which operates through love', it is my hope that I can be saved."[73] But Anselm objects that they had agreed upon investigating the matter *sola ratione,* abstracting from Christ and Christian faith, and therefore requests to proceed *sola ratione.* Boso follows him: "Never mind the fact that you are leading me in a certain bottleneck/anxiety (*in angustias*), it is very much my desire that you should proceed just as you began."[74] The next chapter shows a deepening of Boso's fear. After Anselm has averred that we are always under the eye of God and that we are always forbidden to sin, Boso interjects that "we live very dangerously."[75] And when Anselm maintains that we owe a satisfaction larger than any object that could not have justified a violation of God's will, Boso assents while acknowledging that no human being will be able to offer it. "I see that reason demands this: I also see that it is utterly impossible."[76] The consequence that God can grant no-body bliss is called *nimis gravis* ("exceedingly grave"). And when Anselm announces a further reason for this same consequence, Boso can only appeal to his faith to avoid despair: "If it were not that faith were consol-ing me, this alone would force me to despair."[77] When, however, Anselm declares that he will develop a third argument, Boso claims that he can-not be terrified more than he already is.[78] He repeats only *grave nimis,* when Anselm rejects his argument that man's guilt is diminished because he simply cannot satisfy God by countering that man is himself respon-sible for having incapacitated himself.[79] Shortly afterward, however, Boso is willing to give up the whole rationalistic method since this necessarily seems to lead to the damnation of *miser homuncio* ("wretched little man"); and Anselm must remind him that it was he who had asked so insistently for reason and should therefore stick with it: "Rationem postulasti, ratio-nem accipe" ("You asked for reason: here is reason").[80] Again, Anselm says that the persons who deny the necessity of Christ for salvation and whom Boso represents (*quorum vice loqueris*) have now to demonstrate how salvation would be possible without a God-man. If they are unable to show an alternative, they should either despair or, if they are horrified by this perspective, join the Christians.[81]

It has already been mentioned how the dialogue proceeds: the sec-ond book starts with the argument that God created man with the end of the salvation in mind and hence the God-man is necessary. Boso's emo-tional tension releases and ushers in an outburst of joy at the end of this book, that is, of the whole work: "There is nothing more reasonable, nothing sweeter, nothing more desirable that the world can hear. I indeed derive such confidence from this that I cannot now express in words with what joy my heart is rejoicing. For it seems to me that God rejects no member of the human race who approaches him on this authority."[82] The passage is important not only because of its emotional intensity. The trust regained by Boso is so joyful because not only he himself, but in principle every human being can be saved—a universalist dimension is attached to his certainty of salvation that one does not find in all compa-rable religious experiences of salvation. No doubt this dimension is linked to the rational basis of this certainty: the first predicate Boso uses, anterior to *dulcius* ("sweeter") and *desiderabilius* ("more desirable"), is *ra-*

tionabilius ("more reasonable"). The message is sweet and desirable because it is rooted in reason—Anselm had just appealed to the *ratio veritatis.*[83]

It is quite likely that the emotional reactions of Boso in the dialogue mirror his existential crisis mentioned at the outset.[84] But Anselm would not have integrated them into his work, had he not thought that they allowed him to make a powerful point: the discussion of religious issues is more than an intellectual pastime. In order to follow and trust reason, one needs more than reason alone: the stern majesty of Anselm's "rationem postulasti, rationem accipe" conveys forcefully the idea that not everybody is able to stick to reason. For reason may lead, at least during a phase of transition, to results so terrifying that one needs strength beyond reason to continue with the rational examination of an issue. Even those who no longer share Anselm's conviction that without incarnation every human being would face damnation can quote analogous experiences. Many rationalists, for example, have gone through a skeptical crisis, and if they have overcome it, this was due not to rational resources alone; for before they hit upon rational arguments against skepticism, they already needed a certain trust that a search for such arguments had a serious chance to yield the desired results.[85] Perhaps this is the reason Anselm did not write a real interreligious dialogue—perhaps he feared that an interlocutor who not only, like Boso, pretended to deny, but truly denied Christianity could not have been brought over the abyss of the end of the first book. A faith not yet grounded in reason is not the highest degree of belief, but it may be according to Anselm a psychological *conditio sine qua non* for achieving a higher degree. But Anselm does not speak only about faith. In I, 20 this faith is qualified as operating through love (Gal. 5:6), and the dialogue between a pupil and a master who partly introduces him into his more profound understanding of the faith, partly searches together with him, is a splendid exemplification of this love present in a living tradition.

Terrere, angustiae, periculose, grave, desperare, horrere are the words that describe Boso's increasing anxiety. The term "anxiety" is consciously chosen, for it is etymologically related to *angustiae* (*anxius* stems from *ango* to which also *angustus,* "narrow," belongs). In turn, *angustiae* is related to the German/Danish noun *Angst/Angest,* and the Danish word may remind us of the title of one of the most important treatises of nineteenth-century philosophy of religion—Søren Kierkegaard's *Begrebet Angest (Concept of Anxiety)*. In fact, one can say that Kierkegaard fathoms the emotional states sketched by Anselm in several of his works—despair, for example, in *Sygdommen til Døden (The Sickness unto Death)*, even if the Danish term *fortvivlelse,* due to its accent on splitting in two, allows for conceptual developments precluded by the more pedestrian term *desperatio,* which simply means lack of hope. This proximity of Anselm and Kierkegaard is both surprising and significant. It is surprising because there is indeed an abyss between the rationalist frame of Anselm's philosophical theology and the rejection of rationalism (in its Hegelian form) by the Danish pre-existentialist: a work like *Frygt og Bæven (Fear and Trembling)* is diametrically opposed to the whole program of rational theology; its central tenets are incompatible with Anselm's doctrine of God as well as his ethics. Suffice it to remember that Anselm rejects the idea that God can directly will (not only accept as a means for a higher good) the suffering of an innocent person.[86] It is significant, however, that this does not prevent Anselm from knowing at least the superficies of those emotional states Kierkegaard would analyze in depth. And he not only *theorizes* about them, he *represents* them in the form of a dialogue—a genre marginalized by Kierkegaard, obsessed as he was with subjectivity.[87] By doing so, Anselm achieves three things precluded by Kierkegaard. First, instead of brooding about them, he shows those emotions in action, linked with and checked by an intellectual search. Second, he contrasts them with the tranquility of mind of the other interlocutor, namely, himself; it is this presence of a more mature person that prevents Boso from being completely overwhelmed by them. Third, he does not permit them to have the last word, but overcomes them in Boso's final joy, a joy mediated, as we have seen, by insights into reasons. It would no doubt be interesting to compare the dramaturgy and dialectics of fear and reassurance in *Cur Deus homo* with the one in Anselm's first Meditation, the *Meditation to Bring about Fear (Meditatio ad concitandum timorem)*, which starts with an almost dramatic *"Terret me vita mea"* ("My life frightens me"),[88] and employs a similar, still richer vocabulary of fear, trembling, and despair (*terrere, terror, terribilis, terrificus, horridus, taedere, tremere, plorare, desperare, timere, pertimescere*) that is then abruptly overcome by the appeasing "sweet name" of Jesus.[89]

As a matter of fact, Anselm's first meditation seems no less to reflect the course of *Cur Deus homo* than his third, more famous *Meditation on Human Redemption* (*Meditatio redemptionis humanae*). While the latter chiefly resumes the arguments developed in *Cur Deus homo* and thereby highlights its rational side, Anselm's first meditation captures the development of Boso's emotional states in the dialogue.

A rationalist, Anselm's example shows us, need not be blind to emotions; on the contrary. He knows that the way of reason is risky and that we have to be thankful for a faith that guarantees emotional stability and prevents us from being swallowed by emotions of fear, anxiety, and despair (which nevertheless belong to the way of reason). He furthermore holds that our mind is made for enjoying sweetness and that the most reasonable thing is also the sweetest.

III.

We have seen that Anselm's awareness of the importance of emotional states does not endanger his rationalism, but rather enriches it. But how do the many appeals to God that we find in the Anselmian corpus relate to the autonomy of reason?

Immediately after Anselm has decided to satisfy the desire of Boso and his friends to discuss the issue rationally, he appeals to God's help and the prayers of his friends.[90] At the end of the first book he prays again for God's help, "not putting trust in myself but in God."[91] When later he yields a second time to Boso's "importunity" and embarks upon the study of the above-mentioned intricate problem, he proposes thanking God for all that he might be able to show.[92] The last sentence of his work reads: "But if what we think we have rationally discovered is corroborated by the Testimony of Truth, we ought to attribute this not to ourselves but to God, who is blessed throughout all ages. Amen."[93] A particularly revealing passage is the following. After Anselm has claimed that *ratio inevitabilis* ("an inevitable reason") has led us to the conclusion that the divine and human nature must be united in one person, Boso concurs: "The road, fortified on both sides by reason, along which you are leading me is such that I see I cannot depart from it either to the right

or to the left.”⁹⁴ Anselm, however, objects: “It is not I who am leading
you but the one about whom we are speaking, without whom we can do
nothing, and who is our guide wherever we keep to the way of the
truth.”⁹⁵ The passage is revealing because three possible leaders are
mentioned—first, an inevitable reason, second, Anselm himself, third,
Christ. How do they stand in relation to one another?

An immediate consequence of the passage quoted is the identification of necessary truth and Christ (often referred to as *veritas* in the
Middle Ages). We already saw that Anselm identifies God with moral
goodness (*iustitia*): God is no less identical with truth, truth and moral
goodness being both related to *rectitudo*.⁹⁶ Whenever we grasp a truth
(*viam veritatis tenemus*), that is, whenever we follow reason (*via . . . undique
munita ratione*), and particularly whenever we grasp reasons relating to the
divine itself, God and his logos are operating in us. God being the principle of our reason, it is in using our reason rightly that we come closest
to God and in reflecting on the principle of our reason that we fulfill the
possibilities of our finite reason. This does not mean that God interferes
with the normal course of arguments or that he adds something to
them—if an argument is cogent, it is by itself a manifestation of Truth
and thus of God. Therefore, Anselm could conceive the *Proslogion* as a
prayer, and yet this does not signify that his argument already presupposes the existence of God—Anselm was far too subtle a philosopher to
commit such a vulgar *petitio principii*. But after we have demonstrated the
existence of God, we realize intellectually—and not only through faith—
that our activity would not have been possible without the principle of
all being and reasoning, that is, without God. The existence of God is
not a premise of the argument, but God is the ground of all being and
arguing—as the argument itself shows.⁹⁷ Some may regard it as arrogant
to ascribe to God one's own argumentation. But the last sentence of the
work shows that the ascription is only hypothetical—only as long as the
argument can be validated by truth. What is more, this move implies
greater symmetry: it is not Anselm who leads Boso, but Truth that leads
both of them.⁹⁸ This is, of course, not to say that the insight would produce itself independently of Anselm's and Boso's efforts to arrive at it.

One might object that if God's presence in an argument is reduced
to the argument's being true the point is quite trivial. But obviously,

God's presence has to be located on two levels—the one (just discussed) of which is what Frege calls the *third realm.* The other is to do with Frege's *second realm:* the ideas in individual minds, that is, subjective qualities that vary according to the different subjects. There are, indeed, innumerable arguments that have not been discovered by any finite mind; hence, analyzing an argument does not answer the question why there are subjective ideas correlating to it. This question is particularly difficult to answer when someone discovers an argument for the first time. For one cannot force one's way toward an important discovery,[99] and even if a rationalist will always assume that there is a series of secondary causes that explain why a certain discovery was made by a specific individual at a specific time, those causes, if they can ever be found out, can be considered only ex post in the spectator perspective, not by the person discovering the argument herself. The existential question "Why I and not someone else?" remains unsolved for her. The experience is almost universal among those who open up new intellectual horizons that their discoveries came to them as a gift, as a present, as grace. Anselm has described very well how his greatest philosophical insight (no doubt also one of the most momentous in the whole history of philosophy), the ontological proof, impressed itself upon him when he had already given up the hope of finding the one argument "that for its proof required no other save itself."[100] Of course, he discovered his master argument only because he had an idea of what such an argument would look like, and because in writing the *Monologion,* in teaching, and in reflecting, he had prepared his mind for such a search. But it is still significant that he had failed in his search and had decided to ban this project from his thinking so that he might focus on more promising endeavors. Nevertheless the question came to his mind again and again, very much against his will, which proved unable to get rid of it, until "one day, when I was quite worn out with resisting its importunacy, there came to me, in the very conflict of my thoughts, what I had despaired of finding, so that I eagerly grasped the notion which in my distraction I had been rejecting."[101] We see from this passage that not only Boso, but also Anselm had gone through despair, that he had known contrasting emotions as well as thoughts, and that he had been presented with a gift after he had decided to abandon his project. There is an almost miraculous transformation of opposites into each other—in the moment in which he became tired of the resistance against the thought that still tormented him, the argument he had so long sought in vain offered itself to him. The analogy with Boso's (hypothetical) rejection of the gift of Christ's self-sacrifice is striking and demonstrates that in both the *Proslogion* and the *Cur Deus homo* the autonomy of reason is, for the individual who raises himself to it, a gift from God: if it goes along with his willing according to the right norms, it is at the same time an approach to God, an imitation of the Creator.

CHAPTER 10

Interreligious Dialogues during the
Middle Ages and Early Modernity

Ut credat quod tu, nullum ui cogere tempta;
sola quippe potest huc racione trahi.
extorquere potes fidei mendacia frustra:
ipsa fides non ui, set racione venit.
—Petrus Abaelardus, *Carmen ad Astralabium,* 783–86

One of the defining features of religiosity in the contemporary world is
the fact that almost every religious person is confronted, already in
his immediate life-world, with a plurality of religious offers. This is one
of the necessary consequences of globalization—the expansion of our
historical and geographical horizon, the mixing of people through mi-
grations and journeys, the presence of all possible ideas in a global mar-
ketplace, as realized in its most diffuse form by the Internet, renders the
access to alternative religious traditions something natural and even obvious. In modern European history, however, this is something quite

new. Even after the collapse of the religious unity in the Reformation, most European countries remained for political reasons denominationally homogeneous, and also in a denominationally mixed country like Germany, the principle of *cuius regio, eius religio* guaranteed that in most states within the Holy Roman Empire the large majority of the people belonged to one denomination. Of course, in most European countries there was a Jewish minority, but it was often relegated to a ghetto and almost always excluded from full citizen rights. Furthermore, the Jews did not represent for Christians radical religious alterity since their central sacred book, the Old Testament, was part of the Christian canon. This state of affairs lasted until long into the twentieth century—in his recent autobiography,[1] Johannes Hösle described the closed cosmos of a Southern German Catholic village of the 1930s and the 1940s, in which even Protestantism was something only rumored about and an alternative to the Catholic worldview was radically inconceivable.

The social conditions of such a form of religiosity disappeared in the second half of the twentieth century, and the Second Vatican Council was the remarkable theological attempt to deal with the new situation, which rendered the *extra ecclesiam nulla salus* more and more obsolete and even insulting. A complex theology of non-Christian religions developed, which tried to mediate between the claim to absoluteness intrinsic to most religions (certainly to Christianity) and the plurality of religious traditions. Besides the more traditional exclusivist approach, both inclusivist and pluralist theologies of religion were elaborated.[2] The results of these new theological approaches have been both a greater openness to non-Christian religions and a foundering of the religious certainties that characterized Christianity for almost two millennia. The latter process was met with disapproval by many traditional Christians, and sometimes one cannot avoid the impression that the differences between the more traditionally oriented defenders of a religion and the more "liberal" interpreters of the same religion are even sharper and more embittered than those between people belonging to different religions, as long as they are interpreted, on the meta-level, in a somehow analogous way. In any case, one thing is hardly dubious: a responsible religious education in the twenty-first century must address the issue of the existence of different religions in a far more intensive way than it did before. The capacity of interacting with other religions in a way that tries to learn from them without betraying the commitment to certain absolute principles—a commitment that constitutes the essence of religion—will probably be a crucial competence in a globalized, but for the distant future religiously heterogeneous world.

Fortunately, such a capacity need not be developed from scratch. The medieval world was in some aspects religiously more diverse than the world of early modernity—the fact that the Greek tradition was recovered by the Occident partly through the Arab mediation rendered Islam in the Middle Ages a far greater intellectual challenge for Christians than it was from the sixteenth century onward. (The military successes of the Ottoman Empire were not matched by comparable intellectual innovations, and the scientific revolution certainly loosened the relation of Europe to the non-Christian world.) Not only did Christian medieval theologians and philosophers deal in long treatises with the other two non-Christian monotheist religions, they used the literary genre of the dialogue to show how an intellectually and morally satisfying intellectual encounter with other religions ought to take place. Of course, these dialogues antecede two of the great challenges that profoundly transformed Christianity—the emergence of modern natural science and of modern historical thinking.[3] None of the authors I discuss in the following, not even the historically and philologically erudite Jean Bodin, has the broad and precise knowledge that history of religion and historical theology acquired about other religions as well as about the development of one's own tradition from the eighteenth century onward. Still, I do think that much can be learned from these dialogues. I focus on both the pragmatics of the interreligious exchange (I) as well as—very shortly and superficially—some of the main arguments (II) one can find in those four works that probably are the most original and rich interreligious dialogues from the twelfth to the sixteenth century—Peter Abelard's *Collationes* or *Dialogus inter philosophum, Judaeum et Christianum* (*Dialogue between a Philosopher, a Jew and a Christian*), Ramon Llull's *Llibre del gentil e dels tres savis* (*Book of the Pagan and the Three Wise Men*), Nicholas of Cusa's *De pace fidei* (*On Peace in Faith*), and Jean Bodin's *Colloquium heptaplomeres de abditis rerum sublimium arcanis* (*Colloquium of the Seven about Secrets of the Sublime*).[4]

226 A Rationalist's Tradition

Those four dialogues, which I compare and contrast in the following, are connected with each other: even if it is not clear whether Llull knew Abelard[5]—I regard it as unlikely—Cusanus must have studied Llull's dialogue,[6] and Bodin reacts explicitly, I think, to Cusanus's inter-religious dialogue. In Abelard's dialogue the author is asked in a dream vision to function as judge in a controversy between a Jew, a Christian, and a philosopher not bound by any religious faith, but of Ismaelitic descent (I would not exclude that Abelard might have had in mind one of the Muslim rationalists à la Ibn Tufayl[7]); he does not give any judgment, but listens to a dialogue first between the Jew and the philosopher, then between the Christian and the philosopher. (I do not share the opinion of some that a third part containing a discussion between the Jew and the Christian was ever planned.) Llull's dialogue brings a gentile who despairs out of fear of death in contact with three wise men, namely, a Jew, a Christian, and a Muslim, one of whom—it is not said who—in the first part of the work convinces the gentile of the existence of God and the immortality of the soul; his great pleasure, however, is transformed into even greater despair, when he is asked to convert to one of the three monotheistic religions since he now faces eternal damnation if he does not make the right choice; and so first the Jew, then the Christian, then finally the Muslim present the arguments in favor of their own religion. Even if the gentile at the end declares that he has made his choice, the wise men do not want to hear it so that they may continue to discuss among each other which of the three religions is the true one. Cusanus's work describes a vision in which the hero, easily identifiable with Cusanus himself, is brought to heaven, where he listens to the complaints of angels before God about religiously motivated violence: God, at the recommendation of the Word, asks his angels to bring before him philosophical representatives of the various nations (and thus religions): before the Word, they discuss their religious differences and are then sent back with the order to gather in Jerusalem to agree on one common religion. Finally, Bodin's dialogue, by far the longest, richest, and formally most complex of the works, consists of six books in which seven persons converse first on physical and metaphysical, then on religious matters in the house of a Venetian gentleman, Paulus Coronaeus. The host is a Catholic; his guests are the Lutheran mathematician Fridericus Podamicus, the Calvinist jurist Antonius Curtius, the old Jew Salomon Barcassius, the Italian Octavius Fagnola, who converted to Islam after having been captured by Muslim pirates (he reveals himself as Muslim only in the middle of the fourth book), the defender of a rational theology (closer to Plato than Aristotle) Diegus Toralba, and finally Hieronymus Senamus, also not bound by any historical religion, but defending all of them on the basis of a negative theology and of a skepticism reminiscent of Montaigne, after whom I think he could have been modeled.

I.

The choice of the form in which a philosopher communicates his thought determines far more of its content than historians of philosophy usually realize. The literary dialogue, for example,[8] allows the author to hold back his own opinions in a way that is not feasible in a treatise—at least as long as he himself is not an interlocutor in the dialogue; and even when he is, a distancing from oneself is possible. It has often been debated how Petrus Abaelardus—I mean now not the author, but the person of the *Collationes* asked to function as *iudex,* who clearly has to be distinguished from the real person who wrote the dialogue as well as, albeit to a lesser degree, from the narrator[9]—relates to the *Christianus,* who develops so many of Abelard's tenets, and it has been rightly remarked that the two are consciously distinguished by Abelard the author: the *Christianus* is that side of the real person who identified with the Christian tradition in which he was brought up; Abaelardus, however, is the more complex figure who could lean back from his own religious background and confront Christianity with the Jewish religion as well as with a philosophy not committed to any revelation.[10] Indeed, the *Philosophus,* too, mirrors aspects of the real Abelard, and perhaps this is one of the functions of the nocturnal, dreamlike vision within which the dialogue takes place—namely, to show that at least two of the interlocutors and the *iudex* are facets of Abelard's complex personality.

By rendering unusual hermeneutical efforts necessary, the dialogue engages the reader in a particularly challenging way—even if every text constitutes an invitation to a dialogue between the author and the readers, dialogical texts usually provoke a more interesting dialogue between the author and the readers than, for example, essays. This appeal to the autonomy of the reader can even be increased when the work remains a fragment. Thus a distinctive feature of Abelard's dialogue is its unfinished character. While the traditional view was that Abelard was prevented by his death in 1142 from completing the work written in his last years at Cluny, newer studies have made it more and more likely that the work was written in the 1120s or 1130s.[11] Of course, this poses the question of why Abelard left the work unfinished—or, better, whether the work is really unfinished or whether Abelard consciously decided to break it off. There are indeed arguments for the latter view (which would make of Abelard somehow a medieval predecessor of Rodin)[12]—by suppressing the *iudex*'s final judgment, Abelard could have deliberately chosen an aposiopesis for pedagogical reasons. "In its present form, the *Dialogue* thrusts the reader into the magisterial role: the three interlocutors have presented their cases; those open to learn from cross-cultural discussions must decide the question for themselves."[13] A less radical and perhaps more likely interpretation of the abrupt end is that "Abelard decided to bring the work to a provisional conclusion, leaving it open to him to continue it at some later date if he chose."[14]

However this specific question may be solved, there is little doubt that most dialogues, just by proposing different stances, oblige readers to take a position themselves. This is at least the case when we have a dialogue between partners who are more or less on an equal footing or, better, where the superiority of one of the interlocutors is not as evident as in those dialogues between a teacher and a pupil that constitute the majority of the medieval philosophical dialogues. Klaus Jacobi has rightly remarked that a first rough classification of medieval philosophical dialogues is that of dialogues between teachers and pupils and interreligious dialogues between Christians, Jews, pagans, and philosophers, even if there are transitions between the two forms—notably in Gilbertus Crispinus's *Disputatio Christiani cum Gentili*.[15] Among the four dialogues I want to focus on, certainly Cusanus's *De pace fidei* comes closest to a dialogue between teacher and pupil—for in it not only Peter and Paul, but also the *Verbum caro factum* speaks, and obviously with a voice no less authoritative than that of the normal medieval teacher. Still, in the dialogue beginning in chapter 3 there are seventeen other interlocutors, all of whom are humans, who are more or less on an equal footing with each other (not, however, with the Word and the saints). Naturally, it is of extreme importance to distinguish between those dialogues in which the equality of the partners is only formal and those in which it is essential—that is, between those dialogues where the author clearly opts for the position of one of the interlocutors, even if all are treated by him with respect and they also deal with each other with courtesy, and those where the author does not seem to side with anybody or seems to grant every side a partial truth. Sometimes it may be hermeneutically difficult to find out what the author's intention really was; but since in the cases of all of our authors—differently from Plato, whose dialogues, however, are usually dialogues among radically unequal persons—we have several works that are nondialogical, we are not in too difficult a position. Thus it is obvious to anybody who has looked at, for example, the *Llibre de contemplació en Déu* that Llull did not harbor any doubt about the superiority of the arguments developed by the Christian—despite the fact that in his dialogue the intermediate position of the Christian between the Jew and the Muslim does not signal any special value of Christianity and that the gentile's choice of one of the three monotheistic religions remains secret since the three wise men do not want to know it. Bodin, on the other hand, who in his life wavered between Catholicism, rational theology, perhaps the Reformation—even if the person in Geneva may well have been a namesake of him—and Judaism,[16] does not seem far from the spirit of Gotthold Ephraim Lessing's ring parable in *Nathan der Weise* (*Nathan the Wise*) and even from modern pluralism: the first, second, and sixth books of the *Heptaplomeres* end with the playing of music, and the fourth book begins with a discussion of harmony—suggesting probably that the plurality of religions is wanted by God, insofar as it contributes to the complexity of the harmony of the universe. "I think harmony is produced when many sounds can be blended; but when they cannot be blended, one conquers the other as the sound enters the ear, and the dissonance offends the delicate senses of wiser men,"[17] says Octavius. Or as Toralba puts it: "These discussions would offer no purpose or pleasure unless they took lustre from opposing arguments and reasons."[18] On the other hand, it fits the idea that also this principle is opposed: Senamus thinks that a state without wicked people would be happier than one with both good and wicked ones, and with his usual sarcasm he asks whether there are civil wars even among angels.[19]

As we have seen, the dialogue to which the author invites his reader depends also on the type of the dialogue in which the interlocutors created by him engage. Indeed, literary dialogues are not only aiming at a real future dialogue between the author and his interpreters, they represent a past dialogue, either real or, in most cases, fictitious. Even where a real dialogue may have occurred in the past, the laws of the genre oblige the author to transcend the brute factuality and to idealize it, albeit to varying degrees. Bodin's *Colloquium* comes closest to a real-life dialogue, but this contributes to the lack of concentration of the work, its repetitions and digressions. We have to distinguish from the question of whether there was a real-life basis for the literary dialogue—a question that transcends the literary work—the immanent literary question whether the text pretends to represent a real dialogue or not. Of our four dialogues, for example, only two—Llull's and Bodin's—claim to depict such a real dialogue; Abelard's and Cusanus's dialogues pretend to represent dreams or visions within which dialogues occurred; the ontological status of the dialogue partners is thus, according to the literary text itself, somehow deficient. Even if Llull's and Bodin's texts depict real dialogues, the introduction to the prologue of Llull's *Llibre* clearly shows that he wants the reader to recognize the fictional character of his dialogue, whose frame story is reminiscent of fairy tales. Bodin, on the contrary, wants to convey the impression that his dialogue really took place—the characters are clearly individualized, far more than in Abelard, whose characters are types, but still with some psychologically interesting peculiarities (the types of Llull and Cusanus lack even peculiar traits). The central problems of the dialogue are only slowly and tactfully approached, and the narrator, who claims to have listened to the dialogues as *kōphon prosōpon,* presents himself shortly in the letter to N.T., within which the dialogue is narrated. The letter vies with travel narratives (imitated also in Thomas More's *Utopia*), but since travels constitute an important part of the life experience of the sixteenth century, this only enhances the realistic atmosphere of the dialogue.

What are the formal features of the exchange among the interlocutors within a dialogue? Each of our dialogues presupposes, first and foremost, that the encounter between religions should not occur in the medium of violence. Even if the later Llull defended the idea of the Crusades, his early work, thus the *Llibre del gentil e dels tres savis,* is committed to the idea of peaceful exchange between religions;[20] Cusanus's dialogue is an explicit reaction to the fall of Constantinople,[21] and Bodin's work is an attempt to propose an alternative to the madness of the religious wars of the sixteenth century. Venice is praised at the beginning of the *Colloquium* because of its liberty, which is contrasted with the civil wars of other states,[22] and the work ends with a sharp condemnation of the use of force in religious matters, recently mainly against Jews and Muslims in Spain and Portugal, and with a general agreement on religious tolerance.[23] Even if in Bodin there is no longer the hope that people can come to a consensus in substantial religious matters, there still is an agreement on how one has to deal with persons with whose religion one does not agree. The renouncement of violence is already presupposed by the form of the dialogue: for a real dialogue is different from a strategic bargaining, which may well usher in violence, since it is based on the sincere desire to learn from each other and to arrive together at the truth. For that, certain procedures have to be agreed upon and respected: when in Llull's dialogue first the Christian, then the Jew and the Christian want to contradict the Muslim (who in the first case had ascribed the Christian an interpretation of the Trinity that he had rejected before), the pagan interrupts them—it is not their turn to make objections; only he, the pagan, is allowed to do so.[24]

Nevertheless, the authors of our dialogues are realistic enough to know that power relations remain important in the real dialogues that occur among humans, that particularly in interreligious controversies people tend to hurt each other and that the willingness to subject oneself to the demands of truth is rarely unconditional. Probably Cusanus's dialogue is the most naïve in this respect—since the dialogue presents an absolute, divine authority that cannot be challenged without impiety, Cusanus might have thought to be allowed to abstract from power relations among humans. But the reality of human dialogues is that no one has direct access to the insights of the divine Word, and this leads almost necessarily to differences that are hard to reconcile. Furthermore, there is a certain naiveté in Cusanus's text not so much because it inevitably anthropomorphizes God, who has to be asked by the archangel and the Word to act; the naiveté consists far more in the fact that the *frame* of his dialogue already presupposes the *truth* of Christianity—even if in the course of the dialogue he tries to give rational arguments for the Christian position. Still, this frame is responsible for the fact that an explicit consensus is achieved only in this dialogue—at least in heaven since its implementation in the human council in Jerusalem remains a task.

In contrast, the place where the dialogue described by Llull is supposed to occur is characterized by absolute neutrality—it is a forest with all the properties of the traditional *locus amoenus* (familiar, with a different function, from both Plato's *Phaedrus* and Cicero's *De legibus*), but at the same time allegorically ennobled by the presence of Lady Intelligence and five trees whose flowers stand for virtues, sins, and vices. In this forest, which the power structures of the city do not seem to penetrate, the interaction between the three wise men is determined by complete symmetry, manifested, for example, by the fact that Llull often writes "one of the wise men said"[25]—it is not relevant who takes the initiative. In order to honor the others, nobody wants to begin to expose his religion first—it is the gentile who finally chooses according to a chronological criterion.[26] Of course, there is an initial asymmetry between the three wise men on the one hand and the gentile on the other, but it is somehow inverted at the end, when the gentile not only is able to sum up all the arguments he had patiently listened to,[27] but also shows such a profound religiosity that the three wise men feel humbled by him.[28] A particularly beautiful trait is that the three wise men at the end ask—and grant—forgiveness from—and to—each other for any disrespectful word they might have used against the others' religions.[29]

Certainly the neutrality is insofar apparent, as the method proposed by Lady Intelligence is Llull's specific combinatory method, the so-called Ars, which makes most of his works so tiresome to read. No author can abstract from his own standpoint, and perhaps Abelard is more honest when he makes himself the judge, even if as a Christian he is party to the controversy—particularly since he then leaves the judgment to the reader. It is remarkable that the argumentative styles of the two parts of his dialogue are quite different—the dialogue between the Jew and the philosopher is characterized by less freedom of speech and by a greater inequality than the dialogue between the Christian and the philosopher.

True, in the second part the philosopher who had been the intellectually superior in the first one is in turn led himself by a superior mind, but despite the intellectual asymmetry in both parts the relation between the two interlocutors becomes far more agreeable in the second part—the interlocutors listen with the intent to learn from each other; the Christian, for example, takes the philosopher's objections seriously.[30] Abelard makes it clear that the arrogance of the philosopher as well as secular fears consciously and subliminally limit the freedom of expression of the Jew,[31] while there are no such obstacles in the second discourse. The philosopher revokes his remarks about the madness of the Christians—they were only intended to provoke a frank discussion and are therefore forgiven,[32] but he continues to speak about the Jews in derogatory terms, even as animals.[33] Also, Llull's Jew complains about the fate of his nation;[34] only Cusanus does not deal with the political inequality of the Jews in the Middle Ages, and Cusanus even ascribes to his Peter an aggressive anti-Judaic remark—not too surprisingly given Cusanus's own policies against the Jews.[35] Bodin, on the other hand, who was probably of Jewish descent, has an awareness not inferior to Abelard's of the fears of the Jews. But while the Jew in Abelard is unable to overcome them, in Bodin's *Colloquium* he succeeds in doing so—thanks to the generous encouragement of his host.

In Bodin's work the place of the discourse is the house of one of the interlocutors, but Bodin does much to convince the reader that this fact does not diminish the neutrality of the place. First, the house is a microcosm in which one can find not only all possible books and instruments, but also the pantotheca where in boxes models of almost all basic entities of the world are kept. Second, the host is a man of exquisite character— a man seriously committed at the same time to Catholicism,[36] curiosity, and religious tolerance (possibly modeled after the great Cardinal Gasparo Contarini), of great kindness to his guests whose religious feelings he never hurts (in contrast particularly to the irascible Lutheran Fridericus) and whom he invites again and again to speak freely. His own contributions are not intellectually overwhelming, and he does not speak as much as others, but it is he who gently directs the flow of the conversation and eliminates obstacles where they emerge. One of the most touching passages is when he asks his friends to pray for him.[37] The move is also an astute one because he wants to show that it is pious to pray to the saints; but it is far more than that and contrasts with Fridericus's brutal rejection of Salomon's remark that the Jews pray for the non-Jews.[38] The Muslim Octavius thanks Coronaeus for all the kindness he has done to him—an apostate from Catholicism,[39] and again this contrasts with Curtius's condescension toward the poor Muslims[40] and Fridericus's vulgar comments.[41] When Coronaeus mingles artificial apples with real ones, offers both to his guests, and Fridericus bites into an artificial one, Coronaeus gives him and all the others a subtle lesson—to be more careful with our truth claims regarding complex questions, if even our senses can so easily be deceived.[42] Even if we cannot be sure that Bodin regarded himself as a Catholic when he wrote the *Heptaplomeres* and although it is obvious that, if he did, he lacked the religious certainty of a Coronaeus, one feels Bodin's veneration and even love for this type of person. Probably Bodin's sympathy is not diminished by the fact that Coronaeus, in practice the most tolerant of all interlocutors, in theory accepts the doctrine of the Catholic Church that people ought to be forced to go to public religious services.[43] For Bodin is well aware of the contradictions that belong to human nature—the aggressive Fridericus is theoretically more tolerant than Coronaeus[44]—and practice counts for him more than theory.

Few passages in the *Colloquium* are as intense as when the interlocutors finally begin to talk about religion. Only at the end of the third book the question is put "whether it is proper for a good man to talk about religion,"[45] and when after the already-mentioned discussion on harmony the interlocutors finally face the issue, it proves difficult to motivate Salomon, the Jew, to take part in it. On the one hand, people had agreed that even the crassest superstition is better than the lack of religion,[46] and Salomon is afraid that a conversation about religion may uproot a person's piety without replacing it with something better. He is seconded by Senamus, who on the one hand defends Aristotle, even when there are strong empirical arguments against his theories,[47] but on the other hand is the most skeptically inclined mind and just because of that supports the traditional religion, whatever it may be: "Even if a new religion is better or truer than an old religion I think it should not be proclaimed."[48] But even more important than the altruistic regard for other persons' mental stability is Salomon's fear, rooted in historical experience, that such a discussion may lead to hatred against the Jews. Therefore, Salomon remains silent even after Fridericus explains that only public religious discussions are dangerous, not private ones. Salomon's restraint is understandable, particularly since Fridericus's remarks, comparing him with a viper, are insulting and show that while he wants to convert Salomon to Christianity, he is not at all willing to put his own faith at stake. It is in this situation that Coronaeus declares: "I pledge to Salomon that he will bring to all of us the greatest knowledge and delight through his speech, and nothing will be more gratifying to me than for each among us to enjoy the greatest freedom in speaking about religion."[49] Salomon still wavers and mentions very critically the oldest dialogue between the representatives of two monotheistic religions, Justin's *Pros Tryphona Iudaion dialogos* (*Dialogue with Tryphon the Jew*): "I remember reading a dialogue of Justin Martyr with Trypho the Jew, whom he presents so untutored and foolish that I was annoyed with the work and the foolishness of the writer. Indeed the author decrees victory, just as the braggart warrior standing in the theater." He mentions furthermore his old age that makes it almost impossible for him to change his religious allegiance and continues to be afraid that such religious discussion may destroy his friendship with his interlocutors. Coronaeus reassures him again; Salomon still hesitates, and other interlocutors share his concern that the discussion of religions may endanger public peace. One has to mention that Coronaeus keeps his pledge: when Salomon decides to open his heart and, after further withdrawals, finally raises the sharpest objections against Catholicism in the most vehement form, the other guests become silent because they feel that Coronaeus is hurt; but the gentle host manages to restrain himself and only says: "I thought I would remove the charges and complaints of Salomon, but I think I should defer to another time, lest I seem to have hampered anyone's liberty of speaking."[50]

II.

Far more important than the political arguments against an interreligious dialogue are the epistemological ones—and with their analysis we leave the pragmatic and enter the theoretical level of the works. Toralba regards faith as something distinct from both knowledge and opinion;[51] and while Curtius and Coronaeus think that there is a moral duty to try to convert people belonging to other religions, it is Senamus who asks the decisive question: "Who will be the arbiter of such a controversy?"[52] Fridericus's answer is of touching naiveté: "Christ the Lord! For He said that if three were gathered together in His name He would be in their midst." As Senamus objects, just this is the point of disagreement between Christians and the other monotheistic religions whether Christ is God or not. Curtius—whose level of argument as well as courtesy of manners is far superior to that of Fridericus, as John Calvin's to that of Martin Luther—says something more valid, when he asks for "suitable witnesses and references." Still, Senamus says: "It is doubtful what witnesses are reliable, what records are trustworthy, what bondsmen are secure in determining a certain and sure faith." The next to offer a criterion is Coronaeus, and he is as naïve as Fridericus: "The church will be the judge." It is not hard for Senamus to react. "An even more serious problem is what the true church is? The Jews say that their church is the true one, and the Mohammedans deny it. On the other hand, the Christian makes a claim for his church, and the pagans in India say their church ought to have preference over all others because of its age. And so the very learned Cardinal Nicholas of Cusa wrote he must represent nothing about the Christian church, but by positing the foundation that the church rests on its union with Christ, he assumes that which is the chief point of debate."[53] And indeed Salomon claims that the Hebrews are the one true church of God, while Fridericus limits the truth of this statement to the time before Christ, and Octavius avers that the New Testament has been corrupted. The rationalist Toralba introduces the criterion of the wise men, but it is open to doubt who is wise, as Senamus states. And when finally God himself is claimed to be the final authority Senamus agrees: "Necessarily, the religion which has God as its author is the true religion, but the difficulty is in discerning whether He is the author of this religion or that religion. This is the task and difficulty." Nor do miracles and oracles help, particularly since they can be done and given also by magicians. Neither is the duration of a religion a good criterion.[54]

In fact, the *Heptaplomeres* does not end at all with religious agreement. The interlocutors embrace each other, but decide to hold "no other conversation about religions, although each one defended his own religion with the supreme sanctity of his life"[55]—in sharp contrast to Llull's *Llibre,* at whose only apparently open end the three wise men decide to continue their discussions until they come to an agreement.[56] What are the reasons for this failure—*if* it is a failure, for the civility and friendship of Bodin's interlocutors are the more remarkable, the less they agree substantially?[57] I think at least three factors explain it. First, Bodin makes it clear again and again that not all interlocutors are willing to distance themselves from their faith. Salomon states this, as we have seen, openly; Coronaeus no less;[58] and even if Fridericus and Curtius do not say it explicitly, one feels that the same applies to them. Toralba is the only one who claims explicitly that he is willing to be convinced by better arguments—adding, of course, that it would be a mark of folly to agree too quickly with other people.[59] Second, the interlocutors commit again and again fallacies and circles—Bodin wants to show his intelligent readers how difficult it indeed is to avoid circularities in dealing with religious matters.[60] The aggressiveness with which his interlocutors sometimes claim that the other's religion does not even merit refutation[61] and praise their own belongs to this context. Third and last, Bodin seems to have doubts with regard to the capacity of human reason to settle the questions at stake. Often enough, not only the Old Testament (including Deutero-Isaiah),[62] but even the same facts can be interpreted in different ways—the suffering of the Jewish people can be seen as punishment or as privilege,[63] Jesus' forgiving of sins as a mark of divinity or as a sign of detestable arrogance.[64] It is not clear to me whether Bodin accepts reason as a last standard or sees in the assumption of this standard, too, a form of circularity. Toralba prefers arguments to authorities, which would not be accepted, for example, by Epicureans,[65] but Curtius defends fideism,[66] and Fridericus goes even as far as to say that certain contradictions are only perceived by people without a pure heart[67] and that God is incomprehensible by reason.[68] Even if it is clear that with such statements the Protestants immunize themselves against any criticism, this does not yet entail that Bodin shares Toralba's rationalist optimism; he is at least fascinated by Senamus's skepticism.

Abelard, Llull, and Cusanus, on the other hand, share a common faith in reason. The three of them believe in a possible agreement between religions and know very well that such an agreement can be achieved only on the basis of reason. The main difference between their works and Bodin's dialogue in my eyes consists not in the fact that a "deism" committed to reason alone in the sixteenth century had become a full-fledged alternative to religions based on revelation; for the philosopher in Abelard comes close to the position of deism, and so does the unnamed wise man who develops the common basis of all three monotheistic religions in the first book of Llull's *Llibre*. Still, probably Abelard and certainly Llull believe that a rational religion is not an alternative to Christianity—Christianity for them is *the* rational religion, at least insofar as the rational religion is willing to render explicit what is implied in it. It is not an accident that the main speaker of the first book of Llull's work at the same time belongs to one of the monotheistic religions—he could never have grasped the thought that the rational religion could be true and all the historical religions false. In Cusanus the situation is somehow different because, as we have seen, the frame of the book already presupposes a Christian setting. Still, the bulk of the arguments used by the Word, Peter, and Paul are based on reason. Scripture is almost absent in their debates—Cusanus identifies like Llull the religion of reason with Christianity. One could say that for Abelard with limitations, and for Llull and Cusanus completely, Christianity—interpreted in a certain way—and the religion of reason coincide, and this is indeed a difference from Bodin with his Toralba. For Toralba is inimical to Christianity; he regards the doctrine of the Trinity and Christology as inconsistent theories and is not familiar with interpretations of them that may be compatible with reason or even follow from it. Christianity had radically changed in the course of the sixteenth century—the synthesis of Platonism and Catholicism that one can find also in Marsilio Ficino had collapsed: with the Tridentinum, Catholicism had become more anti-philosophical, and philosophy had become more distant from the traditional religion.

But as important as it is, this is not the most relevant difference. More significant is the fact that in the intellectual universes of Abelard, Llull, and Cusanus there is no intellectual corresponding to Senamus. His presence in Bodin is important not so much because it increases the number of the interlocutors, but because it endangers the project of the identification of one specific historic religion, however subtly interpreted, as the religion of reason—for the plurality of religions is then only mirrored by the plurality of reasons. This might seem an attractive position; but the price for it is very high—as legal positivism is the necessary consequence of the demise of natural law, so a religious authority unchallengeable by reason must be the result of reason giving up its position as final arbiter.

The three earlier authors, as mentioned before, are more or less religious rationalists—they think that reason is the supreme arbiter even in divine matters and that we can come through reason alone to decide what the true religion is; faith and authorities are subordinated to reason. It is hard to see how an interreligious dialogue could otherwise be possible—each side would appeal to its own faith, and the dialogue would fail as it does in Bodin. All three authors are aware of the fact that religious habits and traditions are extremely important and that people are unwilling to shed them; still, they insist that they are able, and more: that they ought to do so, when they are convinced by reason. Abelard's philosopher complains: "There is a love naturally present within all people for their own race and for those with whom they are brought up, which makes them shrink with horror from anything which is said against their faith; and, turning what they have become accustomed to into part of their nature, as adults they doggedly hold whatever they learnt as children, and before they are able to grasp the things that are said, they affirm that they believe them . . . For it is amazing that . . . about faith . . . there is no progress, but rather the leaders of society and ordinary folk, peasants and the educated are considered to have the very same views, and the person who is said to be strongest in faith is the one who does not go beyond the common understanding of people."[69]

Certainly the philosopher is not identical with Abelard, whose epistemological position does not appear to be completely rationalistic—at least in some of his other books. In the *Collationes,* however, the Christian does not really contradict the philosopher's rationalistic creed: "We do not yield to their [i.e., of the philosophers who converted to Christianity] authority in the sense that we fail to discuss rationally what they have said before we accept it. Otherwise we would cease to be philosophers—that is to say, if we put aside rational enquiry and made great use of arguments from authority."[70] For the Christian objects only that certain things may appear rational, even if they are not,[71] and this is not denied by the philosopher who only adds that also authorities err and that there are authorities contradicting each other so that it is reason that must determine what an authority is. The Christian replies that "none of our writers who has good judgment prohibits the faith from being investigated and discussed by argument, nor is it reasonable to accept what is doubtful, unless the reason why it should be accepted is first proposed."[72] And he recognizes that the discussion with a person who does not accept the authority of Holy Scripture can be done only on the basis of reason. "No one can be countered except on the basis of what he agrees to; he will not be convinced save through what he accepts . . . I know that what Gregory and our other learned writers, what even Christ himself and Moses declare, is irrelevant to you: their pronouncements will not compel faith in you."[73] When Abaelardus at the beginning had said that the fact that the philosopher was not obliged to defend any authority made his position easier in the debate, since he could be attacked less, however, he had added that he therefore should not consider it anything great if he appeared to be the strongest in the debate.[74] The commitment to an authority may be a burden, but if it proves possible to defend this authority, as the Christian succeeds in doing, the intellectual achievement is the more impressive. Later the Jew inverts the argument: the Christian is favored by being armed with two horns—the two Testaments—instead of one.[75]

Llull is certainly the most rationalistic of the three—he usually opposes faith to reason in the same way as Plato had opposed *orthē doxa* to *epistēmē*,[76] and he does not know the subtle difference between *ratio* and *intellectus* that characterizes Cusanus's epistemology (even if, probably for pedagogical reasons, it does not play a role in *De pace fidei*). In his dialogue, already before the appearance of the gentile, the three wise men had decided to aim at one religion corresponding to the one God and thus to discuss their faiths according to the methodological principles taught them by Lady Intelligence; for since they could not agree on appealing to authorities, they would have to use necessary reasons.[77] After the conversion of the gentile, one wise man proposes that one should reassume the earlier task, but another objects that humans are so rooted in the faith to which they and their ancestors belong that it would be impossible to change their religious opinions through disputations; they despise arguments aimed at shaking their faith and say that they want to live and die in the faith of their parents. But the first wise man insists that it belongs to the nature of truth to be more strongly rooted in the soul than falsehood; and he avers that there is a religious duty to try to find out what the truth regarding God is. So they agree on hour, place, and method, both of dealing with each other and of arguing, for their next meetings.[78] An expression of Llull's rationalism is that the three wise men do not even want to know how the gentile chose since this could endanger the reliance on reason alone of their discussion.[79] What counts for them is not which religion the gentile chose, but which religion he *ought* to have chosen. Still, Llull does not at all deny the emotional aspects of a conversion, which on the contrary are depicted very well—the gentile weeps both after his conversion to monotheism in general and after his conversion to one of the three monotheistic religions.[80] Llull speaks in this context also about grace and enlightenment—but divine grace is effused when a person is enabled by reason to grasp and internalize salvific truths.

Cusanus's view on the historically realized religions is even more realistic than Abelard's and Llull's. In the introductory dialogue before God an archangel describes the human condition as such that most people are obliged to work hard and to obey the political power. They do not have the possibility to think for themselves, and therefore God sent them prophets to instruct them. But the people did not think to hear the prophets, but in them God himself; in general, human nature tends to regard habit as truth.[81] The central idea of Cusanus is to show that all religions partake, albeit in different degrees, in the one true religion; they have different rites, which should be kept in their difference, for the desire for too much homogeneity is an obstacle to peace[82] and diversity may well increase devotion.[83]

In fact, this is a great difference between Llull and Cusanus: Llull wants to convert everybody to the Catholic Church because he harbors no doubt that all non-Catholics will be damned, while Cusanus seems to accept a plurality of religions with their different rites and customs, as long as they accept the basic tenets of a Platonic form of Christianity. If the contents of the various religions are rightly interpreted, they do not really contradict each other. Cusanus seems to grant that Christianity, too, has to be interpreted in a right way; there are wrong interpretations of the doctrine of the Trinity, and Cusanus himself dislikes the misleading terms Father, Son, and Holy Spirit.[84] Cusanus's approach is clearly inclusivist—in every religion there are hints of the religious truths revealed in Christianity since the basic tenets of Christianity are implied in every religion.[85] For a radical metaphysical monist as Cusanus, an exclusivist, necessarily dualist position cannot be acceptable; somehow he must share the conviction of Abelard that there is no doctrine so false that it does not contain some truth.[86] Without doubt, inclusivism has certain paternalistic traits—it presupposes that the interpreter has the superior stance and that he is able to understand the representatives of other traditions better than they do themselves. When Cusanus writes in his sermon CXXVI that every Jew believes in Christ, whether he wants it or not,[87] one thinks of Karl Rahner's "anonymous Christians"—and of the rage it provoked among non-Christians.[88]

When Abelard, Llull, Cusanus, and Bodin (in the character of Toralba) oppose reasons to authorities, what do they mean by "reason"? On the one hand, both Abelard's philosopher and Toralba oppose natural law and natural religion to the law and religion based on revelation and demanding the fulfillment of rites that cannot be deduced from reason (for example, circumcision). It is characteristic that neither of them appeals to pure reason alone, as Kant would do; both accept the biblical narrative and identify their position with the religion of the patriarchs before Moses. "It is clear that before the actual giving of the law and the observances of the sacraments laid down by law there were many people who made do with natural law, which consists in loving God and one's neighbor, who cultivated justice and lived lives which were most acceptable to God: for example, Abel, Noah and his children, and also Abraham, Lot, and Melchisedech, whom even your law records and greatly commends."[89] Similarly, Toralba says: "I only conclude that Adam and his son Abel had been instructed in the best religion, and after them Seth, Enoch, Methusaleh up to Noah who worshipped in great holiness, to the exclusion of all others, that eternal and only true God, the Builder and Parent of all things and the great Architect of the whole world. Therefore I believe this religion is not only the oldest but also the best of all."[90] According to Toralba, law of nature and natural religion (*naturae lex et naturalis religio*) are sufficient for attaining salvation so that the Mosaic rites are not necessary.[91] Even in his defense of the Decalogue Toralba gives a "natural" justification—the Ten Commandments correspond to the ten celestial orbs.[92] Not revelation, but cosmo-theology grounds morals.

But the opposition to authority and factual rites does not yet clarify what reason is and how it proceeds. Our authors have quite different concepts of reason. Abelard's dialogue differs from the others because it does not confront the Jew with the Christian, but the philosopher with both of them; and the second *collatio* deals almost completely with questions of ethics (including the metaphysics of ethics and the theodicy problem), ignoring the doctrines of Trinity and incarnation. The starting point of this *collatio* is the human desire for happiness; the definition of "good" and the determination of the highest good are the main subjects of the debate. The horizon of the debate is thus what Kant would call "ethico-theology." As the Christian says: "You usually call it 'ethics,' that is 'morals,' and we 'divinity.' We call it thus because of what it aims to grasp—God; you name it from that through which the journey there is made—good behaviour, which you call 'virtues.'"[93] The central idea is that ethics can be elaborated convincingly only if including an eschatological dimension. In this process, however, the Christian rejects popular ideas about heaven and hell as places. God is not local, heaven and hell should not be interpreted so either; in general, the biblical assertions about hell should not be understood literally.[94] While Abelard defends Christ's physical ascension, he insists that it was done only to strengthen our faith, not to increase Christ's glory, and that in any case the statements about Christ being seated at the right hand of the Father are only metaphoric.[95]

If Abelard's dialogue can be called "ethico-theological," Llull's dialogue is certainly "onto-theological." The basis of all his arguments, many of which are repetitive, is the ontological proof.[96] This is an a priori proof, and such a proof is needed by Llull if he wants to rely on reason alone. As in Anselm, the ontological proof is interpreted in its axiological variant: God has all perfections, and that religion has to be regarded as true that ascribes to God the greatest perfection. Having done it elsewhere, I do not want to analyze here in detail Llull's arguments for why the doctrines of the Trinity and incarnation follow from divine perfection—even those who reject them will probably agree with the comparative statement that they belong to the best arguments developed for the specifically Christian dogmas. They have profoundly influenced Cusanus. What Cusanus adds in *De pace fidei,* however, is a transcendental reflection alien to Llull.

The whole dialogue starts by reflecting on what is already presupposed by the philosophers gathered in the heaven of reason. It is wisdom, the object of their search. But there can be only one wisdom; if there were many, they had to partake in the one, for unity antecedes plurality. This wisdom is the divine Logos, which cannot be different from God. "See how you philosophers of various sects agree on the religion of one God—whom you all presuppose, in that you profess to be lovers of Wisdom."[97] Already in Abelard, the Christian had seen in the Logos the bridge from the philosopher's position to Christianity;[98] but this was an isolated remark, while it is Cusanus's aim to deduce the main features of the true religion from the concept of Logos. The Trinity is interpreted as the inner structure of this Logos—it has nothing to do with polytheism, which in fact presupposes the One God in the same way as the cult of the saints presupposes the One Saint.[99] As infinite, God is neither one nor three; the Trinity can best be grasped with the concepts of unity, equality, and connection.[100] Like Llull,[101] Cusanus sees furthermore in the triadic structure of the creatures an allusion to the divine Trinity.[102]

It is important that Cusanus agrees with Jews and Muslims that the Trinity that they deny indeed has to be denied; but rightly understood, the Trinity is implied by them.[103] Far more clumsy is the argument for incarnation, as developed by Peter; it is less satisfying than what we find in other works of Cusanus, as the third book of *De docta ignorantia* where Christ has the function of mediating between God and the universe. The central idea in *De pace fidei* seems to be that human nature can achieve immortality only by union with divine nature[104] and that this presupposes that one person has a wisdom that could not be greater; such a person would then be at the same time human and divine.[105] Cusanus defends against the Muslims the necessity—not the mere historical factuality—of Christ's death; through such a death he is more perfect than he would be without it.[106] It is important that such axiological arguments for the incarnation do not yet determine the question whether the historical Jesus is the incarnate God. Already Llull[107] has a clear awareness that these are two distinct questions, and it is easy to see that the second question is far more difficult to settle than the first: even if we had apodictic arguments for the necessity of incarnation, this would not yet show that Jesus is the Christ. Cusanus's theory seems to entail that God incarnate was omniscient—how could one ever prove that Jesus was?

Ethical questions play the dominant role in Abelard, a minor one in Llull. In Cusanus they appear only at the end of the work, when the nature of human happiness is discussed. Remarkable is the discussion of the Qur'anic paradise that so often has been criticized by Christians; like Llull,[108] Cusanus mentions that it could be interpreted in a nonliteral sense, and that this has indeed been done by Islamic philosophers like Avicenna.[109] Remarkable is Peter's sympathy for Muhammad's difficult task: to overcome the traditional polytheism, the prophet had to entice them by sensual promises.[110] The discussion of the sacraments is initiated by a Tartar who says bluntly how awkward the Eucharist seems from his point of view—namely, as a form of theophagy.[111] Peter is replaced by Paul as discussion leader, who develops a theory of justification through faith that has often been compared with Luther's. Cusanus, however, insists that a faith without works is dead and that the works demanded by God are the same for all people. Our moral duties are not mandated to us in a heteronomous way by different prophets including Jesus—the light that shows them to us is created together with our soul. "The divine commandments are very terse and very well known to everyone and are common to all nations. Indeed, the light that shows us these commandments is created together with the rational soul. For God speaks within us, commanding us to love Him from whom we receive being and not to do unto another anything except that which we want done unto us. Therefore, love is the fulfillment of God's law, and all other laws are reducible to the law of love."[112]

The material content of the law of God is thus similar to what we found defended by Abelard's philosopher and Toralba. And the sacraments? Cusanus reduces their importance radically: what counts is not the sign, but what is signified by it,[113] circumcision does not save, but ought not to be forbidden either,[114] and even without Eucharist salvation is possible.[115] Neither Llull nor Bodin's post-Tridentine Coronaeus would have been able to agree with this new doctrine of the sacraments of the fifteenth-century cardinal.

III.

What can we learn from these dialogues? Allow me to sum up my analysis with the following seven points.

First, the range of possibilities of dealing with each other sketched by our authors is remarkably broad. From the humiliation of the other to the sincere desire to learn from each other to the respect of the person and religion of the other despite the conviction that he is wrong, our authors show us almost everything that in our time as well as in theirs occurs in human interactions dealing with religious questions. It is clear from what they show us that a symmetrical relation is, ceteris paribus, better than an asymmetrical one, that an interreligious dialogue must take place in a neutral arena, that freedom of speech must be guaranteed, even if everybody is well advised to avoid hurting remarks, that procedural rules are indispensable, and that one does not have the right to expect from the other that he give up or correct his religion if one is not willing to do the same. The conviction that the members of the other religion are damned if they do not convert to one's own is, as Llull shows, compatible with politeness, but poisons the openness of the exchange at least in the long run—Llull himself developed obsessive traits in his later life, even if his wrath was more direct against his indifferent fellow Christians than against the Muslims whom he pitied.[116]

Second, such a dialogue is possible only if the interlocutors know much, and are willing to learn more, about the other religions. Abelard is the most ignorant of our four authors—he mentions only the Jew, and what he ascribes to him does not correspond to what contemporary Jews thought about themselves. Llull's knowledge of the Jewish religion is not very profound either; however, his knowledge of Islam was exceptional not only for his time. Suffice it to mention that he spoke fluent Arabic and that possibly he wrote the *Llibre del gentil e dels tres savis* first in Arabic.[117] Cusanus did not know Arabic, but he studied the Qur'an thoroughly, as his *Cribratio Alkorani* demonstrates, and he included in his dialogue far more interlocutors than any interreligious author before him, among them polytheists. Bodin's range is limited to monotheists, but due to the Reformation he adds the interdenominational debate to the interreligious. His knowledge about the different religious traditions is highly impressive, and he seems utterly fair to each of them. Of course, none of our authors is familiar with the very different type of religiosity represented by the East Asian religions such as Confucianism and Buddhism; they became seriously known to the West only in the seventeenth and the nineteenth century, respectively, and they indeed challenged the monotheistic consensus: suffice it to mention Arthur Schopenhauer.

Third, we have seen that Llull and Cusanus are aware of different traditions and interpretations within the other religions—no religion is a monolithic unit. Thus it is morally imperative to try to find the best tradition and to give a charitable interpretation of it—at least if one desires to have one's own tradition treated with an analogous respect. In his *Cribratio Alkorani,* by no means a fair work, Cusanus uses the term *pia interpretatio,*[118] and even if he ascribes it to the Muslims, Jasper Hopkins has made it plausible that Cusanus "meant something akin to charitable construal,"[119] also because he distinguishes between Muhammad's and the Qur'an's intent. As Cusanus praised Avicenna, so today we must remind the Muslims of their own tradition of rationalistic theology—even if it is a fact that has to be taken into account that such a tradition is no longer alive among the powerful people.

Fourth, one has to recognize that also in one's own religion there are irrational, superstitious, and even morally pathological traditions. To overlook them and to point only at the questionable traits of the other religions is manifestly unfair. Far more important than a conversion of others to one's religion is the conversion of oneself to a spiritual interpretation of one's own religion. Cusanus subtly reinterprets his own tradition, and even if his concept of Christianity is not touched by many of Toralba's attacks, the problem of a consistent interpretation of Christology remains a daunting task. Cusanus himself knew that it was far easier to agree on the doctrine of the Trinity than on the Christological dogmas.[120] The Chalcedonian Formula seems inconsistent to many who have thought about it; and the historical approach to Jesus has destroyed many of the traditional evidences of Christology. Still, the idea of a necessary mediation between God and the world remains a profound one, and on its reinterpretation in a way that is both logically consistent and compatible with the historical facts the future of Christianity may well depend.

Fifth, besides the dogmatic the ethical dimension of religions must not be neglected. The sublimity of the Gospel's ethics remains a mark of the divine, and one can easily understand that neither Llull[121] nor Cusanus[122] was willing to regard the Islamic polygyny as of equal value with Christian monogamy. An ethico-theological reconstruction of religion, as proposed by Abelard and elaborated by Kant, must be, if not the core, a central element of any religion of reason. The fulfillment of the moral law must enjoy a higher status than the celebration of religious rites, even if that anthropology errs that does not recognize the need of external symbols for internal moral principles—all of Bodin's characters sing together hymns to God.[123]

Sixth, the failure of Bodin's dialogue shows us that the continuation of an interreligious exchange can be expected only if there is a common ground, and this can hardly be anything other than reason. The destruction of reason will not enhance the interreligious dialogue—on the contrary, as the history of Islam shows, a skeptical philosophy like that of Senamus must paralyze any meaningful interreligious exchange. A rationalist foundationalism does not at all lead to fundamentalism; on the contrary, it is the strongest intellectual bulwark against it. Fideism is the natural reaction when people begin to despair regarding reason; and when they embrace modern hermeneutics, fideism may lead to fundamentalism (a thoroughly modern phenomenon).

Seventh, the main problem of the program sketched here is, of course, its elitist character. None of our authors has an illusion about it—their interlocutors are philosophically or theologically trained, and they know that their logical, hermeneutical, and historical knowledge can be found only in a few. After Toralba's last contribution Salomon remarks: "If we were like those heroes, we would need no rites or ceremonies. However, it is hardly possible and even impossible for the common people and the untutored masses to be restrained by a simple assent of true religion without rites and ceremonies."[124] The intellectual aristocratism of our authors is hardly compatible with the democratic aspirations that lie at the basis of modern nationalisms and contemporary fundamentalisms. People need institutions, and these are jealous of each other. As the wars between Christian nations teach us, it would be furthermore naïve to as-sume that even if a religious unity could be achieved, human aggression would stop. Is there any way to reformulate the idea of the search, based on dialogue and rational arguments, for a common religion so that it may be attractive also for the twenty-first century? I will not venture to an-swer this question but limit myself to the concluding remark that the human prospect would look better than it does if a functional equivalent to it could indeed be found.

CHAPTER 11

—◆·ı◆ı·◆—

Platonism and Anti-Platonism in Nicholas of Cusa's Philosophy of Mathematics

One of the reasons Cusanus so deeply fascinates the historians both of ideas and of philosophy in our time consists certainly in the fact that he can be regarded as a Janus-faced thinker, whose thought simultaneously completes medieval philosophy and anticipates central ideas of modern philosophy and science.[1] Traditional scholastic thought, Raimundus Lullus's peculiar attempt at rationalizing the Trinity and Christology, the speculative ideas of German mysticism, especially, Meister Eckhart's concerning the relation of God and soul, the great discoveries of "Galileo's forerunners" in Paris and Oxford,[2] the conciliarist tradition, the humanists' interest both in a new anthropology and in a new approach to the ancient philosophers—all these have clearly influenced Cusanus, who succeeded in synthesizing them in a system of singular coherence, originality, and depth.[3] In it, we can discover in an embryonic form many of the ideas that will dominate the scientific and philosophical debates of the following centuries, including the mathematical concept of the actual infinite, the new anti-Aristotelian cosmology, the program of a quantitative natural science, the idea of the constitutive gnoseological function of finite subjectivity, and the search for a dialectical logic.

Since I am not at all convinced that there is continuous progress in the history of philosophy, I do not think that it is fair to regard Cusanus as *merely* a transitional figure. The fact that within the triadic structure of *De docta ignorantia* (*On Learned Ignorance*) the idea of the God-man in the third book[4] in a certain sense relativizes the ingenious cosmological speculation of the second book need not be interpreted, as is done by Hans Blumenberg,[5] as a sign of the superiority of Giordano Bruno's cosmological thought. Certainly, Cusanus's project is more remote than Bruno's from the world of modern science, to which teleological structures are alien. But since it is not at all clear that this conception is philosophically the most satisfactory one, the relation between Cusanus and his divulger Bruno could be determined very differently: the triadic structure of Cusanus's first system could be given preference over Bruno's abstract and naturalistic monism since only Cusanus can ground human dignity metaphysically and give man a well-defined place in the cosmos. One could refer—as Franz Brentano did[6]—to the striking similarities between Cusanus's *De docta ignorantia* and Georg Wilhelm Friedrich Hegel's *Encyclopädie der philosophischen Wissenschaften;* in both works, God and nature are treated in the first two books; the dualism is then overcome in a synthetic part, which reconciles God with the natural universe through Christ, or, more generally, the human spirit. While it is unacceptable to ignore the systematic unity of Cusanus's thought and to regard him only as a precursor of various later ideas, it is necessary that a charitable interpretation recognize tensions and even contradictions in the thought of Cusanus. Let us turn for a moment to *De docta ignorantia* and its cosmology and Christology. On the one hand, Cusanus's attempt at rationalizing the incarnation without appealing to the original fall—an attempt deeply influenced by Lullus[7]—deserves our admiration, as does his designation of mankind as the middle of creation—between animals and angels—and, therefore, as the only place in which the unity of the *maximum absolutum* and the *maximum contractum,* the absolute maximum and the contracted maximum, is possible (III 3, PTS I 436ff.). On the other hand, Cusanus has developed in chapter 12 of book II (PTS I 402ff.) the fascinating and, for his time, extremely original idea that other stars may be inhabited by reasonable beings. He does not, however, see that the assumption that there might be other finite, reasonable beings endangers his Christology. For, first, how can we know that man is really the middle of the universe if we do not know these other beings? And, second, who is the mediator who can lead these other beings to God? The disquietingly heretical idea of a manifold incarnation becomes apparent to the careful reader of Cusanus especially since incarnation is not motivated by the original sin.

Cusanus's Christology is not the subject of this essay. Nevertheless, I deemed it appropriate to begin with his Christology, not only because it is so central to his philosophy from *De docta ignorantia* to *De ludo globi* (*The Game of Spheres*), but also because it shows rather clearly the ambiguity that sometimes characterizes our author's attempt at reconciling traditional theological thinking with ideas that will lead to modern science. Such an equivocity we find also in his philosophy of mathematics, which deserves to be thoroughly analyzed since it is undoubtedly a turning-point in the history of the philosophy of mathematics and since its author is without doubt one of the major mathematicians of the fifteenth century.[8] For, on the one hand, Cusanus adopts with great virtuosity the central ideas of the Platonic and neo-Platonic philosophy of mathematics: one can say probably that since Proclus nobody had so deeply appropriated these ideas. It is amazing how detailed the correspondences are that we find between Cusanus's philosophy of mathematics and the esoteric Platonic doctrine to which this form of thought returns. On the other hand, two ideas in Cusanus's philosophy of mathematics stand at a great remove from the traditional Platonic philosophy of mathematics, namely, his concept of the infinite and the interpretation of mathematical entities as creations of the human mind. Are these two ideas compatible with the Platonic background? This seems to be the major problem for everyone concerned with Cusanus's philosophy of mathematics. In the following, I begin with a very brief sketch of the Platonic ideas about the philosophy of mathematics that are still in Cusanus (I). I proceed to thematize the corresponding Cusanian ideas (II), and, lastly, I turn to the anti-Platonic moments in Cusanus's philosophy of mathematics (III). In my analysis, I deal with both his early and late works; I must put aside for now the difficult question whether a development takes place in Cusanus's philosophy of mathematics.[9]

I.

After the works of Hans J. Krämer,[10] Konrad Gaiser,[11] John N. Findlay,[12] Thomas A. Szlezák,[13] and Giovanni Reale,[14] I do not think that it can be reasonably doubted that the Platonic dialogues presuppose a theory of principles, which we can reconstruct with the help of fragments mainly of Aristotle and his commentators and to which the Platonic dialogues often allude, without, however, rendering it explicit. The esoteric doctrines maintain that beyond the sphere of the ideas there are two fundamental ontological principles that through their cooperation constitute the world. Plato calls them the One (*hen*) and the Indeterminate Dyad (*aoristos dyas*), the latter being the principle of plurality and having the great and the small (*mega-mikron*) as its manifestations. A special interest of Plato's consisted in solving foundational problems of the mathematics of his time. It must not be forgotten that the Academy was the center of mathematical research of the time and that Plato was—as were many great philosophers, especially in the idealist tradition (e.g., Proclus, Cusanus, René Descartes, Gottfried Wilhelm Leibniz)—certainly one of the most gifted mathematical minds of world history. The discovery that human reason can grasp truths a priori with absolute certainty was made by him first in the field of mathematics, and this discovery forms the basis of his philosophical program, which is deeply connected with Pythagoreanism. Plato was convinced that for every philosopher a mathematical education was absolutely necessary in order to prepare the mind for the conception of metaphysical truths, and, although it is probably a later invention, the rumor that above the entrance to the Academy was written *"mēdeis ageōmetrētos eisitō," "nobody shall enter without having studied geometry"* is certainly fitting.[15] Plato saw very clearly, however, that mathematics cannot ground its own definitions and axioms, and, therefore, he attempted to establish a metaphysical foundation for mathematics. Although genetically philosophy presupposes mathematics, on the level of validity it is mathematics that presupposes philosophy. In two previous essays,[16] I have tried to reconstruct Plato's philosophy of mathematics and, especially, his attempt at grounding the arithmetic and geometry of his time, the two branches of pure mathematics.[17] With regard to arithmetic, to which he gave a place prior to geometry, Plato justly saw the necessity of grounding the existence of the series of numbers and the main properties thematized by number theory. He thought that his two principles—which are not themselves numbers since they do not ground mathematical entities only—constitute the numbers in the following way: first, the *hen* creates the mathematical number 1 (which, incidentally, Plato does not regard as a number), and then the two principles co-operate in generating the natural numbers out of the mathematical one. Every number is a unity of unity and plurality: it consists of diverse units and is itself a unity. The concrete process of the generation of numbers was not conceived as an iterated addition, but as an iterated dichotomy. To this context belongs the attempt to relate the two main properties of the number theory of his time (even and odd) to the two principles.[18] Odd represents the One, since odd numbers can be indivisible, while even numbers, being necessarily divisible, are manifestations of the Indeterminate Dyad. To understand Cusanus, it is furthermore important to know that Plato assumed the existence of ten so-called ideal numbers, which he distinguished sharply from the mathematical numbers, the latter occupying an ontological sphere located between the ideas and the sensible things since they are neither sensible nor unique: there are many circles and many "threes," but there is only one idea of the circle and one idea of the number 3. It seems curious that Plato ends the series of the ideal numbers with the decad, but this has to do with Pythagorean speculations about the special character of the tetrad and the decad: the three-dimensional physical world can be interpreted as a tetradic unfolding of the point, the geometrical pendant of the One; point, line, surface, and body constitute, in any case, the fourfold fundamental structure of stereometric bodies and of the real world. At the same time, the decad was thought important because of the assumed naturalness of the decadic system, and a connection between the two numbers was produced by the insight that 10 is the sum of 1, 2, 3, and 4.[19] We should not underestimate the importance of such numerological reflections for the metaphysical tradition, even if we must disregard them today: Aristotle's contrived attempt at arriving at ten categories is clearly influenced by this belief in the fundamental importance of the number 10.

We have just touched upon the dimension model of Plato, who also interpreted geometry and stereometry as constituted by his two principles. With regard to concrete geometrical structures, two arguments are particularly important. Plato linked the one right angle to the One, and the infinite plurality of acute and obtuse angles to the Indeterminate Dyad and its two aspects, the great and the small. In a similar way, straight lines, because of their infinite length, were conceived as manifestations of the *aoristos dyas,* while circular lines were linked back to the *hen.*[20]

II.

The kind of philosophical mathematics that we have just treated began with the Pythagoreans[21] and with Plato, who systematized their thoughts and gave them a clear ontological basis. Also, in agreement with Krämer, I am convinced that the central ideas of Plato's esoteric teaching, especially as mediated by what Aristotle writes about them, had a great impact upon the Hellenistic and Late Ancient philosophies—particularly, neo-Platonism.[22] With regard to the philosophy of mathematics, it is evident that arguments of the sort just described can be found in mathematicians and philosophers from Euclid to Proclus (e.g., Hero, Nicomachus, Theo, Jamblichus). It is now interesting to see that Cusanus's works are rich with these ideas. And it shows that Philip Merlan was probably right when he wrote in 1934 that Plato's impact on medieval philosophy was restricted to his esoteric system.[23] In fact, until Friedrich Schleiermacher, the conviction that Plato had an esoteric system was shared by almost all philosophers who were systematically interested in metaphysics, and the *basic* structures of this system were known to them.[24]

Cusanus himself, in chapter XXIV of *De beryllo* (*On Eye-Glasses*), alludes in the context of the doctrine of the Trinity to the "secrets of Plato"[25] and writes in *De principio* (*On the Principle*): "But Plato after the One posited two principles, namely the finite and the infinite."[26] The two passages are significant because they reveal a certain knowledge of the contents of Plato's unwritten doctrine—Plato also called the two principles *peras* and *apeiron,* "the limit" and "the illimited." On the other hand, it is remarkable that Cusanus attributes to Plato certain ideas that are his own, or that belong to later neo-Platonists, but not to Plato himself. In Plato's dualistic theory of principles, triadic structures do not play a major role, and it is wrong to say that, in Plato, the finite and the infinite *follow* the One (which Cusanus assumes to be the only principle): the finite and the infinite, in Plato, are manifestations of the *two* principles, which probably are not opposed in the sense of a strict dualism, but, certainly, cannot be interpreted in the sense that the One subsists without the Dyad.[27] It is this unity of appropriation and critical transformation of elements of Platonic and later neo-Platonic thought that characterizes the whole of Cusanus's philosophy of mathematics.

As is the case for Plato, mathematics has a special importance for Cusanus as preparation for metaphysics—or, better, theology, since for him the true theory of being is grounded in the rational doctrine of God.[28] By way of mathematics, we can overcome the sensible sphere of physics and thereby approach God. The traditional Platonic-Aristotelian order of the sciences[29]—physics, mathematics, and metaphysics (theology)— can also be found in Cusanus (*Trialogus de possest* [*Trialogue on actualized-possibility*], PTS II 344; see also *De beryllo* XXX, PTS III 62). Nevertheless, an important difference between Plato and Cusanus is immediately clear. For Plato, mathematics is also gnoseologically inferior to metaphysics since one of Plato's central axioms is that of the ontological and gnoseological correspondence, which states that the higher something is ontologically, the better it can be known (*Republic,* 477a 2ff.). Cusanus, however, thinks that our knowledge of mathematics is more precise than our knowledge of God—first, because of his anti-Platonic interpretation of the nature of mathematical entities, which I analyze later, and, second, because of his clear awareness of the difficulties of a knowledge of the infinite by a finite being. Mathematics can be used as a starting-point for conjectures about God; the relations between mathematical figures can be interpreted as symbols of God's reality (*De docta ignorantia* I 11, PTS I 228ff.).[30] Mathematics for Cusanus has, therefore, a greater importance than for Plato—without it, Cusanus's doctrine of the absolute could not be grounded. Nevertheless, Cusanus also tries the opposite, namely, to ground the principles of mathematics in general metaphysical categories.

Following Aristotle's *Categories,*[31] Cusanus states several times that quantity is defined by its capacity to assume the more and the less (*De beryllo* XXVI, *Idiota de sapientia* [*The Layman on Wisdom*] II, PTS III 52, 468).[32] Interesting is his idea that not quantity but number is the more universal determination—number, he writes, is not restricted to quantity

(*De docta ignorantia* I 11, PTS I 196).[33] Cusanus argues that without it, no distinction would subsist and, therefore, no distinction between the categories, either: "Reason convinces us that when it [number] is eliminated nothing at all has remained . . . For without otherness, substance would not be something other than quantity or whiteness or blackness and so on; what otherness is, it owes to number."[34] It makes sense, therefore, that Nicholas treats number as prior to geometrical concepts. In this, he follows Plato and anticipates Gottlob Frege.[35]

Platonic is the idea that number is the product of a synthesis of unity and alterity or multiplicity.[36] From this definition of number, it follows that, for both Plato and Cusanus, only natural numbers larger than 1 are numbers: the *monas* is not a number for Cusanus; in it, the ontological category of unity—which, as for Plato, is not identical with the number 1[37]—manifests itself "without being numbered" (*innumerabiliter, De Filiatione Dei* [*On Being a Son of God*] IV, PTS II 628ff.). As for the dyad, which Cusanus considers to be a number and not an ontological principle, it is a very peculiar number: neither unity nor plurality, it participates in unity and is the cause and the mother of plurality (*De principio,* PTS II 248). Not only the number 2, but every number, participates in unity: for although it signifies a plurality, it signifies, first, a plurality of units: "Is not one one once, and two one twice, and three one thrice and so on?"[38] Furthermore, every plurality is a *determinate* plurality, and this determination stems from the ontological principle of unity. "This would be caused by the infinity of that form that is called the power of the unity, since that form, if you look at the two-ity, cannot be larger or smaller than the form of the two-ity, of which it is the most precise model."[39] That the number 10 is 10 and not 6 or 7, that it is one number and not another, is the result of the *monas.* "The decad has all what it is from the monad, without which the decad would neither be one number nor a decad."[40] The last sentence, however, is not without problems, for it says something that Plato would never have said: namely, that 10 is *all* that it is by virtue of the *monas.* Here we see the general tendency of Cusanus to mitigate the dualistic moments in Plato's theory of principles. Although this tendency follows from Cusanus's monotheism and it cannot be denied that there are indeed strong philosophical arguments against every form of dualism (Cusanus deals with them, e.g., in *De principio*[41]), it is one of the greatest problems of Cusanus's philosophy in general (not only of his philosophy of mathematics) that he cannot explain the source of difference. It cannot reasonably be doubted that his usual answer that it stems "from contingency," which we find from *De docta ignorantia* (II 2, PTS I 324) to *De ludo globi* (PTS III 308),[42] is more the renouncement of a solution than a solution: for where does contingency come from? Even less convincing is the argument that plurality arises from the fact that God is in the nothing (*De docta ignorantia* II 3, PTS I 334ff.), for either the nothing is nothing, and then it cannot explain anything, or it is something, and as such must itself be explained.[43]

In his attempt at understanding the relation between unity and plurality, Cusanus often uses the concepts that determine the relation between God and the world: those of *complicatio* (enfolding) and *explicatio* (unfolding).[44] As the line unfolds the point; time, the now; movement, rest; difference, identity; inequality, equality; division, simplicity; so also number unfolds the One (*De docta ignorantia* II 3, PTS I 330ff.; *De ludo globi, Idiota de mente* [*The Layman on Mind*] IV, PTS III 314, 320, 506). But Cusanus concedes that it cannot be conceived how enfolding and unfolding work.[45] In any case, it is fascinating to note that for him number cannot be understood only as an unfolding of unity: in order for a determinate number to arise, the process of unfolding must be stopped. Cusanus calls this interruption "enfolding." "For who counts unfolds the power of unity and enfolds the number into unity. For the decad is a unity enfolded from ten; thus who counts unfolds and enfolds."[46]

The concepts of unity and alterity in Cusanus, as in Plato, are brought into relation with the concepts of odd and even, oddness being linked to unity, evenness to alterity (*De coniecturis* [*On Surmises*] I 9, PTS II 40). Often he says that every number consists of both oddness and evenness.[47] In *De ludo globi,* he explains this peculiar statement in the following way: since it is not possible that a composite thing consists of identical parts, the number 4 should not be interpreted as the sum of 2 and 2. This would capture only its quantity, not its substance, which consists of an odd and an even number: "Therefore the quaternary number consists of the ternary and alterity, the ternary being odd, alterity even, and analogously the binary number consists of the one and alterity."[48] If we want to make sense of Cusanus's statement, we must understand "alterity" as "successor," and, indeed, Plato's Indeterminate Dyad has strong affinities to Giuseppe Peano's concept of successor.[49]

The idea that nothing can be composed of two identical parts would seem to follow from one of the central principles of Cusanus's metaphysics—the principle that Leibniz would later call *principium identitatis indiscernibilium* and that Cusanus anticipates again and again in his works.[50] It is clear, however, that this principle is valid only for the material representations of mathematical entities (*De coniecturis* I 3, PTS II 56) and not for mathematical entities themselves: "And even if the rules are true in their essence in order to describe a figure equal to a given one, nevertheless in actuality equality is impossible in different things."[51] Cusanus recognizes, as does Plato, that in the sphere of mathematical entities, there is a plurality of equal entities, and he distinguishes, therefore, between intellectual and mathematical numbers. The operations of arithmetic (e.g., division and multiplication) cannot be applied to the intellectual numbers. The latter can be interpreted as the ideas of numbers. Of these, there are multiple instantiations.[52]

In agreement with the Platonic tradition, Cusanus favors the numbers 4 and 10.[53] He uses the argument that 10 is the sum of the first four numbers (*De coniecturis* I 5, 13, PTS II 12, 64; *De ludo globi* II, PTS III 306, 338). The number 4 is especially important in the neo-Platonic systematic structure of *De coniecturis* because God, spirit, soul, and matter constitute the four regions of being and because—as already in Plato—it underlies the dimension model. Point, line, surface, and body are the four basic principles of geometry and stereometry; the body describes the empirical world (*De coniecturis* I 10, PTS II 32ff.); only as body is the line actual (*De docta ignorantia* II 5, PTS I 346). Cusanus also tries to discover this fourness in the four quantities, the four modes, and the four figures of Aristotelian syllogistics (II 2, PTS II 92), the four elements (II 4, PTS II 104ff.), the four causes, the four seasons, and the like (*De ludo globi* II, PTS III 306). The number 10 is relevant, of course, because of the ten categories (*De docta ignorantia* II 6, PTS I 350ff.)[54] and the decadic system, which Cusanus does seem to regard as necessary. But it also owes its importance to the fact that with the number 10, Cusanus attempts to bridge the gap between the tetradic options, which we have just treated, and the triadic options, which one expects from a Trinitarian thinker.[55] In both

De coniecturis (I 14ff., PTS II 66ff.) and *De ludo globi,* the importance of the number 10 results not only from its relation to 4, but also from the fact that it is the number that immediately follows 9, the square of 3. Nine are—again as for Lullus—the virtues or degrees of reality that constitute the world: chaos, the virtue of the elements, of the minerals, of vegetation, of sensation, of imagination, of logic, of intelligence, and of intelligibility (*chaos, virtus elementativa, mineralis, vegetativa, sensitiva, imaginativa, logistica, intelligentialis, intellectibilis, De ludo globi* II, PTS III 336). How are 3 and 4 related ? Clearly, 3 is a more divine number than 4. For this reason Cusanus believes that in the created world, 4 is more dominant. It is appropriate that here the middle is not simple, but double: "If therefore in the ordered or created order there cannot be a simple and equal middle, it won't be completed in the ternary progression, but it goes beyond toward composition. The quaternary proceeds immediately from the first progression."[56] In a similar way, 4 (suppose 4 is 0000) can be extended to 6 by doubling the double middle (000000). And if we proceed from 4 to 1, we have seven items (1, 2, 3, 4, 3, 2, 1); if we proceed again in order to reach 4 a second time, we have ten items, so that we reach 10 in this way, too (*De coniecturis* II 7, PTS II 118ff.).

I have already mentioned the dimension model that leads us to geometry and in which the point has the same function as the *monas* in arithmetic. Cusanus often insists on the thought, not to be found in Plato, that the triangle is the simplest polygon; he uses this as an argument for the Trinity (*De docta ignorantia* I 20, PTS I 262ff.; *De coniecturis* I 10, *De possest,* PTS II 36, 322). It is easy to see that this argument is extremely weak. For the simplest body, the tetrahedron, is determined by four points, as Cusanus, of course, knows (*De coniecturis* II 4, PTS II 102ff.). Why, then, should the tetrad not be the measure of God?

Very Platonic is the idea that the one right angle is the measure of the infinite number of obtuse and acute ones, which can always be more obtuse and more acute, and that it is the exact middle between two extremes (*De beryllo* VIII, XXV, XXXIII, *Complementum theologicum* [*Theological Complement*] XII, PTS II 10ff., 48, 72, 692). No less Platonic is the attempt to link straight and curved lines to the positive and the negative principles. There is a peculiar ambiguity in Cusanus, however. For, on the one hand, he subordinates, as does Plato, the straight to the closed circular line, which appears to him more beautiful and uniform: "Thus the curvature of the circle is more similar to it [the infinite straight line] because it is more similar to the infinite than the finite straightness is. All of us who have a mind are affected by the figure of the circle, which appears to us complete and beautiful because of its uniformity, equality, and simplicity."[57]

The circle, with its symmetric, closed structure in which beginning and end coincide, is interpreted as an image of eternity (*De ludo globi* I, PTS III 234f.); and theology is said to be "circular" and "positioned in a circle" (*De docta ignorantia* I, PTS I 270) since the different properties of God, such as justice and truth, coincide. On the other hand, Cusanus writes that the straight line, like the right angle, is unequivocally determined and cannot admit of the more and the less, while there are different degrees of curvature (*Complementum theologicum* VII, PTS III 672).[58] The tension between the two options can be overcome, it seems, only in the infinite circle, "in which straightness coincides with circularity."[59] This leads us to one of Cusanus's most original ideas, which transcends radically the Platonism of the reflections that I have hitherto treated.

III.

If Cusanus's philosophy of mathematics amounted to no more than the foregoing arguments, he would have to be regarded as an intelligent and erudite Platonist, but as nothing more; not much could be learned from him. The originality of both his mathematical and his philosophical thought, however, consists in his combining the classical tradition of Platonic philosophy of mathematics with a concept that is completely anti-Platonic and stems from the intellectual revolution that took place within Christianity and ushered in the concept of the infinite. It is well known that Greek mathematics did not countenance the actual infinite. This refusal explains why the Greeks did not develop the infinitesimal calculus, although Eudoxus's and Archimedes' method of exhaustion could have led in this direction. Plato's philosophy of mathematics reflects this situation very well. For him, the infinite is a manifestation of the *negative* principle, the Indeterminate Dyad.[60] That the squaring of the circle remained one of the major unsolved problems of Greek mathematics was a consequence of its refusal of the actual infinite. For, on the one hand, the Greeks accepted a certain form of the axiom of continuity: they believed that there existed something equal to something given, if there existed something larger and something smaller than it (Plato, *Parmenides* 161d). Now, it is not difficult to inscribe a square into a circle and to circumscribe the same circle with a square. But it is not at all easy to construct a square having the same surface as the circle—in truth, as Ferdinand von Lindemann has demonstrated, it is impossible to carry out such a construction with straightedge and compass in a finite number of steps. It is not an accident that the squaring of the circle was the mathematical problem to which Cusanus dedicated all his mathematical works.[61] But I will not deal with them here. I must limit myself to his *philosophy* of mathematics.

In his philosophical interpretation of the problem of the squaring of the circle, Cusanus states repeatedly that the circle can be regarded as a polygon with an infinite number of sides and angles. According to this conception, the circle is superior to the rectilinear polygons because in it the infinite is present. The application of this interpretation to epistemology is profound: Cusanus compares the relation between our actual knowledge and God to the relation between finite polygons and the circle: "Therefore the intellect, which is not truth, never grasps truth so precisely that it could not be grasped in infinite ways more precisely, relating to truth as a polygon relates to the circle, which is the more similar to the circle, the more angles it has when it has been inscribed to it. However, it never becomes equal, even if it multiplies the angles to the infinite, as long as it does not resolve itself into identity with the circle."[62]

This comparison is excellent, for it does not restrict itself to stating the difference between our opinions and truth. The mere idea of approximation is, in fact, philosophically unsatisfactory since it does not explain how we can know that we are approximating truth if we have no knowledge of truth. How is it possible to assert that we are approaching truth and not receding from it if truth is completely unknown to us? Cusanus's comparison suggests a much more complex and much better idea. We have not yet exhausted truth—and will never exhaust it—but we are already in the presence of truth. We are *viatores,* we are on the way to truth, but in this way we are already embraced by truth, which some-how is always already present.[63]

On the other hand, we have already seen that the circle, notwith-standing its excellence, is limited insofar as the degree of its curvature varies in accordance with the length of its radius. Cusanus sees clearly that both determinations are indirectly proportional (*Complementum theologicum* III, PTS III 658) and draws the important conclusion that a circle with an infinite radius would have a degree of curvature equal to zero and, therefore, would be a straight line. In the infinite, opposites coincide: the straight line is at the same time a closed circle.[64] This idea, which is repeated throughout the work of Cusanus,[65] is first developed in book I of *De docta ignorantia*, whose mathematical parts anticipate as much of later mathematics as the last chapters of book II anticipate of later cosmology. Cusanus here declares in a very Platonic and neo-Platonic way that mathematics can lead us to the cognition of God. Completely anti-Platonic, however, is the contention that *infinite* figures should form the basis of philosophical theology. Cusanus distinguishes among three steps. First, we should analyze finite figures and the relations and qualities that exist in them. Second, we should transfer them to infinite figures, and, lastly, to the concept of the simple infinite that is absolute—which is even "ab-solved" from the determination of being a figure (I 12, PTS I 232). We see that Cusanus never identifies God with the infinite figure—he seems, however, to identify God with the quantitative infinite; we do not find in Cusanus, as we do in Hegel's *Science of Logic,* a distinction between the qualitative and the quantitative infinite.

To regard God as infinite is, of course, a specifically Christian thought. Anselm had called God "maximum," and this is also the first qualification of God Cusanus used in *De docta ignorantia* (I 4, PTS I 204). But already at the beginning, Cusanus says that this maximum is also the minimum, the argument being that the minimum is the *maximally* small—that is, both extremes agree in being extremes.[66] This argument does not prove what Cusanus thinks he has proved; although both extremes have something in common, this does not entail that they are identical. Nevertheless, it is fascinating to see how, with this idea in hand, Cusanus transforms the Platonic theory of principles. In the latter, the negative principle was responsible for the Greater and the Smaller; the One stood in the middle between the two manifestations of the Indeterminate Dyad. Of course, Plato did not assume that the actual infinite existed; the Indeterminate Dyad was only indeterminate and the principle of an infinite progress, whose end did not actually exist. Cusanus makes the actual infinite extremes, the maximum and the minimum, coincide. This maximum, which is at the same time the minimum, is regarded as being the absolute measure (*De docta ignorantia* I 16, PTS I 244); it is, therefore, the true One. Mediated by the coincidence of the two sides of the negative principle, the positive and the negative principles also coincide. It is important to see how the two principles coincide through the positing of the actual infinite. If we assume the actual infinite, then we have reached something that cannot become greater (or smaller): "For only infinity can be neither larger nor smaller."[67] Such an infinite can no longer fall under the rule of the negative principle: it becomes the positive principle itself. "For the beginning of the emanation and the end of the return coincide in the absolute unity, which is the absolute infinity."[68]

One of the most important of Cusanus's concrete insights into the nature of the mathematical infinite is the discovery that in the infinite two sets can be equinumerous, although one is a proper subset of the other. From Proclus's incidental remarks to Bernhard Bolzano's *Paradoxien des Unendlichen* (1851),[69] philosophers have been puzzled by this amazing fact, which received its systematic solution in Georg Cantor's set theory, and, certainly, Cusanus's work has an important place in the history of this thought. In his fundamental work, "Grundlagen einer allgemeinen Mannichfaltigkeitslehre" of 1883, the fifth essay of *Über unendliche, lineare Punktmannichfaltigkeiten* in which Cantor deals with both the philosophical and the historical aspects of his mathematical theory, Cantor explicitly acknowledges Cusanus as a forerunner of his concept of the actual infinite.[70] In fact, Cusanus states several times that a line consisting of an infinite number of units is as long as a line consisting of an infinite number of double units, "for the infinite is not larger than the infinite."[71] Another anticipation of later set theory is his oft-repeated idea that every part of the infinite is infinite (I 14, I 15, I 16, II 1, PTS I 236, 240, 246, 320). Of course, not every subset of an infinite set is infinite—but, certainly, every infinite set has an infinite number of proper subsets, which are themselves infinite. Nevertheless, Cusanus errs in assuming that there can be no quantitative differentiation in the infinite[72]—R (the set of real numbers) is uncountable and, therefore, not equinumerous with Q (the set of rational numbers), which is equinumerous with N. But the smallest part of the continuum is equinumerous with R, and R is equinumerous with R^3.[73] With these results in mind, one can, in fact, make some sense of Cusanus's claim that the infinite line is also a triangle,[74] a circle, and a sphere (I 14f., PTS I 236ff.),[75] even though his argument is only a meta-physical one: in the infinite line, that which the finite line is only poten-tially must become actual. Incidentally, the idea of the identity of the infinite line and the infinite triangle also contains certain thoughts that will lead to projective geometry as it will be developed in the seventeenth century by Gérard Desargues.

The philosophical importance of set theory consists certainly in the fact that it shows that certain ideas that are inconsistent for finite sets become necessary for infinite sets: "You see that what is impossible for quanta becomes in all respects necessary in what is not a quantum."[76] It seems immediately contradictory to assume that a set can be equinumer-ous with a proper subset, and, yet, this assumption is true for infinite sets. The "logic" of infinite sets differs from that of finite sets;[77] this has pro-found consequences for a philosophical theory of the absolute. For if other axioms are valid for the quantitative infinite than for finite quanti-ties, it is appropriate to believe that this is true to an even greater degree of the absolute itself. Although I am far from thinking that Cusanus's theory of God is unsurpassable,[78] I share his belief that, for a philo-sophical theory of the absolute, a logic is needed that transcends the ontological presuppositions of Aristotelian logic, that the *ratio* must be overcome by the *intellectus*.[79] It is plausible that this belief, which makes Cusanus a forerunner of Hegel and of the different theories that can be called dialectical, was mediated by his mathematical studies. It is the mathematics of the infinite that forms the background of the history of dialectical and philosophical mysticism.[80]

Cusanus's theory of the mathematical infinite is even more striking once we understand that he is convinced that the actual infinite *does not exist*.[81] This may come as a surprise after all I have said, but there can be little doubt on this count: Cusanus speaks only in the counterfactual con-ditional of the actual infinite and says again and again that it does not exist. "One does not get to the greatest number than which none can be greater, for it would be infinite."[82] "There cannot be an infinite or simply maximal quantity."[83] But why, then, does he elaborate a theory of something that does not exist?

The answer, I think, is clear to everybody who is familiar with the history of mathematics and, especially, with the categories developed by one of the most brilliant historians of mathematics, Imre Tóth, for understanding this history. According to Tóth, in the history of mathematics, it often happens that certain theories are first developed with the explicit consciousness that they are wrong.[84] They are hypothetical intellectual experiments having the following structure: if these fictitious or imaginary entities existed—which they certainly do not—what would follow? Only in a later step is their existence acknowledged, in a creative act positing the existence of something, the essence of which was already known. The classic instantiation of this structure is to be found in the development of non-Euclidean geometries, which were anticipated by what Tóth calls anti-Euclidean geometries—for example, in Girolamo Saccheri's (1667–1733) *Euclides ab omni naevo vindicatus,* which contains the central theorems of hyperbolic geometry, but in the context of a purported indirect proof of Euclidean geometry. Adopting this usage, we could say that Cusanus is an anti-finitist; he has remarkable theories about the actual infinite, but does not yet believe in its existence.[85]

We have just spoken of the creative acts that posit the existence of determinate mathematical entities. Of course, this expression would seem incomprehensible to all Greek mathematicians and philosophers of mathematics, for in Greece few assumptions went as unquestioned as the belief that mathematical objects pre-exist the human mind. When Euclid sketches a construction, he uses the imperative *perfect* passive (see, e.g., *Elements,* I, 1): this clearly shows that he thinks that the construction has always already been done in a timeless ideal world. Archimedes shares this conviction that mathematicians discover, rather than invent, the mathematical entities with which they deal.[86] A sizeable portion of modern philosophy of mathematics, on the other hand, presupposes a very different ontology: Thomas Hobbes, Giambattista Vico,[87] and Immanuel Kant regard mathematics as creation and construction of the human mind and think that the a priori truth claims of mathematics can only be grounded on this interpretation. The main problem of this position is that it cannot guarantee the ontological validity of mathematics. It leaves the application of mathematics to the empirical world unexplained. Kant draws the logical consequences of this position when he writes that our mathematically structured intuition is merely subjective and cannot grasp the objective essence of the world, that is, of the so-called things-in-themselves. Now, there is no doubt that Cusanus is one of the first philosophers, if not the first philosopher, of mathematics to develop such a "creationist" approach. It is also clear, however, that Cusanus does not question the ontological claim of mathematics; he thinks that the world—and not only our image of the world—is structured mathematically. Are these two beliefs of Cusanus compatible? If so, why?

To begin with the "creationist" passages, Cusanus shares the humanistic belief that man is a human God (*De coniecturis* II 14, PTS II 158). Since one of the main determinations of God in the Judeo-Christian tradition is his creative power, this claim implies that man takes part in God's creative power. Man can create a new world, the world of artifacts, which plays a very important role in Cusanus's philosophy. It is symptomatic that Cusanus favors the creation of new things such as spoons over the imitation of things already existing in nature. "The spoon has no other model outside the idea in our own mind. For even if the sculptor or painter gets his models from objects that he tries to represent, this is not true of me, who makes spoons out of wood and bowls and pots out of clay. In doing so, I do not imitate the figure of any natural thing. For such forms of spoons, bowls and pots are produced only by human art. Thus my art is rather something perfecting than something imitating the created figures, and thus it is more similar to the infinite art."[88]

But artifacts presuppose the existence of matter, which man himself cannot create, while God "does not get the possibility of the things from something which he did not create."[89] This limitation of human creativity is transcended, however, in the production of the purely intellectual world of conjectures and concepts. In the creation of logic, there is no matter that is given; mind precedes even the "possibility of becoming" (*posse fieri*) of this art (*De venatione sapientiae* [*On the Hunt for Wisdom*] IV, PTS I 16ff.). The same is true of mathematics: Cusanus compares Euclid's *Elements* to God's creation (*De beryllo* XXXVII, PTS III 86). In this respect, Cusanus explicitly criticizes Plato and the Pythagoreans, who assumed that the mathematical mind imitates something outside it. According to him, mathematical entities exist in their truth only in mind itself. "For if he [Plato] had considered it, he would certainly have found out that our mind that creates the mathematical objects owns what belongs to its office in greater truth in itself than if it were outside."[90] Especially in the *Idiota de mente,* he develops the idea that numbers, points, lines, surfaces, and bodies are creations of the human mind (III, VI, IX, PTS III 500ff., 522, 554; see also *De venatione sapientiae* XXVII and *De docta ignorantia* I 5, PTS I 128, 210). Mathematical entities do not exist in their own sphere of being, as is the case in Plato, where they mediate between God and nature. They are either in man's mind, where they subsist as in their form, or in the external things themselves (*Idiota de mente* VI, VII, XV; *Complementum theologicum* II, PTS III 530, 538, 602, 652). Since mathematical entities are produced by our mind, animals cannot count (*De docta ignorantia* II 3, PTS I 332; *De coniecturis* I 4, PTS II 8; *Idiota de sapientia* I, PTS III 424). This also accounts for our ability to have complete knowledge of them—Vico's famous theory of the *verum-factum* is already present in Cusanus. While only God can know exactly the nature that he has created, mathematics, man's creation, is accessible to man:

> For in mathematics the entities that proceed from our reason and which we experience as being in us as in their principle, are known by us precisely as our own entities, or as entities of reason, namely with that rational precision from which they issue. Similarly real things are known with the precise divine precision from which they proceed into being. And those mathematical entities are neither substances nor qualities but a kind of concepts produced by our reason, without which it cannot proceed into its own work, namely building, measuring etc. But the divine works that proceed from the divine intellect remain unknown to us in their precise being. And if we know something about them, we conjecture this through the assimilation of a figure to the form.[91]

There are nevertheless important differences between the Cusanian theory and later constructivist philosophies of mathematics. First, it is obvious that Cusanus does not have a clear concept of a priori knowledge; sometimes, he suggests that all human knowledge stems from the mind's reflection on itself.[92] Now, one can certainly say that there are also creative moments in the formation of empirical theories, but if the word "creative" is used in this broad sense, the specific difference between mathematical and empirical knowledge is erased. Second, in Cusanus there are passages stating that mathematical entities are not exclusively subjective, but proceed from the divine mind. These statements aim at explaining why mathematics is applicable to reality. The layman answers the philosopher's question whether plurality (which presupposes number)[93] exists without our mind's consideration. "It exists, but thanks to the divine mind. Therefore as, concerning God, the plurality of things issues from the divine mind, so, concerning us, the plurality of things issues from our mind. For only the mind counts; without mind there is no discrete number."[94] Plurality is in this perspective a category of mind, but, as in traditional Platonism, a category of the divine mind: "Thus, if you consider in an astute way, you will find out that the plurality of things is only a mode of knowledge of the divine mind."[95] We must distinguish between the number created by the divine and the number created by the finite mind—the latter is the properly mathematical number, the image of divine number (PTS III 522; *Complementum theologicum* X, PTS III 686). Only God's mind, we are told, creates being; our mind is assimilative and creates only concepts (*De ludo globi* II, *Idiota de mente* VII, PTS III 322, 534).

With this statement, the originality of Cusanus's philosophy of mathematics seems to fade away, for Plato could have granted, too, that our mind creates *images* of the pre-existent mathematical entities, albeit not the entities themselves. I think that although Cusanus's statements are somewhat irresolute, the best interpretation is the one that succeeds in avoiding ascribing to Cusanus either the traditional Platonic essentialism or modern variants of constructivism. But is there a middle way? I think there is one, and I am convinced that exactly this middle way is the solution at which Cusanus was aiming and which deserves to be taken seriously also by philosophers today. Our concepts cannot be explained as passive reflection of reality; they are constructions. But in these constructions, if they are done intelligently, we grasp the essence of reality, for reality is itself the creation of a divine mind.

We begin by comparing Cusanus with Kant. If Cusanus holds that mathematical entities are created by the human mind, it is clear that, in the framework of his metaphysics, the creativity of the human mind is itself something created. In the human mind, the divine mind creates itself, in a certain sense: "Thus mind is created by the creative art, as if that art wanted to create itself."[96] Kant's theory, on the other hand, is not grounded in such assumptions—the unity of self-consciousness is no longer derived from a divine unity. For Cusanus, however, it clearly is; although in *Idiota de mente* the human mind is no longer regarded as an unfolding of God, it is still an image of the divine enfolding (IIIf., PTS III 500ff.). From that it follows that the structure of the mind is grounded in God—it consists of the unity of the two fundamental categories of unity and alterity, or identity and difference: "For that the mind consists of the identical and the different signifies that it consists of unity and alterity in the same manner in which number is composed of the identical regarding the common trait and of the different regarding the singular features."[97] Now, the passage just quoted tells us that mind is the unity of the same two principles which, according to Plato, constitute mathematical entities. Of course, it is not satisfactory to insist on similarities between number and soul if we are not told at the same time which categorical differences are responsible for the fact that mathematical entities and the soul are not the same—and Cusanus, as most neo-Platonists, fails to do so.[98] But his theory shows very well how Platonism and constructivism are compatible: the human mind creates the world of mathematical entities independently of anything exterior to itself, including a possible world of preexistent ideas. In so doing, it reflects only on itself and unfolds the structures that it finds in itself. But these structures are created by God, and they are created in accordance with the same principles that constitute the basis of God's creation of the divine numbers and the natural world, in which these mathematical structures are realized—although they are realized in a way lacking the precision that can be found in the (divine or human) mind. Between the divine and the human creation of mathematical entities, there is, therefore, a preestablished harmony. Cusanus can, therefore, pass from essentialism to constructivism and from constructivism to essentialism without contradicting himself.[99]

Cusanus is also justified in believing that the a priori science of mathematics applies to nature. For God utilized the four mathematical sciences in creating the world: "God used arithmetic, geometry and at the same time music and astronomy in the creation of the world, arts that also we use when we investigate the proportions of things, elements, and movements."[100] At the same time, Cusanus is convinced that the nature of the sensible does not allow for a perfect reproduction of mathematical entities: "And if the Pythagoreans, and whoever else, had considered this, they would have clearly recognized that the mathematical objects and numbers, which proceed from our mind and are in the way in which we conceive them, are not the substances or principles of the sensible things, but only of notional beings, whose creators we are."[101]

It has been said paradoxically, but rightly, that this renunciation of precision was one of the reasons Cusanus could develop the program of a quantitative science (especially in the *Idiota de staticis experimentis* [*The Layman on Experiments Performed with Weight-scales*]). In the fourteenth century, as has often been the case, the better was the enemy of the good, and the ideal of exactitude suffocated attempts at developing an exact science. Within the framework of Cusanus's ontology, on the contrary, it was impossible to achieve absolute exactitude. This allowed him to be content with less and to initiate the measuring of the world in which we live.[102]

Cusanus is thus one of the fathers not only of modern mathematics, but also of modern science, which dismantled the unity of the medieval world. We saw that these modern moments in his thought are linked narrowly together with the fundamental concepts of Platonism in its various shapes. In his philosophy of mathematics, this led to tensions, which I have tried to display. On the other hand, it is worth considering whether the fact that in Cusanus—and still in Johannes Kepler's work—science has not yet become autonomous, but functions within a philosophical program, is not a reason *for* Cusanus's greatness.[103] Although his synthesis cannot be valid for our time, I am convinced that a synthesis of philosophy, science, and religion is a central need of our culture, and that anyone trying to work toward such a goal will have a great deal to learn from Cusanus.

CHAPTER 12

◆ ·┼· ◆ ·┼· ◆

Can Abraham Be Saved? And:
Can Kierkegaard Be Saved?

A Hegelian Discussion of Fear and Trembling

In this chapter I attempt to answer two questions that appear to stand in tension with one another. First, *can Abraham be saved?* This question is posed by Søren Kierkegaard with gripping intensity, and insofar as I take it up again, I at least recognize that the question *must* be asked, and that Kierkegaard demonstrates his greatness in asking it. On the other hand, my second question—*can Kierkegaard be saved?*—presupposes that Kierkegaard's philosophy is no less problematic than Abraham's behavior. The tension between the two questions can be tolerated only insofar as one holds, *along with* Kierkegaard, that philosophy must reflect on Abraham, indeed, that it cannot ignore the difficulties that he poses, and if at the same time one believes, *against* Kierkegaard, that his own response is not only false, but also entirely unacceptable, and that it poses a new problem itself: how could a philosopher of Kierkegaard's merit have offered such a theoretically absurd and practically dangerous response?

The hope to make sense of both Abraham's deed as well as Kierke-gaard's thought is all the more important the more one is convinced that the world, especially the historical world, does not lack an inherent rationality—that is, the more sympathy one has toward Georg Wilhelm Friedrich Hegel's notion of a system. It is well known that post-Hegelian philosophy is a strong argument against Hegel. This is evident not only if one analyzes the concrete philosophical arguments that we find in writers like Ludwig Feuerbach, Søren Kierkegaard, and Karl Marx, and acknowledges them (something that, in my view, is far more difficult than we think today; for Hegel's critics rarely argue on his level); the simple fact that both political and philosophical history continues after Hegel can itself be seen as an argument against him—at least if no logic can be found in such later developments. Anyone attempting to take Hegel's central ideas seriously therefore should avoid adopting a purely negative attitude toward Hegel's critics. One might state a slight paradox (and since Kierkegaard loved paradoxes, he would not protest): if Hegel were fully justified in spite of his critics, he could not be right; for in that case the history that followed him would make little sense. Only by granting that post-Hegelian philosophy had been aware of several problems that Hegel could not yet accommodate into his system, do we have the possibility of defending the basis of his objective idealism.[1]

I have both an objective as well as a subjective ground for focusing specifically on Kierkegaard among all of Hegel's critics. The objective ground is that Kierkegaard is undoubtedly the most fascinating of all such critics. His personality is one of the most enigmatic in the history of philosophy; were existential radicalism the most important criterion for determining the greatness of philosophers, Kierkegaard could claim first prize among them all. In our own century, only Ludwig Wittgenstein can be compared to him. Indeed, it is no coincidence that Wittgenstein admired Kierkegaard more than any other philosopher of the nineteenth century.[2] His life is characterized by a flawless purity, and in this life one finds a truly wonderful logic. Not only is his life, in a certain sense, a work of art; his philosophical writings are accomplished works of art as well. One certainly cannot deny the poetic quality of Giambattista Vico's language, or G. W. F. Hegel's. But their works are doctrinal writings, not new literary genres. By contrast, Kierkegaard discovered an entirely new form of expression for his philosophical thoughts; since Plato, no philosopher has been such a great poet. That does not mean, of course, that he can also be compared to Plato as a philosopher.

Thus, I come to the second reason for my disagreement with Kierkegaard. In my first book, which deals with the problem of the relationship between philosophy and the history of philosophy,[3] I investigate several structural analogies between various philosophers. In particular, I claim that such an analogy exists between Plato, the neo-Platonists, Nicolaus Cusanus, and Hegel. As far as the first three are concerned, I agree with Egil Wyller, a Norwegian philosopher who exercised a great deal of influence on that book.[4] The agreement ended and the disagreement began with respect to Hegel. In Wyller's view, Hegel's predecessor, namely, Johann Gottlieb Fichte, and later, his critic, Kierkegaard, were among those who carried on the tradition he termed "henological." Of course, the partial differences in our interpretation of the history of philosophy are a function of systematic differences, particularly with respect to the relation between philosophy and religion. My critique of Kierkegaard therefore focuses on *Fear and Trembling*, Kierkegaard's most provocative writing on this problem, rather than his more explicit arguments against Hegel in the *Philosophical Fragments* and, to a greater extent, in the *Unscientific Postscript*.[5] Perhaps this approach can be validated by the fact that Kierkegaard himself probably viewed *Fear and Trembling* as the work that would be the most likely to outlive him;[6] it cannot be doubted, at least, that it is his "most difficult writing,"[7] which therefore requires above all others a philosophical analysis.

This chapter is naturally divided into four parts. First, I sketch an outline of Kierkegaard's argument (I). Then, I show why this argument is unacceptable (II). Third, I offer an alternative response to Kierkegaard's question (III). Finally, I defend the intuition that I take Kierkegaard to be justified in holding against his own concrete formulations (IV). As one can see, the structure is dialectical: the third and fourth parts are in a certain sense a synthesis of the first two. I believe, along with both Hegel and Kierkegaard, that the synthesis is stronger if the thesis and antithesis stand in the most obvious opposition to one another. Thus, if my critique should be too severe, I beseech the reader's patience—it is not my last word on Kierkegaard.

I.

As with almost all of Kierkegaard's works, *Fear and Trembling* mixes a peculiar brand of poetic flourish with philosophical—that is, argumentative—analysis; and in this analysis, literary works play a major role. The subtitle of the work, "Dialectical Lyric," indicates this relation between two forms of expression. Moreover, the pseudonym, Johannes de Silentio, behind which Kierkegaard conceals his identity, suggests that the main point of the text cannot be disclosed.[8] And lastly, Johann Georg Hamann's motto indicates that an implicit meaning lies behind that which is said explicitly. After a rather polemical foreword, Kierkegaard describes the state of mind in which he approaches the tales of Abraham's temptation; he tells four variations on the story, all of which suggest a lack of faith on Abraham's part and thus must be distinguished from that which actually occurs. The "Speech in Praise of Abraham" contrasts the true Abraham with the heroes of the fictitious variations. Following the "Preamble from the Heart," the central text—the "Problemata"—discusses three questions: "Is there a teleological suspension of the ethical? Is there an absolute duty to God? Was it ethically responsible for Abraham to conceal his intentions from Sara, Elieser and Isaac?" It is not difficult to see a *climax* in the three questions: the first transcends the ethical; the second speaks expressly of God; and the third addresses silence as a necessary consequence of the absolute, more than ethical relation of the individual with God.

The starting point for Kierkegaard is the conviction that accepting Abraham's behavior on the basis of our normal ethical understanding is no simple matter. "The ethical expression for what Abraham did is that he was willing to murder Isaac; the religious expression is that he was willing to sacrifice Isaac; but in this contradiction lies the very anguish that can indeed make one sleepless" (29f./60).[9] Neither the church's interpretation of Christianity nor Hegel's philosophical discussion of Christianity can impart meaning to Abraham's willingness to sacrifice Isaac. What confuses Kierkegaard the most is not the fact that modern man is far removed from Abraham, but the fact that one continues to show hypocritical admiration for a man who must be condemned if one were only consistent in one's principles. In order to continue perceiving

Abraham as a model, our ethical categories must be radically altered; if one is not willing to do this, one must distance oneself from Abraham. "So let us either forget all about Abraham or learn how to be horrified at the monstrous paradox which is the significance of his life, so that we can understand that our time like any other can be glad if it has faith" (49/81). Ironically, Kierkegaard depicts a priest, who praises Abraham in his sermons, but would be horrified if someone in his parish were to take him seriously (28ff./58ff.). Kierkegaard undoubtedly grasps a central feature of modern Christianity, which has become much more of a cultural than a religious phenomenon. As a Christian, one has several elements in one's cultural repertoire that are not taken seriously, even though one lacks the courage to clear them from one's path. Such half-heartedness cannot satisfy Kierkegaard's notion of seriousness. "But if one wants to market a cut-price version of Abraham and then still admonish people not to do what Abraham did, then that's just laughable" (50/82). Kierkegaard especially rejects any attempt to rationalize Christianity, for this would necessarily entail a decisive break from those moments in faith that are more basic than reason. While the Danish Hegelians want to go beyond faith with Hegel, Johannes de Silentio would be content if he could only arrive at faith (9ff./41ff.). For him, Hegel is easier to understand than Abraham (32/62f.). Johannes laments the absence of the force of passion in our own time (11/43, 40/71, 62/95, 68/101, 91/126, 109/145), yet he feels this very force in Abraham. He is the hero whose poet he wants to be (17f./49f.).

What is faith? Kierkegaard develops this concept as a third step beyond that which one could call a commonplace philistine mentality, as well as resignation. We can already observe the triadic character of this and many other divisions. Kierkegaard—whose master's thesis, *On the Concept of Irony*, is one of the best books written in Hegel's spirit—also remains, in terms of his conceptual apparatus, a critic of Hegel in debt to Hegel to a much greater extent than he himself was aware. Since the first step is not analyzed in greater detail by Kierkegaard, I will content myself here with a few remarks on the relation of resignation and faith. Resignation—which can result from rejection by a beloved woman—consists in the recognition that we cannot attain that which we desire, in escaping to an internal world, in the dignity of subjectivity as opposed to the contingency of existence, and at the same time, in a melancholy relation to the outer world. "The knight of resignation is a stranger, a foreigner" (47/79), because he has sustained endless suffering. In this way he has surely become invulnerable to harm. "Infinite resignation is that shirt in the old fable. The thread is spun with tears, bleached by tears, the shirt sewn in tears, but then it also gives better protection than iron and steel. A defect of the fable is that a third party is able to make the material" (43/74). Through resignation one experiences death, before one dies (43/75, 105/141); "for only in infinite resignation does my eternal validity become transparent to me" (44/75), as it is expressed in a sentence that reminds us of Martin Heidegger's notion of "being-toward-death."[10]

Faith presupposes all of this—without resignation one cannot become a believer. But faith finds the way back to the world and does not lose its trust in it, or in existence. Faith reverses the movement of the infinite resignation—"having performed the movements of infinity it makes those of finitude" (36/67). "Convinced that God troubles himself about the smallest thing" (33/64), faith returns from eternity to the temporal (19/52). This movement could be called *katabasis,* corresponding to the *anabasis* of resignation. Since the believer, like the philistine, is at home in the world, he can be confused with him (37ff./67ff.); perhaps for this reason "the dialectic of faith is the most refined and most remarkable of all dialectics" (35/66). To have faith means "to exist in such a way that my opposition to existence expresses itself every instant as the most beautiful and safest harmony" (47/78).

All of this explains Abraham's trust in God, and thus why he was willing to sacrifice Isaac without despair. The variations at the beginning of *Fear and Trembling,* on the contrary, offer a glimpse of the different forms that the knight of resignation can take. The moral problem, however, is not thereby resolved: did Abraham have the right to sacrifice Isaac? The difficulty of the question consists in the fact that Abraham is not simply sacrificing himself; he is willing to kill another human being. Had Abraham sacrificed himself instead of Isaac, he would have doubted; he would have been a hero worthy of our admiration—but Abraham does not doubt (21f./54f.). It is equally impossible to say that Isaac's sacrifice takes place for the sake of a higher purpose, as in the case of a tragic collision. If Agamemnon, Jephthah, and Brutus sacrifice their children to save their homeland, it is perceived as something terrible. But it can be rationally analyzed with pure ethical categories—as a conflict between two values. Abraham's deed, however, cannot be justified in this way. The tragic remains within the realm of the ethical. Abraham, however, opens a new dimension—the religious dimension—which forms a third stage, beyond the aesthetic and the ethical. (While *Either/Or* does not yet explicitly mention this third stage, it receives careful treatment in *Stages on Life's Way*.) "Abraham is therefore at no instant a tragic hero, but something quite different, either a murderer or a man of faith. The middle-term that saves the tragic hero is something that Abraham lacks" (53/85). Abraham cannot be understood if we do not give up the Hegelian notion, already present in Greek thought, that the ultimate purpose of the individual is "to abrogate his particularity so as to become the universal" (51/83). Faith is something entirely different:

> Faith is just this paradox, that the single individual as the particular is higher than the universal, is justified before the latter, not as subordinate but superior, though in such a way, be it noted, that it is the single individual who, having been subordinate to the universal as the particular, now by means of the universal becomes that individual who, as the particular, stands in an absolute relation to the Absolute. This position cannot be mediated, for all mediation occurs precisely by virtue of the universal; it is and remains in all eternity a paradox, inaccessible to thought. (52f./84f.; cf. 57f./90f.; 64f./97f.)

All religious people must experience this paradox, and must do so in anxiety—even Mary ("she is not at all the fine lady sitting in her finery and playing with a divine child" [61/94]); even the apostles: "Was it not a fearful thought that this man who walked among the others was God? Was it not terrifying to sit down to eat with him?" (61/94). Thus one must admit "that those whom God blesses he curses in the same breath" (60/94).

Against both Immanuel Kant and G. W. F. Hegel, Kierkegaard maintains that, although every duty is also a duty to God, there is also a direct duty toward God that cannot be reduced to a duty to other humans

(63/96). The knight of faith "addresses God in heaven as 'Thou'" (71/105). We read now that for the faithful, "interiority is higher than exteriority" (64/97). For this reason, communication about faith is impossible (even among the various knights of faith); in faith, the most radical form of egoism coincides with absolute devotion to God (66/99); the universal disappears in this exclusive relation between God and the soul. Thus the knight of faith cannot be assisted by the church either, "for qualitatively the idea of the Church is no different from that of the state" (68/102). Kierkegaard sees no danger that his theory could be misused. Such a fear can only torment him who does not know "that to exist as the individual is the most terrifying thing of all" (69/102). He cannot be responsible for "stragglers and vagrant geniuses" (70/103). All the same, Kierkegaard admits that the knight of faith is, in a certain sense, insane (70f./104, 23/56, 96f./131f.).

While the universal is apparent, the individual is "concealed" (75/109). Thus it immediately follows that the third question must be answered in the affirmative: Abraham must keep his intentions to himself, for no one could have understood him. "The relief of speech is that it translates me into the universal" (102/137)—but we have already seen that Abraham is outside of the universal. Kierkegaard recognizes that the ethical demands candor, particularly because—and here he seems to anticipate the central thought of the discourse ethics—only an open discussion can ensure that we do not overlook any significant argument (79f./114). He also recognizes that not every form of silence is good—it can be demonic. Silence is "the demon's lure, and the more silent one keeps the more terrible the demon becomes; but silence is also divinity's communion with the individual" (80/114f.). I do not have space here to discuss Kierkegaard's category of the demonic; let it suffice to say that it functions as a bridge concept. Just as the category of the "interesting" mediates between the aesthetic and the ethical (75f./109f.), the "demonic" mediates between the ethical and the religious. "In a sense there dwells infinitely more good in the demonic person than in a superficial person" (88/122). Both the demonic person as well as the religious leave the universal behind and close themselves up in their individuality; but the first does this without the authority of God, whereas the other does so in obedience to God. I cannot here analyze the narrative of Agnes and the merman, which illustrates a significant example of the demonic. As he so often does in his works, Kierkegaard again speaks in this fable of the dissolution of his engagement to Regine Olsen. The merman's greatest pain is that he cannot disclose himself and thus must hurt the woman he loves in order to free her from a love that will only condemn her to unhappiness; if he is the cause of misfortune, it is he who suffers most from it. The demon cannot discuss his pain with others because he fears their compassion: "A proud and noble nature can endure everything, but one thing it cannot endure, it cannot endure pity. Pity implies an indignity" (94/129).[11] The merman, however, can and should express himself. There is a solution to his dilemma: to disclose himself and marry Agnes. That is the difference between Abraham and himself. The demon commits a sin by keeping his silence; and "an ethic that ignores sin is an altogether futile discipline" (90/124).

We need to distinguish the demonic from a case in which silence is ethically permitted. Kierkegaard, in contrast to Johann Wolfgang von Goethe, represents Faust as a skeptic who does not want to communicate his corruptive thoughts because he does not want to risk the deterioration of society (97ff./132ff.). He finds himself in an ethical dilemma; for on the one hand the universal demands of him that he speak; on the other hand he has also the ethical duty not to disrupt the certainty of simpler folk. Kierkegaard's Faust thus stands between the tragic hero and Abraham; he must choose between two values, but one value is the negation of the universal, the disclosed. It is still an ethical value at stake, however. That distinguishes Faust from Abraham; and Kierkegaard can only repeat himself: "I cannot understand Abraham, I can only admire him" (101/136).

II.

Each of Kierkegaard's critics must recognize at least two of the philosopher's merits: a contempt for a lukewarm Christianity and an extraordinary depth of psychological analysis. Anyone wanting to understand the notions of anxiety, despair, and the like will always refer back to Kierkegaard.[12] Were it not for his phenomenological analysis of the unhappy subjectivity (developed further by Martin Heidegger, Jean-Paul Sartre, and Karl Jaspers in the twentieth century), we would be without one of the greatest philosophers in this philosophical domain. That does not imply, however, that Kierkegaard can be compared with those philosophers who can claim to have discovered new arguments; indeed, I fear that one cannot even regard him as among the greatest Christian theologians.

In order to begin my critique, it is clear that Kierkegaard always argues disjunctively: *Either-Or* is not only the title of his first and brilliant book, it is his general *forma mentis*. Either Abraham must be condemned or we must recognize the theory of the absolute relation of the individual to the Absolute—this is the central thesis of *Fear and Trembling*. I will show that we do not necessarily have to accept this alternative; if, however, we must accept it, a rational human being can only come to the conclusion that, because Kierkegaard's theory is absurd, Abraham must be condemned. In philosophy, it is not sufficient simply to establish implications or alternatives. The ultimate aim of philosophy consists in making categorical statements, as Plato taught, and as Fichte demonstrates quite convincingly in his work, *On the Concept of the Science of Knowledge*. Kierkegaard, on the other hand, contents himself with offering only an alternative: Abraham's salvation is never proved; but only that he can be saved on the sole condition that we do not take ethics to have the final word. One could say that at least such an alternative is original, but not even that is true. Kierkegaard is not the first to note the difficulty that Abraham's behavior poses for an ethics based on rationality; both Kant and Hegel were attuned to this much earlier.[13] Kant mentions Abraham in *Die Religion innerhalb der Grenzen der bloßen Vernunft* (*Religion Within the Limits of Reason Alone*), and criticizes him in a parenthesis (VI 187). Also, in *Der Streit der Fakultäten* (*The Conflict of the Faculties*), Kant argues that it is impossible to know whether or not it is God speaking to an individual, but that that person can exclude such a possibility if the supposed voice of God commands something that is immoral. "An example may be the myth of the sacrifice that Abraham, acting on divine command, was going to carry out by slaughtering his own son and burning him (the poor child was unknowingly carrying wood for it). Abraham should have answered to this allegedly divine voice: 'It is certain that I should not kill my son, but that you who appear to me are God, I am not certain and cannot be certain,' even though the voice came down from (visible) heaven" (VII 63).

With this critique of Abraham, Kant plays a part in one of the most important trends of early modern philosophy: the eradication of all superstition with theological pretensions. Abolishing superstition was extremely important on both theoretical as well as practical grounds: only thus could reason achieve autonomy, and only thus could the state demand obedience from its subjects. The inevitable consequence of allowing a tale of a divine voice to count as an instance against philosophical arguments or moral and positive laws would be intellectual and political anarchy. Indeed, one does not understand the reason both Thomas Hobbes, in the *Leviathan*,[14] and Baruch Spinoza, in *Tractatus theologico-politicus*,[15] discuss prophets and miracles in such detail if one fails to understand that the modern state could not have developed without having rejected them. Every modern, constitutional state would exact punishment against anyone who behaves as Abraham—just as today, Jehovah's Witnesses are punished for letting their children die rather than undergo a blood transfusion that they consider forbidden by God.

But does a critique of purely subjective religious claims not imply the negation of every theology? One misunderstands the great rationalists if one fails to see that almost every one of them desired to be a rational theologian: René Descartes, Baruch Spinoza, Gottfried Wilhelm Leibniz, and G. W. F. Hegel are deeply religious men—all of whom hold the conviction that God is best served if one rejects an irrational form of religion. For God manifests himself most clearly through reason. (Hobbes himself considers faith in divine voices a remnant of pagan demonology; he would have considered Kierkegaard, who always emphasized that his philosophy alone offered an advance over the Greeks, to be much more pagan than all the rationalists.) One can deny the project of the rational theologians, but certainly not their subjective religiosity: the critique of a voluntarist account of God, put forth by Leibniz, Kant, and Hegel, is grounded in both logical arguments as well as the sense that a God who cannot be conceived by reason cannot be loved, only feared. In the text just quoted from Kant we find a very significant passage—the parenthesis around "visible." By this Kant wants to suggest that the true heaven is not of the sensible realm; the true heaven, in which God resides, is the moral law. We find God when we listen to the moral law, and any excuse that detracts from the latter is irreligious, even when (or perhaps exactly when) it lays claim to a divine command. Kant therefore describes the story of Abraham as a "myth." (Incidentally, I want to point out that in this short text Kant expresses a deep sympathy for Isaac, while Kierkegaard never attempts to see the matter from Isaac's perspective; that is, he does so only in his variations on the story, which do not deal with the biblical Isaac.)

Kant does not yet try to understand how Abraham could believe that Isaac must be sacrificed—in his eyes, Abraham is himself a victim of superstition. By contrast, Hegel has a strong historical interest in the psychology of Abraham, even though he dislikes him. In the first part of *Der Geist des Christentums und sein Schicksal* (*The Spirit of Christianity and its Fate*), sometimes called "The Spirit of Judaism," Hegel attempts to approach Abraham's values and those of Judaism. According to Hegel's interpretation, its fanatic form of monotheism fears nothing more than loving something more than God; thus Abraham must prove to himself that he can kill Isaac. "He could not love anything; the only love that he had, namely, to his son and hope of progeny—the only way to extend his being, the only way of immortality he knew of and hoped for—could depress him, disturb his mind, which detached itself from all, and unsettle it, which once went so far that he wanted to destroy even this love and was reassured only by the certainty of the feeling that this love was only as strong as to leave him with the capacity to slaughter with his own hand his beloved son" (I 279).

We will see that Hegel's historical-psychological interpretation cannot be viewed as correct. But one can probably say of Kierkegaard that he was in no position to love another human being, which explains why he was so fascinated by Abraham. Hegel was wrong about Abraham; but not with regard to Kierkegaard. Moreover, we see here the most important difference between Kant and Hegel: Kant seeks the universal, the divine in the moral law, while Hegel seeks the universal in the world-historical evolution. Kant's philosophy of religion is an ethical theology, while Hegel's is a speculative philosophy of history.

I began by showing that Kierkegaard's alternative is not original. We have already seen that the alternative can be resolved: Abraham, as Kierkegaard understands him, must be condemned (or be seen as a lowly, irresponsible fanatic). Kierkegaard's theory that the religious can defeat the ethical as well as the rational must be rejected. Every claim to validity must be justified by reason; whoever denies this destroys all communication among rational human beings. Kierkegaard knows this; he asserts that his theory cannot be disclosed; he writes under the pseudonym Johannes de Silentio. Why then does he write at all? I do not wish to pursue the question here whether the fact that Kierkegaard drafts his journals in a public language presupposes that his writings can be communicated. In any case, it is clear that *Fear and Trembling* (which was published as a book) presupposes this, and that there is a performative contradiction in trying to communicate that which cannot be communicated and thinking that which cannot be thought. Presumably, that is an argument against negative theology as well; but it is of utmost importance to realize that Kierkegaard's view does not belong to negative theology. This view contains (perhaps unconvincing) arguments for the theory that the Absolute cannot be determined. The neo-Platonists never would have accepted that a definite commandment such as "sacrifice Isaac" could stand in relation to the Absolute—for the abstract Absolute cannot legitimize any action, at least not an action that contradicts fundamental moral principles. Kierkegaard wants much more than negative theology can offer—he wants to justify the absurd. But the idea of justification already presupposes certain principles of reason; justifying their negation is logically impossible. On a practical level, too, society would collapse if we took seriously the absolute relation of the individual to the Absolute. For it cannot be distinguished from madness. In the *Phenomenology of Spirit,* Hegel writes: "By appealing to his sentiment, his inward oracle, that person is done with in relation to the other who does not agree; he must aver that he has nothing further to say to the person who does not find and feel the same in himself; in other words, he treads upon the root of humanity. For its nature is to insist on agreements with others, and its existence consists only in the achieved community of consciousnesses. The anti-human, the beastly, consists in limiting oneself to the sentiment and in being able to communicate through it alone" (III 64f.).

Kierkegaard is a philosopher who is not able to think transcendentally or justify his claims as valid. He constantly confuses psychological inquiry with the question of validity. His phenomenological capability is not tied to a transcendental consciousness. Nevertheless, every phenomenological analysis presupposes categories; and Kierkegaard derives his categories (which are the basis of his classifications) primarily from Hegel, but without wanting to accept the systematic context that ascribes meaning to these categories. He is not the only one to do this (Marx is another famous example); all the same, it is always risky to saw off the branch upon which one sits—it avenges itself.

Kierkegaard's theory that the religious is not simply the ethical is of course correct; there are plenty of moral individuals to be found who are not religious. But he wants to say something more: he believes that an action that is morally prohibited can be justified if it is a religious deed. Even though Kierkegaard is convinced that he is less modern than, say, Hegel, his belief in the independence of the religious is indicative of the tendency of modernity toward autonomy. Modern capitalism does not want the economy to be evaluated on the basis of ethics—business is business. Nor does the modern artist want his art to serve "the Good"— *l'art pour l'art*. And modern science recognizes no objections made on ethical grounds alone. Likewise, the modern religious man seeks the absolute autonomy of religion.[16] Kierkegaard's doctrine of the different stages could at first glance be compared to Max Scheler's value ethics.[17] For Kierkegaard's notion of the "aesthetic" corresponds to the "pleasant" in Scheler's hierarchy of values; the ethical corresponds to the just, and the religious corresponds to the holy. There is a major difference here, however: Scheler's values are all *moral* values, and the conflict between them is tragic in the Hegelian and Kierkegaardian sense. This implies that an objective criterion exists that can determine when an inferior value must give way to a higher. Also, if Scheler's concept of the holy is not particularly clear, he of course never would have accepted Abraham's action. Apart from that, it is remarkable that Kierkegaard's third *Problema* still makes use of the expression "ethically responsible." In truth, this makes little sense, for we have already seen that Abraham's action transcends the ethical. Does Kierkegaard perhaps mean to say that he is responsible in a more than ethical sense? In any case, the fact that

Kierkegaard employs the word "ethical" is an indication of the absoluteness of ethics.

Kierkegaard has a rather peculiar concept of faith. It is not difficult
to see that he is working with two different concepts. On the one hand,
faith (in the "Preamble from the Heart") is the third stage, after the philistine mentality and infinite resignation. On the other hand, faith implies
a readiness to act against reason. The first concept is clearly not identical
to the second. In order to understand the deeper meaning of the first
concept, we must use a broader concept of resignation than Kierkegaard
does. Resignation can be understood as a tension between the ego and
the world. This feeling is a necessary consequence of philosophy since
philosophy involves, first and foremost, placing a question mark behind
everything that had hitherto never been doubted. The peculiar capacity
for abstraction that a philosopher must possess makes it particularly difficult to find one's way back to the world. Nonetheless, there are a few
philosophers who claim they have succeeded in doing so, not only in
thought, but also in life. The philosopher who makes this claim most
energetically is Hegel. His concept of reconciliation corresponds to
Kierkegaard's first concept of faith. I cannot investigate here whether
Hegel's system actually achieves reconciliation with the world. At the
very least, one must admit that, if one understands Hegel correctly, one
comes to understand a great deal of the world in all its abundance. But if
one understands Kierkegaard correctly, one has an important and original
insight into the soul's abyss, but little else—neither nature nor history is
better understood. If we compare the lives of Hegel and Kierkegaard—
for Kierkegaard competes with Hegel on an existential rather than argumentative level—we see on the one hand a man who has a family, who is
integrated into his society, and who clearly has a passion for life, even if
we hardly perceive him as superficial. On the other hand, we see a talented, but curmudgeonly man who could never find his way back into
the world. Kierkegaard is the knight of resignation, and Hegel the knight
of faith. One does not risk too much in supposing that, precisely because
he rejects Kierkegaard's second concept of faith, Hegel could have been
a believer in his own life (in the sense of Kierkegaard's first concept
of faith).

With regard to the second concept it is obvious that the naïvely religious person is not a believer in this sense. Faith that is opposed to reason is a concept of reflection; that is to say, only the individual who has lost immediate religious trust can begin to say that he believes, but does not know. Kierkegaard's concept of faith is possible only as a reaction to rationalist theology and ethics. Historically speaking, it is absurd to assume that Abraham actually could have said, *"Credo, quia absurdum."* Only he who suffers from his own negativity can idealize faith in this way, as Kierkegaard does. The relation between Abraham and God cannot be called faith in Kierkegaard's sense; this relation is indeed more basic than the difference between faith and reason. We must therefore say that Kierkegaard's concept of faith is not only philosophically absurd, but historically absurd as well. One need not have studied hermeneutics to get the feeling that, between the Old Testament and Kierkegaard, or indeed, even between the New Testament and Kierkegaard, there lies an abyss—an abyss created by modern subjectivity.

It is of utmost importance that Kierkegaard does not claim to be historically accurate. Not only does he lack any historical inclination, he is also aware of this. He writes on several occasions that he has no interest in discussing the possibility that Abraham's deed might have a different interpretation within his own milieu than it would have in our day and age. "Or perhaps Abraham simply didn't do what the story says, perhaps in the context of his times what he did was something quite different. Then let's forget him, for why bother remembering a past that cannot be made into a present" (30/60; cf. 33/64, 50/82, 67/100). Of course, Kierkegaard's critique of historicism is in a certain sense justified: One can learn from Gotthold Ephraim Lessing, Immanuel Kant, and G. W. F. Hegel that the historical problem of whether what is stated in the Bible actually took place is not important in answering the question of whether Christianity is relevant for us. The past must become the present—one must recognize, along with Hegel and Kierkegaard, that this is indeed so. This does not imply, however, that we may read into the text only what we already feel or believe—such an interpretation would be historically false and systematically superficial: so much can already be gleaned from Spinoza's critique of Moses Maimonides.[18] We need both: first, we must attempt, by way of historical method, to understand what is intended by the Bible's authors (or by the people about whom they narrate); then, we must try to find a meaning therein. Kierkegaard never attempts the first task. He finds in the story of Abraham something that keeps him constantly occupied, namely, his sacrifice of Regine. For that reason, Abraham (who likely would have had little appreciation for a modern existence such as Kierkegaard) can be seen as a precursor to Kierkegaard. I think along with Hegel that a historicist philosophy of religion is much worse than a speculative philosophy of religion; yet there is something still worse than what historicists have done—namely, Kierkegaard's approach. For even if the historicists do not rise to the universal that is given in reason, they at least find their way into the universal element of a culture's past; Kierkegaard, however, grasps only his own subjectivity. The twofold attack that Kierkegaard wages in both the *Philosophical Fragments* and the *Unscientific Postscript* against both historicist and speculative philosophy of religion cannot be won,[19] even if the absolute individual naturally fails to recognize this, and instead despises those who cannot accept his doctrine: for being the absolute individual means rendering oneself immune to every form of criticism. I cannot give an analysis of the *Philosophical Fragments* here, but I would like to say that in a certain sense of the term Kierkegaard proceeds far more aprioristically than Hegel (or Spinoza); for Hegel knows that the correct historical interpretation often differs from the concept of speculative philosophy. Kierkegaard, on the other hand, claims to be able to discover actual historical truth in his own subjectivity (despite his repeated reminders that he is not interested in factual history). Kierkegaard commits the same error for which he reproaches both Socrates and Hegel: overestimating the value of *anamnesis* and failing to come out of oneself. He never attempts to understand a biblical figure as something different from modern subjectivity—even though this might have helped him understand himself better than the way in which he continuously revolves around himself.

The critique published in *The Corsair* is simply vindictive. But the famous caricature undeniably makes an important point: that the whole world revolves around Kierkegaard. Friedrich W. Korff's ironic book, *Der komische Kierkegaard,*[20] fails to acknowledge Kierkegaard's greatness; but he is correct to point out that there is something grotesque to be found in Kierkegaard's attempt to use (or misuse) God, Abraham, and many others to justify his problematic relationship with Regine. As with Jean-Jacques Rousseau and Friedrich Nietzsche, Kierkegaard is one of those philosophers who cherish speaking about themselves; and one does not deny subjectivity all its rights if one prefers those philosophers who are more discreet, who lose themselves in their work, and who immerse themselves in the riches of a world that is far greater than even the most interesting modern subjectivity. (Indeed, Kierkegaard is without a doubt far more fascinating than the caricatures of him that we find in our century.) He himself writes: "For he who loves God without faith reflects upon himself, while the person who loves God with faith reflects on God" (35/66). If this is true, one must say that Spinoza and Hegel love God faithfully, *but not Kierkegaard.*

One can regard Kierkegaard's view as morality in the Hegelian sense—he avoids traditional mores because he finds them banal and superficial. But he offers no rational alternative, aside from the claim that his own subjectivity is true. This position is immoral, even though Kierkegaard does not aim at mere pleasure, and even though he himself suffers most from a sense of isolation that is the necessary consequence of his critique of both history and rationality. But suffering does not imply that one is in the right—an inner joy is also expected, especially from a Christian, but which is conspicuously absent in Kierkegaard. It is clear that the absolute individual can never love another, or himself, since he has destroyed a necessary condition for intersubjectivity—that is, *rationality.* Even if Kierkegaard recognizes the "deep secret," that "in loving another one should be sufficient unto oneself" (42/73), he nonetheless praises Abraham as "great in that love which is hatred of self" (18/50). And it is but all too evident that Kierkegaard himself was great in exactly this kind of love. Jean Wahl's application of Hegel's category of the unhappy consciousness to Kierkegaard is well known;[21] and one can very well regard Kierkegaard as a far better example of the kind of psychological structure analyzed in *The Phenomenology of Spirit* than the medieval Christianity that Hegel had in mind (III 163ff.).

I want to say, therefore, that continuity between Kierkegaard and the major Christian tradition is hardly discernible: Christianity of the Middle Ages was far removed from Kierkegaard, both emotionally and intellectually. The view, *credo quia absurdum,* is found among only a few philosophers, even if not all of them were radical rationalists like Raimundus

Lullus. A story Lullus tells in his autobiography can be described as "anti-Kierkegaardian" par excellence.[22] He decides to travel to North Africa with the aim of converting Muslims, but at the last moment, he does not follow through with his intention. His failures plunge him into a deep, psychosomatic crisis; he believes he will die and thus requests holy communion. But then he hears a divine voice that instructs him otherwise, for in his sinful state he would only profane the holy sacrament. But Lullus deliberates the matter further and reaches the conclusion that he would appear a heretic if he died without having taken communion; and this would have a negative effect on the fate of all the books he had written with the intention of saving many souls. Thus he takes communion, in spite of the fact that the voice becomes audible to him again and adds that he would face damnation for doing so. Lullus later interprets the voice as a temptation from God; and in choosing the redemption of others' souls over his own, he passed the test. Had he obeyed the voice, he would have demonstrated merely a radical religious egoism. Following reason rather than a voice that commands unreasonable things is the greatest expression of religiosity. No doubt Lullus would have judged Kierkegaard to be someone who acts contrary to the essence of Christianity.

Also, if we analyze Kierkegaard's life, it is much easier to find a rather demonic element in his thinking than something of a distinctly Christian character. Kierkegaard belongs to those philosophers of the nineteenth century who feel that Christianity risks growing listless, and who, in their sincere character, can no longer bear the hypocritical culture of their day, a culture that is no longer Christian, but that still parades itself as such. Nietzsche belongs to this group as well, though the conclusions he draws stand in opposition to those of Kierkegaard. Juan Donoso Cortés might also be mentioned in this context. But Donoso Cortés, the great Spanish Catholic reactionary, was at the same time very much active in the social sphere. In a state of grim despair over the crisis of Christianity, he worked tirelessly to fulfill Christ's commandment to care for the needy. Charity in him has something of a compulsive character. But Donoso Cortés is to be admired, while Kierkegaard's discourse on love comes across as compensation for a personality whose narcissism renders it impossible to assume responsibility for another. Christianity is a religion in which intersubjectivity plays a major role. Kierkegaard, who holds little interest for the social and political concerns of his day, hardly maintains any intersubjective relation aside from his relationships with his father and Regine. With Kierkegaard, subjectivity destroys intersubjectivity: since one can never know whether another has faith (VI 93), a religious community is essentially impossible. Finally, Kierkegaard's battle against the church demonstrates his lack of recognition for the moral duties that he ascribes to his Faust. While it is reasonable to insist that duty to truth be mediated by a duty to society, Kierkegaard attacks without any sense of tact the religious sentiments of individuals who could not afford his luxuriant subjectivity on account of their other responsibilities.

Kierkegaard's God belongs more to the Old Testament than the New; at any rate, his God is no *Deus caritatis.*

III.

The last words in Henrik Ibsen's *Brand* are, as is well known, deeply ambiguous. On the one hand, they indicate that Brand's God is not the true God, and in a certain sense they are a condemnation of his life. On the other hand, it is clear that a God, understood as a *Deus caritatis,* could not condemn; he must understand and recognize even those who are not capable of loving as he loves. We must therefore try to understand both Abraham as well as Kierkegaard better than we have done so far; if we are to be satisfied with our interpretation, Abraham must become something more than a murderer, Kierkegaard something more than a narcissist.

We want to accompany Abraham and Isaac once again to Mount Moriah. What takes place there is perhaps more important for the history of the relation of humans to God and God to humans than either Kant or Hegel believed. Along with Kierkegaard, we want to assume that this journey has a meaning for the modern individual, and indeed for all individuals. But in order to discover this meaning, one must avoid two of Kierkegaard's mistakes: we must adhere to the notion that human sacrifice can never be justified, and that God could never have commanded such a thing. We must recognize, moreover, that previous cultures could have held values different from our own, even though all cultures share common values as well. Kant's moral philosophy and Vico's philosophy of history should be the eyes through which we perceive this mythical journey.

Today we are experienced in reconstructing the past of humankind. Thus it cannot be at all surprising to suppose that Abraham can only be understood if we go beyond the text of the Bible, for the period in which the Elohist writes is long after that in which the sacrifice must have taken place;[23] and it is only likely that his interpretation does not capture what the real figure in an even more distant past must have intended to do.[24] Abraham, rather than the Elohist (whom Kierkegaard perhaps did not interpret so incorrectly), should be our primary interest. In his novel, *Joseph und seine Brüder* (*Joseph and His Brothers*), Thomas Mann presents one of the most fascinating approaches to the Old Testament, whose psychological and metaphysical interpretation inspires my present analysis. Of course, we cannot know whether a person by the name of Abraham actually existed; we cannot rule out that he is a *universale fantastico* in Vico's sense of the term, in other words, that many historical personalities and many historical events are wrapped up into one literary figure. Mann's *Höllenfahrt* (*Descent into Hell*)can bring us into that very mindset that we need in order to understand that this in no way detracts from the value of our story, but rather increases it.

In order to understand what must have taken place in the history of the Jewish religion, we must recall that human sacrifice was a common practice in almost all archaic cultures, and that the sacrifice of one's own children was quite widespread in Semitic culture—in Carthage, for example, it was practiced up until the time of the Romans.[25] Even if such a practice cannot be justified, we do not want to overlook the idea of a deep moral truth manifesting itself in this terrible institution. Bartolomé de Las Casas already understood that human sacrifice is not an expression of contempt for human life.[26] Quite the contrary: precisely because life is the greatest good, it is offered up to the gods; and precisely because one's own children are most precious, they are slaughtered. Only through fear and trembling, which the sacrifice sustains, can an archaic society overcome the centrifugal forces that threaten it—that is Vico's sociological interpretation. But on the moral level, it is equally clear that the sacrifice of something one loves is the clearest proof that one is not dependent on external factors, that one can separate oneself from the world. Without this capacity, a human being can hardly mature. A culture that has lost all sacrificial traditions has lost a central feature of humanity, and it is certainly important that such a culture be reminded of Abraham.

But if Abraham had only complied with the command to slaughter Isaac, he would not have been any more interesting than the Phoenician or Aztec fathers who did the same. He would have been a representative of archaic mores that we would regard, along with Giambattista Vico, G. W. F. Hegel, and Émile Durkheim, with a certain sympathy if our disgust for modern subjectivity had become too strong. But his values would not be our own; and even the critics of morality must realize that there is something greater than traditional conduct within given mores. What is this "something greater"? It is a conduct that overcomes earlier, more primitive mores and makes way for newer and better ones. Abraham is an example of precisely that; he is the first in a line of biblical figures characterized by inspired moral renovation—here we might think of the prophets, and last but not least, of Christ. Abraham can and must be admired, not because he was willing to sacrifice Isaac, but because he was the first to *abolish* the custom of sacrifice.

How, then, are we to understand the voice that initially commands Abraham to sacrifice Isaac, and subsequently, to spare him? After Hobbes, Spinoza, and Vico, it is clear that the voice is not to be interpreted as an objective, acoustic phenomenon. (Kierkegaard himself once attempted to give a psychological explanation of the miracle of Isaac's birth.) Nor is it to be understood as some form of deception. And lastly, it would miss the point altogether if the voice were described as a subjective illusion. Insofar as the archaic individual hears God, he hears the moral law; and this has a much higher reality than daydreams. On the long journey to Mount Moriah (lasting perhaps a thousand years), Abraham (or the various Abrahams) must have developed the profound belief that God could not will the sacrifice of an innocent child. The man who discovers a higher concept of God also enters a higher level of human moral development. He does not err in believing that he hears the voice of God; for the moral development of humanity is not merely subjective; in it, something manifests itself that is greater than a psychological phenomenon, namely, the moral law. The archaic individual can experience its objectivity only as an external power. But how terrible must have been the painful uncertainty over whether it was actually God renouncing the sacrifice due to him, or whether this renunciation was in fact a temptation. It is no simple matter to be a moral innovator, and it is likely even more difficult if the new voice suggests that which one secretly desires. Only someone with a deep loyalty to the other aspects of his mores could have attempted to do away with human sacrifice—only he who knows obedience can be taken seriously when he claims to have heard a new voice.

Why, then, does Abraham warrant more than a purely historical interest? Thank God human sacrifice is no longer practiced today, and thus this history could be consigned to the past. But even if one considers this concrete question resolved, the conflict between the mores of a society and new moral commandments is eternal, for no society can realize everything that the moral law commands. In relation to this conflict, we must acknowledge that Kierkegaard grasps several ethical problems neglected by rationalist ethics, even if they do not constitute a general argument against rationalism. A rationalist ethics (as, for example, discourse ethics) insists on the universal, on the importance of discussion, and on what in Kantian terms can be referred to as the "capacity of publicity."[27] And as we have seen, it is true that whatever cannot in principle be communicated cannot be true. One should openly discuss ethical issues in order to find solutions to them. But that which discourse ethics does not fully appreciate—and what Kierkegaard over-appreciates—is that situations exist in which it is impossible (whether factually or ethically) to discuss publicly what should be done. I will not attempt here to offer a typology of such situations; I will only mention the most important case—namely, when paradigmatic mores are no longer perceived as adequate by a developed moral conscience. One can certainly suppose that the old paradigm will be criticized by a number of persons at once; but it is not unthinkable that only one individual can be found who already stands on the ground of a higher paradigm. There must, of course, be objective arguments for the innovator's view—otherwise he would not be a moral revolutionary, but merely a dangerous criminal, or at best a mad narcissist. That does not mean, however, that he can discuss his insights with others. Nor does it mean that he has developed for himself a precise argument for his point of view—perhaps he has only a moral feeling that could later be articulated as an argument, but is not yet in a position to be developed in rational form. In this situation—and *only* this—can we speak of the absolute relation of the individual to the Absolute. The Absolute remains the universal and the rational; but it is the universal with respect to a future community, and with respect to rational argumentation—not, however, with respect to the norms of contemporary culture. Thus, the individual is completely alone, and it is no doubt an agonizing struggle he has with himself in which he gains the consciousness that he is right—"to contend with the whole world is a comfort, but to contend with oneself dreadful" (102/138; cf. 46/77). In terms of understanding the existential situation of this individual, Kierkegaard is of greater help to us than Kant—even if Kant alone manages to establish the objectivity, that is, the intersubjective validity, of ethics.

I have already mentioned that the moral innovators, at least at the beginning of the history of our moral consciousness, could not have advanced any rational argument. Nonetheless, without them the moral never would have been raised to the level upon which ethical argument is made possible; and if we want to immerse ourselves in their moral struggle, we will always fall back on the Bible. Even if one does not believe in a verbal inspiration of the Bible, one must appreciate the fact that likely no other text contains so many splendid descriptions of the moral innovators' struggles. The prophets are the best known; but Abraham is the first to experience such a struggle, and his story will always empower those who feel that the mores of their culture stand in need of radical reform.

IV.

It is not difficult to guess what Kierkegaard's objection to our reconstruction of moral history would be. He could well make the following criticism (not to mention many others): we seem to presuppose a moral superiority over Abraham insofar as we speak of a *development* of moral consciousness. But this is exactly the kind of thinking that Kierkegaard would not tolerate.

On the one hand, Kierkegaard is mistaken. Vico and Hegel are not wrong in supposing that different cultures hold different values, and that not all of these values can be equally rational. There is progress in human mores, and it would be absurd to deny that the institutions and values that are realized in the modern constitutional state are "higher" or "better" than those that existed in Abraham's day. On the other hand, Kierkegaard suggests something of utmost importance, something that offers a key to properly understanding the rational core of his critique of Hegel. Even if, these days, every philistine adopts certain values that Abraham neither knew nor respected, it would be absurd, indeed blasphemous, to claim that the philistine is a greater moral character than Abraham. For if we evaluate the morality of a person, we not only analyze his or her behavior, we must also situate those behaviors in the context of their respective culture. And the moral innovator is always more noble than his epigones, even though the latter adapt themselves more quickly to the new values than he himself could do since he had first to discover them. Moral values are not only a function of a culture, they are perhaps even more the result of a subjective appropriation. Since those who are born at a later time enjoy the advantage of becoming familiar with higher ethical values earlier, they are far less dependent on the subjective work of appropriation; and precisely this is not only an opportunity, but rather a grave danger. For no one can relieve the individual of the subjective moral appropriation. For this reason, a later culture loses its superiority if, being proud of its superiority, it neglects the subjective appropriation. If the individual does not reiterate the *phylogenesis* in his *ontogenesis,* he can become no better than his predecessors, only the caricature of them. Reaching a decision after a prolonged struggle for particular values is not the same as donning oneself superficially with them; and if those who come later content themselves with the latter, they have no place to speak of progress. "What then is education? I had thought it was the curriculum the individual ran through in order to catch up with himself; and anyone who does not want to go through this curriculum will be little helped by being born into the most enlightened age" (44/75).

Kierkegaard diagnoses precisely this situation in his own time. Even if his critique of Hegel is misguided from an existential point of view (for the young Hegel went through a phase of deep despair), one cannot doubt that the claim made by most Hegelians—that an absolute insight lies at their disposal—is in no way mediated by their existence, and therefore *grotesque* (92/127). One understands Kierkegaard's criticism of each and every professor who lectured on the meaning of doubt without taking on any intellectual or personal risk (58/91, 99/134), and it is certainly right to distinguish between Descartes, who must have expended a great deal of effort to carry out his methodical doubt, and his epigones (9f./41f.). "Conventional wisdom aims presumptuously to introduce into the world of spirit that same law of indifference under which the outside world groans. It believes it is enough to have knowledge of large truths. No other work is necessary. But then it does not get bread, it starves to death while everything is transformed to gold" (27/57f.). It is much more important to ward off the confusion between the subjective appropriation of Christianity's commandments and the cultural Protestantism of Kierkegaard's time. Even if Hans Martensen was on to something when he wrote that Christianity was our second nature,[28] Kierkegaard's critique hits upon an important point: that faith cannot be naturalized, and that the convictions of our society cannot replace the subjective choices for or against Christianity (VI 86f.). To choose Christianity for oneself means more than simply growing up in a Christian society (not to mention a society that can no longer be called Christian). This insight from Kierkegaard is the basis of dialectical theology. Admittedly, the dialectic between morality and mores constitutes one of the fundamental reasons dialectical theology has nowadays become a part of the cultural Protestant tradition—one can of course cite Kierkegaard and Karl Barth with the same absurd pompousness with which Hegel and Schleiermacher were treated after they had become established fixtures of our culture. Subjectivity is not the truth, but beyond my own subjectivity the truth can never be a truth *for me*. Kierkegaard is wrong to deny that human subjectivity is always a part of a culture; but he and all the existentialists are correct in pointing out that something exists that can never be undertaken by another, not even by the most advanced of cultures. *I* am the one who must always take a stance on truth, even if the truth can only be considered truth if there are objective arguments for it.

But Kierkegaard does not suggest simply that understanding something entails more than being aware of what others have said about it. He suggests also that even the deepest subjective understanding is by itself not yet sufficient. With this point we turn from Kierkegaard's critique of the Hegelians to his critique of Hegel himself. While his central criticism that a concrete existence cannot be integrated into a system is certainly correct, it is also superficial. It was never Hegel's intention to systematize all contingencies relevant to an individual's existence, even if he never denies that the universal must exist as the individual. Hegel is convinced, along with Plato and Aristotle, that science and philosophy deal only with the universal. Yet he knows, of course, that a universal characteristic of existence is to exist as individual. As a philosopher, Hegel would have lacked the patience to analyze Kierkegaard's concrete psychological problems, though he likely would have learned to appreciate his more general views. All the same, Kierkegaard recognizes a problem that Hegel could not resolve. Hegel is principally a defender of theoretical life; that is, for him the best approach to reality is the theoretical, contemplative approach. According to Hegel, the philosopher has withdrawn from the struggles of the world, transformed reality into theoretical propositions, and no longer needs to dwell on the question, "what ought I to do?" but rather contents himself in discovering rationality in reality. Kierkegaard never realizes that this approach is a result of Hegel's theological premises (and that his own existentialism is more compatible with an atheist perspective than a theist one): if the world is God's creation, it cannot be chaotic, but must be understood as a cosmos; nor can the historical world lack a hidden logic that transcends the intentions of active human beings. But even if one cannot deny that Hegel's (and Leibniz's) approach to the world is a justifiable position, it goes without saying that it is not the only possible position. We must also live in this world; we must shape it and form it without knowing beforehand the purpose that our actions serve in God's world-plan. Hegel abandons us if we attempt to live as finite beings with respect to a future unknown to us; for Hegel thinks only of the past. If we want to live "forward," thought will not suffice; without *passion,* the concept is powerless. Philosophy cannot be content with mere retrospection; philosophy must be more than a theoretical approach. This is obvious in the case of ethics: the grounding of moral norms cannot replace the task of their appropriation; to have given a speculative justification of Christianity does not imply that one has become a Christian. The existential struggle is more than mere comprehension, even if without the effort of the concept it can only be untruth.

With this insight, Kierkegaard takes up one of the central convictions of Greek philosophy.[29] Plato withholds his esoteric doctrine because he believes it would be lost on those whose personalities are not formed in a certain way; and in general, the Greek schools of philosophy always wanted to be more than just sites for learning true propositions. Plato writes dialogues in order to show what *kind* of individual one must be in order to understand certain truths. Plato does not explicitly instruct—not because he thought that truth could not be articulated propositionally, but because he was convinced that this manner of grasping truth would be of little help to anyone. Only if I discover truth for myself, by thinking through the interlocutors' arguments and considering the relation between these arguments and the characters defending them, can I appropriate truth. Philosophy discusses explicitly that which art suggests; but only by pointing out what a theoretical position holds for a person's own life can art motivate us to become one with philosophical truth. Perhaps we can say that, with Plato, one still finds a unity in that which for Hegel and Kierkegaard is distinct: Hegel represents objectivity, Kierkegaard subjectivity. The divine Plato develops a philosophy that does not appear to differ much from Hegel's in terms of its content, but in a form that is taken up again by Kierkegaard.

A great deal of modernity becomes intelligible, then, if one understands that Plato's synthesis is no longer possible. There exists a yawning abyss between the existential relationship of a disciple that links Socrates and Plato and the business-like structure of our philosophical institutions, and there is good reason to fear that the ideal of equality will gradually displace the education of character. Kierkegaard's (as well as Nietzsche's) existence is a deeply felt protest against this tendency. The end result of this tendency would be a culture that no longer knows what it means to be serious, a culture whose representatives lose sight of what it means to sacrifice themselves. Only by sacrificing himself could Kierkegaard wage a battle against this development—and not only by his teachings, but also by his existence. Only as an unhappy consciousness could Kierkegaard allow his creativity to unfold and say that which he can and must say better than all others. Regine was sacrificed, not on the altar of an irrational God, but on the altar of absolute Spirit; and indeed, on the basis of the simple truth that marriage is not always compatible with a creative life—even more so if the central idea of this life is sacrifice. Whether Kierkegaard's breaking of his engagement can be justified is not an easy question to answer. Nevertheless, one must recognize that Kierkegaard never stops loving Regine; few lovers have dedicated such a great literary-philosophical monument to their beloved with such loyalty.[30] Romantic subjectivity has found no greater expression than in Kierkegaard—therefore he too can be redeemed in the universal. For it is the universal itself that recognizes that truth must be reconciled with subjectivity.

Translated by Jason Miller

CHAPTER 13

———•—·—•—·—•—·—•———

A Metaphysical History of Atheism

Charles Taylor's most recent book, pithily entitled *A Secular Age,*[1] which grew out of the Gifford Lectures of 1999, can in many ways be considered a synthesis of his extensive oeuvre: his outstanding methodology in the history of ideas, trained in Georg Wilhelm Friedrich Hegel's phenomenological approach, is connected with his valuable reflections on the theory of social sciences as well as his strong religious engagement. It also forms a sophisticated theory of secularization that, in terms of differentiation, is unparalleled. Of course, Taylor might have explained everything he had to say in considerably fewer pages since the individual chapters are conceived more as independent essays (ix). Certain examples recur regularly, and occasionally entire sentences are repeated word for word (cf. 360 and 400, 361 and 398). But on account of Taylor's elegant writing, it is nevertheless always pleasant to read his later prose. Particularly fascinating is the "stance" by which he approaches his theme—for he rightly maintains that Edward Gibbon's success has less to do with his material insights than with the dry irony of his "unflappable stance" (241; cf. 272ff., 286ff.).[2] It is clear that Taylor's own approach is opposed to that of Gibbon—he approaches the topic of religion with a genuinely cognitive interest: his aim is not simply to learn *about* religious people, but to learn *from* them. But this intellectual candor, this sincere respect, applies equally to those who in the past century have detached themselves from religion, people whom Taylor tries sympathetically to understand. On all 851 pages of the text, one detects a spirit of Christian charity that is uncommon among modern intellectuals, whether nonreligious or Christian.

After the extensive introduction, in which Taylor distinguishes three different concepts of secularization (as a separation of church and state; as a decline in religious practices; as a shift in the nature of belief due to the availability of alternatives), the first three parts of the book deal with changes in the history of ideas from the world as it was five hundred years ago, when atheism was hardly a common view, indeed, when atheism conceived itself as a view fostered by the devil, up to the present-day situation. He sees in this desire for reform dating back to Hildebrand (Gregory VII) the decisive force that, with the Protestant Reformation, culminates in a new form of discipline for humans and leads to new "social imaginaries."

In this way, Taylor deftly connects studies in the history of ideas with social-historical analyses à la Norbert Elias and Michel Foucault, and is thus able to ban "the specter of idealism" (212ff.) that he presumably sees lingering in John Milbank's alternative theory of secularization (773ff.). Key in this process is for Taylor the genesis of the "buffered self" (37ff., 134ff., 300ff.) that makes the earlier, porous self impenetrable, so to speak, and creates a sharp distinction between the physical and psychical, which he sees as the essence of disenchantment.

The second part deals with deism and the idea of an impersonal order as the pivotal point at which the development of atheism was first made possible. The third part, entitled *The Nova Effect,* discusses the continuous emergence of new positions since the nineteenth century—the radically enlightened views as well as the romantic reaction against a rationalization perceived as spiritually impoverishing. Among these reactions, Taylor rightly draws sufficient attention to the immanent Counter-Enlightenment, as represented by Friedrich Nietzsche (369ff., 636ff.). The fourth part then introduces his actual sociological theory of secularization, which is distinguished from other theories that easily become self-fulfilling prophecies (525, 530, 535). Taylor opposes authors like Steve Bruce and is instead strongly influenced by the well-known sociologist of religion, José Casanova, and his studies on the enduring religious motives of political movements.[3] According to Taylor, only the form changes: "The new structures indeed, undermine old forms, but leave open the possibility of new forms which can flourish" (432). In the first step ("The Age of Mobilization"), institutions, including religious institutions, understand themselves more and more as the product of a conscious, collective deed, rather than, as in the *ancien régime* and its "paleo-Durkheimian polities," an expression of a cosmological order (459ff.). Paradoxically, this also occurs where organizations have to be formed in order to defend the old establishment (445, 462). The second step, however, goes even beyond these "neo-Durkheimian forms": in the age of authenticity there is a commitment to subjective expression that has led, among other things, to a radical reshaping of sexual ethics. Admittedly, the fact that traditional religion no longer conforms to the spirit of the times can itself prove strongly attractive: "The very fact that its forms are not absolutely in true with much of the spirit of the age; a spirit in which people can be imprisoned, and feel the need to break out; the fact that faith connects us to so many spiritual avenues across different ages; this can over time draw people towards it" (533). Therefore, it is wrong to speak of an inevitable demise of religion. In the fifth part, Taylor outlines the conditions of faith in a contemporary context. Modern science indeed offers an immanent framework, but one that is open to various interpretations. It is a peculiarity of our time that we are subjected to influences from opposing directions, seek out a middle path between orthodoxy and atheism (deism being the first of these; 599), and try to make ontological sense of the phenomenal experiences of freedom, of the moral law, and of beauty (609). In certain dilemmas, both sides, the religious and the secular, are involved in analogous ways (e.g., questions about transcendence, self-limitation, the meaning of violence).

The discussion that follows cannot fully address the wealth of fascinating interpretations, particularly of modern French and English intellectual history, which Taylor knows especially well. The breadth of his interests is particularly encouraging in a time in which the essence of philosophy is being undermined by an increasingly narrow specialization; for Taylor is competent, not only in historical, sociological, political, and religious science, but also in theories of art and literature (see, for example, his interpretation of Jacopo Tintoretto's *La Resurrezione* in the Sala grande di San Rocco; 97). Instead, I would like to concentrate on a few central philosophical premises in the book that will shed light on the specific character of Taylor's theory and will perhaps throw into relief an alternative theory. For the telling of history is inevitably influenced by the normative beliefs of the narrator, even if these beliefs are themselves reinforced by the way in which he narrates his story (on the positive circle operating here, cf. 768; concerning the inevitability of "master narratives," cf. 573).

Without the slightest doubt, Taylor is right in maintaining that the standard *subtraction story* does not work (26ff.). Modern atheism is not simply a result of a decline in superstition that left behind a naturalist, that is, nonreligious, view of the world, if only for the simple reason that, first of all, modern science is rooted in a belief in God: "The new interest in nature was not a step outside of a religious outlook, even partially; it was a mutation within this outlook. The straight path account of modern secularity can't be sustained. Instead, what I'm offering here is a zig-zag account, one full of unintended consequences" (95). Still, there is a good deal more to say on this topic than Taylor tells, though he at least points to Nicholas of Cusa's central importance (61, 99, 113). Second, contemporary secular humanism is itself bound to a Christian heritage, without which it would be entirely incomprehensible, perhaps not even possible.[4] "The in fact very exigent demands of universal justice and benevolence which characterize modern humanism can't be explained just by the subtraction of earlier goals and allegiances" (572; cf. 255). Not only do certain value judgments shape humanism; modern atheism would not even have come to pass without moral reasons. I think even Nietzsche, the anti-universalist, demonstrates this quite clearly: he is driven by the pathos of sincerity, and even if the overestimation of sincerity (which is in no way identical with truth) belongs to the era of authenticity, his unconditional will to sincerity, even at the cost of self-destruction, indicates that his atheism cannot be explained merely in terms of subtraction. Nietzsche does not simply return to the ancients (247). The historical nature of the self makes such a return simply impossible.

Of course, this leads to a fundamental objection to every theory of secularization: secularization cannot at all occur for the simple reason that certain value judgments are inevitable, and without a corresponding view of reality, and thus without religion in the broadest sense, there would be no value judgments. From this it follows immediately that it is fundamentally impossible to reduce the religious motives to other kinds of motives, even if in a particular case they might be (self-)deceiving (453, 459, 530). Taylor even considers whether the relative number of intensely religiously motivated people throughout all ages remains the same (91). In *Morals and Politics,* I include religion among the irreducible components of any social system, and then it is unavoidable that both immanentist religions such as Confucianism,[5] as well as worldviews that conceive themselves as antireligious, such as Marxism-Leninism, are designated as "religions."[6] As with Max Weber, Taylor is aware that he cannot really define "religion" (15), but by limiting himself to Latin Christendom, he can understand "secularization" essentially as "immanentization" (16, 429), or even as "de-Christianization." (Of course, the importance of the incarnation doctrine speaks against Taylor's conflation of the two latter terms, as he himself indicates; cf. 144.) Taylor resists the sociological expansion of the concept of religion by functionalists (780f., n. 19), but in other passages he agrees with them (516ff., 714f.). Indeed, at one point he states, "All the above shows that the religious dimension is inescapable. Perhaps there is only the choice between good and bad religion" (708; cf. 427, 768; at 491 atheism is even described as "power of another religious stripe"). Taylor is right when he occasionally remarks that the separation of church and state occurred, among other causes, for religious reasons (532, 797f., n. 43). It resulted in a greater religious freedom. "We shouldn't forget the spiritual costs of various kinds of forced conformity: hypocrisy, spiritual stultification, inner revolt against the Gospel, the confusion of faith and power, and even worse" (513). The example of the United States shows how a state can identify itself with a form of religiosity that transcends denominations and increasingly even different religions (454).[7] In fact, the pluralization of religious forms is the inevitable cost of religious freedom, and with it, a more frequent religious conversion that certainly does not preclude intensive religiosity (833f., n. 19). Taylor, the communitarian, knows that forced solidarity comes to a totalitarian end (466, 485f., 692).

Anyone who believes, along with Taylor, that there is in fact only a choice between good and bad religion will surely have an interest in the question of what makes it possible for us to decide between the two forms. Taylor himself does not address the question head-on, though neither does he conceal his own view. He represents a liberal Catholicism minus the doctrine of infallibility (512), an option that is broadly attractive because it does not try to demonize pre-modern Catholicism in any way and makes glaringly obvious, among other things, the banality of the *pro-choice* position (478f.). However much Taylor dismisses Pius IX's *Syllabus* of 1864 (569f.), he also dismisses a simplistic model of progress, and notes: "But that doesn't mean that Catholics suspicious of democracy in the nineteenth century might not have seen some of its dangers and weaknesses more clearly than we do as children of the twentieth century, who had to defend democracy against various gruesome forms of tyranny" (753). Still, Taylor's remarkable knowledge of Catholic history is not accompanied by a clear analysis of the crucial arguments in the philosophy of religion. Thus, his criticism of deism presupposes the authority of traditional orthodoxy. Taylor does not adequately account for the fact that the standards of orthodoxy have changed—even if he mentions several times the general decline of a belief in hell (13, 223).

Despite his insight into the evolving interpretations of Christianity, however, Taylor never feels compelled to inquire on his own account which tradition actually withstands the test of reason. His own Catholicism is influenced by the French personalism of the twentieth century, as indicated by his fascination with Charles Péguy (745ff.). He seems not to acknowledge that a rather formidable rationalist tendency has long been present within the Christian tradition. Those Enlightened thinkers who no longer wished to recognize the authority of the church could in part be consistently interpreted as the successors to these rationalist theologians; and undoubtedly they were often driven by religious motives—the desire to think independently about God is a direct result of the unconditional significance attached to one's own relation to the divine.[8] And even today, alienation from the church is often enough caused by an objectively unjustified misuse of clerical authority, clearly one of the cardinal sins of the church. Taylor admittedly denies a rationalist philosophy of religion, including even the proofs of God's existence (294,

551).[9] His polemic against the modern epistemological model of justification in the wake of Martin Heidegger seems to confuse origin and validity (559), and it also misconstrues the point of René Descartes' grand foundationalist project when he writes: "And, of course, knowledge of the things of 'this world,' of the natural order precedes any theoretical invocation of forces and realities transcendent to it" (558). For, according to Descartes, of course, the knowledge of God precedes knowledge of the external world. Taylor is certainly right that valuative beliefs underlie Descartes' epistemological project, but in my view that can clearly only mean that such beliefs, too, must be justified by means of the epistemic criteria developed. I am convinced that the idea of an "ultimate foundation" of norms is required in order to warrant the kind of transparadigmatic comparison that Taylor regards as entirely possible (480).

Taylor seems just as little aware that the timelessness of God strongly suggests the idea of an impersonal order as the main content of a divine spirit, a timelessness taught not only by the pagan Platonists, but also by the majority of Church Fathers, who themselves were Platonists (God's timelessness is incompatible with Taylor's metaphor of the tennis player; 277). It may be that deism destroys the crucial tension in Christianity between Platonism and the doctrine of incarnation; but it cannot be denied that deism has exhaustively developed an essential moment of Christianity. And Taylor undoubtedly underestimates the explosive power behind the problem of theodicy in developing the modern concept of God. Certainly Taylor is right that, in "the age of worldviews" (Heidegger), the problem has attained a new level of intensity; for the simple reason that it was more difficult to get by in earlier times, one was content to trust in God as a redeemer, "while accepting that we can't understand how his creation got into this fix, and whose fault it is (presumably ours)" (233; cf. 305f., 388f., 650f.). But such historical references do not solve the problem at hand. One simply cannot understand the religious nature of the enthusiasm for a deterministic system of natural laws without realizing that it helps resolve the theodicy problem—God allows innocent children to die because this simplifies considerably the laws of nature. This is Gottfried Wilhelm Leibniz's famous reply, and even if it is not necessarily heartwarming, it is presumably fair to say that, as of today, no better reply has been offered. Analogously, the tension between divine omnipotence and human free will is neglected, a tension with which both modern theology and religion have struggled. Taylor emphasizes that the doctrine of predestination "seemed to be generated inevitably from a belief in divine omnipotence" (262), and he remarks that Thomas Jefferson's deism was a reaction to the morally repugnant aspects of Calvinism (804, n. 59; cf. 78f.). Still, one would like to know what Taylor himself thinks about this tension: for the impression of its insolubility as well as of the inconsistency of traditional Christology certainly favors religious agnosticism. "But if our faith has remained at the stage of the immature images, then the story that materialism equals maturity can seem plausible" (364).

In connection with the development of the contemporary worldview, it seems important also to discuss the *moral* arguments that have led to doubts about the immortality of the soul. For, in my view, such moral arguments have proven more effective than those that rely on the development of neurological research, the findings of which can always be interpreted in a parallelist manner. With authors like Baruch Spinoza, Pierre Bayle, and Immanuel Kant there is the familiar notion that virtue must be its own reward, that in fact it is morally disgraceful to set one's sights on a reward in the afterlife. One might object that this position underwrites the subjectivist's preference for a solitary heroism, against which Taylor plays off the notion of a highest good consisting of "communion, mutual giving and receiving, as in the paradigm of the eschatological banquet" (702). Still, it is crucial to investigate the history of this argument as it pertains not only to the development of unbelief, but also to the transformation of the Christian conception of the afterlife.

A further morally relevant reason for the crisis of Christianity is certainly the growing acquaintance since the nineteenth century with non-Christian religions and their investigation using the tools of modern historiography. Anyone who accepts ethical universalism (and it speaks well of Taylor that, in spite of his reservations about Kantian formalism,[10] which I share, he stands firmly on the ground of modern universalism: 120, 608, 671), must of course ask himself with what right he can study other religions as an outside observer, so to speak, while refusing to assume a third-person perspective toward his own religion. This question is all the more pressing since the transition into the role of a distant observer, who brackets the search for truth, is fortunately not the only alternative. Johann Wolfgang von Goethe's *Die Geheimnisse* (*The Mysteries*) and Hegel's *Vorlesungen über die Philosophie der Religion* (*Lectures on the Philosophy of Religion*) are impressive examples of an attempt to overcome the provinciality of blindly identifying with one's own religion due to sheer ignorance of other religions, while at the same time avoiding a position of complete neutrality. The search for a natural religion—which, according to Taylor, is one of the three features of deism (221), though he pays less attention to this than the other two characteristics (the physico-theology and the impersonal order)—may have unjustly ignored a wealth of historical traditions. The kind of interreligious dialogue needed today, however, is hardly possible without the regulative idea of such a religion. Taylor of course rejects the idea that commitment to our own religion comes about as the result of comparing all religions (680).

Here is not the place to pursue philosophical arguments for religion. I am much more concerned with the fairly trivial claim that every account of the secularization process presupposes certain views within the philosophy of religion that do not disappear simply by leaving them out of the discussion. If anyone's concept of God differs from that of Taylor, that person will also have a different view of the history of religious thought. Thus he might grant, for example, that Gottfried Wilhelm Leibniz, Gotthold Ephraim Lessing, Immanuel Kant, and German idealism all played a key constructive role in formulating a more sophisticated concept of God. This is, by the way, not just the subjective perspective of a philosopher with hard-nosed rationalist tendencies; the most important modern theology—that of Friedrich Schleiermacher—also emerges partly in response to Kant and Johann Gottlieb Fichte in the context of early romanticism. It is unfortunate that the name of this most original theologian since Thomas Aquinas occurs only once, and indeed, quite in passing (489). Considering the content of their doctrines, I find less regrettable the complete absence of the dialectical theologians of the twentieth century, but in light of their enormous influence, also on Catholic theology, an inclusion of the Protestant history of theology in a book of this scope would have been appropriate. Within Catholic theology, Taylor points to the strides made by Yves Congar, Jean Daniélou, and Henri de Lubac toward overcoming the neo-scholastic tradition by reverting to the Church Fathers and the preparation of the Second Vatican Council (752, 847f., n. 39). Taylor connects with Irenaeus of Lyons his own conception of human education out of a violence that is rooted in man's animal nature but becomes culturally transformed quite early on (668)— of course, he might also have mentioned Lessing.[11]

Things become even more complicated if the discussion about secularization applies, not to Christianity alone, but to religion in general. For, compared with ancient national religions, even Christianity appears to be a secularizing force, as not only Friedrich Schiller recognizes in "Die Götter Griechenlandes" (The Gods of Greece). Taylor himself writes: "There were important Christian motives for going the route of disenchantment" (26; cf. 74, 143, 375). Disenchantment cannot be equated with the decline of religion, as Max Weber wrongly supposed (553). If it is true even of the Reformation that it was both an expansion as well as a limitation of the sacred (79), there remains the question of how to evaluate the transition from national religions to universal religions during the so-called Axial age, a period to which Taylor, following Karl Jaspers, devotes a good deal of attention.[12] On the one hand, Taylor laments the loss of popular cults whose significance he holds, along with Mircea Eliade and especially Victor Turner (47ff.), in high regard. These cults partially survived through the Axial age, even through the period of Christianization up until the nineteenth century. But the blame lies with church authorities for repressing them more and more. Today, paradoxically, it would be the Pentecostal movement that stops this unholy tendency toward "excarnation" that prevailed in the Reformation (614). "A strange turn of events, which would surprise Calvin, were he to return!" (503). "The Great Disembedding," that individualistic dissolution of the organic communities of antiquity, begins with the Axial age (146). On the other hand, Taylor takes into account that only the Axial age made it possible to develop a concept of transcendence, a concept foreign to earlier religions, for which the divine embraced both good and evil. "Seen from another angle, this means a change in our attitude to evil, as the destructive, harm-inflicting side of things. This is no longer just part of the order of things, to be accepted as such. Something has to be done about it" (153). For the first time the need arose of transcending nature and community.

The immanent Counter-Enlightenment seems from this perspective, not as irreligious, but as an attempt to return to an earlier (and more *primitive,* I do not hesitate in saying) form of religiosity, as a form, in Peter Gay's words, of "modern paganism" (771). Here the central question concerning his own position is raised once again: anyone who denies, against Aristotelianism, an immanentist foundation of ethics will recognize in universal religions the crucial breakthrough of a higher form of moral, and thus, also religious, consciousness that finds its clearest conceptual articulation in Kant. Ultimately, the equilibrium model of early modernity (176ff.) is closer to Aristotle's view than to Kant's, according to whom morality can never be reduced to rational egoism or pursuit of happiness. But Taylor rejects a Kantian approach to ethics (282), and even if, following Ivan Illich (737ff.), he views the legal regulation of the church in an excessively negative or perhaps even nomophobic way (cf. 707), one must agree that the ability to overcome rigid ideas about justice, as in the South African Truth and Reconciliation Commission, is superb (705ff.). But does that not imply that forgiveness is a higher moral principle? It is regrettable that Taylor never mentions Rudolf Otto's peerless book, *Das Heilige* (*The Idea of the Holy*), from 1917, which interprets the history of religion from the tension between the experience of the numinous and the moral imperative.

Yet Taylor would probably object to the above alternative account of secularization in the following way: the reconstruction of belief in God from pure reason—be it theoretical or practical—does no justice at all to the social power of religion. Religion certainly is more than a theological insight based on arguments. But after the Enlightenment, religion can hardly be preached in good conscience *without* such arguments. What must be added to the arguments are socially shared emotions, and normally these are evoked only through paradigmatic histories. An interesting question is how, after the erosion of the Bible's authoritative status in the nineteenth century, partly due to the historical method, an existential reappropriation of biblical narratives in great world literature occurred. *Great Expectations* by Charles Dickens, who had Unitarian sympathies, is an excellent example.[13] Religious kitsch, on the other hand, is not only aesthetically impermissible, it threatens to further alienate intelligent people from traditional religions. More important than good stories are of course living examples of faith; the need for these is great, and a single pope like John XXIII might attract more people to traditional religion than various repulsive popes have driven away. "A pope just had to sound like a Christian, and many immemorial resistances melted" (727). Presumably it is also the experience of human fallibility and guilt, such as that experienced in the aftermath of the French Revolution and the totalitarian adventures of the twentieth century, that greatly intensifies doubts about the self-idolization of humans (cf. 598). The environmental catastrophe toward which we are inevitably headed will therefore encourage religious fervor in the strict sense.

Taylor's construction of the history of the "buffered self" is quite successful, and it invites the reader to metaphysical speculation. In *Die Philosophie der ökologischen Krise*,[14] I distinguish between five concepts of nature that ultimately culminate in the Cartesian dualism between *res extensa* and *res cogitans;* analogously, in *Morals and Politics*,[15] I distinguish between five interpretations of the relation between "is" and "ought," which reach an apex in Kantian dualism. In the latter book, I interpret the trend toward the formation of subjective centers not only as a law of the development of conscious states, but rather as a metaphysical blueprint that structures the development of the organic world, and ultimately the emergence of spirit out of the principle of life.[16] Insofar as the self-empowerment of modern subjectivity is an expression of this trend, I see in it, paradoxically, a necessary manifestation of the absolute. Certainly this is not its last appearance, but we have to pursue further Taylor's coy remark that "We might even be tempted to say that modern unbelief is providential, but that might be too provocative a way of putting it" (637).[17] Only the experience of the utter contradiction of a purely secular religion can lead to a deeper relation to God, a relation in which autonomy will come to play a more significant role than in earlier epochs. "Gottes ist der Orient! Gottes ist der Okzident!" ("To God belongs the East! To God belongs the West!"), as Goethe says in the *West-östlicher Diwan* (*West-Eastern Divan*). To God belongs modern secularism as well.

Translated by Jason Miller

NOTES

1. As is common in the Anglo-American world, I use the term "philosophy of religion" to refer to what should be more appropriately called "philosophical theology." For "philosophy of religion" would better fit the discipline dealing with the human phenomenon of religion, a subdiscipline of the philosophy of humankind intersecting with, among others, social philosophy, philosophy of history, and aesthetics. Also, the study of the pathologies of human religion, such as superstition, fanaticism, and sentimentality, belongs to this discipline. I deal here only with metaphysical and epistemological questions related to God.

2. Cf. *Summa theologica* I 1, 2; I 2, 2, II–II 1, 5.

3. Cf. Henricus Denzinger and Adolfus Schönmetzer, *Enchiridion Symbolorum, definitionum et declarationum de rebus fidei et morum* (Barcino: Herder, 1963), n. 2751–56 and n. 2765–69.

4. This intellectual mésalliance is regrettable, given the nihilistic tendencies of Heidegger's philosophy, so well elaborated by Hans Jonas, "Gnosis, Existenzialismus and Nihilismus," in Hans Jonas, *Zwischen Nichts und Ewigkeit* (Göttingen: Vandenhoeck & Ruprecht, 1963), 5–25.

5. The rationalistic strand is not limited to the heterodox movement of gnosticism. Thus it can be misleading to see modern rationalists such as Hegel and Schelling mainly as heirs of gnosticism. There are, however, other common traits. See Peter Koslowski's impressive study *Philosophien der Offenbarung: Antiker Gnostizismus; Franz von Baader, Schelling* (Paderborn: Schöningh, 2001).

6. See *De principiis* I Praef. 2; I 5, 4; III 3, 4; III 5, 3; IV 2, 2; IV 3, 14.

7. See *Contra academicos* I 3, 9 and *De ordine* II 9, 26: authority is important only at the start of the intellectual process. See my interpretation of these and

other dialogues dealing with the relation of reason and authority in *The Philosophical Dialogue* (Notre Dame: University of Notre Dame Press, 2012), 312ff.

8. See Bernd Goebel, *Rectitudo: Wahrheit and Freiheit bei Anselm von Canterbury* (Münster: Aschendorff, 2001).

9. Cf. *A Treatise of Human Nature* III 1, 1.

10. Kant unfolded the argument in the second and third *Critiques*. A modern version of "axiarchism," the idea that values determine being, was proposed by John Leslie, *Value and Existence* (Totowa, NJ: Rowan and Littlefield, 1979).

11. See chapter 5 of this volume.

12. Needless to say, I do believe that Darwinism is compatible with an objective-idealist version of theism. See Vittorio Hösle, "Objective Idealism and Darwinism," in *Darwinism and Philosophy,* ed. V. Hösle and C. Illies (Notre Dame: University of Notre Dame Press, 2005), 216–42.

13. *Nouveaux essais* II 10 §7, in Gottfried W. Leibniz, *Die Philosophischen Schriften V,* ed. C. Gerhardt (Berlin: Weidmann, 1882), 419.

14. Alvin Plantinga, *The Nature of Necessity* (Oxford: Clarendon, 1982), 216.

15. See, for example, René Descartes, *Principia philosophiae* II 36ff.

16. See Josef Schmidt, *Philosophische Theologie* (Stuttgart: Kohlhammer, 2003), 79–105: "Der alethologische Gottesbeweis." An important recent book that uses transcendental arguments for the foundation of a metaphysical view recognizing in spirit the ultimate reality is the latest work by Béla Weissmahr, *Die Wirklichkeit des Geistes* (Stuttgart: Kohlhammer, 2006). A remarkable defense of a spiritualist and theistic metaphysics can be found in a recent work of Germany's best analytical philosopher: Franz von Kutschera, *Die Wege des Idealismus* (Paderborn: Mentis, 2006), 252ff. It starts from the assumption (presumed to be a simple hypothesis) of the intelligibility of being.

17. See my essay "Foundational Issues of Objective Idealism," in Vittorio Hösle, *Objective Idealism, Ethics, and Politics* (Notre Dame: University of Notre Dame Press, 1998), 1–40 and 201–9 (German version, 1986).

18. See my preface to Vittorio Hösle, *Platon interpretieren* (Paderborn: Schöningh, 2004), 19ff. On Plato's natural theology as continuation of the pre-Socratic doctrines, see Markus Enders, *Natürliche Theologie im Denken der Griechen* (Frankfurt: Knecht, 2000).

19. I am aware of the fact that there are irreligious interpretations of Hegel. I defend a different one in my book *Hegels System* (Hamburg: Meiner, 1987).

20. Analogously, from a Kantian point of view, God seems to become identical with practical reason. See the impressive book by Gerhard Schwarz, *Est Deus in nobis: Die Identität von Gott und reiner praktischer Vernunft in Immanuel Kants "Kritik der praktischen Vernunft"* (Berlin: Verlag TU, 2004).

21. See, for example, Giovanni B. Sala, *Die Christologie in Kants "Religion innerhalb der Grenzen der blossen Vernunft"* (Weilheim: Gustav-Siewerth-Akademie, 2000).

22. See my criticism in chapter 12 of this volume.

23. See Luc Foisneau, *Hobbes et la toute-puissance de Dieu* (Paris: Presses universitaires de France, 2000).

24. See the important studies by Dieter Wandschneider, particularly "Letztbegründung und Logik," in *Letztbegründung als System,* ed. H.-D. Klein (Bonn: Bouvier, 1994), 84–103.

25. Cf. *Confessiones* IV 16, 29. Cf. also VII 4, 6.

26. See his essay "Versuch einiger Betrachtungen über den Optimismus," A 4 f, in Immanuel Kant, *Werke* I, ed. W. Weischedel (Wiesbaden: Insel, 1960), 588ff.

27. On this issue, see the excellent reflections by Friedrich Hermanni, *Das Böse und die Theodizee* (Gütersloh: Chr. Kaiser, 2002), 266–91.

28. See Günther Nicolin, ed., *Hegel in Berichten seiner Zeitgenossen* (Hamburg: Meiner, 1970), 261, n. 397.

29. See, for example, the end of the fifth part of René Descartes, *Discours de la méthode,* ed. F. Misrachi (Paris: Union générale d'éditions, 1951), 88. The anti-Cartesian stance of some modern theologians, who oppose the belief in the resurrection of the body to Descartes' doctrine, is misguided, for they, too, need some form of dualism to deal with the interim state between death and resurrection. And once this is granted, it is not easy to explain why resurrection is needed at all. The doctrine that God snatches away the body or at least the brain of dead persons in order to preserve them until resurrection and replaces them by matter that looks the same is an ingenious, but hardly attractive feature of Christian materialism.

30. This is what makes Hegel's stance against immortality so strong. See particularly the early works on religion in G. W. F. Hegel, *Werke* I, ed. E. Moldenhauer and K. M. Michel (Frankfurt: Suhrkamp, 1969–71), 100 and 195, and the anecdote told by Heinrich Heine in Günther Nicolin, ed., *Hegel in Berichten seiner Zeitgenossen* (Hamburg: Felix Meiner, 1970), 234f., n. 363. Of course, metaphysical considerations also play a role; for even if Hegel is not a materialist, his peculiar spiritualism represents a form of monopsychism.

31. Of course, suffering and injustice also cause vices. But it may well be that the value of the positive results far outweighs the negative value of those vices; after all, they are quite natural and do not radically change the value balance that existed before.

32. *Gott als Geheimnis der Welt* (Tübingen: J. C. B. Mohr [Paul Siebeck], 1986). The polemic against what Jüngel calls with Abraham Calov and Karl Barth "mixophilosophicotheologia" (204, n. 1) is misleading, for all disciplines are bound by conceptual analysis and thus none can get rid of philosophy. It is a good idea also for theologians, if they want to speak about necessity, to familiarize themselves with the basic concepts of modal logic.

33. *Cur Deus homo* II 5.

34. "On the Study of the Evidences of Christianity," in Frederick Temple et al., *Essays and Reviews* (London: John W. Parker, 1860), 94–144, 114.

35. *Apologia Pro Vita Sua* (Mineola, NY: Dover, 2005), 198f.

36. This was already said by some ancient Christian apologetics, but nobody has formulated it as beautifully as Dante does in *Paradiso* XXIV 106ff.

37. On the interpretation of the Bible, see chapter 7 of this volume.

38. An impressive overview of the history of Christianity can be found in Hans Küng, *Christianity: Essence, History and Future* (New York: Continuum, 1995).

39. Compare Alexis de Tocqueville's reflections on the "religious terror" caused in him by the triumph of democracy that he cannot help interpreting otherwise than as an expression of the divine will (*De la démocratie en Amérique* I [Paris: GF Flammarion, 1981], 61).

40. See the magnificent reconstruction by Jonathan Israel, *Radical Enlightenment* (Oxford: Oxford University Press, 2001); *Enlightenment Contested* (Oxford: Oxford University Press, 2006); and *Democratic Enlightenment: Philosophy, Revolution, and Human Rights 1750–1790* (Oxford: Oxford University Press, 2011).

41. On this issue, see Vittorio Hösle, *Die Krise der Gegenwart und die Verantwortung der Philosophie* (München: C. H. Beck, 1997), 192ff.

42. "Es ist ganz in der Ordnung, ihm zu verbieten, sie auf die Kanzel zu bringen, und es ist von ihm selbst, wenn er nur gehörig aufgeklärt ist, gewissenlos, dies zu thun" (*Das System der Sittenlehre nach den Prinzipien der Wissenschaftslehre* §18 V, in Johann Gottfried Fichte, *Werke IV,* ed. I. H. Fichte [Berlin: de Gruyter, 1971], 252).

43. See my reflections in *Morals and Politics* (Notre Dame: University of Notre Dame Press, 2004), 721.

44. It is expressed in Paul's letter to the Philippians 2:7.

45. This holds a fortiori for later religious reformers. The cult of its founder in Lutheranism (wisely avoided by Calvinism) must either lead to frustrations, when one studies the figure in more detail, or to absurd imitations (brilliantly caricatured in chapter XII of Thomas Mann's *Doktor Faustus*).

46. *Jesus of Nazareth* (New York: Doubleday, 2007).

47. In Johann Wolfgang von Goethe's last novel, *Wilhelm Meisters Wanderjahre* (*Wilhelm Meister's Journeyman Years*), there is in the gallery of the Pedagogical Province a sharp division between the depiction of the life and that of the death of Jesus—"denn zu jenen Prüfungen ist jeder, zu diesem sind nur wenige berufen" (*Goethes Werke* VIII, ed. E. Trunz [München: C. H. Beck, 1981], 163). Goethe may be right that special training is needed to understand and appropriate the passion, but he is wrong in wanting to exclude from its contemplation most people. For even if tremendous suffering may not befall everybody, every human has the opportunity to witness it in others.

48. See Adolf Harnack, *Das Wesen des Christentums* (Leipzig: J. C. Hinrichs, 1901), 56–65: "Das Evangelium und die Armut, oder die soziale Frage."

49. Probably no other modern author has been able to capture this aspect of Christian ethics as aesthetically perfectly as Charles Dickens. See my essay "The Lost Prodigal Son's Corporal Works of Mercy and the Bridegroom's Wedding: The Religious Subtext of Charles Dickens' *Great Expectations,*" *Anglia* 126 (2008): 477–502.

Chapter 2. *Why Teleological Principles Are Inevitable for Reason: Natural Theology after Darwin*

1. Charles Darwin, *The Autobiography of Charles Darwin 1809–1882,* ed. N. Barlow (New York/London: Norton, 1993), 126.

2. A good overview of classic texts of the debate can be found in *Evolution and Creationism: A Documentary and Reference Guide,* ed. C. C. Young and M. A. Largent (Westport, CT: Greenwood, 2007).

3. Charles Darwin, *The Origin of Species by Means of Natural Selection,* ed. J. W. Burrow (Harmondsworth: Penguin, 1968), 458. (This is the first edition of 1859.)

4. See particularly Richard Dawkins, *The God Delusion* (London: Bantam, 2006).

5. On the philosophical struggles to make sense of the Bible, see chapter 7 in this volume.

6. The intentionalist meaning of "selection" has to be rejected when thinking about natural selection. "In the literal sense of the word, no doubt, Natural Selection is a false term" (Charles Darwin, *The Origin of Species 1876* [= *The Works of Charles Darwin,* ed. P. H. Barrett and R. B. Freeman, vol. 16] [London: William Pickering, 1988], 66).

7. See William Paley, *Natural Theology; or, Evidences of the Existence and Attributes of the Deity, collected from the appearances of nature* (London: J. Faulder, 1809), 1ff., 416ff.

8. Leibniz sometimes uses the balancing argument, even if it cannot prove that the actual world is the best possible; see *Essais de théodicée* §258 (Gottfried Wilhelm Leibniz, *Die philosophischen Schriften,* ed. C. J. Gerhardt, 7 vols. [Berlin: Weidmann, 1875–90], VI 269).

9. A modern version of this belief is forcefully articulated by Jonathan Balcombe, *Pleasurable Kingdom: Animals and the Nature of Feeling Good* (New York: Macmillan, 2006). The contrary position has been urged most forcefully by the pessimist philosopher Arthur Schopenhauer, who sarcastically asks us to compare the pleasure of an animal devouring another with the pain of the devoured one (*Parerga und Paralipomena* §149; *Zürcher Ausgabe: Werke in zehn Bänden,* 10 vols. [Zürich: Diogenes, 1977], 9.317). But the comparison is unfair, for what should be looked at is the pleasure that the animal now devoured enjoyed earlier in its

whole life, not the momentary pleasure of the predator. Schopenhauer further-more believes that, although a violent end is not as common among humankind as among other animals, still human life is more miserable because the pain is not simply transient, but both anticipated and remembered (§153; 1977, 9.318ff.).

10. Charles Darwin, *The Origin of Species* . . . (Harmondsworth: Penguin, 1968), 129.

11. With regard to this issue, Darwin agrees with Schopenhauer (*Parerga und Paralipomena* §173; 1977, 9.351).

12. Charles Darwin, *Variation of Animals and Plants under Domestication,* vol. II (= *The Works of Charles Darwin,* ed. P. H. Barrett and R. B. Freeman, vol. 20 [London: William Pickering, 1988]), 371.

13. Charles Darwin, *The Descent of Man, and Selection in Relation to Sex* (Princeton: Princeton University Press, 1981), I 65ff.

14. Already on February 17, 1861, he had written to Asa Gray: "With re-spect to Design &c . . . I have no real objection, nor any real foundation, nor any clear view.—As I before said I flounder hopelessly in the mud" (Charles Darwin, *The Correspondence of Charles Darwin, Vol. 9, 1861* [Cambridge: Cambridge University Press, 1994], 30). Darwin refers to various earlier letters, as, for example, from November 26, 1860 (*The Correspondence of Charles Darwin, Vol. 8, 1860* [Cambridge: Cambridge University Press, 1993], 496). The correspondence with Gray encompasses in a fascinating mixture botanical, theological, and political issues.

15. See John W. Yolton, ed., *Philosophy, Religion and Science in the Seventeenth and Eighteenth Centuries* (Rochester: Rochester University Press, 1990).

16. Suffice it to point to the end of the second book of Aristotle's *Physics,* where the author rejects the primitive pre-Darwinian theory of Empedocles, who does not yet use differential reproductive rates (198b10ff.). The whole argument works only because Aristotle ignores the concept of natural law, as Hans Wagner rightly observes (*Aristoteles: Physikvorlesung,* ed. H. Wagner [Darmstadt: Wissenschaftliche Buchgesellschaft, 1979], 479).

17. The decline of deism in the nineteenth century has various reasons—one, no doubt, that it had penetrated and transformed orthodox Christianity. It became superfluous. I use "natural theology" as equivalent to "rational the-ology," even if one may argue that natural theology is the subset of rational theology that uses only a posteriori arguments for God's existence. Rational the-ology is broader since it also recognizes a priori arguments such as the ontological and the moral ones.

18. "On the Study of the Evidences of Christianity," in *Essays and Reviews,* ed. Frederick Temple et al. (London: John W. Parker, 1860), 94–144, 114.

19. See *Ethica* I 28. Edwin Curley, *Spinoza's Metaphysics: An Essay in Interpretation* (Cambridge, MA: Harvard University Press, 1969), recognized that by doing so Spinoza anticipated the Carl Gustav Hempel–Paul Oppenheim scheme of explanation.

20. *Ethica* I Appendix.

21. See Matthias Schramm, *Natur ohne Sinn? Das Ende des teleologischen Weltbildes* (Graz/Vienna/Cologne: Styria, 1985), 71. Cf., for example, Kant, *The Only Possible Argument in Support of a Demonstration of the Existence of God,* A 63f. Kant speaks of the parsimony of nature (A 63, 141).

22. See *Principes de la Nature et de la Grace, fondés en raison,* in *Die philosophischen Schriften,* ed. C. I. Gerhardt, 7 vols. (Hildesheim: Olms, 1875–90), VI 598–606, 603. One of the great insights of Kant's aforementioned work is that even the existence of logically necessary laws of nature can be interpreted as a manifestation of divine reason (A 56, 101, 118); thus, he combines Spinoza and Leibniz. Interesting are, for example, his reflections on the geometric properties of the hexagon and its importance in nature (A 95, 141, 152). Compare Darwin, *The Origin of Species . . .* (1968), 247ff. on the bees' comb.

23. This unpublished letter of January 4, 1883, to Francis Darwin is quoted according to Phillip Sloan, "'It Might Be Called Reverence,'" in *Darwinism and Philosophy,* ed. V. Hösle and C. Illies (Notre Dame: University of Notre Dame Press, 2005), 143–65, 143.

24. Whewell's third Bridgewater Treatise is quoted already in the notebooks (C 72 and C 91, in Charles Darwin, *Notebooks, 1836–1844,* ed. P. H. Barrett et al. [Ithaca, NY: Cornell University Press, 1987], 262 and 266) and will offer the first of the two citations placed at the beginning of *The Origin.* The passage can be found at the beginning of the eighth chapter of the third book (William Whewell, *Astronomy and General Physics Considered with Reference to Natural Theology* [Philadelphia: Carey, Lea & Blanchard, 1833], 267).

25. An intermediate step between the general theory and its application to biology was the uniformitarianism of James Hutton and Charles Lyell. See Asa Gray, *Darwiniana: Essays and Reviews pertaining to Darwinism* (New York: D. Appleton, 1884), 109 and Thomas H. Huxley, who called "the 'Origin of Species' the logical sequence of the 'Principles of Geology'" (*Darwiniana: Essays* [New York: D. Appleton, 1896], 232).

26. See C 270, C 267, M 104, M 155, N 101, N 184 (*Notebooks,* 321, 325, 545, 559, 591, 596).

27. David Hume, *Dialogues Concerning Natural Religion* (Indianapolis: Bobbs-Merrill, 1947), 185.

28. M 27, M 30f., N 49 (*Notebooks,* 526, 526f., 576f.).

29. M 136; *Notebooks,* 553.

30. Another important Christian Darwinist was St. George Mivart, whose relations with Darwin, however, quickly worsened after the publication of his *On the Genesis of Species* of 1871.

31. Asa Gray, *Natural Science and Religion: Two Lectures delivered to the Theological School of Yale College* (New York: Charles Scribner's Sons, 1880), 458ff.; *Darwiniana,* 260f..

32. "I declare that you know my Book as well as I do myself," Darwin wrote him on July 22, 1860 (*Correspondence, Vol. 8,* 298).

33. I may mention that the copy of *Natural Science and Religion* I am using (from the Libraries of the University of Notre Dame) is graced by an autographed dedication in Latin by the author to the "amicissimo" B. Peirce—no doubt his Harvard colleague Benjamin Peirce, the noted mathematician, devout Christian, and father of the greatest American philosopher, Charles Sanders Peirce, whose late philosophy of evolutionary love has some similarities with Gray's theory.

34. Already on September 26, 1860, Darwin reacted with the following words to the 1860 articles by Gray: "I do not pretend to be a good judge, as I have never attended to Logic, Philosophy &c; but it is my opinion that you are best reasoner, of any man, let him who he may, that I ever read . . . The two last essays are *far* the best Theistic essays I ever read" (*Correspondence, Vol. 8,* 388). On October 24, 1860, Darwin wrote Gray that Lyell had affirmed: "It would be well worth while if a little Book could be got up by Asa Gray for the theological part is so admirable" (443). Gray's two books deserve indeed to be reprinted today. This great American intellectual might even posthumously contribute to an end of the destructive culture war in the United States about evolution. For he was, as Darwin called him, "a hybrid, a complex cross of Lawyer, Poet, Naturalist, & Theologian!—Was there ever such a monster seen before?" (350). In letters to others, however, Darwin was not so generous. Alluding to Auguste Comte's theory of the three stages, Darwin criticizes in a letter to Charles Lyell of August 1, 1861, Herschel and Gray for being still caught up in the theological state of science (*Correspondence, Vol. 9,* 226f.).

35. In another essay, the theory of occasional direct action is mentioned as a third possibility. But while it is called the most popular, Gray claims that it is the least attractive to thoughtful people (*Darwiniana,* 159). He calls the idea that each organ was executed by God "an idea which has been set up as the orthodox doctrine, but which to St. Augustine and other learned Christian fathers would have savored of heterodoxy" (357). *Natural Science,* 83 also mentions Thomas Aquinas, Leibniz, and Nicolas Malebranche.

36. I have not been able to find out for whom "D.T." stands, which is the name of the interlocutor of "A.G.," which stands for Asa Gray.

37. An analogous argument can be found in Kant's *Universal Natural History and Theory of Heaven:* the mechanical explanation of the genesis of the solar system does not exclude its teleological interpretation (A XXff., 71).

38. The term "ecology" was coined in 1866 by the Darwinian Ernst Haeckel (see Günther Leps, "Ökologie und Ökosystemforschung," in *Geschichte der Biologie,* ed. I. Jahn [Hamburg: Nikol, 2004], 601–19, 601).

39. *The Origin of Species . . .* (1968), 127.

40. See Sara J. Miles, "Charles Darwin and Asa Gray Discuss Teleology and Design," *Perspectives on Science and Christian Faith* 53 (2001): 196–201.

41. See Schramm, *Natur ohne Sinn?* 54 and 164f., who follows Hans Freudenthal.

42. Cf. his text *An mundus perfectione crescat* (Gottfried Wilhelm Leibniz, *Kleine Schriften zur Metaphysik* [Darmstadt: Wissenschaftliche Buchgesellschaft, 1965], 368ff.).

43. In a letter to Gray on June 5, 1861, Darwin rejects the idea of designed variation and writes: "what an enormous field of undesigned variability there is ready for natural selection to appropriate for any purpose useful to each creature" (*Correspondence, Vol. 9,* 162; see also *Vol. 8,* 275, 389).

44. See Ernan McMullin, "Could Natural Selection be Purposive?" in *Divine Action and Natural Selection,* ed. J. Seckbach and R. Gordon (Singapore: World Scientific, 2008), 115–25. Already Darwin made this point: *Correspondence, Vol. 9,* 226.

45. *The Origin of Species . . . ,* 263.

46. *Correspondence, Vol. 8,* 224.

47. See *Essais de théodicée* §114 (ed. Gerhardt, VI 166). Similarly Thomas Aquinas, *Summa theologiae* I q. 19 a. 9 c. and q. 49 a.2 c.

48. Alfred Russel Wallace, *An Anthology of His Shorter Writings* (Oxford: Oxford University Press, 1991), 300.

49. It remains an astonishing fact in comparative philosophy that the thinker who came closest to Hume's criticism is the Indian Ramanuja from the eleventh/twelfth century in the *Sri Bhashya,* an author, of course, unknown to Hume. See Keith E. Yandell, *Philosophy of Religion: A Contemporary Introduction* (London: Routledge, 1999), 205ff. The fact proves a strange convergence of the development of the human mind, one is tempted to say: some teleology in the history of philosophy.

50. Hume, *Dialogues,* 149.

51. Cleanthes' counterarguments partly beg the question and partly make wrong presuppositions (thus he confuses causes with reasons, 190), and since Philo points to the very different problem that the necessity of God may entail the necessity of the world (191) and thus a Spinozian conception, we must here leave it open whether Hume shared all the arguments by Cleanthes, who in the other parts of the dialogue argues embarrassingly badly.

52. For fairness's sake one has to mention that, for example, Paley is aware that the attributes ascribable to the cause of the world are only "beyond all comparison" (*Natural Theology,* 443f.).

53. See also Kant's 1788 essay *On the Use of Teleological Principles in Philosophy,* A 36f.

54. This is not to say that all of his ideas in the field of philosophy of religion are valid. Thus, Kant's criticism does not overturn the ontological proof in

the version proposed by Alvin Plantinga, *The Nature of Necessity* (Oxford: Clarendon, 1982), 197 ff. Its validity and soundness would eliminate the subjective
limitations to which Kant subjects teleological arguments.

55. For a concrete elaboration of the way in which transcendental values
are realized in evolution, see my essay "Objective Idealism and Darwinism," in
Darwinism and Philosophy, 216–42; on a possible teleological interpretation of
evolution toward humans, see Dieter Wandschneider, "On the Problem of Direction and Goal in Biological Evolution," in *Darwinism and Philosophy,* 196–215;
on the overcoming of the dualism between nature and Ought, see Christian Illies, *Philosophische Anthropologie im biologischen Zeitalter* (Frankfurt: Suhrkamp, 2006).

56. See chapter 5 of this volume.

57. We have to distinguish the multiverse conception in a strict modal
sense from Lee Smolin's idea of "cosmological natural selection." Since according to it new "universes" are created by collapsing black holes, they all form a
single world even if some constant parameters may differ in the various "universes." The theory is scientific, not metaphysic, and does not add anything relevant to the well-known fact that only small parts of the world are places for life
and mind. Furthermore, the theory has only little to do with natural selection.

Chapter 3. *Theodicy Strategies in Leibniz, Hegel, Jonas*

1. John L. Mackie, *The Miracle of Theism: Arguments for and against the Existence of God* (Oxford: Oxford University Press, 1982).

2. Compare, for example, Richard Swinburne, *The Existence of God* (Oxford: Oxford University Press, 1979), 200ff.

3. Cf. Max Weber, *Wirtschaft und Gesellschaft* (Tübingen: J. C. B. Mohr
[Paul Siebeck], 1980), 314ff.: second part, chapter 5, §8: "Das Problem der
Theodizee."

4. "wir darin irren, wenn, was nur relativ für Menschen in diesem Leben
Gesetz ist, wir für schlechthin als ein solches beurteilen, und so das, was unsrer
Betrachtung der Dinge aus so niedrigem Standpunkte als zweckwidrig erscheint,
dafür auch, aus dem höchsten Standpunkte betrachtet, halten": "Diese Apolo-
gie, in welcher die Verantwortung ärger ist als die Beschwerde, bedarf keiner
Widerlegung; und kann sicher der Verabscheuung jedes Menschen, der das
mindeste Gefühl für Sittlichkeit hat, frei überlassen werden" (Immanuel Kant,
Über das Mißlingen aller philosophischen Versuche in der Theodizee, A 201). Toward the
end of the treatise, however, the Kantian option for an authentic instead of a
doctrinal theodicy itself gets into an unintended proximity with voluntarism.

5. *Die Fragmente der Vorsokratiker,* Greek and German by H. Diels, ed.
W. Kranz, 3 vols. (Berlin: Weidmann, 1954), 85 B 8. Famous is the classical formulation of the problem in Epicurus; cf. Lactantius, *De ira Dei* 13, 20f.

6. Cf. Richard Schenk, "Daedalus medii aevi? Die Labyrinthe der Theo-dizee im Mittelalter," *Jahrbuch, für Philosophie des Forschungsinstituts für Philosophie Hannover* 9 (1998): 15–35.

7. I follow Edwin Curley, *Spinoza's Metaphysics* (Cambridge, MA: Harvard University Press, 1969), and Jonathan Bennett, *A Study of Spinoza's "Ethics"* (Indianapolis: Hackett, 1984).

8. Arthur Schopenhauer, *Die Welt als Wille und Vorstellung,* addenda to the fourth book, chapter 46, in *Zürcher Ausgabe: Werke in zehn Bänden* (Zürich: Diogenes, 1977), IV 683. Schopenhauer claims to deliver a proof for his thesis; but this proof is inductive and as such fraught with difficulties that are analogous to those of the teleological proof of God. Leibniz, however, derives his thesis deductively from the ontological proof of God. Furthermore, dysteleologies or suffering may be explained by Leibniz by pointing to the simplicity of the laws of nature of our world since this is a positive value; but Schopenhauer cannot use the same argument to explain why the world has not even more suffering than it has.

9. "utrum Deus possit meliora facere ea quae facit."

10. "potentissime et sapientissime."

11. Cf. Stephen Grover, "Why Only the Best Is Good Enough," *Analysis* 48 (1988): 224.

12. Cf. Bernd Gräfrath, *Es fällt nicht leicht, ein Gott zu sein* (München: C. H. Beck, 1998), 60ff. I owe a lot to this book's chapter on Leibniz.

13. *Essais de Théodicée* §416, in *Die philosophischen Schriften von G. W. Leibniz,* ed. C. J. Gerhardt (Berlin: Weidmann, 1875–90), VI 364.

14. I understand "world" as the totality of intra-mundane events here, that is, not as the whole consisting of God and the world (in the aforementioned way).

15. "qui joints ensemble produisent le plus réalité, le plus de perfection, le plus d'intelligibilité" (*Essais de Théodicée* §201, VI 236).

16. "Il suit de la Perfection Supreme de Dieu, qu'en produisant l'Univers il a choisi le meilleur Plan possible, où il y ait la plus grande varieté, avec le plus grand ordre: le terrain, le lieu, le temps, les mieux menagés: le plus d'effect produit par les voyes les plus simples" (*Principes de la Nature et de la Grace, fondés en raison* §10; VI 603).

17. "le plus de puissance, le plus de connoissance, le plus de bonheur et de bonté dans les creatures, que l'Univers en pouvoit admettre."

18. "Cette Cité de Dieu, cette Monarchie veritablement Universelle est un Monde Moral dans le Monde Naturel, et ce qu'il y a de plus elevé et de plus divin dans les ouvrages de Dieu et c'est en luy que consiste veritablement la gloire de Dieu, puisqu'il n'y en auroit point, si sa grandeur et sa bonté n'étoient pas connues et admirées par les esprits: c'est aussi par rapport à cette cité divine, qu'il a

proprement de la Bonté, au lieu que sa sagesse et sa puissance se montrent partout" (*Monadologie* §86; VI 621f.)

19. *Essais de Théodicée* §118; VI 169.

20. This holds at least for the late theory, for instance, in the *Théodicée*. In the *Discours de métaphysique* happiness of spirits still counts as "the principal objective of God" ("le principal but de Dieu"; §V; IV 430).

21. "que le mal excite plustost nostre attention que le bien: mais cette même raison confirme que le mal est plus rare" (*Essais de Théodicée* §258; VI 269).

22. *Causa Dei asserta per justitiam ejus* §58; VI 447.

23. "Allein, man kann die Beantwortung dieser Sophisterei sicher dem Ausspruche eines jeden Menschen von gesundem Verstande, der lange genug gelebt und über den Wert des Lebens nachgedacht hat, um hierüber ein Urteil fällen zu können, überlassen, wenn man ihn fragt: ob er wohl, ich will nicht sagen auf dieselbe, sondern auf jede andre ihm beliebige Bedingungen (nur nicht etwa einer Feen- sondern dieser unserer Erdenwelt), das Spiel des Lebens noch einmal durchzuspielen Lust hätte" (*Über das Mißlingen*, A 203).

24. "Wenn auch die Leibnitzische Demonstration, daß unter den möglichen Welten diese immer noch die beste sei, richtig wäre: so gäbe sie doch noch keine Theodicee. Denn der Schöpfer hat ja nicht bloß die Welt, sondern auch die Möglichkeit selbst geschaffen: er hätte demnach diese darauf einrichten sollen, daß sie eine bessere Welt zuließe" (*Parerga und Paralipomena*, second volume, chapter 12; IX 327).

25. Cf., for example, *De civitate Dei* XII 7.

26. Cf., for example, *De civitate Dei* XI 18 and 23.

27. Cf., for example, *De civitate Dei* XI IIff. and XIII Iff.

28. "Privativum est, quod dicit negationem" (VII 195); contrast Thomas Aquinas, *Summa theologiae* I q. 48 a.2 ad 1; a.3 c. Cf. Rolf Schönberger, "Die Existenz des Nichtigen: Zur Geschichte der Privationstheorie," in *Die Wirklichkeit des Bösen*, ed. F. Hermanni and P. Koslowski (München, 1998), 15–47, 39, about an approximation of this thought by Duns Scotus.

29. "mal métaphysique" (*Essais de Théodicée* §21; VI 115).

30. *Causa Dei . . .* § 68; VI 449.

31. "Goutet-on assés la santé, et en rend on assés graces à Dieu, sans avoir jamais été malade?" (*Essais de Théodicée* §12; VI 109).

32. §23; VI 116f. Cf. also the allusion to the "felix culpa," §10; VI 108.

33. David Hume, *Dialogues Concerning Natural Religion* (Indianapolis: Bobbs-Merrill, 1976), 205.

34. "Die Güte ist, daß die Welt ist. Das Sein kommt ihr nicht zu; das Sein ist hier herabgesetzt zu einem Moment und ist nur ein Gesetztsein, Erschaffensein . . . Die Manifestation der Nichtigkeit, Idealität dieses Endlichen, daß das Sein nicht wahrhafte Selbständigkeit ist, diese Manifestation als Macht ist die Gerechtigkeit; darin wird den endlichen Dingen ihr Recht angetan" (17.58f.;

Hegel is quoted according to *Werke in zwanzig Bänden,* ed. E. Moldenhauer and K. M. Michel [Frankfurt: Suhrkamp, 1969–71]).

35. Cf. his modal-logical considerations in the second chapter of the third section of his logic of essence (6.200ff.) and the Leibniz chapter of his lectures on the history of philosophy (20.233ff.).

36. Cf. Vittorio Hösle, *Hegels System* (Hamburg: Meiner, 1998).

37. "Die Philosophie ist die wahrhafte Theodizee, gegen Kunst und Religion und deren Empfindungen" (20.455).

38. "Unsere Betrachtung ist insofern eine Theodizee, eine Rechtfertigung Gottes, welche Leibniz metaphysisch auf seine Weise in noch unbestimmten, abstrakten Kategorien versucht hat, so daß das Übel in der Welt begriffen, der denkende Geist mit dem Bösen versöhnt werden sollte. In der Tat liegt nirgend eine größere Aufforderung zu solcher versöhnenden Erkenntnis als in der Weltgeschichte" (12.28; cf. also the final sentence of the *Lectures,* 12.540).

39. "si fieri non potest ut detur perfectio quae non augeri queat." I quote the text, which is missing in Gerhardt, according to Gottfried Wilhelm Leibniz, *Opuscules métaphysiques / Kleine Schriften zur Metaphysik* (Darmstadt: Wissenschaftliche Buchgesellschaft, 1985), 368–72, 370. An early very detailed philosophy of history committed to basic Leibnizian ideas is Vico's *Scienza nuova* of 1725.

40. Cf. Dieter Wandschneidet and Vittorio Hösle, "Die Entäußerung der Idee zur Natur und ihre zeitliche Entfaltung als Geist bei Hegel," *Hegel-Studien* 18 (1982): 173–99.

41. Leibniz is still far away from the "school of suspicion" (Karl Marx, Friedrich Nietzsche, Sigmund Freud) that has so relentlessly transformed philosophy. He says it himself: "I do not like to judge people's intentions negatively" ("Je n'aime pas de juger des gens en mauvaise part"; *Discours* §XIX; IV 444).

42. "Wenn wir dieses Schauspiel der Leidenschaften betrachten und die Folgen ihrer Gewalttätigkeit, des Unverstandes erblicken, der sich nicht nur zu ihnen, sondern selbst auch und sogar vornehmlich zu dem, was gute Absichten, rechtliche Zwecke sind, gesellt, wenn wir daraus das Übel, das Böse, den Untergang der blühendsten Reiche, die der Menschengeist hervorgebracht hat, sehen, so können wir nur mit Trauer über diese Vergänglichkeit überhaupt erfüllt werden und, indem dieses Untergehen nicht nur ein Werk der Natur, sondern des Willens der Menschen ist, mit einer moralischen Betrübnis, mit einer Empörung des guten Geistes, wenn ein solcher in uns ist, über solches Schauspiel enden" (12.34f.).

43. 2.35.

44. 12.42.

45. "Die berühmte Frage nach dem Ursprung des Übels in der Welt tritt, wenigstens insofern unter dem Übel zunächst nur das Unangenehme und der Schmerz verstanden wird, auf diesem Standpunkte des formellen Praktischen ein. Das Übel ist nichts anderes als die Unangemessenheit des Seins zu dem

Sollen. Dieses Sollen hat viele Bedeutungen und, da die zufälligen Zwecke gleichfalls die Form des Sollens haben, unendlich viele. In Ansehung ihrer ist das Übel nur das Recht, das an der Eitelkeit und Nichtigkeit ihrer Einbildung ausgeübt wird. Sie selbst sind schon das Übel" (*Enzyklopädie* §472 A; 10.292f.).

46. Cf. Philo in Hume's *Dialogues,* 196: "They have no just reason, says one: These complaints proceed only from their disconnected, repining, anxious disposition . . . And can there possibly, I reply, be a more certain foundation of misery, than such a wretched temper?"

47. About the animals' mode of existence it is said: "The environment of external contingency contains factors which are almost wholly alien; it exercises a perpetual violence and threat of dangers on the animal's feeling which is an insecure, anxious, and unhappy one" (*Enzyklopädie* §368; 9.502; "Die Umgebung der äußerlichen Zufälligkeit enthält fast nur Fremdartiges; sie übt eine fortdauernde Gewaltsamkeit und Drohung von Gefahren auf sein Gefühl aus, das ein unsicheres, angstvolles, unglückliches ist").

48. "Sicut autem melior est natura sentiens et cum dolet quam lapis qui dolere nullo modo potest: ita rationalis natura praestantior etiam misera, quam illa quae rationis vel sensus est expers, et ideo in eam non cadit miseriam" (*De civitate Dei* XII 1).

49. "die innerste Reflexion der Subjektivität in sich gegen das Objektive und Allgemeine, das ihr nur Schein ist" (*Enzyklopädie* §512; 10.317).

50. "Der Ursprung des Bösen überhaupt liegt in dem Mysterium, d.i. in dem Spekulativen der Freiheit, ihrer Notwendigkeit, aus der Natürlichkeit des Willens herauszugehen und gegen sie innerlich zu sein . . . Der Mensch ist daher zugleich sowohl an sich oder von Natur als durch seine Reflexion in sich böse, so daß weder die Natur als solche, d.i. wenn sie nicht Natürlichkeit des in ihrem besonderen Inhalte bleibenden Willens wäre, noch die in sich gehende Reflexion, das Erkennen überhaupt, wenn es sich nicht in jenem Gegensatz hielte, für sich das Böse ist" (*Grundlinien der Philosophie des Rechts* §139; 7.261f.).

51. "er macht . . . die Scheidung des unvernünftigen Tieres und des Menschen aus"; "Sogenannte Natur-, unschuldige Völker—Schlimmer als böse" (7.263).

52. "Das Paradies ist ein Park, wo nur die Tiere und nicht die Menschen bleiben konnen . . . Der Sündenfall ist daher der ewige Mythus des Menschen, wodurch er eben Mensch wird" (12.389). Hegel's interpretation of the fall differs widely from Augustine's and is closer to that of Irenaeus of Lyons, for whom Adam has sinned more out of foolishness than out of malice and must thus be saved. Indeed, according to him the exclusion from the tree of life was not so much a punishment than a reversal of the otherwise ensuing timelessness of sin. Cf. Irenäus von Lyon, *Adversus haereses/Gegen die Häresien III* (Freiburg: Herder, 1995), 281ff. (chapter 23).

53. *Enzyklopädie* §6; 8.47f.

54. 7.26f.

55. "Entwirklichung der Übel, die sich hinter dem Rücken der Leidenden mit Gott versöhnt" (Friedrich Hermanni, "Die Positivität des Malum," in *Die Wirklichkeit des Bösen*, 49–72, 72).

56. I quote Hans Jonas, *Philosophische Untersuchungen und metaphysische Vermutungen* (Frankfurt: Suhrkamp, 1992), 190–208. This text was published for the first time in 1984.

57. 193.

58. "Mit dem Erscheinen des Menschen erwachte die Transzendenz zu sich selbst und begleitet hinfort sein Tun mit angehaltenem Atem, hoffend und werbend, mit Freude und mit Trauer, mit Befriedigung und Enttäuschung" (197).

59. "Denn bei dem wahrhaft und ganz einseitig Ungeheuerlichen, das unter seinen Ebenbildern in der Schöpfung dann und wann die einen den schuldlos andern antun, dürfte man wohl erwarten, daß der gute Gott die eigene Regel selbst äußerster Zurückhaltung seiner Macht dann und wann bricht und mit dem rettenden Wunder eingreift" (204).

60. "Jetzt ist es am Menschen, ihm zu geben. Und er kann dies tun, indem er in den Wegen seines Lebens darauf sieht, daß es nicht geschehe oder nicht zu oft geschehe, und nicht seinetwegen, daß es Gott um das Werdenlassen der Welt gereuen muß" (207).

61. Cf. Vittorio Hösle and Christian Illies, *Darwin* (Freiburg: Herder, 1999).

Chapter 4.   *Rationalism, Determinism, Freedom*

1. John Earman, *A Primer on Determinism* (Dordrecht: Reidel, 1986), 250.

2. Earman, *Primer on Determinism*, 33ff.

3. Cf. Laplace's famous first chapter in the *Essai philosophique sur les probabilités* with the allusion to an "intelligence" able to predict everything.

4. See Hans Primas, *Chemistry, Quantum Mechanics, and Reductionism* (Berlin: Springer, 1981).

5. On the logic behind ancient determinism—which I have to ignore in this essay—cf. Pierre-Maxime Schuhl, *Le dominateur et les possibles* (Paris: Presses Universitaires de France, 1960), and Jules Vuillemin, *Nécessité ou contingence: l'aporie de Diodore et les systèmes philosophiques* (Paris: Edition de Minuit, 1984).

6. See his *Philebus* 26 e; *Timaeus* 28 a, c.

7. Boethius, *De consolatione philosophiae* V 1: "Nam nihil ex nihilo exsistere vera sententia est, cui nemo umquam veterum refragatus est, quamquam id illi non de operante principio, sed de materiali subiecto hoc omnium de natura rationum quasi quoddam iecerint fundamentum. At si nullis ex causis aliquid oriatur, id de nihilo ortum esse videbitur; quodsi hoc fieri nequit, ne casum quidem huius modi esse possibile est, qualem paulo ante definivimus." About chance so

defined it is said just before: "Quis enim cohercente in ordinem cuncta deo locus esse ullus temeritati reliquus potest?"

8. Cf. already the remark in Descartes, *Principia Philosophiae,* I 51.

9. Jonathan Francis Bennett, *A Study of Spinoza's Ethics* (Indianapolis: Hackett Publishing Co., 1984).

10. "Mihi nondum certum videtur, corpora esse substantias. Secus de mentibus," Leibniz writes in his notes on the *Ethica* (Gottfried Wilhelm Leibniz, *Die philosophischen Schriften,* ed. C. J. Gerhardt [Berlin: Weidmann, 1875–90], I 145; all works of Leibniz are quoted according to this edition). On Leibniz's study of Spinoza, see the splendid recent work by Mogens Laerke, *Leibniz lecteur de Spinoza* (Paris: Honoré Champion, 2008).

11. "Nos raisonnements sont fondés sur deux grands *Principes, celuy de la Contradiction . . . Et celuy de la Raison suffisante,* en vertu duquel nous considerons qu'aucun fait ne sauroit se trouver vray ou existant, aucune Enontiation veritable, sans qu'il y ait une raison suffisante, pourquoy il en soit ainsi et non pas autrement, quoyque ces raisons le plus souvent ne puissent point nous être connues" (*Monadology,* par. 31f.; VI 612).

12. "Sans ce grand principe, nous ne pourrions jamais prouver l'existence de Dieu, et nous perdrions une infinité de raisonnements tres justes et tres utiles, dont il est le fondement: et il ne souffre aucune exception, autrement sa force seroit affoiblie. Aussi n'est il rien de si foible que ces systemes, où tout est chancelant et plein d'exceptions" (*Théodicée,* par. 44; VI 127).

13. Similar arguments were developed later by Friedrich Nietzsche, whose awareness of the methodological problems linked with determinism is, however, very limited—Nietzsche was not, whatever his other merits may have been, talented in the "harder" branches of philosophy; his reflections on epistemology are dilettante and even self-contradictory.

14. "vermöge welcher nichts für sich Bestehendes und Unabhängiges, auch nichts Einzelnes und Abgerissenes, Objekt für uns werden kann" (Arthur Schopenhauer, *Werke in zehn Bänden* [Zürich: Diogenes, 1977], par. 16; V 41).

15. "Wer nun einen Beweis, d.i. die Darlegung eines Grundes, für ihn fordert, setzt ihn eben hiedurch schon als wahr voraus, ja, stützt seine Forderung eben auf diese Voraussetzung. Er geräth also in diesen Cirkel, daß er einen Beweis der Berechtigung, einen Beweis zu fordern, fordert" (par. 14; V 38).

16. Section IV; VI 107. A similar explanation of the anti-deterministic convictions is given by Hume (*Treatise,* II.III.II). Alvin Plantinga's ingenious free will defense, based on his splendid retrieval of *de re* necessity (*The Nature of Necessity* [Oxford: Clarendon, 1982], 164ff.), does not solve the theodicy problem better than Leibniz's compatibilist solution. For Plantinga also has to answer the question of why God chose to create a world with Adolf Hitler, even if we grant him that this man had a remarkable trans-world depravity.

17. I do not distinguish in this essay between the proposition P ("Everything can be explained in a deterministic way") and the proposition Q ("Our

world is a deterministic system"). P and Q are not strictly equivalent (cf. Franz von Kutschera, *Grundfragen der Erkenntnistheorie* [Berlin: de Gruyter, 1982], 279ff.), but one needs only to introduce all the independent laws presupposed by P as axioms of a theory in order to get Q.

18. This point has been made particularly forcefully by Peter van Inwagen. See, for example, his essay, "The Incompatibility of Free Will and Determinism," *Philosophical Studies* 27 (1975): 185–99.

19. Peter F. Strawson, "Freedom and Resentment," *Proceedings of the British Academy* 48 (1962): 187–211.

20. This suspicion is omnipresent in Ludwig Wittgenstein's *Über Gewißheit*.

21. "Von außen, objektiv betrachtet, ist der Wille kausal gebunden; von innen, subjektiv betrachtet ist der Wille frei" (Max Planck, "Vom Wesen der Willensfreiheit," in *Vorträge und Erinnerungen* [Darmstadt: Wissenschaftliche Buchgesellschaft, 1979], 301–17, 310).

22. Ulrich Pothast, *Die Unzulänglichkeit der Freiheitsbeweise* (Frankfurt: Suhrkamp, 1980). Pothast also edited important texts on our problem in the volume *Seminar: Freies Handeln und Determinismus* (Frankfurt: Suhrkamp, 1978). I owe much to the two books.

23. Karl R. Popper, "Indeterminism in Quantum Physics and in Classical Physics," *British Journal for the Philosophy of Science* 1 (1950): 117–33, 173–95.

24. Besides Planck in the above-mentioned essay Stuart Hampshire has also defended the argument; cf., for example, his book *Freedom of the Individual* (London: Chatto & Windus, 1965), chapter 3.

25. Abraham I. Melden, *Free Action* (London: Routledge, 1967), and Anthony Kenny, *Will, Freedom, and Power* (Oxford: Blackwell, 1975).

26. R. E. Hobart, "Free Will as Involving Determination and Inconceivable without It," *Mind* 43 (1934): 1–27.

27. Some philosophers of causality argue that it is our own intervention in the physical realm that generates the idea of causality that could never be deduced from the relation between bodies and that therefore our self-determination is a clearer concept than that of normal causality. While this may be genetically true, it does not yet solve the validity question; furthermore, the allegedly more evident idea has to do with the cause-effect connection between our body and an external body, not with the internal self-determination of the self.

28. An important example is Roderick M. Chisholm, *Human Freedom and the Self* (Lawrence: University of Kansas Press, 1964).

29. See Vittorio Hösle, *Die Krise der Gegenwart und die Verantwortung der Philosophie* (München: C. H. Beck, 1997), 234ff.

30. Heinrich Rickert, *System der Philosophie. Erster Teil: Allgemeine Grundlegung der Philosophie* (Tübingen: J. C. B. Mohr, 1921), 302f.; Joseph Boyle, Germaine Grisez, and Olaf Tollefsen, *Free Choice* (Notre Dame: University of Notre Dame Press, 1976).

31. Theodor W. Adorno—whose contribution to our problem is generally garrulous and confused—rightly reproaches Kant for a repressive desire to punish (Theodor W. Adorno, *Negative Dialektik* [Frankfurt: Suhrkamp, 1973], 257).

32. "Mit ebenso viel oder wenig Recht, wie sich jemand mittels dieser Beschreibung von seinen Entscheidungen distanziert, könnte er sich überhaupt von sich selbst distanzieren" (*Die Unzulänglichkeit*, 392).

33. See my account of punishment in *Morals and Politics* (Notre Dame: University of Notre Dame Press, 2004), 678ff.

34. I have to agree, however, that the phenomenon of remorse is a serious problem for determinism. But it is not insoluble since the essence of true remorse can be interpreted as directing us toward a change of our past behavior that contradicted practical reason.

35. "C'est qu'il est faux que l'évenement arrive quoyqu'on fasse; il arrivera, parce qu'on fait ce qui y mene; et si l'évenement est écrit, la cause qui le fera arriver, est écrite aussi. Ainsi la liaison des effects et des causes, bien loin d'établir la doctrine d'une necessité prejudiciable à la practique, sert à la détruire" (*Théodicée,* Préface; VI 33).

36. See Karl-Otto Apel, "Das Problem der philosophischen Letztbegründung im Lichte einer transzendentalen Sprachpragmatik," in *Sprache und Erkenntnis, Festschrift für G. Frey,* ed. B. Kanitscheider (Innsbruck: Amoe, 1976), 55–82.

37. See already Sextus Empiricus, *Adversus Mathematicos,* IX 204.

38. The concept of the best possible world presupposes quite a lot—for example, that there is only one world with a maximal axiological value. This presupposition is very strong, but I will not discuss possible alternatives here. If one drops it, then some form of *liberum arbitrium indifferentiae* has indeed to be ascribed to God, or one has to give up the idea that only the actual world is real.

39. *Théodicée,* Discours preliminaire, par. 37, VI 71.

40. "que Dieu luy même ne sauroit choisir ce qui n'est pas bon et que la liberté de cet Estre tout puissant ne l'empeche pas d'estre determiné par ce qui est le meilleur."

41. "Estre determiné par la raison au meilleur, c'est estre le plus libre. Quelqu'un voudroit-il estre imbecille, par cette raison, qu'un imbecille est moins determiné par de sages reflexions, qu'un homme de bon sens? Si la liberté consiste à secouer le joug de la raison, les foux et les insensés seront les seuls libres, mais je ne crois pourtant pas que pour l'amour d'une telle liberté personne voulût estre fou, hormis celuy qui l'est déja" (II 21, par. 49f.; V 184).

42. *Nouveaux Essais* II 21, par. 25; V 168. The same argument is found in Schopenhauer's *Über die Freiheit des menschlichen Willens* (section III; VI 82).

43. "Schon der Wortbedeutung nach läßt Religiosität keine Wahl zwischen Entgegengesetzten zu, kein *aequilibrium arbitrii* (die Pest aller Moral), sondern

nur die höchste Entschiedenheit für das Rechte, ohne alle Wahl" (Friedrich Wilhelm Joseph Schelling, *Über das Wesen der menschlichen Freiheit* [Stuttgart: Reclam, 1974], 111).

44. See, for example, Karl R. Popper and John Eccles, *The Self and Its Brain* (Berlin: Springer, 1977), and Hans Jonas, *Macht oder Ohnmacht der Subjektivität?* (Frankfurt: Insel, 1981).

45. See already the famous letters of Princess Elisabeth of Bohemia to Descartes and Spinoza's criticism of Descartes in the preface to the fifth book of the *Ethica*.

46. Schopenhauer interprets with a certain plausibility parapsychological phenomena as an extension of the power of the mind upon the own body to other bodies in *Über den Willen in der Natur* (*On the Will in Nature*) (V 307).

47. *Principia Philosophiae* II 36.

48. One could try to argue that the conservation laws are only idealizations, that the changes caused by the *res cogitans* are minimal or even, as Hans Jonas claims, that there is a deviation from the laws in both directions—both in perception and in action—so that the two forms cancel each other. But all these solutions are utterly unsatisfying.

49. Cf. Leibniz's criticism of occasionalism in the *Systeme nouveau de la nature et de la communication des substances*: "In order to solve problems it is not sufficient to use the general cause and to have come in what one calls Deum ex machina" ("pour resoudre des problemes, il n'est pas assez d'employer la cause generale, et de faire venir ce qu'on appelle *Deum ex machina*," IV 483).

50. His omniscience is easier to defend, as already Lorenzo Valla showed in *De libero arbitrio*. Molina's doctrine presupposes knowledge of the compatibility of divine omnipotence and human freedom.

Chapter 5.   *Encephalius: A Conversation about the Mind-Body Problem*

1. This is an attempt to render the German pun: "ist eine Qual, ja durchaus ein Quale" (note of translator).

2. Martin Heidegger (note of translator).

3. Johann Gottlieb Fichte and his followers (note of translator).

4. "Letter of Lord Chandos to Francis Bacon," an artistic manifest by Hugo von Hofmannsthal (note of editor).

5. Saul A. Kripke (note of translator).

6. This is a reference to Donald Davidson's theory (note of translator).

7. Jaegwon Kim (note of translator).

8. Colin McGinn (note of translator).

9. Franz von Kutschera from Regensburg (note of translator).

10. The description referred to is in *Wind, Sand and Stars,* a novel by Antoine de Saint-Exupéry (note of editor).

11. "The Flypaper," a one-page text by Robert Musil describing, in minute detail, the struggle for survival of flies that are caught on a piece of flypaper (note of editor).

12. An untranslatable German pun: "ein solches Quale der Qualle zu unterstellen" (note of translator).

13. Karl R. Popper and John C. Eccles (note of translator).

14. Thoas, king of Tauris, in act 1, scene 3, of Goethe's *Iphigenia in Tauris* (note of editor).

Chapter 6. *Religion, Theology, Philosophy*

1. Cf. Max Weber, *Wirtschaft und Gesellschaft* (Tübingen: J. C. B. Mohr [Paul Siebeck], 1980), 245: "Eine Definition dessen, was Religion 'ist,' kann unmöglich an der Spitze, sondern könnte allenfalls am Schlusse einer Erörterung wie der nachfolgenden stehen" ("A definition of what religion 'is' cannot be offered at the beginning, but at most at the end of a discussion like the following").

2. The German words *Wissenschaft* and *wissenschaftlich* include here also the humanities, once called in English, too, "moral sciences" (note of translator).

3. "Supponit denique nobis licere secundum nostras praeconceptas opiniones Scripturae verba explicare, torquere, & literalem sensum, quamquam perspectissimum sive expressissimum, negare, & in alium quemvis mutare" (Baruch deSpinoza, *Opera,* ed. C. Gebhardt, 4 vols. [Heidelberg: C. Winter, 1925], III 115).

4. David Hume, *The Philosophical Works,* ed. T. H. Green and T. H. Grose, 4 vols. (London: Longmans/Green, 1874–75), IV 331. Cf. also 332.

5. "Die Ausbildung geoffenbarter Wahrheiten in Vernunftswahrheiten ist schlechterdings nothwendig, wenn dem menschlichen Geschlechte damit geholfen seyn soll. Als sie geoffenbaret wurden, waren sie freylich noch keine Vernunftswahrheiten; aber sie wurden geoffenbaret, um es zu werden" (§76; Gotthold Ephraim Lessing, *Die Erziehung des Menschengeschlechts* [Berlin: Voß, 1785], 37).

6. It is important that Kant in §76 of the *Critique of Judgment* himself recognizes that the ontological proof may be valid for beings with a different epistemic apparatus than the one he ascribes to humans, thus for God himself. His objection to the ontological proof is fundamentally epistemological, not logical.

7. Cf. my more detailed but still insufficient deliberations in *Die Krise der Gegenwart und die Verantwortung der Philosophie* (München: C. H. Beck, 1997), 143ff., where I appraise and advance Apel's ideas about the ultimate foundation from an ontological perspective.

Chapter 7.   *Philosophy and the Interpretation of the Bible*

1. In the Dimensions of Philosophy Series edited by Norman Daniels and Keith Lehrer one misses a philosophy of hermeneutics.

2. Hans W. Frei, *The Eclipse of Biblical Narrative: A Study in Eighteenth and Nineteenth Century Hermeneutics* (New Haven/London: Yale University Press, 1974).

3. Frei, *Eclipse of Biblical Narrative*, 3.

4. Cf. the second book of *De doctrina christiana* (*On Christian Doctrine*) and particularly III 1.

5. *Confessiones* I 13: "Tenere cogebar Aeneae nescio cuius errores oblitus errorum meorum."

6. III 5: "Non enim sicut modo loquor, ita sensi, cum adtendi ad illam scripturam, sed visa est mihi indigna, quam Tullianae dignitati compararem."

7. V 14: "Maxime audito uno atque altero et saepius aenigmate soluto de scriptis veteribus, ubi, cum ad litteram acciperem, occidebar. spiritaliter itaque plerisque eorum librorum locis expositis iam reprehendebam desperationem meam illam dumtaxat, qua credideram legem et prophetas detestantibus atque irridentibus resisti omnino non posse." For Ambrosius's moral and allegorical interpretation of Scripture, see, for example, his *De Cain et Abel* (*On Cain and Abel*) I 4f.

8. VI 4: "Et tamquam regulam diligentissime commendaret, saepe in popularibus sermonibus suis dicentem Ambrosium laetus audiebam: littera occidit, spiritus autem vivificat, cum ea, quae ad litteram perversitatem docere videbantur, remoto mystico velamento spiritaliter aperiret, non dicens quod me offenderet, quamvis ea diceret, quae utrum vera essent adhuc ignorarem."

9. VI 5: "Nec audiendos esse, si qui forte mihi dicerent: 'unde scis ilios libros unius veri et veracissimi dei spiritu esse humano generi ministratos?' id ipsum enim maxime credendum erat . . . ideoque cum essemus infirmi ad inveniendam liquida ratione veritatem et ob hoc nobis opus esset auctoritate sanctarum litterarum, iam credere coeperam nullo modo te fuisse tributurum tam excellentem illi scripturae per omnes iam terras auctoritatem, nisi et per ipsam tibi credi et per ipsam te quaeri voluisses. iam enim absurditatem, quae me in illis litteris solebat offendere, cum multa ex eis probabiliter exposita audissem, ad sacramentorum altitudinem referebam eoque mihi illa venerabilior et sacrosancta fide dignior apparebat auctoritas. quo et omnibus ad legendum esset in promtu et secreti sui dignitatem in intellectu profundiore servaret, verbis apertissimis et humillimo genere loquendi se cunctis praebens et exercens intentionem eorum, qui non sunt leves corde, ut exciperet omnes populari sinu et per angusta foramina paucos ad te traiceret."

10. VII 20: "Ubi enim erat illa aedificans caritas a fundamento humilitatis, quod est Christus Iesus? Aut quando illi libri me docerent eam?"

11. VIII 12.

12. Gillian R. Evans, *The Language and Logic of the Bible: The Earlier Middle Ages* (Cambridge: Cambridge University Press, 1984), vii.

13. Evans, *Language and Logic of the Bible,* 164f.

14. Cf. F. Stegmüller, *Repertorium Biblicum Medii Aevi,* 11 vols. (Madrid: CSIC, 1940–80).

15. *De ebrietate (On Drunkenness)* 144.

16. Beryl Smalley, *The Study of the Bible in the Middle Ages* (Oxford: Clarendon, 1941), 3.

17. *De opificio (On the Creation)* 3.

18. *De principiis (On First Principles)* IV 3, 5.

19. Cf. *De civitate Dei (City of God)* XIII 21: "Haec et si qua alia commodius dici possunt de intellegendo spiritaliter paradiso nemine prohibente dicantur, dum tamen et illius historiae veritas fidelissima rerum gestarum narratione commendata credatur." See also XVII 3 and *De doctrina christiana* III 5/9 and 10/14. Even a wrong interpretation is accepted as long as it enhances charity: "Quisque vero talem inde sententiam duxerit, ut huic aedificandae caritati sit utilis, nec tamen hoc dixerit, quod ille quem legit eo loco sensisse probabitur, non perniciose fallitur nec omnino mentitur" (*De doctrina christiana* I 36/40).

20. *Confessiones* XII 26.

21. XII 23.

22. XII 31: "Sensit ille omnino in his verbis atque cogitavit, cum ea scriberet, quidquid hic veri potuimus invenire et quidquid nos non potuimus aut nondum potuimus et tamen in eis inveniri potest."

23. Cf. Gregorius Magnus, *Moralia in Iob (Morals on the Book of Job),* Praefatio, 2: "Sed quis haec scripserit, ualde superuacue quaeritur, cum tamen auctor libri Spiritus sanctus fideliter credatur. Ipse igitur haec scripsit, qui scribenda dictauit . . . Si magni cuiusdam uiri susceptis epistolis legeremus uerba sed quo calamo fuissent scripta quaereremus, ridiculum profecto esset non epistolarum auctorem scire sensumque cognoscere, sed quali calamo earum uerba impressa fuerint indagare."

24. Cf. Evans, *Language and Logic of the Bible,* 133–63. Abelard is crucial.

25. Nevertheless, for Hugh of St. Victor, the last function of the study of the Bible is a moral one: *De institutione novitiorum (On the Formation of Novices),* cap. VIII (PL 176, 933f.).

26. *Summa theologiae* I q. 1 a. 10 c.

27. I q. 1 a. 9 ad 2: "Ut mentes quibus fit revelatio, non permittat in similitudinibus permanere, sed elevet eas ad cognitionem intelligibilium."

28. I q. 1 a. 10 ad 1: "Et ita etiam nulla confusio sequitur in sacra Scriptura: cum omnes sensus fundentur super unum, scilicet litteralem . . . Non tamen ex

hoc aliquid deperit sacrae Scripturae: quia nihil sub spirituali sensu continetur fidei necessarium, quod Scriptura per litteralem sensum alicubi manifeste non tradat."

29. I q. 1 a. 10 c: "Illa vero significatio qua res significatae per voces, iterum res alias significant, dicitur sensus spiritualis; qui super litteralem fundatur, et eum supponit."

30. I q. 102 a. 1 c: "Ea enim quae de Paradiso in Scriptura dicuntur, per modum narrationis historicae proponuntur: in omnibus autem quae sic Scriptura tradit, est pro fundamento tenenda veritas historica, et desuper spirituales expositiones fabricandae." See also I/II q. 102 a. 2 and a. 6 ad 4.

31. I q. 68 a. 1 c: "Primo quidem, ut veritas Scripturae inconcusse teneatur. Secundo, cum Scriptura divina multipliciter exponi possit, quod nulli expositioni aliquis ita praecise inhaereat quod, si certa ratione constiterit hoc esse falsum, quod aliquis sensum Scripturae esse asserere praesumat: ne Scriptura ex hoc ab infidelibus derideatur, et ne eis via credendi praecludatur."

32. A good example for the criticism of the political abuse of an allegorical reading of the Bible can be found in Dante, *De monarchia* (*On Monarchy*) III 4.

33. Gillian R. Evans, *The Language and Logic of the Bible: The Road to Reformation* (Cambridge: Cambridge University Press, 1985), 82.

34. Cf. Gerald L. Bruns, *Hermeneutics Ancient and Modern* (New Haven/London: Yale University Press, 1992), 139ff.

35. Nikolaus von Kues, *Philosophisch-theologische Schriften,* ed. L. Gabriel, 3 vols. (Wien: Herder, 1964–67), II 408ff.

36. *Tractatus theologico-politicus,* cap. 1, in Spinoza, *Opera,* ed. C. Gebhard, 4 vols. (Heidelberg: C. Winter, 1925), III 18.

37. Cap. 1; 28f.

38. Cap. 1; 23.

39. Cap. 2; 33f. A sociological explanation of Amos's stylistic peculiarities is already found in Jerome and Aquinas (*Summa theologiae,* II/II q. 173 a. 3 arg.1).

40. Cap. 2; 35ff.

41. Cap. 2; 40f.

42. Cap. 2; 43 and cap. 4; 64.

43. Cap. 3; 53.

44. Cap. 7; 98: "Eam autem, ut hic paucis complectar, dico methodum interpretandi Scripturam haud differre a methodo interpretandi naturam, sed cum ea prorsus convenire." See also 102.

45. Cap. 7; 99ff.

46. Cap. 7; 113ff.

47. Cap. 9; 134: "Ex his itaque clarissime sequitur veram annorum computationem neque ex ipsis historiis constare, neque ipsas historias in una eademque convenire, sed valde diversas supponere. Ac proinde fatendum has historias

ex diversis scriptoribus collectas esse, nec adhuc ordinatas neque examinatas fuisse."

48. *Scienza nuova seconda*, 208f., 361f., 412, 901. (I refer to the paragraph numbers introduced in Nicolini's classical edition and adopted by almost all subsequent editions.)

49. *Scienza nuova seconda* 408.

50. *Scienza nuova seconda* 417ff.

51. *Scienza nuova prima* 28, 192, 293; *Scienza nuova seconda* 585, 794.

52. David Hume, *The Philosophical Works*, ed. T. H. Green and T. H. Grose, 4 vols. (London: Longmans/Green, 1874–75), IV 331 and 332.

53. *Der Streit der Fakultäten*, A 102f. On the very different analysis of the story in Søren Kierkegaard's *Frygt og Bæven* (*Fear and Trembling*), see chapter 12 of this volume.

54. *Die Religion innerhalb der Grenzen der bloßen Vernunft* (*Religion Within the Limits of Reason alone*), B 186ff./A 177ff.

55. B 189ff./A 180ff.

56. B 199f./A 190.

57. Kant quotes this rule in *Kritik der reinen Vernunft* (*Critique of Pure Reason*), B 370/A 314. On the history of this rule, cf. Hans-Georg Gadamer, *Wahrheit und Methode* (*Truth and Method*) (Tübingen: J. C. B. Mohr [Paul Siebeck], 1975), 182ff.

58. *Der Streit der Fakultäten* A 49ff., particularly 54ff.

59. *Der Streit der Fakultäten* A 63ff.

60. *Fichtes Werke,* ed. I. H. Fichte, 11 vols. (reprint Berlin: de Gruyter, 1971), V 71.

61. V 123f.

62. Georg Wilhelm Friedrich Hegel, *Frühe Schriften* I, ed. F. Nicolin and G. Schüler (Hamburg: Meiner, 1989), 413.

63. Hegel, *Frühe Schriften,* 271.

64. Hegel, *Frühe Schriften,* 277.

65. The first edition for a broader public is Thomas Jefferson, *The Life and Morals of Jesus of Nazareth* (New York: W. Funk, 1940).

66. Georg Wilhelm Friedrich Hegel, *Werke,* ed. E. Moldenhauer and K. M. Michel, 20 vols. (Frankfurt: Suhrkamp, 1969–71), XVII 201.

67. XVI 35ff., XVII 199f., 321.

68. XVI 265ff.

69. XII 389: "Das Paradies ist ein Park, wo nur die Tiere und nicht die Menschen bleiben können."

70. XVIII 94: "Wir Lutheraner—ich bin es und will es bleiben— . . ."

71. VIII 27ff. (preface to the second edition of the *Encyclopedia*) and XX 54f.

72. On Paulus, see Albert Schweitzer, *Geschichte der Leben-Jesu-Forschung* (Tübingen: J. C. B. Mohr, 1951), 49–58.

73. Schweitzer, *Geschichte der Leben-Jesu-Forschung,* 643–46.

74. David Friedrich Strauss, *Das Leben Jesu, kritisch bearbeitet,* 2 vols. (Tübingen: Osiander, 1835–36), II 735: "Die Menschheit ist die Vereinigung der beiden Naturen, der menschgewordene Gott, der zur Endlichkeit entäusserte unendliche, und der seiner Unendlichkeit sich erinnernde endliche Geist."

75. 2 vols. (Stuttgart: Kröner, 1905), II 382–90.

76. Epistle 73 to Oldenburg.

77. Charles Darwin, *The Autobiography of Charles Darwin 1809–1882,* ed. N. Barlow (New York/London: Norton, 1993), 87.

78. *Der Antichrist* (*The Antichrist*) 28 (Friedrich Nietzsche, *Sämtliche Werke,* Kritische Studienausgabe in 15 Bänden, ed. G. Colli and M. Montinari [Berlin: de Gruyter, 1980], VI 199): "Die Zeit ist fern, wo auch ich, gleich jedem jungen Gelehrten, mit der klugen Langsamkeit eines raffinirten Philologen das Werk des unvergleichlichen Strauss auskostete. Damals war ich zwanzig Jahre alt: jetzt bin ich zu ernst dafür."

79. When in *Der Antichrist* (32; VI 204) it is said of Jesus "*Das Verneinen* ist eben das ihm ganz Unmögliche," it is hard not to think of Nietzsche's wish: "Ich will irgendwann einmal nur noch ein Ja-sagender sein!" (*Die fröhliche Wissenschaft* [*The Gay Science*] 276; III 521). Neither Jesus nor Nietzsche want to say "No."

80. *Jenseits von Gut und Böse* (*Beyond Good and Evil*) 263 (V 218).

81. *Jenseits von Gut und Böse* 247 (V 191).

82. I 8 and 143 (II 28f.; 139).

83. 68 (III 64).

84. *Jenseits von Gut und Böse* 52 (V 72).

85. *Morgenröte* 84 (III 79f.). "Hat diess jemals Jemand *geglaubt,* der es behauptete?"

86. *Menschliches, Allzumenschliches* II/2 85; *Morgenröte* 68; *Der Antichrist* 42ff. (II 591; III 64ff.; VI 215ff.).

87. *Der Antichrist* 47f. (VI 225ff.).

88. Cf., for example, Heinrich Zimmermann, *Neutestamentliche Methodenlehre* (Stuttgart: Katholisches Bibelwerk, 1968).

89. XXIV 103ff. "Dì, chi t'assicura / che quell'opere fosser? Quel medesmo / che vuol provarsi, non altri, il ti giura." "Se il mondo si rivolse al cristianesmo, / diss'io, sanza miracoli, quest'uno / È tal che gli altri non sono il centesmo." The argument can already be found in Augustine, *De civitate Dei,* XXII 5, and in a rudimentary form in Arnobius, *Adversus gentes* (*Against the Heathens*) II 44.

90. Cf. Gadamer, *Wahrheit und Methode,* 170: "daß zwischen der Philologie und der Naturwissenschaft in ihrer frühen Selbstbesinnung eine enge Entsprechung besteht, die einen doppelten Sinn hat."

91. "Aber indirekt ist doch überall, wo man sich um das Verständnis—z. B. der Heiligen Schrift oder der Klassiker—bemüht, ein Bezug auf die Wahrheit

wirksam, die im Text verborgen liegt and ans Licht soll. Was verstanden werden soll, ist in Wirklichkeit nicht ein Gedanke als ein Lebensmoment, sondern als eine Wahrheit" (173).

92. "Jedenfalls teilt das Verstehen in den Geisteswissenschaften mit dem Fortleben von Traditionen eine grundlegende Voraussetzung, nämlich, sich von der Überlieferung angesprochen zu sehen. Gilt denn nicht für die Gegenstände ihrer Forschung—so gut wie für die Inhalte der Tradition—daß dann erst ihre Bedeutung erfahrbar wird?" (266).

93. Gadamer, *Wahrheit und Methode,* 277ff.

94. "Nicht nut gelegentlich, sondern immer übertrifft der Sinn eines Textes seinen Autor" (280).

95. "Die Heilige Schrift ist Gottes Wort, und das bedeutet, daß die Schrift vor der Lehre derer, die sie auslegen, einen schlechthinnigen Vorrang behält" (313).

96. "Wenn der Philologe den gegebenen Text, und das heißt, sich in dem angegebenen Sinne in seinem Text versteht, so versteht der Historiker auch noch den großen, von ihm erratenen Text der Weltgeschichte selbst, in dem jeder überlieferte Text nur ein Sinnbruchstück, ein Buchstabe ist, und auch er versteht sich selbst in diesem großen Text . . . Es ist das wirkungsgeschichtliche Bewußtsein, worin sich beide als in ihrer wahren Grundlage zusammenfinden" (323).

97. "Denn das ist gewiß richtig, daß gegenüber der wirklichen hermeneutischen Erfahrung, die den Sinn des Textes versteht, die Rekonstruktion dessen, was der Verfasser tatsächlich im Sinne hatte, eine reduzierte Aufgabe ist. Es ist die Verführung des Historismus, in solcher Reduktion die Tugend der Wissenschaftlichkeit zu sehen und im Verstehen eine Art von Rekonstruktion zu erblicken, die die Entstehung des Textes gleichsam wiederholt" (355).

98. Cf. 279: "daß ihre Aufgabe überhaupt nicht ist, ein Verfahren des Verstehens zu entwickeln, sondern die Bedingungen aufzuklären, unter denen Verstehen geschieht."

99. Cf. Emilio Betti, *Die Hermeneutik als allgemeine Methodik der Geisteswissenschaften* (Tübingen: J. C. B. Mohr, 1962), 34f., 43ff.

100. A similar fallacy with regard to natural sciences can be found in the first part (3).

101. Cf. Vittorio Hösle, *Wahrheit und Geschichte* (Stuttgart-Bad Cannstatt: Frommann-Holzboog, 1984), my essay "Truth and Understanding: Analytical Philosophy (Donald Davidson), Phenomenology (Hans-Georg Gadamer), and the Desideratum of an Objective Idealist Hermeneutics," in *Between Description and Interpretation: The Hermeneutic Turn in Phenomenology,* ed. A.Wierciński (Toronto: The Hermeneutic Press, 2005), 376–91, and my "Hermeneutics" in the 2012 edition of the *Princeton Encyclopedia of Poetry and Poetics.*

102. One could name here also Karl Rahner, *Hörer des Wortes* (*Hearer of the Word*) (München: Kosel, 1941), a book that shares with Gadamer's work Heidegger's influence.

103. Christian authors have often claimed to be inspired; see, for example, Nicholas of Cusa's letter to Cardinal Julian at the end of *De docta ignorantia* (*On Learned Ignorance*): "Credo superno dono a patre luminum" (ed. cit. I 516).

104. Cf. Thomas Söding, *Mehr als ein Buch. Die Bibel begreifen* (Freiburg/Basel/Wien: Herder, 1995).

105. Cf. Rudolf Bultmann, *Neues Testament und Mythologie* (München: Chr. Kaiser, 1985).

106. Cf. Erich Auerbach, *Mimesis* (Princeton: Princeton University Press, 1953), 40ff.

107. Cf. Robert Alter, *The Art of Biblical Narrative* (New York: Basic Books, 1981) or Barbara Green, *"What Profit for Us?" Remembering the Story of Joseph* (Lanham/New York/London: University Press of America, 1996). Also see Robert Alter, *The Art of Biblical Poetry* (New York: Basic Books, 1985). In both of his books "biblical" refers only to the Old Testament.

108. *The Western Canon* (New York: Harcourt Brace, 1995), 490.

Chapter 8.   *To What Extent Is the Concept of Spirit* (Geist) *in German Idealism a Legitimate Heir to the Concept of Spirit* (Pneuma) *in the New Testament?*

1. For its intermediary status from the point of view of the theory of science, see V. Hösle, *Morals and Politics* (Notre Dame: University of Notre Dame Press, 2004), 438f.

2. *The Historical Figure of Jesus* (Harmondsworth: Penguin, 1993). Not yet completed is the magisterial work, planned to consist of five volumes, by John P. Meier, *A Marginal Jew* (New York: Doubleday, 1991ff.). I am aware of the fact that the caution of the historical method leads to the result that one often sees successful predictions (like that regarding the destruction of Jerusalem) as being issued post factum, which is something that in reality is not at all necessary—otherwise one would have to date the conclusion of the first volume of Alexis de Tocqueville's *De la démocratie en Amérique* to 1950 rather than to 1835. (Nevertheless Luke 21:20 is too precise to have been written ante factum.) But the reverse is correct: mistaken predictions are very old. That the early church had an imminent expectation is obvious, and since its partial disappointment is already obvious in the first letter to the Thessalonians (4:13ff.; cf. also John 21:22f.; 2 Peter 3:3ff.), one would hardly have projected it back on Jesus, if he had not himself shared it. Certainly he can have been radically misunderstood by his immediate disciples, but then we must give up all hope of ever arriving at the historical figure. No, one of the ideas that we can ascribe to Jesus with a probability

beyond reasonable doubt was wrong, and his depiction of judgment and of damnation was probably not compatible with modern moral principles. Furthermore, the historical Jesus seems to have envisioned a universal diffusion of his message only occasionally, incidentally, perhaps increasingly after disappointments with the Jews. A pericope like Mark 7:24ff./Matthew 15:21ff. is something that one would hardly have newly invented in a time of a flourishing mission to the pagans. A fundamental danger for the historical method admittedly consists in the fact that it sometimes believes that the *epistemologically* most sustainable hypotheses regarding the views espoused by an author also constitute the *ontologically* central components of his system of ideas. With this it admittedly commits an elementary fallacy. Jesus may very well have considered some of his ideas to be much more meaningful than others that we can ascribe to him with much greater probability.

    3. Compare Marie E. Isaacs, *The Concept of Spirit* (London: Heythrop College, 1976), 10ff. It would go beyond the limits of this essay to inquire whether the idea of a divine spirit (which arises from the insight that spirit is the most divine part of humans) is connected in a special way with the axial age. Clearly it is not limited to the Jewish religion; think of Anaxagoras's theory of Nous, but also the much earlier *spenta mainyu* (holy spirit) of Zarathustra, which gives the name to the third Gatha (Yasna 47–50).

    4. Edward W. Winstanley has given an old and still useful list of all the passages with *pneuma* in the New Testament in his book *Spirit in the New Testament* (Cambridge: Cambridge University Press, 1901).

    5. See Christian Schütz, *Einführung in die Pneumatologie* (Darmstadt: Wissenschaftliche Buchgesellschaft, 1985), 157: "Jesus selber hat vermutlich nur wenig vom Geist gesprochen" ("Jesus himself probably spoke little of the spirit"). I am grateful to this book for much information.

    6. Luke 11:20 has "with the finger of God." Robert P. Menzies has good arguments for why it is Matthew and not Luke who follows Q (*The Development of Early Christian Pneumatology with Special Reference to Luke–Acts* [Sheffield: JSOT Press, 1991], 185ff.).

    7. *Das Johannesevangelium: Ein Kommentar* (Tübingen: J. C. B. Mohr [Paul Siebeck], 1980), 495: "In dieser ersten Vershälfte wird deutlich vorausgesetzt, daß jenes, was der Geist lehren wird, über die Botschaft des irdischen Jesus hinausgehen wird; man könnte vielleicht sagen: soweit hinausgehen wird, wie die Korrekturen und Zusätze des Evangelisten über die Tradition, die ihm in seiner Vorlage zu Gebote stand. Hier spricht ein klares Bewußtsein davon, daß zwischen dem, was der irdische Jesus sagte und tat, und der Botschaft des Geistes eine Zäsur besteht . . . Johannes hat die Enderwartung, die für Mk noch als ein kosmisches Ereignis in einer unbestimmten Zukunft lag, derart radikalisiert, daß die chronologische Zeit ausgeschaltet wird und mit ihr jene Veränderung innerhalb der Welt, auf die Mk und die erste Christenheit warteten."

8. Johannes S. Vos, *Traditionsgeschichtliche Untersuchungen zur paulinischen Pneumatologie* (Assen: Van Gorcum, 1973), 145. On the prehistory of Paul's concept formation, compare also Finny Philip, *The Origins of Pauline Pneumatology* (Tübingen: Mohr Siebeck, 2005).

9. Compare Hermann Gunkel, *Die Wirkungen des heiligen Geistes nach der populären Anschauung der apostolischen Zeit und nach der Lehre des Apostels Paulus* (Göttingen: Vandenhoeck & Ruprecht, 1888), 77: "Paulus sieht in einer Fülle von christlichen Funktionen Geisteswirkungen, welche das Judentum und die ältesten Gemeinden nicht für Wirkungen einer übernatürlichen Kraft gehalten haben" ("Paul recognizes in a variety of Christian functions effects of the spirit, which Judaism and the oldest communities did not consider effects of a supernatural force").

10. It is also found in 1 Peter 3:18; 4:6. The spirit is not a mere principle of life, but is also contrasted to the *psychikos . . . anthrōpos* (1 Cor. 2:14; cf. James 3:15 and Jude 19) and differentiated from *psychē* as well as from *sōma* (1 Thess. 5:23).

11. Compare Wolf-Dieter Hauschild and Volker H. Drecoll, *Pneumatologie in der Alten Kirche* (Bern/New York: Peter Lang, 2004).

12. Cf. Elizabeth A. Dreyer, "An Advent of the Spirit: Medieval Mystics and Saints," in *Advents of the Spirit: An Introduction to the Current Study of Pneumatology*, ed. B. E. Hinze and D. L. Dabney (Milwaukee: Marquette University Press, 2001), 123–62. Meister Eckhart's biblical hermeneutics is a particularly important link to German idealism.

13. I am referring to the convincing subdivision of Hans Küng, *Christianity: Essence, History, and Future* (New York: Continuum, 1995).

14. See his "Erklärung" from August 7, 1799 (*Kant's gesammelte Schriften,* vol. XII [Berlin/Leipzig, 1922], 371). Kant himself, of course, in other contexts insists on the tension between letter and spirit.

15. Georg Wilhelm Friedrich Hegel, *Werke in zwanzig Bänden* (Frankfurt, 1969–71), 2.9. All of the passages that I am citing are from this edition, including the late lectures, which are now available in critical editions, since Hegel's development over the individual years is not thematic.

16. Friedrich Wilhelm Joseph Schelling, *Philosophie der Mythologie, Erster Band: Einleitung in die Philosophie der Mythologie* (Darmstadt: Wissenschaftliche Buchgesellschaft, 1976), 264 ("mehr aus tief religiöser und sittlicher Erregung als wissenschaflichem Geist hervorgegangen, hatte die alte Metaphysik unangetastet stehen lassen, war aber eben dadurch unvollendet geblieben") and 266 ("Glauben an die Offenbarung als bloß äußere Autorität, worein unleugbar die Reformation zuletzt ausgeartet"). Schelling nevertheless praises the early reformers who, unlike his contemporaries, the Pietists, had not picked out individual Bible passages, but had acted "in accordance with the spirit of Christianity," "and because they have encountered the spirit, they have been victorious" (*Philosophie der Offenbarung,* 2 vols. [Darmstadt: Wissenschaftliche Buchgesellschaft, 1974], II 101: "und eben weil sie den Geist getroffen, darum haben sie gesiegt"). The late

philosophies of Fichte and Schelling cannot be discussed here. The statement must suffice that they cannot be designated as irrational even if they deviate markedly from Hegel's idea of a system. Schelling writes in the same text, shortly after the above-cited passage: "Also Christianity demands overcoming, but not of reason itself (for then all understanding would cease), but only of the merely natural reason" (267: "Auch das Christenthum verlangt Ueberwindung, aber nicht der Vernunft selbst [denn dann hörte alles Begreifen auf], sondern der bloß natürlichen"). "If there should lie in us something transcending all reason, we will be able to speak of it only after the science of reason has been completed, and it is still far from that point" (269: "Wenn in uns selbst etwas alle Vernunft Uebertreffendes liegen sollte, so wird von diesem erst dann die Rede seyn können, wenn die Vernunftwissenschaft bis an ihr Ziel geführt ist, davon sie aber noch weit entfernt ist"). At any rate, his relatively traditional Christology is very different from that of Fichte and Hegel, against whom he turns in the *Philosophie der Offenbarung* (II 101ff.). One of the problems of his Christology (not the only one) is that Schelling does not really take modern New Testament research seriously: he considers the letter to the Hebrews to be Pauline (320) and presents a philologically unacceptable interpretation of John 21 (328ff.).

17. See chapter 7 of this volume.

18. Johann Gottlieb Fichte, *Von den Pflichten der Gelehrten: Jenaer Vorlesungen 1794/95,* ed. R. Lauth, H. Jacob, and P. K. Schneider (Hamburg: Meiner, 1971), 58.

19. Fichte will interpret in the sixth lecture of *Die Anweisung zum seligen Leben, oder auch die Religionslehre* (*Way to a Blessed Life, or also Doctrine of Religion*) of 1806 the prologue of the Gospel of John in accordance with his own philosophy. See Daniel Weidner, "Geist, Wort, Liebe: Johannes um 1800," in *Das Buch der Bücher—gelesen: Lesarten der Bibel in den Wissenschaften und Künsten,* ed. S. Martus and A. Polaschegg (Frankfurt: Peter Lang, 2006), 435–70.

20. I can refer to my book: *Hegels System* (Hamburg: Meiner, 1998), 638–62.

21. *Philosophie der Offenbarung,* I 248ff.

22. On the second point, see, for example, Haenchen, *Das Johannesevangelium,* 493: "Es ist längst aufgefallen, daß der Begriff Sünde im vierten Evangelium zwar 16mal vorkommt, aber dennoch keine entscheidende Rolle spielt" ("It has already been noted a long time ago that the concept of sin occurs 16 times in the fourth gospel, but nevertheless does not play a crucial role").

Chapter 9.   *Reasons, Emotions, and God's Presence in Anselm of Canterbury's Dialogue* Cur Deus homo

1. On Llull's rationalism, see Vittorio Hösle, "Einführung," Raimundus Lullus, *Die neue Logik: Logica nova,* ed. Ch. Lohr, trans. V. Hösle and W. Büchel (Hamburg: Meiner, 1985), ix–lxxxii. His followers include Ramon Sibiuda and

Nicholas of Cusa. Even if Cusanus's epistemology, due to his distinction between *ratio* and *intellectus,* is more complex than Llull's, no other author has influenced him more profoundly than Llull. This holds also for his interreligious
dialogue *De pace fidei;* see chapter 10 in this volume.

2. See Karl Barth, *Fides quaerens intellectum: Anselms Beweis der Existenz
Gottes im Zusammenhang seines theologischen Programms* (München: Zollikon, 1931,
1958).

3. For Boso, cf. Bernd Goebel, "Boso von Montivilliers," in *Biographisch-
bibliographisches Kirchenlexikon,* ed. T. Bautz (Nordhausen: Traugott Bautz, 2004),
vol. 23, 112–14; the most extensive modern text on Boso is Adolphe-André
Porée, *Histoire de l'Abbaye du Bec* (Evreux: Charles Herrissey, 1901), vol. 1,
280–314.

4. Using the categories introduced by Edward M. Forster, *Aspects of the
Novel* (San Diego: Harcourt Brace, 1955), 67ff., one could call them "round"
characters in contradistinction to the "flat" ones of the earlier dialogues.

5. For Anselm's conception of monastic friendship, see Richard Southern, *Saint Anselm: A Portrait in a Landscape* (Cambridge: Cambridge University
Press, 1990), 138–65.

6. *Epistola* 174, *Sancti Anselmi Cantuarensis Archiepiscopi opera omnia,* ed. F. S.
Schmitt, 6 vols. (Seckau/Rome/Edinburgh: Thomas Nelson, 1938–61; quoted
as "S", giving volume, page, and line numbers), IV, 56, 3–5: "cuius conscientiam
sic novi, ut nullum hominem supra me diligat, et quem tantum diligo, ut nesciam
quem plus diligam."

7. *Epistola* 209, S IV, 104, 6–8: "Novit dulcedo dilectionis tuae erga me
dulcedinem dilectionis meae erga te, et novit affectus meus erga te affectum
tuum erga me." (English translations of Anselm's letters are taken from *The Letters of Saint Anselm of Canterbury,* trans. W. Fröhlich, 3 vols. [Kalamazoo, MI: Cis-
tercian Publications, 1990–94].)

8. Milo Crispinus, *Vita venerabilis Bosonis,* Patrologia Latina 150 (Paris:
Migne, 1854), 723–32, 726 B: "quia magis amaret cum illo vivere in solitudine
quam sine eo in magnis divitiis."

9. Eadmer, *The Life of St. Anselm, Archbishop of Canterbury,* ed. R. W. Southern (Oxford: Clarendon, 1996), 61 (ch. 34): "Miratus ergo hominem est, et nimio
illius amore devinctus."

10. Eadmer, *Life of St. Anselm,* 61 (chapter 34); cf. Milo Crispinus, *Vita venerabilis Bosonis,* 725C–D.

11. Thus the abbot of Cluny, Petrus Venerabilis (1094–1156), who was
interested in interreligious dialogues and had the Qur'an translated into Latin,
recounts that in a dream he encountered a deceased acquaintance and asked
him: "But are the things we believe of God certain? Is there no doubt that the
belief that is ours be the true one?" (Petrus Venerabilis, *De miraculis* [Turnhout:
Brepols, 1988 (CCCM 83)], 145 (II, 25); cf. Peter Dinzelbacher, *Vision und
Visionsliteratur im Mittelalter* (Stuttgart: Anton Hiersemann, 1981], 44–45). Again,

a few decades after Anselm's death, the nun Elizabeth of Schoenau (1129–65) gives an account of her spiritual crisis that culminated in her question: "But can all this be true what is written about Him [Christ]?" (Ferdinand W. E. Roth, *Die Visionen der Heiligen Elisabeth* [Brünn: Verlag der Studien aus dem Benedictiner- und Cistercienser-Orden, 1884], 1, 2, 4). And as early as in the middle of the eleventh century, Otloh of St. Emmeram (1000–1070) relates how, following the insinuations of a "demonic voice," he doubted the reliability of the scripture and eventually even the existence of God (Otloh of St. Emmeram, *De temptationibus suis,* Patrologia Latina 146 [Paris: Migne, 1884], 29–58, 33AB); cf. Jay Rubenstein, *Guibert of Nogent: Portrait of a Medieval Mind* (New York: Routledge, 2002), 76f.

    12. Cf. Eadmer, *Life of St. Anselm,* chapter 19.

    13. Cf. *Cur Deus Homo* (CDH) I, 1, S II, 48, 11–15.

    14. CDH I, 1, S II, 49, 3–6.

    15. CDH I, 2, S II, 50, 6: "non tam ostendere quam tecum quaerere."

    16. See the classification by Klaus Jacobi, "Einleitung," in *Gespräche lesen,* ed. K. Jacobi (Tübingen: Narr, 1999), 9–22, 12. Gilbertus Crispinus's *Disputatio Iudaei et Christiani* (ed. B. Blumenkranz [Utrecht/Antwerp: Spectrum, 1956]) is usually considered the first interreligious dialogue of the Middle Ages; cf. Anna S. Abulafia, *Christians and Jews in the Twelfth Century Renaissance* (London/New York: Routledge, 1995). Gilbert was a friend of Anselm and like him had been a pupil of Lanfranc at Bec.

    17. See, for example, René Roques, "La méthode de S. Anselme dans le Cur Deus homo," *Aquinas* 5 (1962): 3–57; *St. Anselm's Proslogion,* ed. Max J. Charlesworth (Notre Dame: University of Notre Dame Press, 1965, 1979), "Introduction," 30–40 ("Faith and Reason in the Cur Deus Homo"); Gillian R. Evans, "Cur Deus homo: The Nature of St. Anselm's Appeal to Reason," *Studies in Theology* 31 (1977): 33–50.

    18. See, for example, Marilyn M. Adams, "Fides quaerens intellectum: St. Anselm's Method in Philosophical Theology," *Faith and Philosophy* 9 (1992): 409–35, 411–14.

    19. CDH I, 1, S II, 48, 16–18.

    20. CDH, Commendatio operis ad Urbanum Papam II, S II, 40, 10–12.

    21. How to gain mathematical convictions—which are to be sharply distinguished from their proofs, although they facilitate the discovery of them—is a problem discussed for the first time at the beginning of Archimedes' *Method Concerning Mechanical Theorems.*

    22. For an interpretation along these lines, see Michel Corbin, "La nouveauté de l'incarnation: Introduction à l'Epistola et au Cur Deus Homo," Anselme de Cantorbéry: *Lettre sur l'incarnation du verbe: Pourquoi un Dieu-homme,* ed. M. Corbin and A. Galonnier (L'oeuvre de S. Anselme de Cantorbéry, vol. 3) (Paris: Cerf, 1988), 58–61.

23. Jean Bodin, *Colloquium heptaplomeres,* ed. L. Noack (Schwerin: Bärensprung, 1857, reprinted Stuttgart-Bad Cannstatt: Frommann-Holzboog, 1966), 131f.

24. CDH, Praefatio, S II, 42, 12–14; English translations from Anselm's works are for the most part taken (at times in a slightly altered fashion) from Anselm of Canterbury, *The Major Works,* ed. B. Davies and G. R. Evans (Oxford: Oxford University Press, 1998); sometimes they are our own.

25. Cf. S II, 106, 19–21: "Ut enim aliquantulum loquar non quasi de illo qui numquam fuerit, sicut hactenus fecimus, sed velut de eo quem et cuius facta novimus." A contrast between *ratio* and *experimentum* with regard to Jesus may be found in CDH II, 11, S II, 111, 26–112, 4.

26. CDH II, 22, S II, 133, 8–11. See also CDH II, 19, S II, 131, 7–10.

27. CDH II, 22, S II, 133, 5–8. It is controversial who the *pagani* are supposed to be. For a defense of the thesis that they are to be considered as Muslims, see René Roques, *Anselme de Cantorbéry: Pourquoi Dieu s'est fait homme* (Paris: Cerf, 1963), 72; however, Charlesworth, "Introduction," in *St. Anselm's Proslogion,* 32–33, suggests that this is wrong. For the intellectual-historical background of *Cur Deus homo,* see further Julia Gauss, "Anselm von Canterbury: Zur Begegnung und Auseinandersetzung der Religionen," *Saeculum* 17 (1966): 277–363; Anna S. Abulafia, "Christians Disputing Disbelief: St. Anselm, Gilbert Crispin and Pseudo-Anselm," in *Religionsgespräche im Mittelalter,* ed. B. Lewis and F. Niewöhner (Wiesbaden: Otto Harassowitz, 1992), 131–48; Klaus Kienzler, "Cur Deus homo—aus der Sicht des mittelalterlichen jüdisch-christlichen Religionsgespräches," in K. Kienzler, *Gott ist größer. Studien zu Anselm von Canterbury* (Würzburg: Echter, 1997), 122–40.

28. CDH I, 10, S II, 67, 1–2: "qui credere nihil volunt nisi praemonstrata ratione."

29. Cf. CDH I, 16, S II, 74, 14; I, 20, S II, 88, 4–10; I, 25, S II, 96, 6–15.

30. Cf. CDH I, 1, S II, 47, 8–11; 48, 16–24; II, 15, S II, 116, 8–12; II, 18, S II, 127, 12–16.

31. CDH I, 3, S 11, 50: "Quamvis enim illi ideo rationem quaerant, quia non credunt, nos vero, quia credimus: unum idemque tamen est quod quaerimus."

32. CDH I, 4, S II, 51, 21–52, 6: "Quapropter cum has convenientias quas dicis infidelibus quasi quasdam picturas rei gestae ostendimus, quoniam non rem gestam, sed figmentum arbitrantur esse quod credimus, quasi super nubem pingere nos existimant. Monstranda ergo prius est veritatis soliditas rationabilis, id est necessitas quae probet deum ad ea quae praedicamus debuisse aut potuisse humiliari; deinde ut ipsum quasi corpus veritatis plus niteat, istae convenientiae quasi picturae corporis sunt exponendae." Cf. also Anselm's reaction in II, 8, S II, 104, 16–27. Boso's criticism does not entail that beauty cannot accompany truth; on the contrary, Anselm himself enjoys the *pulchritudo* of philosophical

arguments, and Boso later recognizes the compatibility of rationality and beauty (CDH I, 1, S II, 49, 17–26; I, 3, S II, 51, 11–12; II, 8, S II, 104, 28).

33. Boso contrasts *conveniens* and *necessarium* again in II, 16, S II, 119, 11–15.

34. See Roques, *Anselme de Cantorbéry,* 80ff.; and Jasper Hopkins, *A Companion to the Study of St. Anselm* (Minneapolis: University of Minnesota Press, 1972), 48–49.

35. CDH I, 10, S II, 67, 2–4: "Sicut enim in deo quamlibet parvum inconveniens sequitur impossibilitas, ita quamlibet parvam rationem, si maiori non vincitur, comitatur necessitas."

36. CDH I, 1, S II, 49, 7–13. Thus, at the end of his life, Anselm began to write a treatise on modal logic, apparently with a view to establishing certain principles and distinctions that he had used in *Cur Deus homo*; the first draft of the first few chapters of this treatise has been edited by Franciscus Salesius Schmitt as the *De potestate* or *Lambeth Fragments* (Anselm of Canterbury, *Ein neues unvollendetes Werk des hl. Anselm von Canterbury: De potestate et impotentia, possibilitate et impossibilitate, necessitate et libertate,* ed. F. S. Schmitt [Münster: Aschendorff, 1936]; cf. *Memorials of St. Anselm,* ed. R. Southern and F. S. Schmitt [Oxford: Oxford University Press, 1991]).

37. CDH I, 2, S II, 50, 7–10: "non alia certitudine accipiatur, nisi quia interim ita mihi videtur, donec deus mihi melius aliquo modo revelet." Cf. I, 18, S II, 82, 5–10.

38. CDH II, 18, S II, 129, 14–16.

39. CDH II, 19, S II, 131, 14–45: "maiores atque plures quam meum aut mortale ingenium comprehendere valeat huius rei sint rationes."

40. CDH I, 24, S II, 94, 19–22.

41. CDH II, 17, S II, 126, 5–7.

42. CDH I, 2, S II, 50, 12–13.

43. CDH I, 12, S II, 70, 14–30, a passage reminiscent of Plato's *Euthyphro* 10a, which Anselm, however, could not know. This rejection of a theological voluntarism is a necessary presupposition of Anselm's Christological argument. In I, 13, S II, 71, 15–27, God is even identified with the *summa iustitia.* In II, 10, S II, 108, 23–24, Anselm anticipates the later principle of sufficient reason: "quia deus nihil sine ratione facit."

44. CDH I, 19, S II, 86, 14–15: "ut, etiam si velim, non possim dubitare." (The point is somehow analogous to Spinoza's criticism of Descartes, *Ethica* II, 49 cor.) Anselm also avers that we are morally obliged to hold certain beliefs: CDH I, 12, S II, 69, 16; I, 13, S II, 71, 26.

45. CDH I, 8, S II, 59, 10–13. Cf. the similar passage II, 15, S II, 116, 4–12.

46. CDH I, 25, S II, 95, 18–23; 96, 2–4: "Quod enim necessaria ratione veraciter esse colligitur, id in nullam deduci debet dubitationem, etiam si ratio quomodo sit non percipitur."

47. Cf. *Monologion* 64, S I, 74, 28–75, 16. This certitude includes our knowledge of the incomprehensibility in question: "rationabiliter comprehendit incomprehensibile esse" (75, 11–12).

48. CDH II, 16, S II, 122, 17–21. See also II, 16, S II, 120, 12–13, where Anselm rebukes Boso for asking a question the answer of which is implicit in what has already been said.

49. We go even beyond Eileen Sweeney, "Anselm und der Dialog," *Gespräche lesen*, 101–24, 123: "So läßt Anselm zu, was Sokrates nie tut, daß der Schüler möglicherweise einsichtigere Fragen und bohrendere Schwierigkeiten aufstellt, als der Lehrer in Angriff zu nehmen wagte. Schüler und Lehrer bei Anselm stehen mehr oder weniger auf gleichem moralischem Grund, und in gewissem Sinne tauschen sie auf höherem intellektuellen Grunde mehrfach die Plätze: Intellektuelle Einsicht oder spirituelle Entwicklung finden sich teils mehr auf seiten Anselms, teils mehr auf seiten des Schülers."

50. CDH II, 16, S II, 116, 16–24. Anselm does not contradict Boso's claim that Mary, too, has been conceived *in iniquitatibus*; he is, however, going to point out later that, before conceiving the God-man, she has been purified through the death of her son even before it occurred.

51. CDH II, 16, S II, 117, 3–6; 15–17: "Qua vero ratione sapientia dei hoc fecit, si non possumus intelligere, non debemus mirari, sed cum veneratione tolerare aliquid esse in secretis tantae rei quod ignoramus . . . Quis ergo praesumat vel cogitare quod humanus intellectus valeat penetrare, quam sapienter, quam mirabiliter tam inscrutabile opus factum sit?"

52. CDH II, 16, S II, 117, 18–22: "Nec peto ut facias quod nullus homo facere potest, sed tantum quantum potes. Plus enim persuadebis altiores in hac re rationes latere, si aliquam te videre monstraveris, quam si te nullam in ea rationem intelligere nihil dicendo probaveris."

53. CDH II, 16, S II, 117, 23. The same term was already used in CDH I, 2, S II, 50, 3. If we remember the use of this term in the preface to the *Proslogion*, where Anselm describes that he could not get rid of the desire to find one cogent argument for the existence of God since "magis ac magis nolenti et defendenti se coepit cum importunitate quadam ingerere" (S I, 93, 15–16), until he finally found his master argument, it becomes clear that the term is not used in a derogatory sense. On the contrary, Boso now plays the same function that Anselm's own ambition twenty years earlier had played.

54. CDH II, 17, S II, 126, 3–4. Cf. the similar remark in I, 18, S II, 84, 2–3.

55. CDH, Commendatio operis ad Urbanum Papam II, S II, 41, 1–5.

56. CDH I, 18, S II, 82, 10–16. This passage is from the discussion about the number of the elect angels and humans, a discussion that suffers from the fact that Anselm does not seem to consider that God certainly knew in advance also the number of the elect angels.

57. See, for example, CDH I, 9, S II, 62, 16–27 on Philippians 2:18.

58. S I, 235, 8–12: "Vide ne ullatenus putes, cum in divinis libris legimus aut cum secundum illos dicimus deum facere malum aut facere non esse, quia negem propter quod dicitur, aut reprehendam quia ita dicitur. Sed non tantum debemus inhaerere improprietati verborum veritatem tegenti, quantum inhiare proprietati veritatis sub multimodo genere locutionum latenti."

59. CDH II, 22, S II, 133, 12–13: "Si quid diximus quod corrigendum sit, non renuo correctionem, si rationabiliter fit."

60. CDH I, 7, S II, 55–59; II, 19, S II, 131, 17–24.

61. CDH II, 8, S II, 103, 28–30 and 144, 9: "non est opus disputare."

62. See, for example, Jan Rohls, *Geschichte der Ethik* (Tübingen: J. C. B. Mohr [Paul Siebeck], 1991), 136: "Anselm will zwar mit ausschließlich rationalen Argumenten die Notwendigkeit der Menschwerdung Christi für die Genugtuung aufweisen, aber der von ihm vorausgesetzte Begründungsrahmen ist der frühmittelalterliche Feudalismus." More recently, however, David Brown, "Anselm on Atonement," in *The Cambridge Companion to Anselm,* ed. B. Davies and B. Leftow (Cambridge: Cambridge University Press, 2004), 279–302, 286, has contended that interpreting the *Cur Deus homo* argument "in terms of Anselm's reliance on feudal imagery . . . is much less plausible than is usually claimed."

63. See Bernd Goebel, *Rectitudo: Wahrheit und Freiheit bei Anselm von Canterbury* (Münster: Aschendorff, 2001), 232–50.

64. CDH I, 11, S II, 68, 15–19; II, 15, S II, 115, 12–21. See also Goebel, *Rectitudo,* 435–44.

65. This is because in Anselm's eyes, sin only exists in the rational will (cf. *De conceptu virginali* III, S II, 142, 12: "Quod non sit peccatum nisi in voluntate rationali"). He therefore concludes: "if an infant is generated even in wicked concupiscence, the sin is no more in the seed than it would be in the spittle or blood, if someone in ill-will were to spit or bleed. For the blame attaches not to the blood or spittle but to the ill-will . . . Indeed, there is no sin in these infants, because they do not have that will, without which they can have no sin; however, sin is said to be in them, because with the seed they assume the necessity that when they become human beings they will sin" (VII, S II, 149, 6–13: "si vitiosa concupiscentia generetur infans, non tamen magis est in semine culpa, qua est in sputo vel sanguine, si quis mala voluntate exspuit aut de sanguine suo aliquid emittit. Non enim sputum aut sanguis, sed mala voluntas arguitur . . . Quippe non est in illis peccatum, quia non habent sine qua non inest voluntatem; et tamen dicitur inesse, quoniam in semine trahunt peccandi, cum homines iam erunt, necessitatem").

66. CDH II, 18, S II, 127, 30–128, 2; II, 19, S II, 130, 26–131, 2.

67. CDH I, 21, S II, 89, 1–17; II, 14, S II, 113, 21–31.

68. CDH II, 21, S II, 132, 8–28.

69. CDH I, 25, S II, 95, 24–96, 3.

70. CDH II, 13, S II, 113, 5–15.

71. CDH I, 11, S II, 69, 3–4: "quamvis aliquantulum me terreas."

72. S II, 74, 11.

73. S II, 87, 30–88, 1: "Si rationes tuas considero, non video quomodo. Si autem ad fidem meam recurro: in fide Christiana, 'quae per dilectionem operatur,' spero me posse salvari."

74. CDH I, 20, S II, 88, 9–10: "quamvis me in angustias quasdam ducas, desidero tamen multum ut, sicut incepisti, progrediaris."

75. CDH I, 21, S II, 89, 24: "nimis periculose vivimus."

76. CDH I, 21, S II, 89, 29: "Et rationem video sic exigere, et omnino esse impossibile."

77. CDH I, 22, S II, 90, 6: "Nisi me fides consolaretur, hoc solum me cogeret desperare."

78. CDH I, 23, S II, 91, 1–2.

79. CDH I, 24, S II, 92, 32–93, 3.

80. CDH I, 24, S II, 94, 10.

81. CDH I, 25, S II, 95, 1–6.

82. CDH II, 19, S II, 131, 3–6: "Nihil rationabilius, nihil dulcius, nihil desiderabilius mundus audire potest. Ego quidem tantam fiduciam ex hoc concipio, ut iam dicere non possim quanto gaudio exultet cor meum. Videtur enim mihi quod nullum hominem reiciat deus ad se sub hoc nomine accedentem."

83. CDH II, 19, S II, 130, 29.

84. The *Vita venerabilis Bosonis* depicts Boso as suffering from *cogitationum tumultibus,* as *turbatus* and *mente confusus* before consulting Anselm; cf. Milo Crispinus, *Vita venerabilis Bosonis,* 725.

85. See already Augustine, *Soliloquia,* 1.6.12.

86. Cf. CDH I, 7, S II, 57, 10–13.

87. See Vittorio Hösle, "Interpreting Philosophical Dialogues," *Antike und Abendland* 48 (2002): 68–90, 80.

88. S III, 76, 4.

89. S III, 79, 85.

90. CDH I, 2, S II, 50, 4–5.

91. CDH I, 25, S II, 96, 16–20; 18: "non in me, sed in deo confidens."

92. CDH II, 16, S II, 117, 23–24.

93. CDH II, 22, S II, 133, 13–15: "Si autem veritatis testimonio roboratur, quod nos rationabiliter invenisse existimamus, deo non nobis attribuire debemus, qui est benedicus in saecula amen."

94. CDH II, 9, S II, 106, 5–6: "Sic est via qua me ducis, undique munita ratione, ut neque ad dexteram neque ad sinistram videam ab illa me posse delineare."

95. CDH II, 9, S II, 106, 7–8: "Non ego te duco, sed ille de quo loquimur, sine quo nihil possumus, nos ducit ubicumque viam veritatis tenemus."

96. According to Anselm, every truth is a form of *rectitudo, iustitia* being a subspecies of *rectitudo;* see *De veritate,* esp. XII.

97. This is Anselm's own interpretation of his argument. In *Proslogion* 14–16, reflecting upon his proof of God's existence and attributes, he writes: "Could [my soul] understand anything at all about You save through 'Your light and Your truth'? . . . For how great is that light from which shines every truth that gives light to the understanding! How large is that truth in which is everything that is true and outside of which nothing exists save nothingness and falsity . . . Truly I do not see this light since it is too much for me; and yet whatever I see I see through it, just as an eye that is weak sees what it sees by the light of the sun which it cannot look at in the sun itself" (S I, 111, 17–112, 24: "Aut potuit omnino aliquid intelligere de te, nisi per 'lucem tuam et veritatem tuam'? . . . Quanta namque est lux illa, de qua micat omne verum quod rationali menti lucet! Quam ampla est illa veritas, in qua est omne quod verum est, et extra quam non nisi nihil et falsum est! . . . Vere ideo hanc non video, quia nimia mihi est; et tamen quidquid video, per illam video, sicut infirmus oculus quod videt per lucem solis videt, quam in ipso sole nequit aspicere"). For an interpretation of Anselm's proof along these lines (an interpretation that does not need to deny the argumentative nature of *Proslogion* 2–4), see also John Hick, "Introduction," in *The Many-Faced Argument,* ed. J. Hick and A. McGill (New York: Macmillan, 1967), 215–18: "The Hegelian Use of the Argument."

98. Even a mathematician can argue in a similar way: Georg Cantor "could write . . . that he was not the creator of his new work, but merely a reporter. *God* had provided the inspiration, leaving Cantor responsible only for the way in which his articles were written, for their style and organization, but not for their content" (Joseph W. Dauben, *Georg Cantor* [Cambridge, MA: Harvard University Press, 1979], 146).

99. Even if one of the reasons Descartes was so proud of his discovery of analytic geometry was that he believed that he had discovered a method that would allow him to find the proofs of geometrical theorems very quickly (*Discours,* René Descartes, *Œuvres,* vol. VI, ed. C. Adam and P. Tannery [Paris: Cerf, 1902], 20f.), one has to recognize, first, that analytical geometry only *facilitates* the discovery of *some* theorems—there is no algorithm that leads to proofs—and, second, that the discovery of such a method can never be the result of its application.

100. *Proslogion,* Preface, S I, 93, 6–7: "quod nullo alio ad se probandum quam se solo indigeret."

101. *Proslogion,* Preface, S I, 93, 16–19: "Cum igitur quadam die vehementer eius importunitati resistendo fatigarer, in ipso cogitationum conflictu sic se obtulit quod desperaveram, ut studiose cogitationem amplecterer, quam sollicitus repellebam."

Chapter 10.   *Interreligious Dialogues during the Middle Ages and Early Modernity*

1. Johannes Hösle, *Vor aller Zeit: Geschichte einer Kindheit* (München: DTV, 2000); Johannes Hösle, *Und was wird jetzt? Geschichte einer Jugend* (München: C. H. Beck, 2002).

2. A good overview of the contemporary discussion, and a criticism of the popular trichotomy of theologies of religion, can be found in Richard Schenk, "Debatable Ambiguity: Paradigms of Truth as a Measure of the Differences among Christian Theologies of Religion," *Jahrbuch für Philosophie des Forschungsinstituts für Philosophie Hannover* 11 (2000): 53–85.

3. See chapter 7 of this volume.

4. My ignorance of Arabic forces me to ignore all analogous works written by non-Christians, such as Yehuda Halevi's *Kuzari*.

5. Fernando Domínguez, "Der Religionsdialog bei Raimundus Lullus," in *Gespräche lesen: Philosophische Dialoge im Mittelalter,* ed. K. Jacobi (Tübingen: Narr, 1999), 263–90, 266.

6. See Eusebio Colomer, *Nikolaus von Kues und Raimund Llull* (Berlin: de Gruyter, 1961), 115, even if Llull's *Llibre del gentil e dels tres savis* is not found, in either Catalan or Latin, in Cusanus's library. On Cusanus's study of Abelard, see Rudolf Haubst, "Marginalien des Nikolaus von Kues zu Abaelard," in *Petrus Abaelardus,* ed. R. Thomas (Trier: Paulinus, 1980), 287–96. (Cusanus's marginal notes, however, do not demonstrate any knowledge of the *Collationes.*) Specifically on the relations between Llull and Cusanus in interreligious matters, see Walter A. Euler, *Unitas et pax: Religionsvergleich bei Raimundus Lullus und Nikolaus von Kues* (Würzburg: Echter, 1990), and Eusebio Colomer, *Nikolaus von Kues († 1464) und Ramon Llull († 1316): ihre Begegnung mit den nichtchristlichen Religionen* (Trier: Paulinus, 1995).

7. See Peter von Moos, "Abaelard: *Collationes,*" in *Hauptwerke der Philosophie: Mittelalter,* ed. K. Flasch (Stuttgart: Reclam, 1998), 129–50, 133. He excludes this possibility too quickly. Abelard was fascinated by Islam's religious tolerance; when he considered emigrating to a Muslim country (*Historia calamitatum* 12), he probably had knowledge of the rationalists among the Muslims.

8. On the multiple variations of the genre, see my essay "Interpreting Philosophical Dialogues," *Antike und Abendland* 48 (2002): 68–90, as well as my book *The Philosophical Dialogue* (Notre Dame: University of Notre Dame Press, 2012).

9. See Hartmut Westermann, "Wahrheitssuche im Streitgespräch: Überlegungen zu Peter Abaelards 'Dialogus inter Philosophum, Iudaeum et Christianum,'" in *Gespräche lesen,* 157–97, 166f. I owe much to this splendid article.

10. See the excellent "Introduction" in Peter Abelard, *Collationes,* ed. and trans. John Marenbon and Giovanni Orlandi (Oxford: Oxford University Press, 2001), xvii–ciii, livf. I quote Abelard according to this edition and translation,

giving first the paragraph number and then the page number, so that the users of other editions may easily find the passage.

11. On the date of the *Collationes,* see Westermann, "Wahrheitssuche im Streitgespräch," 157ff., as well as Marenbon, "Introduction," xxviiff.

12. It was first proposed by Constant Mews, "On Dating the Works of Peter Abelard," *Archives d' histoire doctrinale et littéraire du moyen âge* 52 (1985): 73–134. See also Jean Jolivet, *La Théologie d'Abélard* (Paris: M. Arnold, 1997), 88ff.; Klaus Jacobi, "Einleitung," in *Gespräche lesen,* 9–22, 20.

13. Marilyn McCord Adams, "Introduction," in Peter Abelard, *Ethical Writings,* trans. P. V. Spade (Indianapolis/Cambridge: Hackett Publishing Company, 1995), xiii.

14. Marenbon, "Introduction," lxxxviii.

15. Jacobi, "Einleitung," 12.

16. Bodin, of course, was never a Jew—even if his maternal ancestors may have been—"but rather a profound Judaiser who had a spiritual kinship with the Jews which was rooted in a shared prophetic monotheism" (Paul L. Rose, *Bodin and the Great God of Nature* [Genève: Droz, 1980], 191).

17. Jean Bodin, *Colloquium of the Seven Secrets of the Sublime,* ed. Marion L. D. Kuntz (Princeton: Princeton University Press, 1975), 145. Since the only complete edition of the Latin original is from 1857 (by L. Noack; reprint Stuttgart-Bad: Cannstatt, 1966) and Kuntz consulted for her translation manuscripts unknown to Noack, her translation, which contains many critical notes on the text, is also a contribution to the Latin original, of which a new edition is highly desirable. Hugo Grotius, Queen Christina of Sweden, Pierre Bayle, Hermann Conring, Jacob Thomasius, and Gottfried Wilhelm Leibniz had to read this work of Bodin still in manuscript form. (In 1720, a printing of the book had already begun in Leipzig, but it was stopped by the authorities.) I also give the passages in Noack's edition. (The passage just quoted is on p. 112.) On the importance of harmony and of the new chromaticism of Renaissance music for the *Heptaplomeres,* see Kuntz's erudite "Introduction," xiii–lxxxi, lxiiff.

18. Kuntz, 148: Noack, 115.

19. Kuntz, 150; Noack, 116.

20. See Ramon Llull, *Llibre del gentil e dels tres savis,* ed. Antoni Bonner (Palma de Mallorca: Patronat Ramón Llull, 1993), 207. For most readers it will be easier to look up the Latin translation *Liber de gentili et tribus sapientibus,* which was done during Llull's life; for that, one has still to consult the famous Moguntina, that is, the eighteenth-century edition of Llull's Latin works since the work has not yet appeared in the new critical edition. See Raymundus Lullus, *Opera,* Tomus II (Mainz: Mayer, 1722; reprint Frankfurt: Minerva, 1965), 21–114: there 113. (I give the pages of the reprint, not of the original edition.) A complete English translation by Anthony Bonner can be found in the first of the two volumes of Ramon Llull, *Selected Works* (Princeton: Princeton University

Press, 1985), an abridged version in the later reader: *Doctor illuminatus: A Ramon Llull Reader,* ed. A. Bonner (Princeton: Princeton University Press, 1993).

21. Nicolai de Cusa, *De pace fidei cum epistula ad Ioannem de Segobia,* ed. R. Klibansky and H. Bascour (Hamburg: Meiner, 1959), chapter 1, 3. The most recent English translation of the work is *De pace fidei and Cribratio Alkorani,* ed. J. Hopkins (Minneapolis: Arthur J. Banning Press, 1990). See in the letter to John of Segovia the appeal against war and for a spiritual exchange: 97, 100.

22. Kuntz, 3; Noack, 1.

23. Kuntz, 467ff.; Noack, 355ff.

24. *Llibre,* 160, 180; *Liber* 93, 102. See the agreement *Llibre* 46/*Liber* 41, an agreement that is supposed to avoid the arousal of antipathy.

25. *Llibre,* 13, 14, 207, 208; *Liber,* 25, 26, 113, 114.

26. *Llibre,* 46; *Liber,* 41.

27. *Llibre,* 198; *Liber,* 109.

28. *Llibre,* 205; *Liber,* 113.

29. *Llibre,* 208; *Liber,* 114.

30. *Collationes,* §147, 157.

31. See the self-deprecatory remarks of the Jew, *Collationes,* §10f., 13 and §15f., 19ff.

32. *Collationes,* §63, 81.

33. §69, 87. Bodin's Senamus, who, too, has anti-Judaic inclinations (Kuntz, 152f., 206; Noack, 118, 159), calls all uncultivated people "animals" (Kuntz, 442; Noack, 336).

34. *Llibre,* 67; *Liber,* 51.

35. Chapter 12, 39. On the anti-Judaism in Cusanus's own ecclesiastical policies, see Kurt Flasch, *Nikolaus von Kues: Geschichte einer Entwicklung* (Frankfurt: Klostermann, 1998), 350f. I owe much information to this book.

36. He is called *religiosissimus* by Senamus (Kuntz, 465; Noack, 354).

37. Kuntz, 438; Noack, 333.

38. Kuntz, 254; Noack, 194.

39. Kuntz, 241; Noack, 184.

40. Kuntz, 434; Noack, 330.

41. Kuntz, 420; Noack, 319: after Curtius has mentioned Christian Church Fathers, Octavius quotes Muslim authorities; Fridericus's reaction is: "Non video cur theologorum christianorum clarissima lumina cum ista Mahummedanorum fece debeant comparari." See his analogous comment on the Talmud in Kuntz, 354; Noack, 269.

42. Kuntz, 233; Noack, 178. Fridericus is called by the narrator in this context ironically and benevolently *homo minime malus.*

43. Kuntz, 467f.; Noack, 355f.

44. Kuntz, 471; Noack, 358.

45. Kuntz, 143; Noack, 111.

46. Kuntz, 162f.; Noack, 124.
47. Kuntz, 29ff., 74ff.; Noack, 21ff., 59ff.
48. Kuntz, 165; Noack, 126. See also Kuntz, 422; Noack, 320f.
49. Kuntz, 165f.; Noack, 127.
50. Kuntz, 208; Noack, 160.
51. Kuntz, 169; Noack, 129f.
52. Kuntz, 170; Noack, 131.
53. Kuntz, 171; Noack, 131. Bodin has a passage from *De concordantia catholica* (I 2) in mind, but he may also refer to chapters 13 and 16 of *De pace fidei*. The editors of Cusanus's work write in their erudite *praefatio*: "Guillelmus Postellus nec non Ioannes Bodinus in operibus Cusani versabantur: quorum etsi neuter ipsum laudat *De pace fidei*, tamen utrumque hunc quoque librum cognovisse haud absonum videtur" ("Guillaume Postel and Jean Bodin were familiar with the works of Cusanus; and even if neither of them quotes *De pace fidei*, it makes sense to assume that both knew also this book," xliii).
54. Kuntz, 330ff.; Noack, 252ff.
55. Kuntz, 471; Noack, 358.
56. *Llibre,* 209; *Liber,* 114.
57. See Günter Gawlick, "Der Deismus im *Colloquium Heptaplomeres*," in *Jean Bodins Colloquium Heptaplomeres,* ed. G. Gawlick and F. Niewöhner (Wiebaden: Harassowitz, 1996), 13–26, 25f.: "Von den Sieben wird keiner zu einem Glaubenswechsel oder gar zum Ausstieg aus der Offenbarungsreligion bewegt, und auch vom Leser wird weder das eine noch das andere erwartet. Keine Religion erweist sich als stärker denn die andere, und selbst der Deismus, der den kleinsten gemeinsamen Nenner aller Religionen enthält, ist und bleibt nur eine unter mehreren Optionen.—So hat denn das *Colloquium* m.E. nicht den Deismus zum Ergebnis, sondern etwas anderes, viel Bescheideneres: Gesprächsteilnehmer und Leser bleiben bei der Religion, mit der sie ins Gespräch bzw. in die Lektüre eingetreten sind, nun aber mit verändertem, erweitertem Bewußtsein.—Das scheint nicht sehr viel zu sein; es ist aber auch nicht so wenig, daß man sagen müßte, das *Colloquium* lohne nicht die Mühe intensiven Studiums" ("None of the seven is brought to the point to give up the religion of revelation or even to change his own faith, nor is the reader expected to do the one or the other. No religion proves to be stronger than the other, and even deism, which contains the least common denominator of all religions, is and remains only one among various options.—Thus, in my eyes, the *Colloquium* has not deism as its result, but something else, much more modest: interlocutors and readers stay with the religion, with which they entered the conversation and the reading respectively, but now with a changed and extended awareness.—This does not seem to be very much; but it is not so little either that one ought to say that the *Colloquium* does not deserve the effort of intense study").
58. Kuntz, 205, 435; Noack, 158, 331.

59. Kuntz, 327; Noack, 249.

60. See Kuntz, 268, 277, 292, 383; Noack 205, 212, 223f., 289.

61. Kuntz, 221, 266; Noack 169, 204.

62. Kuntz, 384; Noack, 290.

63. Kuntz, 262; Noack, 200f. Abelard, *Collationes,* §15, 19ff.; *Llibre,* 69; *Liber,* 52.

64. Kuntz, 310. See also the criticism of auricular confession, Kuntz, 391; Noack, 295.

65. Kuntz, 171, 252, 394, 397, 399, 421, 460; Noack, 132, 193, 297f., 300, 302, 319, 350.

66. Kuntz, 252, 354; Noack 193, 269f.

67. Kuntz, 298; Noack, 228.

68. Kuntz, 359; Noack, 273. See also Kuntz, 396; Noack, 299. Interesting are also his remarks, Kuntz, 463; Noack, 352.

69. §7f., 9ff.

70. §70, 89.

71. §72, 93.

72. §77, 97.

73. §78, 99.

74. §5, 7.

75. §10, 13.

76. See my interpretation of Llull's philosophy in my "Einführung," in *Raimundus Lullus, Die neue Logik. Logica nova,* ed. Ch. Lohr (Hamburg: Meiner, 1985), ix–xciv.

77. *Llibre,* 12; *Liber,* 25.

78. *Llibre,* 209; *Liber,* 114.

79. *Llibre,* 206; *Liber,* 113.

80. *Llibre,* 43, 198; *Liber,* 39, 109.

81. Chapter 1, 5f.

82. Chapter 19, 61.

83. Chapters 1, 19, and 7, 62.

84. Chapter 8, 25.

85. Chapter 9, 26 about the doctrine of the Trinity as implied by Isaiah.

86. *Collationes,* §5, 7. Abelard quotes Augustine (*Quaestiones Evangeliorum* 2, 40), but, as Marenbon notes, he "is using Augustine's comment in almost the opposite way to what its author intended."

87. Nicolai de Cusa, *Sermones III (1452–1454). Fasciculus I, Sermones CXXI–CXL,* ed. R. Haubst and H. Pauli (Hamburg: Meiner, 1995), 23: "credit igitur, sive velit, sive nolit, Christum . . . Et ob hoc fides Judaica implicite semper Christum continebat."

88. An East Asian student in one of my courses said this about Rahner's position: "I am not sure I like the condescension of this anonymous Buddhist."

89. §20, 25. See also §48ff., 59ff.

90. Kuntz, 183; Noack, 141. The argument from age is implicitly rejected by Abelard's philosopher, when he states that he expects to find more truth in the Christian than in the Jewish religion since the former is younger and an intellectual progress is never guaranteed, but still likely (*Collationes,* §65, 81ff.). The Muslim in Llull seems to imply that a later prophet is more authorized than an earlier one, but is confronted with the objection that in this case Muhammad would have to be replaced by a new prophet, and so on: *Llibre,* 164; *Liber,* 95.

91. Kuntz, 186; Noack, 143.

92. Kuntz, 190; Noack, 146.

93. *Collationes,* §67, 83.

94. §161–98, 171–203.

95. §174f., 185ff.

96. This becomes particularly evident in *Llibre,* 100; *Liber,* 66.

97. Hopkins, 40; chapter 5, 14.

98. *Collationes,* §71, 89.

99. Chapter 6, 16.

100. Chapter 8, 21ff.

101. *Llibre,* 97; *Liber,* 64f.

102. Chapter 8, 25f.

103. Chapter 9, 27f. A similar distinction between the belief in Trinity ascribed by the Muslims to the Christians and their real belief is to be found in Llull, *Llibre,* 114f., 160f.; *Liber,* 73, 93, and analogously with regard to incarnation (*Llibre,* 140; *Liber,* 81).

104. Chapters 13 and 14, 40f. and 46.

105. Chapter 12, 35ff.

106. Chapter 14, 44ff. Again, Cusanus follows Llull, *Llibre,* 140; *Liber,* 84.

107. *Llibre,* 165f; *Liber,* 95: Jesus' divinity is "proven" by the success of Christianity.

108. *Llibre,* 196f; *Liber,* 109. The Muslim, however, rejects this interpretation as heretical. Llull seems to suggest that there is a more intellectual interpretation of Islam, but that it is not widespread.

109. Chapter 15, 48ff.

110. Chapter 15, 49. In Llull's *Llibre,* 162f.; *Liber,* 94 the Muslim argues that the divine mission of Muhammad is proven by his fight against the polytheists, but the pagan rejects this thought. Cusanus is more willing, at least in *De pace fide,* to grant a positive function, willed by God, to Muhammad.

111. Chapter 16, 51.

112. Hopkins, 65f.; chapter 16, 55.

113. Chapter 16, 52.

114. Chapter 16, 55f.

115. Chapter 18, 60f.

116. Already *Llibre,* 121, 155; *Liber,* 76, 91 the Christian says that Christians deserve to be punished by God for their misdeeds more severely than non-Christians. It speaks for Llull's sense of respect for the other religions that he has his Muslim make an analogous point: *Llibre,* 169; *Liber,* 97.

117. That remains in my eyes a plausible interpretation of *Llibre,* 5f.; *Liber,* 21, despite the objections of Antoni Bonner in his "Introducció" to his Catalan edition, xv–liv, xviiif. He is forced to assume a Llull before Llull, whom nobody else has ever mentioned. And even if he may have existed in the East, is it likely that the autodidact Llull knew his work?

118. Nicolai de Cusa, *Cribratio Alkorani,* ed. L. Hagemann (Hamburg: Meiner, 1986), 125.

119. See his "Introduction" to his aforementioned translation, 24.

120. See the letter to John of Segovia, 98.

121. *Llibre,* 196; *Liber,* 109.

122. *De pace fidei,* chapter 19, 61.

123. Kuntz, 90, 144, 312; Noack, 71, 112, 238.

124. Kuntz, 462; Noack, 352.

Chapter 11. *Platonism and Anti-Platonism in Nicholas of Cusa's Philosophy of Mathematics*

1. I will refer to the Latin text of a Latin-German edition of Cusanus's works: Nikolaus von Kues, *Philosophisch-theologische Schriften,* ed. L. Gabriel, D. Dupré, and W. Dupré, 3 vols. (Wien: Herder, 1964–67) (= PTS). I am quite aware of the defects of this edition (with regard also to the Latin text, which I once corrected), but in the German world it is the most widely used. The English translation is always mine.

2. I have in mind Thomas Bradwardine, Jean Buridan, and Nicole Oresme. See Anneliese Maier, *Studien zur Naturphilosophie der Spätscholastik,* 5 vols. (Roma: Edizioni di Storia e letteratura, 1949–58), especially vol. 1: *Die Vorläufer Galileis im 14. Jahrhundert.*

3. See Ernst Cassirer, *Individuum und Kosmos in der Philosophie der Renaissance* (Darmstadt: Wissenschaftliche Buchgesellschaft, 1963), 34ff., and Pauline M. Watts's introduction to her translation of Nicholas of Cusa, *De Ludo Globi: The Game of Spheres* (New York: Abaris, 1986), 13–51, especially 39ff.

4. On Cusanus's Christology, which pervades all his works, see Rudolf Haubst, *Die Christologie des Nikolaus von Kues* (Freiburg: Herder, 1956).

5. See the fourth part of *Die Legitimität des Neuzeit* (Frankfurt: Suhrkamp, 1966).

6. *Geschichte der mittelalterlichen Philosophie im christlichen Abendland* (Hamburg: Meiner, 1980), 95.

7. See Eusebio Colomer, *Nikolaus von Kues und Raimund Llull* (Berlin: de Gruyter, 1961). See also my introduction to Lullus's *Die neue Logik: Logica Nova,* ed. Ch. Lohr (Hamburg: Meiner, 1985).

8. Cusanus started studying mathematics in Padua with Paolo Toscanelli, one of the best Italian mathematicians of the time. About him, see Gustavo Uzielli, *La vita e i tempi di Paolo dal Pozzo Toscanelli* (Roma: Ministero della pubblica istruzione, 1894), and Giovanni Celoria, *Sulle osservazioni di comete fatte da Paolo dal Pozzo Toscanelli e sui lavori astronomici suoi in generale* (Milano: Hoepli, 1921); on his famous correspondence with Columbus, whom he encouraged to attempt his great voyage, see Henry Vignaud, *Toscanelli and Columbus* (London: Sands, 1902); on humanist mathematicians in general, see Paul L. Rose, *The Italian Renaissance of Mathematics: Studies on Humanists and Mathematicians from Petrarch to Galileo* (Geneva: Droz, 1975). Cusanus dedicated his *De transmutationibus geometricis* (*On Geometric Transmutations*) to Toscanelli (see the cordial introductory remarks in *Opera,* 3 vols. [Paris: Aidibus Ascensianis, 1514, reprint Frankfurt: Minerva, 1962], II, Fo. XXXIII). He was acquainted with the important mathematician and astronomer Georg von Peurbach to whom he dedicated *De quadratura circuli* (*On the Squaring of the Circle*). His specific mathematical achievements are not the subject of this essay: see Moritz Cantor, *Vorlesungen über Geschichte der Mathematik,* 4 vols. (Leipzig: Teubner, 1880–1908), II 170–87, and the works of the best expert on Cusanus's mathematics, Josef E. Hofmann. He is the translator of as well as the author of the introduction and notes to *Nikolaus von Kues: Die mathematischen Schriften* (Hamburg: Meiner, 1952), and of many essays on Cusanus's mathematical writings, such as "Mutmaßungen über das früheste mathematische Wissen des Nikolaus von Kues," *Mitteilungen und Forschungsbeiträge der Cusanus-Gesellschaft* 5 (1965): 98–136, and "Sinn und Bedeutung der wichtigsten mathematischen Schriften des Nikolaus von Kues," in *Nicolò Cusano agli inizi del mondo moderno* (Firenze: Sansoni, 1970), 385–98; see also his *Geschichte der Mathematik,* 3 vols. (Berlin: de Gruyter, 1953–57), I 89–100. Although Cusanus lacked the necessary rigor, his mathematical creativity is remarkable, and with Regiomontanus (who was certainly technically superior to him and who sharply criticized his mathematical errors), Cusanus is one of the two greatest mathematicians of the fifteenth century. Important are his insight into the fact that $3\,^1/_7$ is only an *approximation* of π and his study of Archimedes, whose work he knew in the Latin translation of Jacob of Cremona (see *De arithmeticis complementis* [*On Arithmetical Complements*], *Opera,* II Fo.LIIII and *De mathematicis complementis* [*On Mathematical Complements*], II Fo.LIX). Other influences on Cusanus include Euclid (in the translation of Adelhard of Bath and Campanus of Novara) and the mathematical works of Albert of Saxony and Thomas Bradwardine.

9. In general, I see no *fundamental* changes in the mature Cusanus, although certainly important modifications and elaborations are apparent. Hans G. Senger, *Die Philosophie des Nikolaus von Kues vor dem Jahre 1440: Untersu-*

chungen zur Entwicklung einer Philosophie in der Frühzeit des Nikolaus (1430–1440) (Münster: Aschendorff, 1971) has shown convincingly that many of Cusanus's fundamental ideas can be found already in early sermons—in any case, before the famous experience of enlightenment during the journey back from Greece of which he speaks at the end of *De docta ignorantia* (PTS I 516). Where we find striking discrepancies—as between the triadic Christocentric structure of *De docta ignorantia* and the fourfold neo-Platonic system of *De coniecturis*—it is difficult to resolve the ambiguities chronologically since Cusanus already in *De docta ignorantia* quotes *De coniecturis* (II 1, 6, 8, III 1, PTS I 318, 350, 352, 370, 426). It seems much more probable that Cusanus, whether rightly or wrongly, thought that the two systems were compatible than that he changed his mind. This is, in my eyes, valid also with regard to Josef Koch's suggestion (*Die Ars coniecturalis des Nikolaus von Kues* [Köln/Opladen: Westdeutscher Verlag, 1956], 16) that in *De coniecturis* Cusanus replaced a metaphysics of being with a metaphysics of the One. An explicit self-critique can be found in *De apice theoriae* (*On the Summit of Contemplation*) with regard to *De possest* (PTS II 364ff.), but, although the change from *possest* to *posse* entails important consequences, it shows only that Cusanus never stopped searching for new names for the same object.

10. *Arete bei Platon und Aristoteles* (Heidelberg: Winter, 1959); *Platone e i fondamenti della metafisica* (Milano: Vita e pensiero, 1982).

11. *Platons ungeschriebene Lehre* (Stuttgart: Klett, 1963, 1968).

12. Plato, *The Written and Unwritten Doctrines* (London: Humanities Press, 1974).

13. *Platon und die Schriftlichkeit der Philosophie* (Berlin/New York: de Gruyter, 1985).

14. *Per una nuova interpretazione di Platone* (Milano: Vita e pensiero, 1987).

15. *Johannes Philoponus in Aristotelis de anima* 117, line 26 Hayduck. See Gaiser, *Platons ungeschriebene Lehre*, 446f.

16. "Plato's Foundation of the Euclidean Character of Geometry," in *The Other Plato,* ed. Dmitri Nikulin (Albany: State University of New York Press, 2012), 161–82 (German original in 1982); "On Plato's Philosophy of Numbers and Its Mathematical and Philosophical Significance," *Graduate Faculty Philosophy Journal* 13, no. 1 (1988): 21–63 (German original in 1984). In the following, I restrict myself to summing up the main results.

17. In truth there is a third, since Plato, in the seventh book of the *Republic,* distinguishes geometry from stereometry. But, although this distinction still plays a role in the architecture of Euclid's *Elements,* one can say that it is not very important systematically and that it was rightly given up rather early. The two applied mathematical sciences of the *quadrivium* are music and astronomy. See Philip Merlan, *From Platonism to Neoplatonism* (The Hague: Nijhoff, 1960), 88ff.

18. Compare *Parmenides* 142bff. and Oskar Becker, "Die Lehre vom Geraden und Ungeraden im Neunten Buch der Euklidischen Elemente," in *Zur*

Geschichte der griechischen Mathematik, ed. O. Becker (Darmstadt: Wissenschaftliche Buchgesellschaft, 1965), 125–45, 142.

19. See Hermann Diels and Walther Kranz, *Die Fragmente der Vorsokratiker,* 3 vols. (Berlin: Weidmann, 1954), 44 B11, 47 B5, 58 B15.

20. See Gaiser, *Platons ungeschriebene Lehre,* Test. 37f. Plato does not seem to have seen that there is a certain tension between these two interpretations. For if the one right angle corresponds to the One, then one would expect that the straight line would also be interpreted as manifestation of the One: for there is only one degree of straightness, but there are many degrees of curvature. In fact, Aristotle says that we know the straight and the curved by the straight (*De anima* 411a5).

21. Pythagoras is called by Cusanus "the first philosopher both according to the name and the matter itself" ("primus et nomine et re philosophus," *De docta ignorantia* I 11, PTS I 230) and Plato is praised because he followed him: "Nor do I believe that anyone has achieved a more reasonable method of philosophizing [than Pythagoras], and because Plato imitated him, he is rightly considered great" ("Neque arbitror quemquam rationabiliorem philosophandi modum assecutum [quam Pythagoram], quem, quia Plato imitatus est, merito magnus habetur," *De ludo globi* II, PTS III 342). But, of course, for Cusanus the truth of this philosophical tradition is not justified by its age or its name: in the sixth chapter of *Idiota de mente,* the layman—with whom Cusanus clearly identifies (PTS III 580)—answers to the philosopher's remark that he seems to be a Pythagorean: "I do not know whether I am a Pythagorean or something else: but I do know that nobody's authority leads me, even if it tries to move me" ("Nescio an Pythagoricus vel alius sim; hoc scio, quod nullius auctoritas me ducit, etiam si me movere tentet," III 522).

22. *Der Ursprung der Geistmetaphysik: Untersuchungen zur Geschichte des Platonismus zwischen Platon und Plotin* (Amsterdam: Schippers, 1967); *Platonismus und hellenistische Philosophie* (Berlin/New York: de Gruyter, 1971); "Die Ältere Akademie," in *Die Philosophie der Antike,* vol. 3: *Ältere Akademie-Aristoteles-Peripatos,* ed. H. Flashar (Basel/Stuttgart: Schwabe, 1983), 1–174.

23. "Beiträge zur Geschichte des antiken Platonismus II: Poseidonios über die Weltseele in Platons Timaios," *Philologus* 89 (1934): 213: "daß der Einfluß Platons aufs Mittelalter ungefähr gerade so weit reicht wie die Kenntnis dieses Systems" ("that Plato's impact on the Middle Ages extends approximately as far as the knowledge of this system"). To show in detail how much of Plato's esoteric teachings was still known in the Middle Ages remains an important research task in the history of philosophy.

24. Through which channels these ideas came to Cusanus is not entirely clear. Of course, Plato, Aristotle, Proclus—whose Euclid commentary, however, does not seem to have been known by Cusanus (it occurs no more than any of the works of the other neo-Platonic philosophers of mathematics in Jakob Marx's *Verzeichnis der Handschriften-Sammlung des Hospitals zu Cues bei Bernkastel a./*

Mosel [Trier: Schaar & Dathe, 1905])—Pseudo-Dionysius the Areopagite, and the *Liber XXIV philosophorum*, are important sources, but probably they are not the only ones. Nikolai Stuloff, "Mathematische Tradition in Byzanz und ihr Fortleben bei Nikolaus von Kues," *Mitteilungen und Forschungsbeiträge der Cusanus-Gesellschaft* 4 (1964): 420–36, names some Byzantine authors, such as Michael Psellos and Nikolaos Rhabdas, but the similarities between their ideas and those of Cusanus may be due to common sources and not to a direct influence of their thoughts on Cusanus. The latter, however, can certainly not be excluded since Cusanus was acquainted with several Byzantine Platonists. See Paul O. Kristeller, *Renaissance Concepts of Man and Other Essays* (New York: Harper & Row, 1972), 86–109: "Byzantine and Western Platonism in the Fifteenth Century" (103f. are devoted to Cusanus).

25. *secreta Platonis,* PTS III 46.

26. "Plato autem post unum posuit duo principia scilicet finitum et infinitum," PTS II 248.

27. See Vittorio Hösle, *Wahrheit und Geschichte: Studien zur Struktur der Philosophiegeschichte unter paradigmatischer Analyse der Entwicklung von Parmenides bis Platon* (Stuttgart-Bad Cannstatt: Frommann-Holzboog, 1984), 459ff.

28. The complete knowledge of God, if it were possible, would imply a complete knowledge of everything: *Idiota de mente* III, X (PTS III 500, 566).

29. Aristotle accepts this order in the treatise *Metaphysics* K 7, but gives it up in the latter treatise E 1.

30. See also the first chapter of the *Complementum theologicum,* PTS III 650. This work tries to evaluate theologically *De mathematicis complementis,* which was dedicated to Pope Nicholas V.

31. Aristotle's meta-categories are, of course, influenced by Plato's theory of principles. See Philip Merlan, "Beiträge zur Geschichte des antiken Platonismus I: Zur Erklärung der dem Aristoteles zugeschriebenen Kategorienschrift," *Philologus* 89 (1934): 35–53.

32. In *Idiota de mente* II (PTS III 492ff.), Cusanus ascribes, again in a very Platonic way, the more and the less to the sensible world, in which "only the most simple form itself shines in various ways, more in one object, less in another, and in none precisely" ("non nisi ipsa simplicissima forma varie relucet, magis in uno et minus in alio et in nullo praecise").

33. The concept of proportion presupposes immediately the concept of number: *De docta ignorantia* I 1, PTS I 196; *Idiota de mente* VI, PTS III 524. On proportion and number in Cusanus, see Werner Schulze, *Zahl Proportion Analogie: Eine Untersuchung zur Metaphysik und Wissenschaftstheorie des Nikolaus von Kues* (Münster: Aschendorff, 1978), 74ff.

34. "Eo [numero] sublato nihil omnium remansisse ratione convincitur . . . Neque alia res substantia, alia quantitas, alia albedo, alia nigredo et ita de omnibus absque alietate esset; quae est, numero est" (*De coniecturis* 14, PTS II 8ff.).

35. See *De beryllo* XVII, PTS III 26: "The one or the monas is simpler than the point" ("Unum seu monas est simplicius puncto").

36. "Omnem constat numerum ex alteritate et unitate constitui," we read in *De coniecturis* (I 11, PTS II 38), and in *Idiota de mente* he calls number "simplicitatis et compositionis sive unitatis et multitudinis coincidentiam" (VI, PTS III 524). Cusanus answers the question of what distinguishes number from other unities of unity and alterity no better than does Plato. In *De coniecturis* II 2, PTS II 90, harmony is also defined as "unitatis et alteritatis constrictio," and we will see that a similar definition is given of the soul.

37. Cusanus says that God, who is the absolute unity, is "a power more enfolding than that of the One and the point" ("virtus magis complicativa quam unius et puncti," *De ludo globi* II, PTS III 314). In the *Complementum theologicum* X (PTS III 684), he distinguishes clearly between unity and the One, which is created by unity; it is remarkable that he connects unity with limitation, for Plato already called the *hen peras*. "Thus unity is a principle that limits and at the same time makes something one. By making something one, it limits, and by limiting, it makes one" ("Sic [unitas] est principium terminans simul et unum faciens. Unum faciendo terminat et terminando unum facit"). Nevertheless, Cusanus in his definition of number combines the two different types of definition that I have distinguished within the Platonic–neo-Platonic tradition ("On Plato's Philosophy of Numbers," 31f.).

38. "Nonne unum est unum semel, et duo est unum bis, et tria est unum ter, et sic deinceps?" (*Idiota de sapientia* I, PTS III 424).

39. "Hoc enim ageret infinitas formae illius, quae vis dicitur unitatis, quod, dum ad dualitatem respicis, forma illa non potest esse nec maior nec minor dualitatis forma, cuius est praecisissimum exemplar" (*Idiota de sapientia* I, PTS III 446).

40. "Habet enim denarius omne id quod est a monade, sine qua nec denarius unus quidem numerus nec denarius foret" (*De filiatione* IV, PTS II 628; see *De ludo globi* II, PTS III 290).

41. See, especially, the subtle argument at PTS II 216, which goes back to Proclus's *Commentary on the Parmenides* (*Opera inedita,* ed. V. Cousin [Paris: Durand, 1864; reprint Frankfurt: Minerva, 1962], 725, lines 20ff.) and to Plato himself (*Parmenides* 147ef.). A similar argument can be found in *De ludo globi* II (PTS III 288).

42. In the latter passage, he says that even alterity does not belong to the *essence* of two-ity: "Nec est de essentia binarii alteritas, licet eo ipso, quod est binarius, contingat adesse alteritatem."

43. Nor is it satisfactory to answer that unity and otherness (or plurality) coincide in God (see, e.g., *De docta ignorantia* I 24, PTS I 280; *De coniecturis* II 1, PTS II 80), for the question remains: what led to their dissociation? A possible answer could lie in Cusanus's doctrine of the Trinity. For in order to explain the

real differences in the world, we need a certain "ideal" difference in God himself, and such a difference can be found in the generation of equality by unity.

44. Cusanus uses also the word *evolutio*: "Linea itaque est puncti evolutio" (*Idiota de mente* IX, PTS III 556; see *De ludo globi* I, PTS III 228).

45. "Excedit autem mentem nostram modus complicationis et explicationis" (*De docta ignorantia* II 3, PTS I 334). The concept of unfolding is especially important for describing the relation between the different dimensions since Cusanus knows very well that the line cannot be conceived as a sum of points: "The point is so close to nothing that if you add a point to a point not more will result than if you add nothing to nothing" ("Adeo enim prope nihil est punctus, quod si puncto punctum addas non plus resultat quam si nihilo nihil addideris," *Complementum theologicum* IX, PTS III 678; see *De ludo globi* I, PTS III 228).

46. "Nam qui numerat, explicat vim unitatis et complicat numerum in unitatem. Denarius enim est unitas ex decem complicata; sic qui numerat explicat et complicat" (*Idiota de mente* XV, PTS III 605). This is in accordance with the general ontological principle "the identical calls the non-identical to the identical" ("Vocat igitur idem non-idem in idem," *De genesi*, PTS II 398).

47. Cf. *Idiota de mente* VI, PTS III 522, 530: "compositionem numeri ex unitate et alteritate, ex eodem et diverso, ex pari et impari, ex dividuo et individuo."

48. "Unde quaternarius ex ternario et altero componitur, ternarius est impar, alter par, sicut binarius ex uno et altero" (PTS III 340).

49. See my essay "On Plato's Philosophy of Numbers," 40f.

50. This principle is for Cusanus one of the reasons for our incapacity to know the world exactly. For no measurement can be really exact since no two things are absolutely identical. Were we able to know exactly one thing, then we could know the whole world, since everything is determined by its relation to the whole. The second reason is that a complete knowledge of the world presupposes a complete knowledge of God, which we cannot achieve (*De docta ignorantia* I 3, II 5, PTS I 200ff., 344ff.).

51. "Et quamvis regulae verae sint in sua ratione datae figurae aequalem describere, in actu tamen aequalitas impossibilis est in diversis" (*De docta ignorantia* II 1, PTS I 314). One must understand in this way *De docta ignorantia* I 17, PTS I 250: "it is impossible that two finite lines are exactly equal" ("nullae duae lineae finitae possunt esse praecise aequales").

52. "Triplum enim complicat numeros multos triplos" (*De coniecturis* I 11, PTS II 42). Possibly, this distinction corresponds to that between the number that proceeds from the divine mind and the mathematical number created by us, which is its image (*Idiota de mente* VI, PTS III 522).

53. Also the product of both, 40, has a certain importance for Cusanus, especially since it is the sum of 1, 3, 9, and 27 (*De coniecturis* I 16, PTS II 68ff).

54. In *Idiota de mente* X, PTS III 566, Cusanus sketches the idea that the nine non-substantial categories can be deduced from the concept of multiplicity, but does not carry out the derivation: "For it is understood with difficulty how this occurs" ("Nam quemadmodum hoc fiat, difficulter cognoscitur").

55. Very important for Cusanus are categorical triads, such as unity, equality, connection (*De docta ignorantia* I 7ff., PTS I 214ff.) or possibility (or matter of the universe), soul (or form of the universe), spirit of the whole (II 7ff., PTS I 354ff.; together with God, they constitute the *four* universal modalities of being). The latter triad is regarded as more universal than the ten categories (*De aequalitate* [*On equality*], *Idiota de mente* XI, PTS III 366ff., 576). Like Lullus, Cusanus interprets the three dimensions of space (*De apice theoriae,* PTS II 382) and the syllogism—especially, the mode Barbara of the first figure—in a Trinitarian way (*De genesi* [*On Genesis*], PTS II 432). See Rudolf Haubst, *Das Bild des Einen und Drei-einen Gottes in der Welt nach Nikolaus von Kues* (Trier: Paulinus, 1952), 203ff.

56. "Si igitur non potest esse in ordinato seu creato ordine simplex et ae-quale medium ideo nec in ternaria progressione concluditur, sed ultra progreditur in compositionem. Quaternarius autem est immediate a prima progressione exiens" (*De ludo globi* II, PTS III 340). It is not difficult to see the similarity to Hegel's concept of the "broken middle" (*gebrochene Mitte*); see Vittorio Hösle, *Hegels System,* 2 vols. (Hamburg: Meiner, 1987), I 147ff.

57. "Quare ei [rectitudini infinitae] similior est circularis curvitas, quia similior infinito quam finita rectitudo. Afficimur igitur omnes mentem habentes figura circulari, quae nobis completa et pulchra apparet propter eius uniformitatem et aequalitatem et simplicitatem" (*Complementum theologicum* VII, PTS III 672).

58. See also in the same work IV, VIII, XIII, PTS III 664, 676, 700, where Cusanus favors the straight line, while in III and IX, PTS 660 and 680, he gives the circle preference over the polygons. In *De docta ignorantia* I 18 (PTS I 252ff.), Cusanus compares the relation of the infinite straight line, the finite straight line, and the finite curved line to the relation of being, substance, and accidents and quotes Aristotle (*De anima* 411a5): "The straight is the measure of itself and the curved" ("Rectum est sui et obliqui mensura"). See also *De venatione sapientiae* XXVI, PTS I 118.

59. "in qua coincidit rectitudo cum circularitate" (II, PTS III 656).

60. In his erudite study on the Greek concept of the infinite, *L'infinito nel pensiero del Greci* (Firenze: Le Monnier, 1934), Rodolfo Mondolfo wrongly levels this radical difference between the Greeks and the moderns. Certainly, some later ideas are anticipated by the Greeks, but this does not make the transition smooth and continuous.

61. Also, in his philosophical writings, Cusanus often names the problem—see, for example, *De coniecturis* II 2; *De possest,* PTS II 88, 316; and *De beryllo* XVII, PTS III 54. Even for this interest of Cusanus, Lullus is one of his major sources: see Joseph E. Hofmann, *Die Quellen der cusanischen Mathematik I. Ramon Lulls Kreisquadratur* (Heidelberg: Winter, 1942).

62. "Intellectus igitur, qui non est veritas, numquam veritatem adeo praecise comprehendit, quin per infinitum praecisius comprehendi possit, habens se ad veritatem sicut polygonia ad circulum, quae quanto inscripta plurium angulorum fuerit, tanto similior circulo. Numquam tamen efficitur aequalis, etiam si angulos usque in infinitum multiplicaverit, nisi in identitatem cum circulo se resolvat" (*De docta ignorantia* I 3, PTS I 202).

63. Less felicitous is Cusanus's application of the relation of polygon and circle to the two natures of Christ (*De docta ignorantia* III 4, PTS I 448). For he identifies the human nature of Christ with a maximal polygon. There can then be no difference between human and divine nature, so that Cusanus is in danger of becoming a monophysite. See Jasper Hopkins's well-taken critique in his introduction to his English translation: Nicholas of Cusa, *On Learned Ignorance* (Minneapolis: Banning, 1981), 1–43, especially 36ff.

64. In the smallest circle, there is another peculiar coincidence since there is no difference between the center and the periphery (*De ludo globi* II, PTS III 296).

65. *Idiota de sapientia* I, II, *Complementum theologicum* IIf., PTS III 444, 470ff., 656ff.

66. In *De possest,* we find, with respect to movement, the more concrete idea that a top, moving with an absolute speed, would seem to be at rest since no change could be perceived (PTS II 290ff.).

67. "Solum enim infinitas non potest esse maior nec minor" (*Complementum theologicum* III, PTS III 658).

68. "Principium enim ipsius fluxus et finis refluxus coincidunt in unitate absoluta, quae est infinitas absoluta" (*De coniecturis* II 7, PTS II 118).

69. See Oskar Becker, *Grundlagen der Mathematik in geschichtlicher Entwicklung* (Freiburg/München: Alber, 1954), 272ff., who quotes Proclus's Euclid commentary (on definition I 17), and Maier, *Die Vorläufer Galileis im 14. Jahrhundert,* 155ff. (on medieval thinkers who dealt with the problem).

70. *Gesammelte Abhandlungen mathematischen und philosophischen Inhalts,* ed. E. Zermelo (Berlin: Springer, 1932), 165–209, especially 205: "Ebenso finde ich für meine Auffassungen Berührungspunkte in der Philosophie des *Nicolaus Cusanus*. . . Dasselbe bemerke ich in Beziehung auf *Giordano Bruno,* den Nachfolger des *Cusaners*" ("I also find points of contacts with my conceptions in the philosophy of *Nicholas of Cusa* . . . I remark the same with regard to *Giordano Bruno, Cusanus's* successor").

71. "cum infinitum non sit maius infinito" (I 16; see II 1, PTS I 246, 320).

72. I 14: "there cannot be a plurality of infinites" ("plura infinita esse non possunt"), II 1, *Complementum theologicum* III, PTS I 236, 320, III 660.

73. A good introduction to set theory is Herbert B. Enderton, *Elements of Set Theory* (New York: Academic Press, 1977).

74. Cusanus speaks of a triangle with three right angles (I 12, PTS I 232): does he have spheric triangles in mind? Menelaus had been translated already in

the twelfth century by Gerhard of Cremona, and not too long after *De docta igno-rantia* Regiomontanus, following Georg von Peurbach's suggestions, gives an independent exposition of plane and spheric trigonometry in *De triangulis omni-modis* (*On Triangles of All Kinds*) (1462–64).

75. At I 19, PTS I 258, these geometric determinations are connected with ontological categories: the line with essence, the triangle with trinity, the circle with unity, and the sphere with actual existence.

76. "in quibus [non-quantis] quod in quantis est impossibile, vides per omnia necessarium" (*De docta ignorantia* I 14, PTS I 238). *Quanta* for Cusanus are necessarily finite since he does not believe in the mathematical actual infinite.

77. Incidentally, this was Cantor's main argument against the traditional denial of the actual infinite: see "Über die verschiedenen Standpunkte in bezug auf das aktuelle Unendliche," in *Gesammelte Abhandlungen*, 370–77, especially 371f.: "Alle sogenannten Beweise wider die Möglichkeit aktual unendlicher Zahlen sind, wie in jedem Falle besonders gezeigt und auch aus allgemeinen Gründen geschlossen werden kann, der Hauptsache nach dadurch fehlerhaft, und darin liegt ihr *prōton pseudos,* daß sie von vornherein den in Frage stehenden Zahlen alle Eigenschaften der endlichen Zahlen zumuten oder vielmehr aufdrängen" ("All so-called proofs against the possibility of actually infinite numbers are, as can be shown in each single case separately and can be concluded also on general grounds, faulty mainly because from the beginning they ascribe to or even impose on the numbers in question all properties of finite numbers; in this their *prōton pseudos* consists").

78. The first problem concerns Cusanus's unacceptable identification of the absolute with the quantitatively infinite, two concepts that Cantor rightly al-ways distinguished (see "Über die verschiedenen Standpunkte," 375, and Jo-seph W. Dauben's excellent book, *Georg Cantor: His Mathematics and Philosophy of the Infinite* [Cambridge, MA/London: Harvard University Press, 1979], 120–48: "Cantor's Philosophy of the Infinite").

With regard to the *second* problem, that of the validity of the principle of non-contradiction, see Hösle, *Hegels System,* I 156ff. Cusanus thinks that the prin-ciple is valid only for the *ratio,* not for the *intellectus.* Now, in my eyes, there is one form of the principle of non-contradiction—namely, the one stating that self-contradictory theories must be false—which is absolutely valid, for its denial would do away with the possibility of immanent critique (Cusanus, in fact, rec-ognizes that without it apagogic proofs would not be possible: *De coniecturis* II 2, PTS II 88). But this does not necessarily entail that propositions of the structure "A & not-A" (see, e.g., *De docta ignorantia* I 19, PTS I 260) are always false and even less that theories contradicting axioms that are valid for the finite, and for the finite only, are inconsistent.

79. The complete incapacity of understanding this point demonstrates the intellectual weakness of John Wenck's *De ignota litteratura*—now available in the

new edition and translation by Jasper Hopkins, *Nicholas of Cusa's Debate with John Wenck* (Minneapolis: Banning Press, 1984).

80. See Dietrich Mahnke, *Unendliche Sphäre und Allmittelpunkt: Beiträge zur Genealogie der mathematischen Mystik* (Halle: Niemeyer, 1937), 76ff. and passim.

81. Therefore, Ludwig von Bertalanffy—a mind, in some respects, congenial to Cusanus—exaggerates, when he writes: "Cusanus war der erste Mensch, dem sich der Gedanke der Unendlichkeit eröffnete" ("Cusanus was the first man to whom the idea of infinity presented itself"; *Nikolaus von Kues*, ed. Ludwig von Bertalanffy [München: Müller, 1928], 15). It is at least necessary to interpret the "presenting itself" of an idea as being considered without being accepted. On Cusanus's concept of the infinite, see Siegfried Lorenz, *Das Unendliche bei Nicolaus von Cues* (Fulda: Fuldaer Actiendruckerei, 1926).

82. "Non devenitur tamen ad maximum, quo maior esse non possit, quoniam hic foret infinitus" (I 5, PTS I 208).

83. "Non posse esse quantitatem infinitam seu maximam simpliciter" (*Complementum theologicum* XII, PTS III 694). It follows from this that Cusanus cannot have believed that the physical world is actually infinite—and, even less, that there are infinite worlds: in the passage "if there were infinite worlds" ("etsi essent infiniti mundi," *De quaerendo deum* [*On Seeking God*], PTS II 600), the conditional is counterfactual. His criticism of medieval cosmology remains revolutionary even if we do not ascribe to him theories that are Bruno's and not his. He wants only to say that the world could not be larger—but only because it cannot be infinite; he shares the intuitionistic belief that the negation of the finitude of the world does not entail that the world is actually infinite. See especially *De docta ignorantia* II 1, PTS I 320: "and according to this consideration [the universe] is neither finite nor infinite" ("et hac consideratione [universum] nec finitum nec infinitum est"). Similar is his attitude with regard to time. Although he does not believe that a finite amount of time has elapsed since creation (and although in this regard he openly contradicts "Genesis"), he distinguishes, of course, the eternity of God from that of the world (*De genesi*, PTS II 404ff.; *De ludo globi*, PTS III 314ff.; Sermon 4, *Cusanus-Texte I, Predigten, 2/5: Vier Predigten im Geiste Eckharts*, ed. Josef Koch [Heidelberg: Winter, 1937]).

84. See, especially, *Die nicht-euklidische Geometrie in der Phänomenologie des Geistes* (Frankfurt: Heiderhoff, 1972).

85. In the *Grundlagen*, Cantor shows very well that in Leibniz there is still no clear acceptance of the actual infinite, but that there are both affirmations and negations of it (179f.).

86. See the letter to Dositheus at the beginning of *On the Sphere and Cylinder.*

87. Vico speaks of "verum factum"—true is what we make. On the prehistory of this principle, which seems to begin with Cusanus, see Rodolfo Modolfo, *Il "verum-factum" prima di Vico* (Napoli: Guida, 1969).

88. "Coclear extra mentis nostrae ideam aliud non habet exemplar. Nam etsi statuarius aut pictor trahat exemplaria a rebus, quas figurare satagit, non tamen ego, qui ex lignis coclearia et scutellas et ollas ex luto educo. Non enim in hoc imitor figuram cuiuscumque rei naturalis. Tales enim formae cocleares, scutellares et ollares sola humana arte perficiuntur. Unde ars mea est magis perfectoria quam imitatoria figurarum creatarum, et in hoc infinitae arti similior" (*Idiota de mente* II, PTS III 492).

89. "non colligat ex aliquo quod non creavit possibilitatem rerum" (*De genesi,* PTS II 414).

90. "Nam si considerasset hoc [Plato], repperisset utique mentem nostram, quae mathematicalia fabricat, ea, quae sui sunt officii, verius apud se habere quam sint extra ipsam" (*De beryllo* XXXII, PTS III 66).

91. "Nam in mathematicis, quae ex nostra ratione procedunt et in nobis experimur inesse sicut in suo principio, per nos ut nostra seu rationis entia sciuntur praecise scilicet praecisione tali rationali a qua prodeunt. Sicut realia sciuntur praecisa praecisione divina, a qua in esse procedunt. Et non sunt illa mathematicalia neque quid neque quale, sed notionalia a ratione nostra elicita sine quibus non possit in suum opus procedere scilicet aedificare, mensurare, et cetera. Sed opera divina, quae ex divino intellectu procedunt, manent nobis uti sunt praecise incognita. Et si quid cognoscimus de illis per assimilationem figurae ad formam coniecturamur" (*De possest,* PTS II 318).

92. See *Complementum theologicum* II, PTS III 652: "Whatever the mind sees, it sees it in itself" ("Quaecumque igitur mens intuetur in se intuetur"). Misleading at *Compendium* VIII, PTS II 708, is the comparison of the relation between God, the Creator, and the world, to the relation between a cosmographer and his map, for the second activity is certainly a posteriori. Cusanus hints at the difference with the word *anterioriter:* "But [God] is the craftsman and the cause of everything, and the cosmographer believes that He relates to the whole world, but in an antecedent way, as he himself does to the map" ("Sed omnium [Deus] est artifex et causa, quem cogitat sic se habere ad universum mundum anterioriter, sicut ipse ut cosmographus ad mappam").

93. At *De ludo globi* II, PTS III 308, however, Cusanus says that God does not need (as man does) number in order to distinguish differences.

94. "Est, sed a mente aeterna. Unde sicut quoad Deum rerum pluralitas est a mente divina, ita quoad nos rerum pluralitas est a nostra mente. Nam sola mens numerat; sublata mente numerus discretus non est" (*Idiota de mente* VI, PTS III 526).

95. "Unde si acute respicis, reperies pluralitatem rerum non esse nisi modum intelligendi divinae mentis" (PTS III 528).

96. "Unde mens est creata ab arte creatrice, quasi ars illa se ipsam creare vellet" (*Idiota de mente* XIII, PTS III 592).

97. "Nam mentem esse ex eodem et diverso est eam esse ex unitate et alteritate eo modo, quo numerus compositus est ex eodem quantum ad commune,
et diverso quantum ad singularia" (VII, PTS III 532; see *De ludo globi* I, PTS
III 248).

98. Although creationism in its Cusanian and a fortiori in its more modern
forms is alien to Platonism, the idea that there are deep ontological correspondences between mathematical entities and the soul can be found in Plato himself
and in several neo-Platonists. See Gaiser, *Platons ungeschiebene Lehre*, 95ff. and
Merlan, *From Platonism*, 11ff.

99. See Karl Jaspers, *Nikolaus Cusanus* (München: Piper, 1964), 81: "Eine
forschend aufgefundene, an sich bestehende, ideale Gegenstandswelt des
Mathematischen und eine vom Geist konstruktiv hervorgebrachte sind Aspekte
derselben Sache. Was wir hervorbringen, ist zugleich gefunden" ("A world of
ideal mathematical objects subsisting in itself and found by research and a world
produced constructively by the mind are aspects of the same thing. What we
produce, we at the same time find"). Clearer is Wolfgang Breidert, "Mathematik
und symbolische Erkenntnis bei Nikolaus von Kues," *Mitteilungen und Forschungsbeiträge der Cusanus-Gesellschaft* 12 (1977): 116–26, 125: "Indem der menschliche
Geist die *mathematicalia* erschafft, expliziert er nur das ursprünglich in ihm Einge-
faltete. Dabei ahmt er, getreu dem Imitationsprinzip, Gott bei seiner Schöpfer-
tätigkeit nach" ("By creating the *mathematicalia*, the human mind unfolds only
what was originally enfolded in it. In doing so, it follows God in his creative activity, faithful to the principle of imitation").

A similar structure is to be found in Cusanus's fascinating value theory,
which he develops at the end of *De ludo globi,* book II. Of course, it is God who
determines the value of things, but this value has to be recognized by a finite
spirit, and the value of this finite spirit, without which the creation could not be
appreciated, is inferior only to the value of God himself: "If you consider deeply,
the value of the intellectual being is the highest after the value of God. For the
value of God and of all things is in the power of the intellectual being in a conceptual and discrete way. And even if it is not the intellect that grants being to
value, still without intellect not even the existence of value can be grasped. For
without intellect one cannot know whether there is a value" ("Dum profunde
consideras intellectualis naturae valor post valorem Dei supremus est. Nam in
eius virtute est Dei et omnium valor notionaliter et discretive. Et quamvis intellectus non det esse valori, tamen sine intellectu valor discerni etiam ni quia est
non potest. Semoto enim intellectu non potest sciri an sit valor," PTS III 346).
However subtle Cusanus's theory of the relation of divine and human mind is, it
has to be acknowledged that Cusanus does not answer the question (it does not
even strike him as a problem) of how the human *liberum arbitrium*—in which he
believes—is compatible with a world that he sometimes seems to regard, as does

Leibniz, as the best possible one (although he thinks that God's freedom entails that he could have created a better one).

100. "Est autem Deus arithmetica, geometria atque musica simul et astronomia usus in mundi creatione, quibus artibus etiam et nos utimur, dum proportiones rerum et elementorum atque motuum investigamus" (*De docta ignorantia* II 13, PTS I 410).

101. "Et si sic considerassent Pythagorici et quicumque alii, clare vidissent mathematicalia et numeros, qui ex nostra mente procedunt et sunt modo, quo nos concipimus, non esse substantias aut principia rerum sensibilium, sed tantum entium rationis, quarum nos sumus conditores" (*De beryllo* XXXII, PTS III 68).

102. See Maier, *Studien zur Naturphilosophie der Spätscholastik*, vol. 4: *Metaphysische Hintergründe der spätscholastischen Naturphilosophie,* 1955, 402: "Hier liegt in der Tat die ausschlaggebende Schwierigkeit: eine mathematische Genauigkeit erschien unsern Philosophen von vornherein als unerreichbar, und sie haben darum grundsätzlich auf jedes Messen verzichtet. Ein Rechnen mit ungefähren Maßen, d.h. mit Näherungswerten, mit Fehlergrenzen und vernachlässigbaren Größen, wie es der späteren Physik selbstverständlich wurde, wäre den scholastischen Philosophen als ein schwerer Verstoß gegen die Würde der Wissenschaft erschienen. So sind sie an der Schwelle einer eigentlichen, messenden Physik stehengeblieben, ohne sie zu überschreiten—letzten Endes, weil sie sich nicht zu dem Verzicht auf Exaktheit entschließen konnten, der allein eine exakte Naturwissenschaft möglich macht" ("Herein indeed consists the decisive difficulty: mathematical precision was regarded as unachievable from the outset by our philosophers, and thus for reasons of principle they refrained from all measuring. Calculating with approximated measures and values, with margins of error and negligible magnitudes, as it became natural for later physics, would have appeared to the scholastic philosophers to be a serious violation of the dignity of science. Thus they stayed at the threshold of a proper, measuring physics without passing it—ultimately because they could not decide to renounce exactness, a renouncement that alone renders exact science possible"). This renunciation is Cusanus's merit in Albert Zimmermann's view ("'Belehrte Unwissenheit' als Ziel der Naturforschung," in *Nikolaus von Kues,* ed. K. Jacobi [Freiburg/München: Alber, 1979], 121–37, 124ff.).

103. This remains true if we recognize that many of the limitations inherent in Cusanus's scientific and mathematical work are imputable to his universal interests: "Als genialer Kopf mit dem Stempel des Erfinders ausgezeichnet war aber nur Einer, nur Cusanus, und für die Mängel seiner Erfindungen ist vielleicht verantwortlich, daß er nicht ausschließlicher Mann der Wissenschaft, in erster Linie Mathematiker, sein durfte" ("A genius with the mark of the inventor there existed [in the time from 1400 to 1450] only one, namely only Cusanus, and perhaps the cause of the faults in his inventions is the fact that he could not be

exclusively a scientist, primarily a mathematician," Moritz Cantor, *Vorlesungen über Geschichte der Mathematik*, II 194).

Chapter 12.   *Can Abraham Be Saved? And: Can Kierkegaard Be Saved? A Hegelian Discussion of* Fear and Trembling

1. I refer here to my work *Hegels System: Der Idealismus der Subjektivität und das Problem der Intersubjektivität*, 2 vols. (Hamburg: Meiner, 1987).

2. See Wittgenstein's letter to M. O'C. Drury, quoted in Alastair Hannay, *Kierkegaard* (London: Routledge, 1982), ix.

3. *Wahrheit und Geschichte: Studien zur Struktur der Philosophiegeschichte unter paradigmatischer Analyse der Entwicklung von Parmenides bis Platon* (Stuttgart/Bad Cannstatt: Frommann-Holzboog, 1984).

4. See Egil A. Wyller, *Enhet og Annethet: En historisk og systematisk studie i Henologi. I–III* (Oslo: Dreyer, 1981); *Den sene Platon* (Oslo: Tano Forlag, 1984).

5. For Kierkegaard, and especially his critique of Hegel, see Käte Nadler, *Der dialektische Widerspruch in Hegels Philosophie und das Paradoxon des Christentums* (Leipzig: Meiner, 1931); James Collins, *Kierkegaard's Critique of Hegel* (Bronx, NY: Fordham University Press, 1943); Max Bense, *Hegel und Kierkegaard: Eine prinzipielle Untersuchung* (Köln: Stauffen Verlag, 1948); Niels Thulstrup, *Kierkegaard's Relation to Hegel* (Princeton: Princeton University Press, 1980); *Kierkegaard's* Fear and Trembling: *Critical Appraisals,* ed. Robert L. Perkins (University: University of Alabama Press, 1981). The most important Kierkegaard bibliographies are Jens Himmelstrup, *Søren Kierkegaard: International bibliografi* (København: Nyt Nordisk Forlag, 1962); Aage Jørgensen, *Søren Kierkegaard-litteratur 1961–1970* (Aarhus: Akademisk Bokhandel, 1971); Aage Jørgensen, *Søren Kierkegaard-litteratur 1971– 1980* (Aarhus: Jørgensen, 1983).

6. See *Søren Kierkegaards Papirer, Anden forøgede Udgave ved N. Thulstrup, Tiende Bind, Anden Afdeling* (København: Gyldendal, 1968), 16: "Oh, if I am dead— Fear and Trembling alone will suffice for an immortal name of an author. Then it will be read and translated into other languages" (September 1849).

7. Emanuel Hirsch, *Kierkegaard-Studien,* 2 vols. (Gütersloh: Bertelsmann, 1930–33), 635.

8. Here I cannot address the problem of how Kierkegaard's pseudonyms relate to each other and to the author's intention. See Mark C. Taylor, *Kierkegaard's Pseudonymous Authorship: A Study of Time and the Self* (Princeton: Princeton University Press, 1975).

9. Kierkegaard is quoted from the following edition: *Samlede Værker,* 20 vols. (København: Gyldendal, 1963), with both Roman and arabic numerals. When no Roman numeral is given, I refer to the fifth volume, which contains *Frygt og Bæven* (as well as other works). A printing error in V 35 is corrected on

the basis of another edition: Søren Kierkegaard, *Frygt og Bæven. Sygdommen til Døden. Taler,* ed. L. Petersen and M. Jørgensen (København: Borger, 1989). For this translation of the chapter the standard English translation by Alastair Hannay is used: Søren Kierkegaard, *Fear and Trembling* (Harmondsworth: Penguin, 1985); thus, also the corresponding pages in English are given after a solidus. One obvious oversight was corrected. I do not give the Danish original, since only few readers could understand it.

10. See Martin Heidegger, *Sein und Zeit* (Frankfurt am Main: Klostermann, 1977), §46 ff.

11. Cf. the related passage in Hegel's *Vorlesungen über Ästhetik (Lectures on Aesthetics)*: "But the noble and great man does not want to be pitied and lamented in that way. For insofar as only the miserable part, the negative aspect of the misfortune is pointed out, there is a disparagement of the unhappy person" (XV 525; my translation). Hegel is quoted according to the edition: Georg Wilhelm Friedrich Hegel, *Werke in zwanzig Bänden* (Frankfurt am Main: Suhrkamp, 1969ff.).

12. See *The Concept of Anxiety* and *The Sickness Unto Death.*

13. Kant is quoted according to the so-called *Akademie-Ausgabe:* Kant's *Gesammelte Schriften,* 29 vols. (reprint Berlin: Georg Reimer, 1968); the translation is mine.

14. See Thomas Hobbes, *Leviathan* (Harmondsworth: Penguin, 1968), chapters 2, 12, 32–47.

15. See *Tractatus theologico-politicus* (Baruch de Spinoza, *Opera,* ed. C. Gebhardt, 4 vols. [Heidelberg: C. Winter, 1925], vol. III), chapter 1ff.

16. Jon Hellesnes, "Det socialhygieniska tänkesättet," *Ord & Bild* 3 (1991): 93–100, has recently analyzed scientism, moralism, and aestheticism as three consequences of this process of emancipation. Accordingly, Kierkegaard's view could be called "religionism."

17. See Max Scheler, *Der Formalismus und die materiale Wertethik* (Bern/München: Francke, 1980).

18. See *Tractatus theologico-politicus,* chapters 7, 15.

19. The fundamental contradiction in *Philosophical Fragments* consists in the fact that on the one hand Kierkegaard wants to defend historical facticity from the autonomy of reason, which, on the other hand, he has to use to attack historicism. "It immediately becomes obvious that the historical in a more concrete sense is indifferent" (VI 56). But if it is truly the case that God could not favor anyone in a particular time, those who lived before Christ must have had the possibility of knowing God. Kierkegaard's ahistorical Christianity has substantially less content than Hegel's reconstruction in the *Lectures on the Philosophy of Religion.*

20. Stuttgart/Bad Cannstatt: Frommann-Holzboog, 1982.

21. Jean Wahl, *Etudes Kierkegaardiennes* (Paris: F. Aubier, 1938).

22. See my analysis of the *Vita coaetanea* in my introduction to Raimundus Lullus, *Die neue Logik: Logica Nova,* ed. Ch. Lohr (Hamburg: Meiner, 1985), xxf.

23. For the sources of the Old Testament, see, for example, Werner H. Schmidt, *Einführung in das Alte Testament* (Berlin/New York: de Gruyter, 1979).

24. Cf. *Das Alte Testament Deutsch,* ed. Artur Weiser, vol. 2/4: *Das erste Buch Mose. Genesis,* translated and explained by Gerhard von Rad (Göttingen: Vandenhoeck & Ruprecht, 1972), 188–94: 22, 1–19, esp. 189: "Auch diese Erzählung— die formvollendetste und abgründigste aller Vätergeschichten—hat nur einen sehr lockeren Anschluß an das Vorhergegangene und läßt schon daran erkennen, daß sie gewiß lange Zeit ihre Existenz für sich hatte, ehe sie ihren Ort in dem großen Erzählungswerk des Elohisten gefunden hat. So steht also auch hier der Ausleger vor jener nicht unkomplizierten Doppelaufgabe: Er muß einerseits den Sinngehalt der alten selbständigen Erzählung ermitteln, dann aber natürlich auch der schon verhältnismäßig früh vollzogenen gedanklichen Verbindung mit einem ganzen Komplex von Abrahamsgeschichten Rechnung tragen" ("Also this story—the most elaborate and deepest of all stories about the Fathers—has only a very loose connection with the precedent ones and manifests thereby that it existed for a long time separately, before it found its place in the Elohist's large narrative work. Thus also here the interpreter has to face a not uncomplicated double task: on the one hand, he must reconstruct the meaning of the old independent tale, but then of course also render justice to the intellectual connection, drawn relatively early on, with a whole complex of Abraham stories").

25. Von Rad, *Das erste Buch Mose. Genesis,* 193, writes: "Es mag deutlich geworden sein, daß die Erzählung in ihrer mutmaßlichen ältesten Fassung die Kultsage eines Heiligtums war, und als solche hat sie die Auslösung eines eigentlich von der Gottheit geforderten Kinderopfers durch ein Tieropfer legitimiert" ("It may have become clear that the tale in its probable oldest version was the cult legend of a sanctuary, and as such it justified the replacement of the sacrifice of a child, as it was originally demanded by the deity, with the sacrifice of an animal"). Cf. Exodus 34:19f.

26. See Bartolomé de Las Casas, *In Defense of the Indians,* ed. S. Poole (De Kalb: Northern Illinois University Press, 1974), 221ff., esp. 234. Las Casas speaks expressly of Abraham.

27. Kant, *Zum ewigen Frieden,* VIII 381.

28. Hans L. Martensen's book, which Kierkegaard criticizes in *Philosophical Fragments,* is *Den christelige Daab* (København: Reitzel, 1843).

29. See Pierre Hadot, *What is Ancient Philosophy?* (Cambridge, MA: Harvard University Press, 2002).

30. This text was originally delivered as a lecture at the University of Oslo on July 11, 1991. In discussions after the lecture, Egil Wyller emphasized the importance of Kierkegaard's *Kjerlighedens Gjerninger* (*Works of Love*) in better understanding his concept of love. Doubtless, this work, published under his own

name, contains a masterful Christian ethics on the basis of Kant's ethical universalism and intentionalism. But it still recognizes the idea that God can demand something that transcends practical reason—an idea that thus cannot be ascribed to Johannes de Silentio alone, but belongs also to his author. The impossibility of founding a moral community on Kierkegaard's premises holds also for the later work, whose main difference from *Fear and Trembling* seems to consist in a rejection of the hopes of the knight of faith and in a return to the pure interiority of the knight of resignation.

Chapter 13. *A Metaphysical History of Atheism*

1. All page numbers in the text refer to Charles Taylor, *A Secular Age* (Cambridge, MA: Harvard University Press, 2007). The writing of the book still in the twentieth century becomes obvious when the nineteenth century is called "the last century" (168). "One, two, three! Time runs very quickly, and we with it." ("Einzweidrei! Im Sauseschritt/Läuft die Zeit, wir laufen mit," from Wilhelm Busch's *Julchen*.)

2. Analogously, he writes about religion: "But I'm talking about the underlying attitudes. Once one frames these as doctrines, one betrays them, loses the nuances that they incorporated" (511).

3. José Casanova, *Public Religions in the Modern World* (Chicago: University of Chicago Press, 1994).

4. Taylor is aware of the difficulty of grounding his claim to necessity (247, 267).

5. The Chinese religion that appealed to Enlightened thinkers of the eighteenth century becomes a problem in the nineteenth century, which is more fascinated with India than China. Cf. Friedrich Wilhelm Joseph Schelling, *Philosophie der Mythologie,* 2 vols. (Darmstadt: Wissenschaftliche Buchgesellschaft, 1976), II 521ff.: "The Chinese nation, even if it is not younger than any of the various mythological nations, does not show in its ideas anything that recalls the mythology of other peoples. We could say: it is an absolutely unmythological people" (521). Nonetheless, according to Schelling, even though it is absolutely unmythological, it only seems unreligious (522, 539f.). Schelling, who sees in myth "a form of enchantment" (II, 596), recognizes that the history of *religion* is continually characterized by repression of *mythology* (consider the Iranian religion: II 204f.) and that Christianity "itself plays a part" in overcoming mythology and even in undermining the old belief in revelation (I, 260). Christianity was therefore itself a factor in this disenchantment, to employ a technical term found, not originally in Max Weber, but already in Nietzsche (for example, in *Jenseits von Gut und Böse* [*Beyond Good and Evil*], 239). "Isn't it clear that in the same time and in the same relation in which nature gradually rids itself of every form

of divinity and degenerates into a merely lifeless aggregate, even the living monotheism dissolves more and more in an empty, indeterminate theism without content?" (II 104f.).

6. V. Hösle, *Morals and Politics* (Notre Dame: University of Notre Dame Press, 2004), 265f., 467ff. From this it follows that I avoid the concept of secularization as much as possible; as far as I can tell, the word occurs only once (590).

7. This is certainly the reason that the United States is less secularized (in the second sense of the word) than Europe: "In Europe it was easier to link religion with authority, with conformity to society-wide standards, not to speak of hostile divisions between people, and even violence" (529; cf. 149). But Taylor allows that this cannot be the full explanation: "A fully satisfactory account of this difference, which is in a sense the crucial question facing secularization theory, escapes me" (530). In my view, the enormous influence of skeptical intellectuals in Europe plays a role unlike anything in the United States, which, on account of the lack of an aristocracy, hardly has public intellectuals. Arthur Schopenhauer and Giacomo Leopardi were successes in Europe already in the nineteenth century, but Herman Melville, who felt similarly, first gained prominence in the twentieth century.

8. Cf. chapter 1 of this volume.

9. The proofs of God in the Middle Ages, Taylor writes, were only considered valid within a lived tradition (293f.). But this is a modern projection, not the medieval self-interpretation. See chapter 9 of this volume, where, among other things, an argument is given against Karl Barth's analogous interpretation of Anselm. Of course, reasons do not exclude deep emotions, as Taylor seems to suggest (288).

10. Thus Taylor is a value pluralist, but he exaggerates in attributing to John Rawls and Ronald Dworkin a belief in "the myth of the single, omnicompetent code" (52). For in truth it is monotheism that is averse to the kind of value pluralism that finds natural expression in ancient polytheism. Certainly there are conflicts of values (704f.), but it would be self-defeating for any ethical doctrine to give up the hope that the various value combinations form a kind of connex, transitive quasi-order. Thus, in my view, Taylor's polemic against a priori principles (448) does a disservice to theism.

11. Taylor is of course correct in maintaining that the mechanism of projection underlying human violence (686) is not foreign to secular humanism, which has much more of a problem with "useless" people than Christianity (684).

12. Of course, also prior to the Axial age, there were serious changes in the history of religion, even within the same culture. It is not at all easy, in fact it is often impossible, to measure their contribution to secularization. Consider, for

example, the emerging separation of the sacred area as *temenos* in the dark centuries of Greece in contrast to the palace temples of the Mycenaeans. Does this separation *revalue* or *devalue* the divine? Presumably it does both at the same time, for on the one hand, the religious aims to be conceived as an independent category, and on the other, it inevitably claims to impact the entire social world.

13. Cf. Vittorio Hösle, "The Lost Prodigal Son's Corporal Works of Mercy and the Bridegroom's Wedding: The Religious Subtext of Charles Dickens' *Great Expectations*," *Anglia* 126 (2008): 477–502.

14. Vittorio Hösle, *Die Philosophie der ökologischen Krise* (München: C. H. Beck, 1991), 25ff.

15. *Morals and Politics*, 5ff.

16. *Morals and Politics*, 226.

17. Thus, even one who agrees with Brad Gregory, *The Unintended Reformation: How a Religious Revolution Secularized Society* (Cambridge, MA: Belknap Press, 2012), that secularization is an unintended outcome of the Reformation, may come to a more positive view of Protestantism than does Gregory in his important study.

SOURCE CREDITS

1. "The Idea of a Rationalistic Philosophy of Religion and Its Challenges," *Jahrbuch für Religionsphilosophie* 6 (2007): 159–81; German translation: *Wiener Jahrbuch für Philosophie* 42 (2010): 33–57.

2. "Why Teleological Principles Are Inevitable for Reason: Natural Theology after Darwin," in *Biological Evolution: Facts and Theories,* ed. G. Auletta, M. LeClerc, and R. A. Martinez (Roma: Gregorian & Biblical Press, 2011), 433–60; German translation in: *Post-Physikalismus,* ed. M. Knaup, T. Müller, and P. Spät (Freiburg/München: Alber, 2011), 271–305.

3. "Theodizeestrategien bei Leibniz, Hegel, Jonas," in *Pensare Dio a Gerusalemme,* ed. A. Ales Bello (Roma: Lateran University Press, 2000), 219–43 as well as *Leibniz und die Gegenwart,* ed. F. Hermanni and H. Breger (München: Wilhelm Fink, 2002), 27–51; Portuguese translation: *O Deus dos filósofos modernos,* ed. M. Oliveira and C. Almeida (Petrópolis: Vozes, 2002), 201–22; Hungarian translation: *Mérleg* 41 (2005/3): 283–310; English translation by Benjamin Fairbrother: *Philotheos* 5 (2005): 68–86.

4. "Rationalism, Determinism, Freedom," in *On Quanta, Mind and Matter: Hans Primas in Context,* ed. H. Atmanspacher, A. Amann, and U. Müller-Herold (Dordrecht: Kluwer, 1999), 299–323; German translation: *Jahrbuch für Philosophie des Forschungsinstituts für Philosophie Hannover* 10 (1999): 15–43.

5. "Encephalius: Ein Gespräch über das Leib-Seele-Problem," in *Das Leib-Seele-Problem Antwortversuche aus medizinisch-naturwissenschaftlicher, philosophischer und theologischer Sicht,* ed. F. Hermanni and T. Buchheim (München: Wilhelm Fink, 2006), 107–36; English translation by James Hebbeler: *Mind and Matter* 5, no. 2 (2007): 135–65.

378   Source Credits

6. "Religion, Theologie, Philosophie," in *Auf neue Art Kirche sein. Wirklich-keiten—Herausforderungen—Wandlungen. Festschrift für Bischof Dr. Josef Homeyer,* ed. W. Schreer and G. Steins (München: Bernward bei Don Bosco, 1999), 210–22; Hungarian translation: *Mérleg* 37 (2001/1): 35–49; Portuguese translation: *Veritas* 47, no. 4 (2002): 567–79; English translation by Benjamin Fairbrother: *Philotheos* 3 (2003): 3–13.

7. "Philosophy and the Interpretation of the Bible," *Internationale Zeitschrift für Philosophie* (1999/2): 181–210; German translation: *Jahrbuch für Philosophie des Forschungsinstituts für Philosophie Hannover* 12 (2001): 83–114; Hungarian translation: *Mérleg* 38 (2002/3): 250–79; Italian translation: *Itinerari* 3 (2008): 3–41.

8. "Inwieweit ist der Geistbegriff des deutschen Idealismus ein legitimer Erbe des Pneumabegriffs des Neuen Testaments?" *Zeitschrift für Neues Testament* 25, no. 13 (2010): 56–65; English translation by Jeremy Neill: *Philotheos* 11 (2011): 162–74. Italian translation: *Humanitas* 67, no. 4 (2012): 697–710.

9. "Reasons, Emotions and God's Presence in Anselm of Canterbury's Dialogue *Cur Deus homo,*" *Archiv für Geschichte der Philosophie* 87 (2005): 189–210.

10. "Interreligious Dialogues during the Middle Ages and Early Modernity," in *Educating for Democracy: Paideia in an Age of Uncertainty,* ed. A. M. Olson, D. M. Steiner, and I. S.Tuuli (Lanham: Rowman & Littlefield, 2004), 59–83.

11. "Platonism and Anti-Platonism in Nicholas of Cusa's Philosophy of Mathematics," *Graduate Faculty Philosophy Journal* 13, no. 2 (1990): 79–112; *Aristotelica et Lulliana . . . Charles H. Lohr . . . dedicata,* ed. F. Domínguez, R. Imbach, T. Pindl, and P. Walter (The Hague: Brepols, 1995), 517–43.

12. "Kan Abraham reddes? Og: Kan Søren Kierkegaard reddes? Et hegelsk oppgjør med, 'Frygt og Bæven,'" *Norsk Filosofisk Tidsskrift* 27 (1992): 1–26; English translation by Jason Miller: *Belief and Metaphysics,* ed. C. Cunningham and P. M. Candler (London: SCM-Canterbury Press, 2007), 204–35.

13. "Eine metaphysische Geschichte des Atheismus," *Deutsche Zeitschrift für Philosophie* 57 (2009): 319–27; English translation by Jason Miller: *Symposium. Canadian Journal of Continental Philosophy* 14, no. 1 (2010): 52–65.

Chapters 4 and 6 were also reprinted in my volume *Die Philosophie und die Wissenschaften* (München: C. H. Beck, 1999), chapters 11 and 12 in my volume *Philosophiegeschichte und objektiver Idealismus* (München: C. H. Beck, 1996).

INDEX

Abelard, Peter
  Carmen ad Astralabium, 223
  Collationes/Dialogus inter philosophum,
    Judaeum et Christianum (Dialogue
    between a Philosopher, a Jew and a
    Christian), 225–26, 227–28, 230,
    232–33, 237–40, 241, 242–43,
    244, 245, 246, 248–49, 351n.6,
    355n.86, 356n.90
  on ethics, 242–43, 245
  Historia calamitatum, 351n.7
  intentionalism of, 213
  on Islam, 351n.7
  rationalism of, 3, 203, 237–40,
    242–43, 244–45, 248
Abraham and Isaac, 171, 291–300,
  373n.24
  Hegel on, 283–84, 291
  Kant on, 281–82, 283, 291
  Kierkegaard on, 272–73, 274,
    275–76, 277–80, 281, 283,
    284–85, 287–89, 336n.53
  and values of previous cultures,
    291–95, 296
  and voice of God, 293–94
Acts
  1:15, 193
  2:4, 192
  6:3, 192
  6:10, 192

  7:59, 191
  8:29, 192
  8:39, 192
  9:17, 193
  10:19, 192
  10:44ff., 193
  10:47, 193
  11:16, 193
  13:4, 192
  13:9, 193
  15:8, 193
  15:28, 193
  16:6, 192–93
  16:18, 191
  Pentecost event, 192
Adorno, Theodor W., 72, 330n.31
Aeschylus, 54
Agassiz, Louis, 36
agnosticism, 76
Albert of Saxony, 358n.8
Ambrose, St., 15, 159, 333n.8
American Journal of Science and Arts, 37
Amos, 167, 335n.39
analytic philosophy, 112
Anaxagoras's theory of Nous, 340n.3
animism, 111, 124–25
anomalous monism, 111–18, 121–24
Anselm of Canterbury
  on authority of scripture, 211–12
  on authority of the church, 212

VITTORIO HÖSLE

is Paul G. Kimball Chair of Arts and Letters

in the Department of German Languages and Literatures and concurrent

professor of philosophy and political science at the University of Notre Dame.

He is the director of the Notre Dame Institute for Advanced Study.

He is the author or editor of many books, including

The Philosophical Dialogue: A Poetics and a Hermeneutics (2012)

and *Morals and Politics* (2004),

both published by the University of Notre Dame Press.